FRANCESCO PETRARCH

LETTERS OF OLD AGE
(RERUM SENILIUM LIBRI)

VOL. 2: BOOKS X-XVIII

FRANCESCO PETRARCH

LETTERS OF OLD AGE
(RERUM SENILIUM LIBRI)

VOL. 2: BOOKS X-XVIII

Translated by
Aldo S. Bernardo,
Saul Levin &
Reta A. Bernardo

ITALICA PRESS
NEW YORK
2005

FIRST PUBLISHED 1992
COPYRIGHT © THE JOHNS HOPKINS UNIVERSITY PRESS

FIRST PAPERBACK EDITION
COPYRIGHT © 2005 BY ALDO S. BERNARDO

ITALICA PRESS, INC.
595 MAIN STREET
NEW YORK, NY 10044

Library of Congress Cataloging-in-Publication Data

Petrarca, Francesco, 1304-1374.
    [Correspondence. English. Selections]
    Letters of old age = Rerum senilium libri / Francis Petrarch;
translated by Aldo S. Bernardo, Saul Levin, Reta A. Bernardo
        p. cm.
Translation of: Rerum senilium libri, I-XVIII.
Includes bibliographical references and index.
    ISBN 1-59910-005-3 (pbk.: alk. paper)
    I. Petrarca, Francesco, 1304-1374—Correspondence.
2. Authors, Italian—To 1500—Correspondence.
I. Bernardo, Aldo S. II. Levin, Saul. III. Bernardo, Reta A.
IV. Title. V. Title: Rerum senilium libri.
PQ4496.E29E23   1992
851'.1–dc20   91-18097

Printed in the United States of America
5 4 3 2 1

Cover Art: Ambrogio Lorenzetti, Good Government in the Countryside. Palazzo Pubblico, Siena. Detail. Scala/Art Resource, New York.

FOR A COMPLETE LIST OF MEDIEVAL & RENAISSANCE TEXTS
VISIT OUR WEB SITE AT: HTTP://WWW.ITALICAPRESS.COM

CONTENTS

BOOK III

BOOK IV

BOOK V

BOOK VI

BOOK XI

BOOK XII

BOOK XIII

BOOK XVII

BOOK XVIII

Sen. X, 1.

To Sagremor de Pommiers, formerly a knight-at-arms, now a Cistercian monk,* an exhortation to persevere.

I have enjoyed your live conversation and your letters. If I may pass over our daily conversations which were many and varied over many years, you, who were once my dearest friend in the world and now far more dear in Christ, can testify that talking to you has been my first, greatest, and nearly my only solace for that demanding and difficult journey, that disagreeable itinerary we undertook together with great labor and considerable danger through foreign lands. Yet I have never heard nor could I have heard or read anything from you or about you that was more joyful or more welcome than what I have just read written by your now saintly fingers. I had really been anxious and concerned about your welfare, perceiving that you on the one hand, to use Augustine's words, were on the verge of giving birth to a new life, and on the other, fearing the well-known ties of your former life. I was awaiting word of how you would break away from them, and what would be the outcome of your recent idea, and here now you have escaped from the world. O happy, happy wayfarer who have found the shortcut, you have prudently completed the dangerous road of life before nightfall in a safe hospice, and I, along with everyone else, realize through how many hardships and dangers you labored, but no one knows better than you.

Now, I believe, you marvel silently that you are alive and managed to stand up against such odds, as you look at your earthly, mortal body, but the truth is that, just as there often is no animal more fragile, so at times there is none tougher than man. Thus, at times thrown to the ground by the slightest blows, he quickly yields up his soul as though it were not his and barely a part of him. We hear how certain men have been killed by an unbearable joy or even by some silly exhilaration, others by a grief arising at time from great causes, at times from small, trivial ones, and still others by a laugh or by a single seed from a raisin, or finally, as happened in

---

* An official courier of the emperor Charles IV, he was instrumental in keeping communications open between P. and the emperor. He accompanied P. to Prague in 1356 when summoned by the emperor. P.'s admiration and respect for Sagremor culminate in this letter as a result of Sagremor's decision to enter the religious life. This is the only letter to him.

the death of the senator Fabius, by one hair that he had swallowed while drinking milk: I ask, can there possibly exist more trifling causes of death? On the other hand, man so clings sometimes to the breath of life, unconquered either by wounds or by cave-ins; sometimes, when he is thought to have breathed his last, he so summons it back, as we have even seen and read about many people, that nothing whatsoever seems more enduring than this little human body. You are among such men; and so that you may see more clearly, turn your mind briefly at this point, and, after the rush of your precipitous life, stop awhile and, looking back, reflect once again in your memory the paths you have followed, weigh your actions, count the years, examine your anxieties, and meditate upon your desires. Then you will understand how peaceful a home you have reached through the many turns of the rocky road, how calm a shore you have reached through the stormy seas, and you will render thanks to your Leader who led you through the midst of sandbanks and through Scylla and Charybdis, among the Sirens and the rocks, to safety on your fortunate ship; and to add to your natural astonishment, do not consider those who swim to safety from the storms of this life, consider, rather, those who drown, who, because they do not come into sight, seem to be few, although they are many.

A day, or rather, my whole life, will not suffice to list the misfortunes of men, not only ordinary men, but illustrious ones. I shall refer to one from among the illustrious and another from among the multitude since I knew both, and although they were once very well known by the two of us, you have perhaps not yet heard about their misfortunes. Our Luchino [dal Verme] from Verona (alas, what a fine and great man he was, what a lover of virtue, and how he cared for us whom he never called by our regular names but liked to call you son and me brother!) following his devoted friendship and his military glory, and wishing to add a heavenly dimension to his fleeting earthly glory, set off against the Turks, and there on the shore of the Black Sea ended his days in a most honorable mission and holy expedition, but far from his homeland, even though he died a natural death. Unless my devotion deceives me, it was a pitiful and costly death for all Italy. His remains were taken to Constantinople so that nothing would remain to us of so great and expert a commander except his memory, our mourning, and one young son who we hope will be most like his father in excellence of spirit. Then there was that German, Martin, the courier, who would often go back and forth to the Emperor with a message, and who was lately in the forests of Germany, which we have both crossed with him as a companion, and you later criss-crossed so often by yourself; there he fell into the hands of robbers or foes and was stabbed to death. But note that as often as you came through safely, that is how often you might have perished.

Recognize the liberating hand of Christ which was pierced by a nail for all those who hope in Him, and which snatched your head and mine so often from death, not in order to make us immortal, but to allow us to die better. Recall, I beg you, that time when, ringed by an escort of armed men with mounted arbalests ready to shoot, we traveled with sword in hand many a German mile daily, although the guides were no protection at all and we were in much danger from others, had we not hidden from the robbers who were searching everywhere and made invisible by Him of whom it is written, "He protected me in the day of trouble in the hiding place of His tabernacle" [Ps. 27:5]. And again, "Let their eyes be darkened so that they may not see, and bend their backs forever" [Ps. 69:24]. But then we were many, something perhaps to cheer us but hardly to escape danger. Later on, with only your servants you ventured far into those areas time and again in the worst storms. I could say that for a long time it was an annual undertaking for you, if I did not know that you completed that hellish journey seven times in one year, which hardly anyone would believe possible.

But why am I recalling this one thing, except that it happened more often to you not by choice, but by order of your lord? Is there indeed any place, either east or west, across our seas that you have not been to? When you were younger, how many seas did you cross, and how many times? What foreign land did you not visit? What dangers did you not encounter while often I would say to you, "You will not be equal, dear friend, to so many hardships, for your body is not made of iron; but—as it is written—God, that heavenly artisan, clothed you with flesh and skin, and made you from bones and sinews"? What shall I say now? Look, it has been found to be not only of iron, but of steel and something beyond that, which you will ascribe not to your nature but His mercy. He who shaped you strengthened you with an invisible coat of adamant against all hardship and placed His hand upon you, knowing what He would do with you; for His wonderful foreknowledge, which is beyond us, knows all things, both the most recent and the most remote. In short, from your mother's womb He destined you for this end. He knew you long before you were born and long before you were formed in the womb, and, for your salvation and everyone else's, dreaded neither the recesses of a virgin's womb nor the gibbet of the cross, and He allowed you to be harassed by so many hardships that ultimately you would understand, when at rest, the difference between serving God and, I would not say serving men, but commanding them: the former certainly is sweet, safe, happy; the latter bitter, dangerous, wretched.

Therefore, I should like you to be sufficiently aware of the past so that you will not be ungrateful to your Lord, since you were grateful and faithful to so many ingrates who were not your lords. Moreover, I urge you to have little esteem for all the attractions of the cheating world and its false, fleeting pleasure; along with the Apostle forget the past, and reaching out to what lies ahead, strive with all your might toward heavenly things. Rise up, the Lord will give you His right hand, raise up your spirit and open your misty eyes overcome by the sleepiness of the flesh and the misty smoke of mortal things, rub them and see what you have escaped from, and you will be amazed and tearfully say, "Now I have begun, this change was wrought by the hand of the Most High; were it not that the Lord has helped me, my soul would have been close to dwelling in hell." Seldom has Christ ever been more clearly with anyone than with you, as you will easily sense if, looking back on the course of onrushing time and the flight of passing life from adolescence until now, you will enumerate your trials and dangers undertaken for vanity, along with their happy ending and the grave failings of many.

For this is what hurls soldiers down in war and sailors into the deep: no one counts those who were killed or shipwrecked, but instead everyone counts the victors' prizes and the gains of those who return; as the saying goes, consider the happy ones in order to appear happier to yourself. Remember also those whom you once served, what you did for men's love which is hard to win and very easy to lose, and often, when won, is harmful. So do something now for Him whose love is obtainable only by piety, is always useful and lasts forever. Consider what you did, think what you did for those terrible taskmasters who belittle or overlook even great merits and bypass them with no reward, while exaggerating and chastising the slightest faults. Do something for Him who has never sent off any good man without a reward, whereas for those who returned to Him He had laid aside their many wrongdoings without punishment. You have loved some who did not love you; love Him who loved you before you knew Him, who, when loved, has never failed to love, since He often has loved without being loved, and by loving

He has made Himself loved. Love Him whom to love is the highest virtue, by whom to be loved is the highest happiness; you have served proud mortals; serving them was a menial debasement. Start serving Him who is kind and humble of heart, and who will never again die now; serving Him is to be a king.

If freedom is the highest reward for faithful service, how great will be kingship along with freedom? You know what great things you have done for this new Caesar and for the Roman Empire, not to mention lesser lords; and although your fidelity and labors were very well known to him, how often did I place them before his eyes so that they could not be ignored and would be vouched for in my poor letters, but you have seen what good either your actions or my words have done for you. Therefore, keeping in mind that those long labors were in vain, now do yourself good by taking it easy, for whatever you do for Christ (and do as much as you can!), it will be rest compared to the toils of the world—I call this a fruitful repose while that other was but sterile labor, not only sterile but deadly.

Thus, you who were going to hell on the most demanding path are now going to heaven by the most peaceful course—a most happy turn of events. You were the servant of men, you will be the friend of Christ. You used to be a soldier for the world, now you will be a soldier for God. The payment for that soldiering was war, hardship, and dust, din, deaths, wounds, and finally hell, but payment for this is peace and rest, solitude and silence; the goal of earthly soldiering was to feed and adorn the body, that bait for worms, as if it were a banquet to set before a king, to stuff it to the brim with gold and gems and to wrap it up in the whitest linen, while slighting the soul, the temple of God. The goal of this spiritual militia, instead, is to tend the soul, to wear the body down and bring it back under control, to bind it with the chains of obedience and afflict it with hairshirt, and finally, like an enemy from whom, having suffered much, you have much to fear in order to keep it imprisoned and shackled. That earthly army supplied you now with gory weapons, now with showy clothing either to terrify the enemy or to please the ladies; this one dresses you in a humble, faded cowl to scare off the demons and please God. That army taught you to spur strapping horses by exerting pressure with your shins; this one teaches you to arouse the faltering soul with the goads of charity and hope toward the prize of salvation, but to scorn horses and yourself, and recall those horrifying words of David which mad knights do not heed: "In the strength of the steed he will not delight, nor will he be pleased with the fleetness of the man" [Ps. 147:10]. Finally, that militia promised you remorse and hidden fears and vain praises of men and hard-won boasting; this one promises the lasting purity and safety of your spirit, and scorn for human praise, so that your soul may be praised in the Lord and may glory in the Lord, who has snatched her from such great evils, and along a straight path has led her, sharing in such very good things, to life.

O holy home of the Cistercians where these things are done! O happy school of the Cistercians where such things are learned! O happy you who beyond that holy threshold have found yourself, whom you had lost, and one good kind, generous, and wealthy Lord, instead of many poor, evil, and harsh ones, One who gives abundantly to all without finding fault, who when asked for what is right refuses nothing; and if He delays giving it, that is because He wishes to make it do more good, and often He does not even wait to be asked, but anticipates our prayers, just as He goes beyond our deserts! You have a Lord who will not deceive you, not slander you, not despise you, but value you all the more, the more you despise yourself. You have a Lord who will not harm you or allow you to be harmed, not expose you to danger or labor, unless it is just and pious and meritorious and useful and delightful and honorable; you have a Lord who does not rule over this or that city or over a temporal kingdom or empire coveted by another, but holds in His palm heaven, the sea, the earth, and all that is in them, which He created, who rules with his nod, whose kingdom will have no end, but who is not demanding or arrogant because of such great power.

Never was a humble friend of yours more intimate than He will be, if you want Him wholeheartedly and sincerely. For with Him nothing can be feigned, nothing shared. He wants it all. He wants to share your heart and soul with no one; He is a jealous God. If perchance you love another, unless it is in Him or for His sake, He becomes angry, and disdains any partner—and with reason, for He has no peer. And He says about Himself: "See that I am alone, and there is no God besides Me" [Deut. 32:29]; and it is said about Him: "For there is no other but You" [2 Sam. 7:22]. And again, "There is no one like You among the gods, O Lord" [Ps. 86:8]—how much less among men. However many mere kings rise up on earth, however many men wish to be called lords, there is really one King of kings and one Lord of lords. And if sometime you willingly gave yourself wholly to a man who had no hold on you except your consent, now give, or rather, give back to God your entire body and soul, your thoughts and works that are His. And if perchance you snatched them from Him to give them to another, He, if implored, will come in order to strip the unworthy possessor and get back what is rightfully His, and retrieve your loyalty for you; and therefore if you deprived Him of the first fruits of your life, at least give Him back the rest of it, complete, in good faith. He makes a generous settlement with his debtor and willingly forgets the rest.

Indeed, if Cicero says in praise of Julius Caesar that he used to forget nothing save wrongs done, how much more worthily is it said in praise of Christ, of whom, were He not forgetful of wrongs done but mindful of us and of His own mercy, the prophet would vainly have said: "When You will be angry, You will recall Your mercy" [Hab. 3:2]. And again: "Remember Your compassion, O Lord, and Your mercies down through the ages" [Ps. 25:6]. And still again: "Do not recall the misdeeds of my youth and my ignorance," and immediately after that: "In Your mercy remember me" [Ps. 25:7]. Believe me, He will remember you and your wretchedness, and He will, unbidden, remember His mercy. And why not? Who would not gladly recall and reflect upon the best thing he has? Who in unlocking his storehouses would not more frequently and avidly examine what is most precious there? If Caesar's eulogist, about whom I was just speaking, says in his honor that none of his many, many virtues was more admirable or pleasing than his mercy, how much more worthily does it apply to Christ, about whom it is written: "The earth is full of the Lord's mercy" [Ps. 33:5]; "the Lord is kind to all, and His mercy is over all His works" [Ps. 145:9]; "it is because of God's mercy that we are not destroyed" [Lam. 4:9]. On the other hand, do not doubt that He will forget your offenses, provided you wish to forget all your evil inclinations and evil habits; I say He will forget and erase your iniquity, and, as far as the east is from the west, will distance them from you, and He will cleanse you of your sin and cast it out so that, though sought, it will not be found. He who promised has not deceived: "He will lay aside our iniquities and will now hurl our sins into the depths of the sea" [Mic. 7:19]. Nor will He stop this until He has fulfilled all that, so that where sin abounded will abound grace—which we know He has done in many cases, and we trust He will do. In short, you will find in Him more than you would ever dare to hope or wish for, unless it depended on yourself. For He Himself demands no condition as long as one places oneself in the hands of the Lord.

Thus, He will gladly receive you as you return, as though you owed nothing; and perhaps all the more gladly, all the more joyfully was that son welcomed back who returned after wasting his patrimony, and the more exultantly was the sheep welcomed back that was lost in the desert, and the drachma that was lost at home; and altogether the greater the joy over one sinner who repents than over ninety-nine righteous men who do not need to repent. This was not written to incite righteous men to sin, but to draw the wicked ones back from despair. Come to Him trustingly; do not let fear or shame impede you, or hold you back. But pull them along with you, for dread and abasement are good company for a sinner, and acceptable to God provided they do not shut out hope and faith. Have fear concerning yourself, but hope concerning your Lord; you will find Him well-disposed toward you if you confess sincerely that you are guilty and He is your Lord; in one day you have suffered more trouble and more insolence and wrath from a man who is mortal like yourself, and perhaps going to die a worse death than you, than you are going to suffer for all time from the Lord of all. No greedy doorkeeper, no arrogant hatchetman will keep you out; you will be able to approach Him and speak with Him day and night. He will always listen to you, and if you seek anything properly, He will hear you out, although it may not be necessary to seek many things; and we have learned one thing is necessary, as He says: "The heavenly Father knows the things we lack, and is aware of our needs; let us therefore first seek that one thing, namely, the kingdom of God, and all these others will be granted us besides" [based on Matt. 6:32–33].

But if ever He should perchance appear too stern or slow, wait, take it easy, do not distrust Him, do not get upset or sick and tired of waiting, do not let impatience come anywhere near you; you will get either what you want or what is good for you. But if perchance, as very often is the case in the halls of mortal masters, you believe that you need an intercessor with the Lord, there is always a direct and easy path to His grace. You do not need money, nor trickery, nor flattery, but piety and faith. There is the Virgin Mother whose kindness has never been equaled under the sun, and whose gentleness has never been equaled in our entire race. Her humility is such that it made her worthy of heaven, and it was able to bend the Lord of heaven to earth, since God, soon to become man, seems to have considered her alone paramount while preparing for Himself a fitting mother from our species. Finally, all the virtues so stand out in her that, except the soul of her Son alone, they have never been so excellent in any other soul; she presents the prayers of the faithful, though sinners, to her Son, and with pitying insistence seeks forgiveness for them. For though she hates sins, she does not hate sinners, but rather takes pity on them, cherishes their conversion, and longs for their salvation, recalling that from their sin and the wretchedness that is born of sin divine mercy bent down and created the stuff of such great honor and felicity for her as to make her the mother of God while remaining a virgin; nothing in the entire world was ever more fruitful and nothing more chaste.

If by chance, as sometimes happens, especially in great courts, there is need for another intercessor with the intercessor, and you think this pious expedient necessary for you, the best remedy is near: you have Bernard, the prince of your order, who I am persuaded loves you and enjoys your presence, and desires that in his home, which you preferred to the world, you should be well and happy. Call upon him, no one is readier to bring help, no one, as we believe, is more pleasing to Our Lady, no one is more a friend. Kind generals love to be on hand for their trusty recruits; so, in brief, you have intercessors, you have ready access, you have silence and leisure, you have solitary and holy places, you alone have everything, in short, unless you fail yourself, which I hope you will not do. You were not lazy in the world and in the eyes of men, when laziness is often useful and zeal is harmful; you will not be lazy in the monastery before the eyes of God, where zeal is always useful and laziness deadly. Out there, everything revolved around transitory and vain things, as you now see, here, your eternal salvation; it is an obvious error of the world and blindness of the crowd to pursue little fleeting things, and to look down on great, enduring ones. But you will err no more in this; you have tried everything, sifted things one by one, and you will hold on to what is best. Though still young, you saw things that many aged men have not seen; unless I am mistaken, there is nothing you have not experienced; it is your responsibility to see to it that nothing is wrong with your will.

Therefore, not to distract you any longer from praying, persist in this: that each day you reveal your invisible sickness and the hidden wound of your soul to the heavenly Physician; hidden, I say, to others, for nothing is hidden to God who searches the heart and the innards, yet loves to have what He sees revealed to Him, and hates it to be hidden. Nor should the magnitude of your wretchedness frighten you from this, for He is a much greater comforter than you are a wretch. Our wretchedness is indeed great, but God's mercy is infinite. Nor have any doubt that you seek something too great or unusual; while I realize it is great, or rather, for you, the greatest, for Him it is tiny; if you are a sinful man, He is "the Lamb of God who takes away the sins of the world" [John 1:29], who has not come to call the righteous but the sinners. Will not the One who, with His burden, relieves the world of the weight of so many sins, relieve one man? If you are sick and do not feel well, He says: "Those who are well do not need a physician, but those who are ill do" [Luke 5:31]. If your conscience is leprous, He does not shudder at lepers who have lain down in your home, lest anyone doubt whether He would enter the dwelling of a leprous mind when invited; He also cleansed lepers, and to the leper who said to Him, "Lord, if you will, you can cleanse me," He replied, "So be it; be clean" [Matt. 8:2, Luke 5:12]; and, sooner than it was said, He dispelled the leprosy itself simply by extending His hand full of blessing.

But if our adversary has seized in your soul some right of sinning by your doing so over and over, the Lord himself freed those possessed by demons. If even now your little boat is being struck by the storms of temporal things and by the swells of your past life, still He calmed storms and saved Peter from drowning in the waves, and snatched Paul from shipwreck three times; if your will is so stooped and turned earthward that it cannot look up, if you are lame, if your feelings are paralyzed and cannot raise themselves up, if your hands are withered and incapable of works of piety, He straightened up those who were bent and lame and paralyzed, He restored withered limbs with healing moisture. And if perchance, shrunken by long illness, you cannot help yourself and have no one else to help you, it was that very same One who bade a sick man, immobile for thirty-eight years, to rise; and he rose carrying his cot on his shoulders. If any heat of former passions still grips your soul like a fever, by touching with His hand, He healed Peter's mother-in-law, who was gravely ill with fever. If an insatiable dropsy presses on your mind, He cured those with dropsy. If your inner eyes are blind, He made the blind see. If your ears are deaf to warnings from heaven, if your lips are silent either in the praises of God or in the confession of your sins, He made the deaf to hear and the dumb to speak. If, finally, you are dead because of sin, if you are infected with evil habits, He awakened the dead and returned to life bodies dug up from graves after four days of rotting. Therefore, you will seek nothing that He has not granted and that He will not most willingly grant; seek fearlessly but reverently what you need; once more, as I have said, only one thing is necessary, whereas many are harmful and useless.

And do not fear that you may be rude; He himself taught such rudeness. He says, "Ask and you shall receive; seek and you shall find; knock and it shall be opened to you" [Matt. 7:7; Luke 11:9].

Speaking of the pagan gods, the Satirist says, "Man is dearer to them than to himself" [Juv. 10.350]—he aspired to the truth, but did not reach it. For since all the pagan gods are demons, man is doubtless not dear to them, but hateful, and they begrudge every happiness and every holy joy, and rejoice in our misery and grief. If you want to say this correctly, change the word "gods" to the one true God: man is indeed dearer to Him than to himself, for he is always dear to Him who, as it is written, loves everything that is, and hates nothing of what He has created; nor is there any doubt that He should in the first place love man, who was made in the beginning in His image and likeness, whom later He deigned to want to be made like him. As we read, He was made in the likeness of man, and, having taken on his form, He cannot as man not love what He is; therefore, He loves more and has loved earlier as One who is much better and older; He is all love and eternity; He has loved us before we loved Him or ourselves, indeed even before we came into existence. For unless He had loved, He would not have created, so He deserves to be loved, or rather to be loved in return, having been the first to love and outdoing us in both love and time, of whom John the Apostle says: "Let us love the Lord because He Himself loved us first" [1 John 4:19]. And Paul says: "Christ loved us and sacrificed Himself for us" [based on Gal. 2:20]. But why seek other witnesses? He, our Lover and our God, speaking of his Father, says: "God so loved the world that He gave His only begotten Son" [John 3:16], meaning by "world" nothing more than man, but man is not always so dear to himself as he is to God. For although the same Apostle does say: "No one will ever hate his own flesh" [Eph. 5:29], still it has often been obvious from the outcome that many in loving their soul hate their flesh, and that for them it has been either outright hatred or love having the effect of hatred. Being thus beloved and dearer to your Lord than to yourself, seek with confidence and without hesitation, for you are seeking from One who loves you and has what you seek, One who is eager and accustomed to give and denies nothing worthy of being given. I repeat this knowingly, for if it has been said plausibly of an earthly ruler, how much more plausibly of the heavenly One who, after giving everything to man that can be desired, and, what is best, happiness and Himself, is still left with His treasures all undiminished. Indeed I would say they are increased, except that what is complete and perfect admits of no addition or increase.

Certainly every day something is added to the number of divine gifts, and His mercy, which cannot be greater, becomes more evident; therefore, although you will seek something above your merits, although you, as all of us, are unworthy of such a great gift, He will not consider this, and does not ask what it befits you to receive, but what it befits Him to give. Seneca censured this in Alexander, King of the Macedonians, but in our eternal King it certainly cannot be censured by anyone, but should rather be praised by everyone. For if He were to ask what it befits us to receive, He would give us either nothing or punishment; therefore, He looks at Himself, measures Himself, and has mercy on us according to His great mercy, not our works; for by grace we were saved through faith, and this is not our doing—for it is a gift of God, as the Apostle says—nor through our good works, lest anyone boast; but each of us has done what is characteristic of a sinner, while He does what is characteristic of a Redeemer. So leave all distrust behind, let the hope of salvation abide; whoever you may be, what you seek anyhow is not unworthy of being given. For you seek neither harm for anyone, nor vain advantages for yourself, empty wealth, inglorious honors, fragile power, but the mercy of God and the salvation of your soul, which, once achieved, will make you much richer than any kings with all their pomp in which they, who are dust and ashes, blindly strut.

But enough of this; let this be the gist of it, and I will end on it. Once you had many lords, earthly princes and kings, through whom you could have perished; now you have one Lord through whom you can be saved, and He is uplifted above all the kings of the earth, He is awesome and takes away the life-breath of princes, He is the dread of earthly kings. Therefore, worship Him and love Him, so as to fulfill the meaning of your name: for whatever else I seem to have written at some time according to my subject's demands, holy love cannot be of this world, since it is written: "Do not love the world nor the things that are in the world since all that is in the world is the concupiscence of the flesh and the concupiscence of the eyes, and the pride of life" [1 John 2:15–16]. And again, "Adulterers, you do not know that the friendship of this world is an enemy to God" [James 4:4]. Hence, so that you may be worthy of your name Sagremor, love heaven and yearn for the Lord of heaven, seek Him of whom it is said: "Always seek His face" [Ps. 105:4]; and once you have found Him, latch on to Him and embrace Him with the very arms of your soul; follow Augustine's advice, do not fear to throw yourself at Him; He will not move back and let you fall; throw yourself confidently, He will pick you up and heal you. And you already feel this, I think; you are already beginning to be healed by Him who, since the works of God are perfect, will complete, believe me, what He begins, will not grow weary, nor slow down, nor seek excuses, but will accompany you to the end. He will not abandon you either in life or in death, but will be with you especially then to receive the spirit that He created, to be borne by His angels to the peaceful dwellings, and through His priests will commit your body to the earth, to be taken up again on the last day so that your happiness will be complete. And so, you who worked so hard for a little passing gain, now a little pleasant labor, indeed serving the best of Lords with much respite, will earn infinite and eternal rewards. Thinking this over earnestly, and comparing the past and future, you will never feel either sadness or fatigue or numbness. And I am saying so much to you today not because you are in need of all this, but because in speaking to you I shall hear myself; one learns by teaching. Often advice given to another benefits the giver.

However, your inciting me with your words, but much more with your example, is an act of love. That you seek a letter of mine, as if you had need of encouragement to persevere in such a noble beginning, that, dear friend, is humble and courteous, like everything you do; for in truth what is in me besides your esteem and my loyalty from which you can expect much help, whether real or verbal? I could repeat what I once wrote in an enormous letter to my brother, who had entered a Carthusian monastery by the same path as you have now entered a Cistercian monastery, a letter I later enlarged and addressed to him and to his brethren, but this does not seem either necessary for you or easy for me [*Fam.* X, 3].

Of the two things you request, aside from the letter, I did what the majority of those who call themselves friends do—either nothing or very little. So I did the minimum; I sent the seven psalms that I long ago composed for myself in my misery. I wish they were as edifying as they are inelegant, for I tried to make them both. You will read them as they are and do so more patiently if you will remember that they are what you asked for, and that I dictated them many years ago in less than one day. My book, *De uita solitaria*, which you request as solace for your solitude, I cannot send for the present, for I had only two copies and no more, to begin with. You took one of them with you that last time you left to give to my tried and true Father, to whom it is dedicated [P. de Cabassoles], whose joy at receiving it you read on his face and I in his letter. The other remains with me, and although my judgment does not make as much of it as his love did, still I would not like to be left without it. But if by chance a dependable copyist—a real rarity, I admit—comes along, you may expect, I dare say, that I shall do readily and willingly that and whatever else I can for your comfort, especially so that you may move forward in your pursuit of religion and peace of mind and love of Christ. When, dear brother, through holy sighs and pious tears—which are the most efficacious way to break the hardness of sin and to quell and avert the wrath of God and receive His grace— you feel on very good terms with Him, I will ask you to pray for me so that, whatever the end of my life, it be good and pleasing to Him in whom, as He Himself knows, my last, or rather, my only hope rests. Live well, mindful of our friendship, and farewell.

Venice, March 18 [1367-68].

Sen. X, 2.

To Guido Sette, Archbishop of Genoa,* on how times change.

I know that opinion of Flaccus is against me where, discussing with the ways of old men, he calls them stubborn and complaining, admirers of time gone by, when they were boys [Ars P. 173-74]. I do not deny that it is indeed so, but while perhaps contradicting what I have often said elsewhere, I am not now contradicting Horace's epistle, for although I am a complainer and an admirer of olden times, this praise of the old or complaint about the new will be true. Often through lips accustomed to lying, the truth rings out. While a speaker may detract from the Truth, she herself inspires confidence; I say, and I hope you will agree; I say, I regret, and, if it befits a man, I bewail: why are we living out our old age in years that are so much worse than they were in our youth, unless, as I surmise, a man's life is like a tree's—just as it withstands the threats and storms of heaven, so does man withstand with greater toughness the hardships of the world and the storms of life, which he could not have withstood in his more tender years.

But this consolation is appropriate for us, not so for others. For as we grow old, countless others are just growing up, and while we were growing up, some were growing old; and it can happen that, whereas a peaceful old age awaits our juniors, our predecessors had a troubled childhood. Therefore, passing over the others, I come to our situation; while by living we certainly may have become tougher at bearing ills, we have become more vulnerable to many things and more resentful of everything, as no one will deny. There is nothing more resentful than old age. Although it has learned to control and hide emotions, it still feels, as no age does more deeply, being weary and consumed by life's vexations. This is my opinion, which I have arrived at not by listening or reading, but by experience; I do not know whether you agree, but certainly the truth itself, brighter than the sun, will force you to agree with what I have started saying about the deterioration and ruin of our times.

I think it will not be disagreeable or useless even now to recall

---

* One of P.'s earliest friends, whose father had moved his family to Avignon at the same time as did P.'s father. Reared together in the papal court, they sealed a friendship that lasted their entire lives. This is the only letter to him.

past time a little; so then, cast your glance backward with me as far as you can. The first part of our lives you spent at your home and I in my exile [in Arezzo]. You will not find great things to say for that period when the light of reason and intelligence was so slight. At that dividing line between infancy and childhood we were by chance both transported at nearly the same time into Transalpine Gaul, the province now called Provence and formerly Arelatensis. We were immediately united in friendship, as is normal at that age, but it was to last until the end; and we embarked on the same course of life. Here I say nothing about your Genoa through which we passed then, and within whose borders you were born, and where you now sit on the highest episcopal seat (you know all this, and I, for my part, wrote an extensive letter to the doge and council of that city, a letter I know you saw and approved [*Fam.* XIV, 5]). The destination of our childhood journey was the city called Avennio by the ancients, and Avignon by the moderns. Since the city was cramped because the Roman Pontiff [Clement V], and the Church with him, had recently emigrated there and was not to return to her See even after sixty years, and it lacked housing at that time and was overflowing with the scum of the earth, our elders decided that it would be best for the women and children to move to a nearby place. We two, who were still boys and smooth-cheeked, were included with the others in that move, but were sent elsewhere, to a grammar school. The name of the place was Carpentras, which was a small city, but the capital of its little province. You remember that period of four years: how much joy we found there, how much carefreeness, what peace at home, what freedom in public, what fun in the fields, what silence! I believe you must certainly feel as I do; I am still grateful to that time, or rather to the Author of all times, who gave me such tranquil days that, far from any storms of life, I might drink the bland milk of childhood learning, fit for the weakness of my mind, to grow stronger and ready for more solid food.

But one might say that we have changed, and hence everything around likewise seems to us changed; the same thing seems different to a healthy eye and palate than to a sick one. We have changed, I confess, for who is there of flesh and blood, or even of iron or stone, that would not change in so long a time? Statues of bronze and marble yield to time, man-made cities and castles that hug the mountaintops, and, even more devastating, solid rocks from the mountains themselves—all these tumble down. What, then, must I expect a man to do, a mortal animal built of fragile limbs and enclosed in his thin skin? But is the change so great as to take away the judgment or the senses while the soul remains? I quite believe that if that past age were to return to us as we are today, it would not at all appear to us as it did then; were I to say that the years have done nothing at all to it, still it will surely appear different. Nevertheless, was it not far better and more peaceful than it is now? Or because the eyes perhaps do not discern the wheel spokes on Myrmicides' chariot, that tiny masterpiece—which they say a fly covered with its wings—or because the eyes are too dim to count ants' feet and other parts whose fineness defies the keenest human vision, or to read clearly and quickly through that *Iliad* which, Cicero says, was copied so minutely that it was all on one nutshell, why should they be so dim that they do not see the cities, the streets, the citizens, their ways, their dress, the houses, the churches? Are our minds so dull that they do not recognize that everything has been changed and spoiled? And did we not later often see that little town so different from what it once was that not to see such an enormous change in everything could rather seem the sign of a deranged mind?

Not many years after we left, it became what it had not been before, the tribunal seat of the entire province, or, to put it more accurately, the home of devils. Leisure, happiness, tranquillity came to an end; everything was filled at once with the turmoil and clamor of the court. What is the point of blaming the change on us who went elsewhere, and, as we moved from place to place and our age advanced, we could, of course, change, and no doubt we did; but now its own people no longer recognize the city, as we learn from the frequent complaints of those we know. Someone may respond that this change was for the sake of justice, which seldom can be administered without shouting. But I am discussing the change itself, not its cause. Has it served the cause of justice that after many years that same city and the surrounding region, which seemed very safe and nearly exempt from attack and beyond the reach of Mars, out of respect for the Apostolic See that holds sway over it, were not only attacked by an army of marauders, but laid waste and brought to the extremes of misery? If anyone, while we were boys, were to prophesy that it would ever happen there, would he not have been considered a hateful, and even a mad, prophet?

But let me keep things in order; and though I could discuss major matters, yet I would much rather speak with you about things that we saw together, so that your memory might support my assertions. We also, then, left that city together, for what did we do separately for a large part of our lives? In our teens we moved to Montpellier, at that time a very flourishing city, to study law, and spent another four years there. At that time the ruler was the King of Majorca in the Balearic Isles, except for a very small corner subject to the King of France who, as the mighty are always nasty neighbors, seized control of the entire city in a short time. But even then, what tranquillity, what peacefulness, what wealth of merchants, what swarms of students, what an abundance of teachers! Now, instead, we and the residents who saw both periods perceive what a dearth there is of all these things, and what a change in both the public and the private sphere.

From there we went on to Bologna, than which I think there could be nothing happier in the whole world, and nothing freer. You must remember the great gathering of students, the order, the alertness, the majesty of the teachers. You would have thought that the ancient jurists had come back to life; today there is hardly any one left, but a universal ignorance has invaded the city in place of so many great minds. Would that it had entered as an enemy and not as a welcome guest, and if as a guest, not as a citizen or, what is most frightening, as a queen, since everyone appears to me to have thrown up their hands and surrendered their weapons! Furthermore, what an abundance of everything there was then, what fertility, so that in all countries it had come to be nicknamed "fat Bologna"! I admit it is beginning to revive and grow fat again under the pious guardianship of this Supreme Pontiff [Urban V], but, at this point, if you examined not only its vitals, but its very marrow, you would find nothing thinner, nothing drier. That fine man [Androino Cardinal de la Roche] who was recently sent to govern it as legate-at-large, as they say, referred to this wittily, since it was his wont to joke about troubles. When I came to visit him three years ago, and he welcomed his humble guest with open arms and much too graciously, we began discussing various matters, and I asked about the state of affairs of the city. He replied, "This, dear friend, was once Bologna, but now it is Macerata [afflicted]," playing on the name of the town in the Piceno.

You sense, I think, that it is bittersweet for me to dwell upon these evils and the memory of good things; there lingers in my memory, and, I believe, in yours, a fixed, indelible imprint of that time when I lived there as one of the students; already a more passionate age had arrived as I entered adolescence and was more daring than I should have been and had been. I used to go with my peers; we would wander afar on holidays, so that often sunset would find us in the country, and we would return in the dead of night, and the gates were wide open; and if somehow they were closed, the city had no wall anyhow: a fragile palisade, already split apart by age, surrounded the fearless city. What need was there for a wall or even a palisade in such profound peace? There were therefore many entrances instead of just one, and everyone picked the most convenient one; there was nothing difficult, nothing suspect. For there to be any need of walls, towers, fortresses, armed guards, a night watch, it took first the poison of an internal tyranny, then the plots and assaults of external enemies. Why compel my pen to linger on Bologna as I dredge up the familiar past, if not because the recollection of that old Bologna is so fresh for me that each time I happen to see it I believe I am dreaming and cannot trust my own eyes, that now for so many years war has replaced peace,* slavery freedom, poverty wealth, grief joy, laments songs, gangs of bandits dancing girls, to the point that except for the towers and churches still standing and looking down upon the wretched city from their lofty pinnacles, what used to be called Bononia looks now for a long time like anything but Bononia, the good land?

But let us now leave Bologna. After four years there I returned home, I mean the home that my luck—oh, that it had been good!—had substituted for the one I had lost on the Arno. That place on the muddy banks of the Rhone, from beginning to end, seemed to many and above all to me the worst in the world, not so much on account of itself, but because all the filth and lewdness of the whole world empty into it and thicken and jell. And although in my opinion always the same, yet it has become so much worse that—as only an utterly shameless liar would dare deny—if that old city were compared with its present self, it could seem the best in the world. Not to dwell on particulars, I must say that while there was no faith and no charity, and as was said of Hannibal, "nothing true, nothing holy, no fear of God, no oath, no religion" [Livy 24.4.9], even so, in that place which ought to have been the stronghold of the true religion, not because of its own merits but because of being chosen by the head of the Church, there was anyhow, at least outwardly, a good deal of security and freedom. These have so completely perished that, among other things, it is dominated by the publicans' yoke until now unheard-of and unknown there; and because of the grave fear of enemies thundering endlessly on all sides, it has been necessary to surround the city with new fortifications and to block the

* We emend *pati* to *paci.*

gateways with arms even at midday, when everything had been open throughout the night. Nor did that avail; rather, being unprotected by weapons and fortifications, its safety had to be ransomed with gold and entreaties. I believe that was done or allowed through God's will, so that His Vicar and advisers would be drawn to remember and long for the bride who had been too long neglected. You see that this has already happened to the Pontiff, either because of this or his natural virtue; the others who are more stubborn will either be softened by God or by death, which already seems to have begun. Yet if these ills have struck the head, let the limbs bear them more patiently; and let no one marvel if respect for the absent Pontiff does not restrain those whom he was unable to control when he was present and they were on his threshold. And lest the old habit of evil nullify the recent good and, by pecking away at spirits as yet unsettled, perchance bring on an urge to return there, that region, we know, is now more than ever exposed to pillage.

Before I go any further, I shall say something that is weighing upon me, and I shall attempt today what I would not wish to come true—to become young by speaking with you. You know how in the bloom of surging life which—as I mentioned before— we spent in the straw of the grammar school as if in a bed of roses, my father and your uncle, who were then almost the same age as we are now, came as usual to Carpentras, that small town I just mentioned. And your uncle, like a newcomer, once got the idea of visiting the celebrated source of the Sorgue, because, I believe, it was nearby and a novelty. It was long known; and if one may boast to a friend, that is, to one's other self, about a trifle, it has become somewhat better known because of my long residence there and my poetry. When we heard about it, with boyish eagerness we had our hearts set on being taken along. Since we could not safely be trusted on horseback, we were each assigned a servant to ride the horses, and, as is done, to hold us in the saddle. And so, when at last my mother, the best of all I have seen, mine by birth but yours too through love, was barely convinced though full of fears and warnings, we set out with that wonderful man. The mere recollection of him is a joy; you bear his name and surname, but have added a great deal of learning and fame.

When we came to the source of the Sorgue (I remember it as if it were today!), I was thrilled by the unusual panorama, and I said as best I could with those childish thoughts of mine, "Here is the perfect place for me; someday, given the chance, I shall choose this over the great cities." This I said then silently to myself; but later, when I reached manhood, I made it known to everyone by clear signs and in whatever leisure the world did not begrudge me. For I spent many years there, but they were often interrupted by business that called me away, and by the difficulties of the times; still, I enjoyed such peace and pleasure that, since I learned what it is to live, that has been almost the only time I truly lived; all the rest was but punishment. Though indivisible in spirit, we were by that time led apart by our pursuits: you followed the law and the courts, I sought leisure and the shade of the country; you acquired honest wealth in a public career, while—strange to say—it so chased after this solitary fellow, this refugee who despised it, into the thickest woods, that I have incurred envy. Why need I describe to you now that rural silence, that incessant babble of the sparkling river, the lowing of cattle in the echoing valleys, and those choruses of birds in the branches, not only by day but at night? You know all this, and although you dared not follow me all the way in this, still as often as you could steal yourself from the city throngs, which was all too seldom, you would eagerly take refuge there as in a port from the storm.

How often, do you think, the dark night would find me alone, far off in the fields, how often would I rise in the middle of the night throughout the summer, and, after reciting the nightly office in praise of Christ, go out at times into the fields, especially in the moonlight, and at times into the mountains—all alone, not to disturb the servants who were sound asleep? How often at that hour, unaccompanied, not without a thrill of delight, I would enter that enormous cavern of the river's source when it is hair-raising to enter even with a group by daylight. If one were to ask where I found so much confidence, the fact is I have no fear of shadows and ghosts, never was a wolf seen in that valley, there was nothing to fear from men; plowmen sang in the fields, fishermen watched silently in the river, and they outdid one another to please me, and offered every kind of service at all hours, since they knew that their master, the lord of the area, was not only a friend to me, but a very dear brother and father [Philippe de Cabassoles]. There were well-wishers everywhere, enemies nowhere; and so, considering everything, I had convinced myself, and you backed me and felt the same way, that if the whole world were shaken by war, that place would remain untroubled and peaceful. What made me believe this was the respect for the Roman Church, as I have said, and—much more than that—the proximity [to Avignon], but above all the poverty of the place; for that is the most untroubled thing in the world and can scoff at greed and warfare.

If you did not know what* has happened since then, you might marvel: while I was still there, packs of wolves from elsewhere had begun to burst even into the village houses, to make carnage of livestock and to keep the people themselves bewildered and shuddering. Not only were they pests, but a foretaste and a portent, I believe, of the armed wolves that were to come. In fact, not long after I left there, a small band of robbers, foul and notorious, counting on the inhabitants' cowardice, ransacked and pillaged everything; and finally, to show indeed that they were consecrated thieves and that they duly sacrificed part of their spoils to Laverna, the goddess of thieves, they took the village unawares, right on Christmas Day, carried away what they could, and consigned everything else to the flames. They set fire to that little refuge of mine, from which I scorned the palace of Croesus; but the old vault withstood the flames since the damnable robbers were in a hurry. A number of books that I had left behind had been taken by my overseer's son, who already had a foreshadowing that this would happen, into the stronghold which the bandits thought impregnable, as it is; but as it was, not knowing it was undefended and empty, they went away. Thus, the books were unexpectedly saved from their evil clutches, as God provided that so noble a prey not fall into such foul hands.

After that, go and rely upon the dark recesses of Vaucluse! Nothing is closed off, nothing too high, nothing too dark for thieves and bandits; they penetrate everything, they foresee everything, and they search everything! There is no place so well protected and so elevated that armed greed and lawless rapacity cannot scale. But so help me God, as I consider the present state of that place and recall the past, I can scarcely believe that it is the same place where I used to wander at night over the mountains, alone and carefree. Perhaps I have said more about this than it merits, reckoning not the insignificance of that place in the country, but the sweetness of my solitude; in order to link old happenings to new ones so as to prove how things have changed, I have abandoned the order; but I am turning back.

Well then, in the fourth year, after I returned from Bologna, I visited Toulouse, the Garonne valley, and the Pyrenees, together with that man whom I have often praised but never as much as he deserved [Giacomo Colonna, Bishop of Lombez]. The weather was often stormy, but the company was so cheerful. What shall I say

---

* We emend *quid* to *quod*.

about these places except what I have said about the others? In name Toulouse is the same, Gascony and Aquitaine are the same, but in fact they are all entirely different, and, aside from the ground beneath them, they no longer resemble their former selves. Three years after my return from there, prompted by youthful eagerness and an urge to see the world, I visited the city of Paris; on that journey and on the way back I was so spurred by youthful enthusiasm that I toured the furthest corners of the kingdom, and Flanders, Brabant, Hainaut, and lower Germany. When I recently returned there on business, I scarcely recognized anything at all as I looked upon the wealthiest kingdom turned to ashes and hardly a single house left standing except for those surrounded by city walls or fortresses. I wrote and spoke of this at length to that old gentleman, Pierre de Poitiers [Bersuire], who has since passed away, but would have been happier to pass away a little sooner.

Where is that Paris which, though always less than its reputation and owing much to the lies of its inhabitants, was nonetheless a great city beyond any doubt? Where are the swarms of students, the enthusiasm of the University, the wealth of the citizens, the universal cheer? You do not hear the shouting of disputants, but of warriors; you do not see piles of books, but of arms; not syllogisms or sermons, but the shouts of sentries and the crash of battering-rams echoing against the walls; the cries of eager hunters cease, the noise is at the city walls, the woods are still, the people hardly safe even in the cities; the tranquillity that seemed to have found its temple there has given way and disappeared completely; nowhere is there so little security, nowhere so many perils. Who, I ask, would ever have guessed that the French King [John II], though the most invincible of men as far as he himself is concerned, would be conquered, led to prison, and ransomed at a huge price? Yet, the perpetrator of this horror made it more tolerable: the King was conquered by a king, although a lesser one [Edward III]. But what is utterly distressing and shameful was the fact that the King himself and his son [Charles V], who now rules, were prevented from returning to their country and forced to bargain with the bandits, in order to travel in safety through their own lands. Who, I say, would ever have dreamed of it—imagine*—in that happy realm, let alone have thought of it! How will posterity believe this if, as human affairs are so unstable, that kingdom were at some time or other restored to its

---

* We emend *autumno* to *autumo*.

former stature? For us it is not something we believe; we see it.

But after returning from there, that is, from my first trip to Gaul, once again after four years, I went for the first time to Rome; although by that time and long before that it was nothing but a kind of sketch and death-mask of ancient Rome, attesting to its past greatness by its present ruins, there were still some noble sparks in its ashes; now the ashes are quenched and ice-cold. There was only one phoenix reborn from the ashes of the former ones, that grand old man, Stefano Colonna, father of my lord whom I mentioned above, and of a great, illustrious, but much too ill-fated family, a man whom I often celebrated along with his family—and he deserves it. There were others for whom those ancestral ruins, at any rate, were dear, but none of them now survives, either there or anywhere on earth.

After another four years I journeyed to Naples, and although I have often since then returned to Rome and Naples, the first impressions still cling to my memory. Robert was then King of Sicily, or rather of Italy, or better king of kings, whose life was the joy of the kingdom, and whose death its downfall. He did not live very long after my departure. Surely, if heaven intervened and he was forbidden to repair the growing evils as he was wont to, hardly anyone is granted a more timely death, so that to me such a death seems to have come at the very height of the life's happiness. Four years later—and it seems that I was then experiencing life four years at a time!—upon returning there, which I never would have done except that I was so bidden by Clement, who was then the Roman Pontiff, I did indeed see the walls and the squares, the sea, the port, the surrounding vine-clad hills, and, further off, Falerno on this side and Vesuvius on that side, and also Capri, Ischia, Procida, those wave-beaten islands, and Baiae which steams even in the winter months; but I did not find the Naples I knew. I did notice the seeds of many calamities and clear signs of impending disaster, and I regret being so accurate a prophet. What I felt about it I reported not only orally, but in letters, while fortune was already thundering, but not yet shooting its lightning bolts; and it all was fulfilled so soon afterward, along with so many other evils, that my own prophecy, however terrible, was surpassed by an infinite series of evils that are much easier to deplore than enumerate.

Not long before that time, in these lands where as a young man I had been a carefree student and where I now returned as a man, drawn by the friendship of him to whose memory I am still much indebted [Azzo da Correggio], I saw all of Cisalpine Gaul which I had barely seen earlier, and not as a traveler, but as a resident of many cities, Verona among the first, and soon Parma and Ferrara, finally Padua where I was drawn again by the chain of friendship, which I cannot seem to break. There was another excellent man [Giacomo da Carrara the younger] whose downfall I shall never recall without grieving, and who, though a most eminent and famous man everywhere, long solicited the friendship of an insignificant outsider whom he had known only by name, and, as he himself used to say, had never seen except once, and that was only in passing; for a long time he desired my friendship as though he were about to acquire through me something great for himself and for his state, and—I have a feeling—as though I would have permanent residence in that city while he lived; after he passed away, I continued the residency although with interruptions for compelling reasons. Well, this city, from the time I first came to it, was so shattered by that recent frightful plague; since then, because of the foresight and dedication of his first-born and because of the unbroken peace until now, one must recognize that among all the other cities it stands firm and is not downcast. But compared to what it was the year before I came, that is, before the plague began, it is, like all the others, much smaller and altogether different.

Later I came to know Milan and Pavia. And what do you want me to say? Of them all, not one is what it was—I do not mean many centuries ago, but within recent memory; for I speak of things I have seen, not things I have read or heard. Milan itself, the city which I read was flourishing mightily fifteen hundred years ago, and which I believe has never flourished more than in our age, is no longer flourishing as it was, although it still stands upon its size and power, and, as they say, its own weight. Question its residents, and they will confess that all this is so, and will add something of their own, even sadder. What shall I say of Pisa, where I spent the seventh year of my life, or of Siena? What of Arezzo, dear to me as the place of my birth and my first exile, or of neighboring Perugia, or of others? The condition of all of them is the same. Today they are not what they were yesterday, so that while the change in things is marvelous, the speed of it is incredible and stupendous.

I could guide you around this* way through the whole of Italy, or rather all of Europe generally, and everywhere I would find new support for my position; but I fear that I would weary myself and

* We emend *modo* to *hoc modo*.

you and others, should there be any who will hear and read this colloquy of ours—if I were to lead you with my pen through all the lands where the change is both dreadful and evident. Still I have enjoyed—I know not whether this is the appropriate term for it, except that there is a certain enjoyment in lamentation—and have really felt like wandering with you in words over the past years and distant lands, especially those in which I was with you once upon a time, and retracing with my pen the journeys that we took together on foot or by ship.

However, under no circumstances can I retrace all these things in memory without mentioning my ancestral home [Florence]. Indeed, what else is she if not a clear proof of this dismal fluctuation, since only yesterday, in perfect keeping with her name, she flowered in everything to the point of envy, not only among other Italian cities, but among the cities of Christendom; lately, being stricken by continual evils from without, by conflagrations and factions* and plagues within, she serves, pitiably disfigured, as warning to all mortals, especially to her own citizens, of how much hope one must place in things that perish.

Here some contentious person would perhaps object. For there is a breed of men who, being too weak to defend the truth and unable to keep quiet, attack it with quibbles, and make this their trade. Since it cannot be denied about the cities that I have mentioned, one will admit that this is true, but perhaps not so about others, and that in this regard there is no change of the whole because the dwindling of one is equaled by the growth of another. To this I reply: show me the opposite even in one city in the west or north, and he will have won. For certainly this very city from which I am now writing you, and where I have finally taken up residence, in search not so much of pleasure but of quiet and safety—I mean Venice—may be prosperous and peaceful compared to all the others on our continent because of its location and its citizens' wisdom; but it was also more prosperous at the time when I first came here from Bologna as a youngster for a visit with my teacher. And neither would you hear the citizens denying that this is so, although I myself will not deny the fact that it has grown somewhat, indeed a great deal, in the number of buildings.

But if the quibbler draws me further away, I shall admit that I know not what is happening among the Indians and Chinese, but

---

* We emend *intersectis* to *intus sectis*.

Egypt and Syria and Armenia and all of Asia Minor show no more increase in wealth and no better lot than we do. For the downfall of Greece is ancient, while that of the Scythians [Russians] is recent; as a result, from where lately huge quantities of grain would be brought every year by ship into this city, today ships from there come laden with slaves whose wretched parents eagerly offer them for sale; already a strange and enormous crowd of slaves of both sexes, like a muddy torrent tainting a very clear stream, taints this very beautiful city with Scythian faces and hideous filth. If they were not more acceptable to their buyers than they are to me, and if they were not more pleasing to their eyes than to mine, these repulsive youths would not crowd our narrow streets; nor would they, by bumping into people so clumsily, annoy the visiting foreigners who are accustomed to better sights. Instead they would be plucking the scanty grass with their teeth and nails on the stony soil of their Scythia, with parched and pale Hunger; that is where Naso put her [*Met.* 8.797–800]. But enough of this.

My opponents will insist and say that I unfairly complain about the changes, as though they were only in this age, whereas they are in all ages. But I am not complaining at all, knowing that from the beginning of time everything goes round and round, nothing stands still. Nor do I say, why do you think earlier times were better than the present? "For this kind of question is foolish," as Solomon says [Ecclesiastes 7:11]. Many may be the reasons known to God, and some perhaps to men. I do not complain then that the times have changed, nor do I seek the causes, but I do acknowledge the change against the opinion of our young people who, having been born among these ills and having seen nothing else, contend in their ignorance and disbelief that nothing was ever different, and ascribe the utterly obvious and lamentable change of the times to the change in our minds and biases. That I gladly acknowledge, but this change has nothing to do with the other one; for a huge wheel that has been pushed spins none the less rapidly just because an ant is meanwhile walking slowly along it.

Finally it will be charged that this change is not in things nor in times nor even in the world, but only in men. This too I would not deny in part, knowing that the word "world" often means "men" for whom without doubt the world was created, and whose needs it serves; and certainly many causes for these kinds of changes are in men themselves. If someone were to dig deeper, perhaps all of them are, but some are in the open, others hidden. That piety, truth, faith, and peace are in exile; that impiety, falsehood, faithlessness, discord, and war reign and rage throughout the world; that criminal bands of robbers wander as they please like regular troops, devastating and sacking whatever is in their path; and that cities are to no avail for stopping them, nor kings; that morals are corrupt, studies depraved, and manners spoiled—all this makes it clear that the entire root of the evil is nowhere but in men, although, as I have already said, I am now arguing not about the causes but only about the facts, which were certainly not the same when we were children and teenagers.

Occasional wars were waged between kingdoms or peoples over boundaries or injuries. Nowhere in our time was any "company" organized against the entire human race. There were certainly companies of merchants; we ourselves saw them; through them my fatherland above all flourished. The great volume of commodities that were brought to people through them is hard to tell, harder to believe; for through them almost all of our world was governed, and all the kings and princes were sustained by their wealth and counsel. We used to see companies of another kind, the pilgrims who in great numbers sought the holy places, Jerusalem and Rome. Thieves traveled singly and fearfully, at night; there were no "companies" of thieves deployed in the fields by day, no armed "company commanders" who made themselves renowned for the slaughter of whole nations and their own savagery. It is twenty-five years since this frightful name thundered in our ears; and how quickly this evil has spread and how far, we see. The suffering citizens and peasants, or rather, kings and prelates, all the way up to the Supreme Pontiff, have experienced it; and he [Urban V], as I mentioned above, found himself almost besieged by them on the Rhone, whence he has recently departed and emerged after being subjected to a shameful ransom. He himself did not bear it in silence, but complained gravely and justly to his advisers; nor did I keep silent in writing to him. Who, then, does not recognize or who denies this unspeakable change of times? Anyone who would has either no sense or no shame. The frightening, sinister gleam of these terrible recent events striking the eyes cannot be ignored. Since the suffering world now endures every day what no man had ever heard of a little while ago, what about other things? The word "plague" had been heard and read about in books; a universal plague that was to empty the world had never been seen or heard of. For the past twenty years it has so ravaged all lands that if perchance it lets up or slackens somewhere, it really does not disappear anywhere—so much so that daily, when it seems to have departed, it returns and attacks those fooled by the brief respite. This too, if I am not mistaken, attests to the divine wrath and to human sins, which, if they ever were to end or slacken, heavenly punishments would also abate.

Similarly, the word "earthquake" had been heard and read about, but we would turn to the historians for information about it, and to the scientists for its cause. Nervous people would imagine some rumblings at night, rare indeed and dubious, and most like a dream; but in our age no one had felt a real earthquake. It is now twenty years since both calamities struck at the same time, on the twenty-fifth of January, in the afternoon just before sunset: our Alps, which—as Maro says, seldom move [G. 1.475]—shook all over; and a large part of both Italy and Germany quaked so violently that some ignorant people, for whom the event was quite singular and never thought of, believed that the end of the world was near. I was sitting alone at the time in my library in Verona; and, although I was not completely ignorant of such a thing, nevertheless, struck by the suddenness and novelty of having the floor shaking under my feet, and the books tumbling upon one another from all sides, I was dazed. Stepping out of my room, I saw my servants, and, soon after, the townspeople, trembling and staggering; a deathly pallor was on everyone's face.

The very next year Rome was shaken so hard that towers and churches collapsed; parts of Etruria also were shaken, and, out of deep concern, I wrote about it then to our Socrates [Ludwig van Kempen, *Fam.* XI, 7]. Seven years later, lower Germany and all of the Rhine valley had tremors, at which time Basel was destroyed, not so much a large city as a beautiful one and, it seemed, soundly built; but nothing is sound against nature's onslaught. I had left there a few days earlier, after waiting for a whole month for our dear Emperor [Charles IV], a good and kind ruler but slow in everything; finally I had to go to the most remote, uncivilized land [Prague] to find him. I had it in mind to write about the earthquake to John [von Ringingen], the venerable Archbishop of that city, because I have not forgotten that he had received me with great hospitality; but whether or not I wrote him, I cannot recall; no copy of the letter is still in my possession. In any event, on that day it was reported that on both banks of the Rhine eighty or more castles were leveled to the ground. In our early years it would have been a memorable portent if a shepherd's flimsy hut had quaked. But the frequency of calamities has shaken the fear and astonishment out of mortals. In these happenings too, there emerges the change about which I am speaking, from hidden causes, as I said, unless these too, like the other calamities, result—as we must believe—from men's sins, which are without measure or number; but the difference is that the former are men's doing, whereas the latter are by the consent or at the behest of God because of human crimes. If these were ever to cease, so would His scourges.

In short, whatever the causes of evils and whoever the agent, this is the truth. So you see, Father, that in one day I have piled up before your eyes all our years, very unequal in their deserts, but equal in number, as I recently admitted in good faith in writing to a friend. Whether you do the same or, as some old men are wont to do, you hide your age a little even now as you look back upon your youth, I do not know. Live happily and farewell; remember me.

[Venice, 1367].

Sen. X, 3.

To Paolo de Bernardo of Venice,* sailing abroad; best wishes for a safe return.

I have joked with you, dear friend, and am not sorry to have done so; with my joking I extorted a good letter from you. Why need I say much? I feel that everything you say is true. I know I am loved by you as much as any man can love another. And I suspect that your marriage will not interfere with our friendship, but further it; for while marriage is sometimes a charming burden, it is never a light one: the more it hinders you, the more sweetly will you sigh for me. Nor would I interpret your silence as proof that your heart is cooling toward me, for I always interpret for the good whatever my friends do. If you are regularly in conversation with me, either face to face or by letter, when absent, I shall believe you are indulging your true feelings; but if you are less regular, it will be because you know I am so busy. The one will be for me a sign of your warm love for me, the other of your tact, bashful and considerate. There is, therefore, no reason to fear that my opinion of your conduct has at all diminished—not to mention my love for you. You are always the same and always firmly in my heart.

There now remains for me to wish you bon voyage and a happy return, since you are about to take a trip overseas. May calm seas and favorable winds from the west as you go, and from the east as you return, be granted you, not by Neptune nor by Aeolus, a poor king of the Aeolian Isles in Trojan times—the one is reported to have won the temporal dominion of islands and seashore by drawing lots with his brothers, and the other the bag of storms—but by Christ, the almighty ruler of land and sea and heaven, about whom it is written, "He brings forth winds from His storehouses" [Ps. 135:7], and again, "He encloses the waters of the sea as in a bottle and the deep in His storehouses" [Ps. 33:7], He who rules the winds and the waves; may He, I say, accompany you and return you safely to us, whom you leave behind along with your dear consort, all of us full of yearning for you. And with her we say to you, as you are

---

* A young Venetian friend of P., whose admiration for P. was so great that he boasted of having copies of 100 letters written by P. He played an important role in early Venetian Humanism. This is the only letter to him.

about to embark, what Achilles' wife said in Statius: "Go safely and come back true to us" [*Ach.* 1.942]. Farewell.

Padua, August 29 [1362].

Sen. X, 4.

To Donato Apenninigena [Albanzani], grammarian,* a consolatory letter on the untimely death of [Donato's] son and likewise of [Petrarch's] grandson.

Three sad letters in a row I have received from you in these past few days. The first touched my spirit, but the second shook it and the third shattered it. No news—I hope—can overwhelm me any more, nor you, if you listen to me. I was preparing for you a word of comfort, or rather a brief reminder, for what need have you for a comforter, you who are accustomed to comfort others and myself? Yet we have often seen outstanding physicians seek the help of another physician for their own illnesses, and the most eloquent lawyers the advocacy of other pleaders from abroad in their own case, whence that well-worn saying, "For your own cause seek an advocate." Cato the Elder, to be sure, was a man tough in body, and he relied on the incomparable strength of his mind, and trusted greatly in his old-fashioned eloquence and keen intelligence; we read that he never sought anyone to defend him in the forty-four times that he was accused by his rivals—no one was ever on trial more than that. He always defended himself and was always acquitted by the judges. Nevertheless, if you look at experience generally, hardly ever can the human mind take care of itself when besieged by its own ills as not to need a friend's advice and dependable help.

But what must be pounded into slow, obtuse minds, and with no positive result, keen intellects can grasp after cursorily being shown the same thing. In this regard, it is astonishing that for bodily illnesses a doctor is sent for at once, but not so for mental illnesses, which are without a doubt both more dangerous and more easily curable: for many bodily illnesses are incurable whereas none of the mind is, provided the afflicted one wants to be cured. Wherefore Flaccus marvels at this wrongheadedness, and rightly. Cicero also marvels, and he delicately seeks and admirably resolves the cause of this misconception on the third day of his Tusculan retreat, unless my memory fails me. Therefore, in order not to seem to be philosophizing out of turn with you in your present state, I refer you to that work.

* See V, 4.

Whatever it was that I was preparing on your son's illness, my starting point was that you should not lose heart and tremble, as they say, before the bugle, but walk upright between hope and fear, ready for either eventuality. I was mulling this over after the first message, but the second and the third made me change my mind, no longer reporting illness but death. Some would say that my task is all the harder; on the contrary, I feel that most if not all of it has been dispelled. It was too much, I acknowledge, for you to be steadfast at the sight of your own flesh and blood, your dearly beloved son, so weak and wracked by terrible pain. But I had begun to advise and admonish you to do so courageously, and to endure in another what you would have endured bravely in yourself, if we can call "another" the one you had begotten, nourished, taught, and shielded with all you had. However you felt about it, I was urging you to show in your son's plight the patience and constancy that many famous men had once displayed in their own plight and thereby earned signal glory. I dared not forbid you to show a spirit of compassion toward the suffering boy lest it seem contrary to nature. But, whatever might happen to him, I thought of saying that you should not collapse but stand upright; and that whether He who had given him to you willed to prolong His gift or to snatch it away, you along with me should thank God for what He gave and for what He took away.

For I too did and am doing thus lately for the grief in my own family; the model, to be sure, that is being suggested here for you is humble, but it is from a friend. I could cite the sons of heroes, except that ordinary things of our own are likely to be dearer to us than other people's treasures. The one I am recalling—apart from the fact that everything of mine is yours—was your godson, since you lifted him from the holy font. Suffer me to join my fresh, raw wound to yours so that together we may seek a wholesome poultice for both. And do not whisper to yourself that "the wounds are not equal; I miss my son, you your grandson." I swear by Christ and by the truth of friendship that I loved him more than a son. I did not beget him, but what of it? My Francesco and Francesca did who, as you know, are each no less dear to my heart than I am myself. Thus, having been born of the two who are dearest to me by far, he was twice dearer to me than if he had been my begotten son. You gave yours an ancient and honorable name, we gave ours a plain, humble one; or rather, you named both. Your Solone augured a great career, if fate had allowed it, ours got the name of both his parents and me at the same time. So, to the three of us was added this fourth Francesco, who was a huge comfort to our lives and the hope and joy of our house.

In order, I suppose, to make my grief* all the keener, he was endowed with talent and rare bodily grace—you would have said he was born a prince. He seemed destined to equal his father in comeliness but surpass him in talent. What I would call his worst feature was so like my face that those who did not know his mother would have simply taken him for my son. Everyone said so, and I remember you once declared to me in a letter, when he was hardly a year old, that you had seen my face in his, and that from this you had conceived some great hopes for him. This resemblance, so striking despite the great difference in age, had made him dearer to his own parents and dear to everyone around; especially the great lord of Liguria was so fond of him that, although shortly before, with dry eyes, he had witnessed the untimely death in infancy of his only son, he could scarcely hear about the passing of ours without weeping.

As for me, while I see clearly, and have seen from the very start, that he has effortlessly gained eternal happiness, and that I have been freed of no little trouble, and that in one stroke we are both better off, nevertheless, I confess I could not help but be upset because I have been robbed of so much sweetness of life. And if I were now of the same disposition as a few years ago, believe me, I would overwhelm all my friends, and you above all, with wailing and groaning; nor does it matter that I was grieving over a baby. For often such children are more deeply loved since, besides our natural instinct, the very innocence and purity of their age endear them to us, whereas, when they grow up, their superior attitude and their disobedience taint our love with resentment and turn us against them. It was, therefore, not any regard for his age, but for my own, that held me in check. While it is unseemly for a man, and especially an old man, to weep for mortal things, since it befits him to be hardened by time and by the experience of similar misfortune, and calloused against all blows—I use my own words and Tully's—I shall not do something I know I will promptly be ashamed of, as today I am ashamed of many letters which, overcome with grief over the deaths of my dear ones, I once poured forth in my tenderer years, too weakly, although lovingly. I hope henceforth to be free from womanish weaknesses at least. Were the whole world to collapse upon me alone, it will crush me, if not joyful and unmoved, at least

---

* We emend *dolorem* to *dolerem*.

uncomplaining and erect. I have learned that complaints are useless, and that there is nothing more useful than patience, in what cannot be changed. I read this long ago, but did not believe it. Now, if I were to read this nowhere, but the opposite everywhere, I would not believe it.

So that you may know the whole story about my weakness, I ordered a marble tomb for my little boy in the city of Pavia, and had it inscribed in gold letters with six elegiac couplets—something I would hardly do for anyone else, and would not want anyone else to do for me. But I, who checked my tears and my complaints, was so overcome by my feelings that since there was nothing else I could offer that boy who had gone to heaven and was no longer concerned about earthly things, I was unable to control myself from offering this final, empty tribute; even if it is of no use to him, it gave me satisfaction. This dedication to him was meant for the sake not of tears, as Maro says, but to preserve his memory, not so much in myself who had no need of any stone or poetry, as in those whom chance may bring there, so that they may know how dear he was to his family from the very beginning of his life. Though there is the Ciceronian saying, in the eighth book of the *Philippics*, that no other courtesy can be rendered to the dead than a statue or a tomb [actually based on *Phil.* 9, esp. 14–15], with us there is a certain greater courtesy, namely, prayers poured out to God for the soul and salvation of a departed one, and surely my little one has no need for these. Nevertheless, since in the sight of God not even the heavens themselves are spotless, and a day-old infant on earth is not without sin, I also implore His mercy in his behalf so that, now that he is torn from my embrace, He may fondle him lovingly in His embrace. The love for that little one so filled my breast that it is not easy to say whether I ever loved anyone else so much.

See, dear friend, how upset I am as I undertake to comfort others. But to you I am not "another," nor you to me. And so I comfort you as I can, and myself no less, though unworthy of comfort. Many have comforted others, and some themselves, with books or treatises. I am struggling to do both at the same time, which I hope will be more gratifying to you, whatever the remedy that is offered by one suffering man to another; for it is easy for a healthy man to comfort a sick one with words. No one's solace penetrates a saddened mind more than that of a fellow sufferer, and therefore the most effect words to strengthen the spirits of the bystanders are those which emerge from the actual torments. Only he who has been, or at least could have been, wretched with the same kind of wretchedness in his own family or in himself, does not know how to pity fully the wretched; whence that horror and shock of Aeneas, which Virgil seemed to me to have drawn straight from nature: "My dear father's picture came to me" [*Aen.* 2.560], as he saw the king, a man of the same age, cruelly wounded, gasping his life away. Just as that queen, herself an exile, out of pity had declared to the exile,

> Being acquainted with grief, I learn to succor
> The wretched [*Aen.* 2.630],

so I succor and comfort you, dear friend, in what time there is, and to the best of my ability, and I comfort myself since we share everything: hopes, fears, joys, and grief. And so, as I have said, I combine our wounds in order to prepare the salves.

I could search for a remedy through the gardens of all the philosophers and poets, and pick from here and there choice gems of thought for you; I could also go inside the recesses of my meager mind, seeing if I find anything of my own that might be there—except that the words of others are known to you, while my own have been applied previously in similar wounds and friends' sicknesses: to offer another's words to one who knows them is arrogant, to repeat my own superfluous, and to think up new ones in a flash is difficult. Besides, we know that unexpected ills need an immediate remedy, and it would be more helpful to bind a wound quickly in an emergency, and to treat it with any plain, handy, ordinary medicine than to waste time searching for exotic antidotes while the danger from the neglected wound gets worse; and I am afraid that I may not already be too late in this case, because all your letters have reached me so slowly, considering how near your home is to mine.

Of all that can be said for our comfort—and it is enough to fill huge books—this, unless I am mistaken, is the gist: our yearnings must be raised above this earth, and our minds armed in order not to be terrified at the sight of the enemy or throw up our hands at the appearance of something dreadful without any actual blow of fortune, and separate the mind from the senses, and thought from habit, as Cicero so elegantly says [based on *Tusc.* 1.38]. If we can do this, there will be nothing wretched in all that the multitude considers most wretched. There is nothing I am about to say to you today that does not apply to me. Eager and perhaps still moist, our eyes seek our babies, those sweet pledges of loves, and our wounded hearts sigh deeply. It was certainly human for them to die, nor did it happen before its time, since no day is assigned for that. It is human for us to wish for the comfort that we have been deprived of, the light of our eyes, the support and hoped-for assistance of my old age which is already here, and of yours which is imminent.

And so? Just as it is human to miss them, so it is womanish to weep. That is, Nature excuses us for missing them, since she has injected something listless and watery into our spirits. And she has set this in full view so as to be manifest in everyone, and especially in weaker men. On the other hand, that same Nature censures this softness, since she has put a certain firm, manly quality squarely in our minds, but quite deeply, so that it cannot be dug up, brought to light, and applied to our troubles, except with the aid of virtue. The former quality is by itself obvious to the senses, the latter is scarcely accessible to reason without effort, that is, the mind has to be separated from the senses, and forced into those innermost recesses where invincible constancy and masculine thoughts dwell. Thus, we weep easily, and we are comforted with the greatest difficulty. To weep for one's dear ones is now an ancient and unshakable custom, covered by the veil of devotion; and in the name of devotion it has been excused, or rather praised, confirmed not only by the folly of the multitude but by the sayings and examples of great men as well. How much Octavia grieved over Marcellus, her pride and joy, made famous by Virgil's poetry but still mortal! There was no end to her grief other than the end of her life. If we make allowance here for her sex, and turn away from ignorant men who are too many, how much did Nestor, the wisest of the Greeks, weep over his Antilochus, who was killed by the hand of Hector? He upset his comrades with his pathetic question as to why he had lived on to that day. And he blamed Nature herself for endowing him with too much vitality, How much, finally, did our dear Paolo Annibaldeschi mourn over his son not long ago; he was not the least of the Roman nobles, but by far the foremost among all who grieve; and surpassing* in a sad victory all examples of mourning, he alone out of all those who come to mind, with no outside force but only his grief, in the midst of weeping, died as his breath suddenly stopped; the wretched father followed his all too dear son, accompanying him to the grave.

Theodosius Macrobius, a man of endless curiosity, meticulously examining Maro's pathos, refers to that passage, certainly applicable here, where Mezentius, the Etruscan exile, says after his son was

---

* We emend *suspirans* to *superans*.

killed, "Now the wound goes deep" [*Aen.* 10.850] and comments, "And what else is to be understood by this except that this deep wound was the loss of a son" [*Sat.* 4.4.23]. And again, when Mezentius says,

This is the only way you could destroy me [10.879],

Macrobius remarks, "This too must be understood to mean that to lose a son is to die" [4.4.24]. Then there are those who teach you that a son's death is not only a wound to a father, but his death. There are a thousand such examples to which the entire multitude, wherever it may be, with one voice agree. These are the errors that circulate among the ordinary opinions of men, and, as though swallowed with nurses' milk, with no attempt in the meantime to correct them, they grow daily and pursue us from infancy to old age. But if we are men, if we differ in some way from the multitude, nothing vulgar or plebeian becomes us from now on. For why do we seek a name that stands out, if we adhere to ordinary opinions. A unique reputation is acquired by unique talents and undertakings. He is a fool who hopes to achieve the glory of the few by following in the footsteps of the many. Each pathway has its own end. If worthy ends attract a mind, it welcomes steep and demanding trails; it is along these that I would lead you and me.

I confess it is hard not to be touched by the deaths of one's dear ones, nor do I forbid anyone to be touched lest I myself be harder; it is also hard not to collapse; however hard it may be, it is certainly praiseworthy, desirable, and virtuous, which it would not be were it not hard and demanding, but the love of praise and virtue softens the hardness. What are we to do, you ask? I have already said it: the mind must be separated from the senses, and thought from habit, and raised to the loftiest stronghold of reason. There is where calmness dwells, there everything is secure and tranquil. From there we shall see everything underneath our feet: the world, the multitude, opinions, cares, actions, and Fortune, if she exists, and her snares and those of the world uncovered. For they were set to take us unawares so that the excessive love for our dear ones and the brief joy would be punished by the lasting sorrow and longing that we feel. But we, like brave men, shall range our forces against the enemy, once we have caught on to their tricks, and shall resist their attacks and turn upon them what they were scheming against us. For we shall succumb neither to longing nor to grief, but be grateful to God and happy that we have had our babies, and resigned to having lost or rather sent them on ahead, placing them in His safekeeping, as though they were too frail.

You recall how Metabus, in flight, feared for his baby daughter whose name your Camilla bears, as a river halted him; and he was baffled, and pondering at length; so he finally hurled her across the river bound to his spear, and unencumbered thus, plunged in and swam across much greater ease, and

> Triumphantly the spear with the child
> He plucked out of the grassy turf,

as Maro relates [*Aen.* 11.565–66]. We too, dear friend, are fleeing at a rapid pace, and our enemies are pressing from behind, and there is a swollen whirlpool in the way, and already we too have hurled to the opposite shore our dear burdens that were pressing, however sweetly, upon our shoulders and delaying our journey. They have been snatched from the thousand dangers and thousand miseries of this death that the dead call life; we shall find them there when we have escaped from here.

You have read, I believe, how Antigonus, King of the Macedonians, was once caught in a dangerous storm with his children; and after he had barely survived it, he warned them never to expose themselves to risks together lest they perish together. But what about you? Speaking to you, I speak to myself; do you grieve that your son has been taken from you for such a short time? Do you not rather rejoice that he is there where he fears nothing and desires nothing, subject to no evil, and abounds in all good things that shall have no end; that he is there where you both wish you already were and wished that he would arrive in his time, but you wanted it to be postponed and delayed for a long while? That is what I sense; I can see your heart. But there is nothing more foolish than to seek a postponement of a desired good, and to place certain happiness in doubt, voluntarily besetting it with inescapable miseries—and, good God, how very short is that reprieve we procure with such pains! Who in the world is so greedy for life and fearful of death except the most cowardly buffoon who, faced with certain death, humbly begs for one moment's delay? And what else, I ask, is life than a very fleeting moment, not only this life of ours—whose brevity everyone argues and complains about—but whatever life is said to be the longest; for in truth no life is long, and nothing is long at all that has an end. So if (this is true) of what is called the age of the primal men, not of Arganthonius, King of Tartessus who (as Cicero writes in his ignorance of sacred history) lived a hundred and twenty years, nor of the Ethiopians and the Indians, nor of any of the others whom Valerius mentions in his discussion of old age, but not even of Methuselah himself or of whoever else of that series of long-lived ancestors, what can you expect from this life?

A thousand years are not only as the passing of yesterday in the eyes of God, as the royal prophet [David] says, but also in the eyes of men, although they seem to be something, or even a great deal, when one ponders or anticipates them. And yet, when they have passed away, what more do they contain, I ask you, than the lone moment when I print one letter at a time on the paper, and which has passed as the pen dwells upon the letter, and it is no longer here? But I omit the miseries of too long a life, to which no voice, no pen has ever done justice. Measure and judge how great these are, since there have been those who said it is best not to be born, and next best to die as soon as possible; and this opinion has found support not only among philosophers, but even among saints, and while it is possible to have doubts about the first part, I should think there is hardly anyone with doubts about the second.

Although I do not deny that what has happened has quite a bitter taste for you, it has still been good for you, and lucky in any case for your little boy. With one sigh he left behind innumerable griefs, he had a clear and open path to heaven; had it been entrusted to you, he would perhaps have found it rough or blocked. Therefore, be careful lest, as happens to many others, you wish evil upon your beloved son, for this is nothing more than "to ruin by loving," to use the words of Flaccus [*Carm.* 1.8.2-3]. I ask you, what price would you have paid, were you perchance tossed with him in a shipwreck, to see your beloved son on the dry shore so that, whatever might befall you, he would be safe and sound? And yet, he now lives securely, whereas you and all of us are being tossed about on a great sea, and struggling to avoid a foul shipwreck. He rests in peace and is not only safe but blessed in a place from which, even if he could, he would not want to return, and indeed would refuse; for he has been moved from his earthly parents to his heavenly Father by an amazing shortcut. Why then do you weep? Why torture yourself? Would you rather leave your son here, alone and orphaned, and you depart worried and saddened? See how happily and innocently he has departed, escorted by angels; you will depart more secure and happier.

Therefore, let that confused and discordant murmur of false opinions within the soul finally cease; let the massed phantoms of things that we have absorbed with the ears and eyes of the flesh go away, as well as those that hinder the eyes of the mind from viewing the truth. Let us reflect upon the unexpected and changing turn of events, on the unexpected falls, on the unpredictable dangers that mock the wretched and always hover no less over the heads of those who are called happy, on their griefs and perpetual fears and cares and anguish, losses, worries, disgraces, privations, sicknesses of the body and the mind, and open and hidden blows of a gnawing conscience, all of which are no easier to count than the grains of sand on the seashore. Besides these, let us meditate upon life disturbed by crises and restless with troubles, and time—so brief, fleeting, and never halting—which fills so many people with disgust, and old age stealing over us unawares, and finally death, the uncertain hour of certain death, and the ultimate, the most wretched disappearance of shadowy happiness, the sad ending of false joy.

If you loved your son, if you love yourself, you will rejoice that he has been snatched from these evils, and you relieved of these cares; and, reflecting upon all that could have befallen him, which also befalls the sons of kings, you will tremble. It is not a great thing to live, my dear Donato; if it were, the same could be said of flies and worms. Nor does human happiness depend upon a long life. Otherwise deer and crows would be very happy, or the Arabian phoenix which, in my opinion, is famous not because of its age, but because of its extreme rarity and beauty. What is great is rather to live well, to die well; but he lives well who leads, as much as possible, a life without vices and abounding in virtues; he dies well who does not die completely. While the first of these is beyond a child in that virtue, which that age is incapable of, is required for living well, still your son did not lack a noble disposition, which is nothing more than a sort of virtue in the bud, so to speak. The other merit was there to the full: to die well, namely, without any grave sin, without evil thoughts and desires, and without any offenses against God or neighbor. Beware not to mourn as dead the one who has had the best thing that life holds: a good ending of life in God's grace.

But I now also sense what is troubling you—the wish, shared by all parents, which, once implanted by nature, can scarcely be uprooted by virtue. You intended him to survive you, and were providing for what could happen to him long after you pass away—hard toil indeed for a father, and often useless, a long-lasting, heavy anxiety, but wasted; and whereas men's thoughts, as the Psalmist says, are vain, I know none more vain than this; you hoped to stuff him with book-learning, for which many go mad, and with wealth, for which almost all do. The first of these you could, by Jove, have showered upon your son from your own stores, as you have often done for so many others, but to get the second there certainly was need of labor: you wanted to advance him, a goal for which so many toil. You wished to see him married, a state in which very few are at ease, and, finally, to see his children, and, as goes the human heart, his children's children; and if you do not know what a spur this is to parents, your son himself has shown you. In a word, unaware of fate, you were trying by all means to have him live a little longer (since no one here lives long) and thereby run into hardships, and what is worst, perhaps an eternal death, or certainly some signal grief which a longer life can scarcely avoid. For were everything to go as desired, something very rare in human experience, it is still frightening to recall how ambiguous and often terrible those things turn out that at first seemed most favorable. Every road is good that leads to a happy ending, and the shorter the better; but assuredly, whatever a father strives for in behalf of his son aims at what your son has already reached, namely, a wished-for happy death; for although the roads of life are many, this is the goal of them all, to which hardly anything could be added and a great deal subtracted by the prolonged life you prayed for.

Lay aside your groans; there is no reason for groaning, but there are some for rejoicing. You had a mortal son on earth, you now have an immortal one in heaven. You were concerned for him; now he is for you, since he realizes now how much you loved him and he sees, in the face of Him who sees all things, your feelings which he could not see up to now, and he in turn prays to God for you. A favored intercessor, worthy prayers, a willing listener—never was your son more helpful to you than he is now. I shall say more: he was once a burden, though a dear one; he is now beginning to be your protector, which happens here rarely or not at all; you have a son for whom you have nothing to fear and much to hope. Again I say, why do you weep? It is time to rejoice and wipe your eyes; for you can, unless you choose not to and knowingly promote your own ill.

Rest assured then that all these sobs and tears and wailings are not natural to everyone, but are weaknesses in individuals. For if they were common to everyone, all without exception would weep for the death of their loved ones, and all would carry on just as much. Instead, not everyone weeps, nor does everyone weep to the same extent, nor do those who weep less therefore love less—not even those who do not weep at all. Indeed, whereas strong things resist the hardest blows, weak things are broken at the slightest impact; it is not the strength of the one that does it, but the weakness of the other. And if Maro writes that love never has its fill of tears, he is speaking of impure love which is an overpowering passion of the mind; and undoubtedly his very verses clearly indicate that he is speaking of cruel love. We speak of noble, devoted love in which devotion alone is called for, a certain sweetness of mind, a mild sigh now and then, and joyful recollection of the departed ones, but without passion, without sorrow, without tears which come forth not so much from manly devotion as from womanly weakness.

And that you may clearly see that it is so, Octavia wept inconsolably, as we have said, as did Nestor; but it was not so with Cornelia, nor with Cato, and yet in each case it was the same love, the same reason for loving and the same for grieving. They were of the same sex, and their loss was the same, except that Octavia lost one but Cornelia lost more. What, therefore, made the difference in weeping was only the difference in spirit, on which depend all the differences in our behavior and appearance. As you heard, Paolo Annibaldeschi also wept until he died, but not Stefano Colonna, that unmatched man of our time, who, as Paolo's relative and fellow citizen, ought to have served him as an example of how not to succumb to sorrow. For three years on end, he lost three fine sons, one after the other; finally, a little before Paolo's decease, he heard of the passing of his first-born, a phenomenal man, and of the grandson born to him, also an incomparable youth, both of whom had met their end at the same time in the uprising [of Nicola di Rienzi]; he did not shed a single tear nor utter a word of complaint or a note of sadness, but at the first report, fixing his eyes a short while on the ground, he finally said, "God's will be done. It is certainly better to die than to suffer the yoke of one boor." By this he meant Nicola [di Rienzi], the Tribune of the city of Rome who was then leader of the people and had wrought disaster on the very threshold of the city.

Here I survey a few things done by men and women of antiquity and of our time, so that both sexes would have a model of endurance and composure. And how many other examples there are, either recent or ancient, of those who endured hardships with dignity and fortitude! But since all the books are full of ancient examples, and you have no need of my guidance to know where to look for them—and often too they have been introduced in my writings when the subject demands—I shall only touch upon one recent example, but famous and known by all. It may be written up by someone, but is worthy of higher eloquence and surely of a more cultivated style. Robert, King of Sicily, or rather, if you consider true excellence, the king of kings (let it be said without offending anyone of our time), who in his old age loved me in my youth that I, now old, might love him in his grave, had an only son, Charles, Duke of Calabria, father of the queen [Joan I] who now reigns and has long reigned not in peace but amidst the greatest upheavals and civil disturbances in the kingdom. This son of a great king grew up with immense renown for his extraordinary valor and especially for his righteousness. Sharing with his elders this patrimony of virtues, he had chosen for himself this claim to glory so that, whereas his great grandfather had been held the bravest, his grandfather the most generous, and his father the wisest, he himself should be held the most righteous; and so he was. Although it is inborn in everyone to love their sons, still, in this case, if you consider on the one hand the royal father, the power of paternal love, and his concern for so fine a successor, and on the other the son—and such a son!- who, over and above his outstanding virtue, than which nothing in the world is more attractive, was not only the first-born but the only son of his father, and not only the heir apparent but the only heir, you will understand how dear he must have been to him. Well, this son, in the flower of his youth and with everyone expecting and hoping for great things from him, was overtaken by sickness. The attentive king sat by him not only as a father but as a doctor, for he was, among the many things in which he surpassed all kings, also an outstanding physician, but physics and all the medicines and doctors are hushed at the coming of death; and so the young prince passed away amidst the deepest grief and wailing of the entire kingdom. The father alone did not weep, when all were weeping.

As soon as the funeral was over, he, unaltered in countenance and dress, consoled the grieving nobles and people with a magnificent oration. He was as praiseworthy as Aemilius Paullus who, in like circumstances, is said to have consoled the Roman people. Although Paullus had lost two sons and Robert only one, Paullus had two left, whom he had let other families adopt, and he knew he was very dear to them; for no artificial act can cancel out nature. In losing one, Robert had lost all, nor did he have any comfort in adversity, any hope of begetting another child. Yet on the same day he attended to royal business, heard and judged lawsuits, made decisions on whatever needed to be done, not as a grieving king, but rather as a cheerful king's consolatory emissary or substitute. But enough about this man.

I pass over Job, known in every by-way, whose words, should

always be remembered by bereft parents and all who are sad and afflicted: "The Lord has given, the Lord has taken away; as it pleased the Lord, so has it been done; blessed be the name of the Lord" [Job 1:21]. I shall add David as an ancient example both of a king and of a wise man, who, though a very great man, wept over Amnon, his first-born and so loved by him all the more, but guilty of incest and killed in sin; and afterward he wept grievously, as we read, over another son, Absalom, a most handsome youth, but his brother's murderer, a ruthless rebel even against his father, and killed with his soul in that dangerous condition. Nevertheless, we read that that same king wept and fasted when his baby became sick; but after the child passed away, he took food and ceased weeping, giving as the reason for his behavior that perchance God, out of pity for a weeping father, might save his son for him and restore him to life; once death had come, weeping was idle and useless. He said, "I will go to him, but he will not come back to me" [2 Sam. 12:23]. And he consoled himself and his wife, the child's mother, an act and a saying that are wise and grave, worthy of their author, and—unless I am mistaken—worthy of imitation by you.

I shall add still another reason: that not to suffer along with an ailing son is not becoming to a father, but once he is freed from his pains and has already overcome death to enjoy the blessings of the true life, it is not only unbecoming for a father to weep, but a friend as well. Such being the case, all that feeds sadness must be erased, or better, torn out, indeed uprooted from the spirit. What then? Am I telling you to forget your son in order to overcome your grief? I would flatly tell you this if you could not remember him without grief. I would prefer for myself and for you a happy forgetfulness to a mournful recollection. And, by Jove, forgetfulness, as they say, is good for lovers, and for this reason poets consecrate the soporific and utterly amnesiac poppy to Orpheus,* while Lethean Cupid also has his rites. But this applies only in the case of mad love; for those who love devotedly it is out of the question to forget what ought to be remembered. Far be it from me, then, to tell you to do this.

Augustus is reported to have placed in his bedroom a hallowed portrait of his great-grandson, who passed away at the same age as your son; and each time he entered, he would kiss it, and although it perhaps may appear too tender for such a great prince, love has no respect for great power. Hence paternal love or recollection is

* P. confuses Orpheus with Morpheus.

not forbidden to you, but only grief, groans, and complaints. I want you to speak of him, think of him, love him, and remember him. Remember him not bitterly, but sweetly as befits a believer, not as someone dead, but as one who is now for the first time beginning to live and spending a most happy eternity in the fatherland where he has arrived from his brief exile. Reflect upon him with joyful spirit, and recall his appearance as best you can, and think that he was given to you for a while not without reason, and taken from you for a while not without reason. You will see him again, if you have any faith, no longer needing food from you or clothing, nor any help whatsoever. Think that in the meantime you have lost nothing, but have gained an intercessor with God. For now your child loves you even more than he used to, as I was saying, because now for the first time he understands how you love him. If you would rather have him still living in this vale of tears—well, if it is for your sake, you love yourself, not him; but if it is for his sake, you hate him. To love both as you ought, bear his happiness joyfully and your loss bravely.

With these thoughts and similar ones I comfort myself, and with these thoughts console yourself too, since a learned and pious mind needs nothing further, nor even this. And whatever you hear from me, believe that our Giovanni [Boccaccio] has said it, for he has borne your calamity as though it were his own, and wishes you to bear your grief [as philosophically] as he bears his own. We beg you, imagine us always to be one at your right and the other at your left. If you do this, we hope you will grieve no more than is right. Farewell.

[Padua, 1368].

Sen. X, 5.

To the same person,* on the same subject, and the undemanding nature of [Petrarch's] friendship.

Bittersweet for me was the visit of our Antonio, whom you begot through the flesh and I through the mind. In itself it was sweet; at first sight, though, it was bitter because of the memory of his only brother who was snatched away, but if we are wise, that too will be sweet. For we believe that nothing bad happened to him, and we trust that much good has befallen him. If there is anything harsh in this kind of death, it falls upon the survivors. We know, indeed, that to weep over this is not so much piety as weakness, for what is it but envy to mourn those who have been snatched from wretchedness and exile, and returned to the happiness of their fatherland? In this I am glad that my lengthy letter, unless you are beguiling me, has benefited you. But I fear that you may be beguiling me as well as yourself, and repaying my love with a charming lie. Still, I did write it in order to be helpful, just hoping that, along with my handwriting, my very brow and remembered image, though I was not there, would have some influence on you. If it did, fine. If not, take measure of my bare thoughts.

But I have nothing to add now except my prayers; and, if many ideas do come to mind, there is no time to trim them and stitch them together. I beg you, then, if you love me and Giovanni [Boccaccio], who was with me when I wrote all that, and who will be with you when you read this, or rather is always with both of us at the same time, I beg you, indeed I charge and adjure you by all the saints, by us two here whom you hold dearest on earth, unless we are mistaken, and by the sacred trust of friendship and all that we and you hold holy and sweet: accept not only calmly but joyfully that your child has moved from misery to happiness, and do not grieve that he already has his rest while you seek a companion for your struggles. But if your breast still swells with sighs, or your eyes are wet with tears, if your brow is darkened by even a thin cloud of sadness, bring to mind that idea of Cicero that is so effective, especially for the one who grieves; here is the gist of it: this grief of yours certainly will not last forever. For you are not one who wants to die amidst tears, like that unhappy father [Paolo Annibaldeschi],

* See V, 4.

or grow old like that wretched mother [Octavia] whom I named in my other letter; prolonged weeping, as wise men like to say, is either feigned or foolish. Accordingly, a revolution of the moon or the sun will put an end even to great affliction; therefore, consider how becoming it is, how worthy of a man, that a little time has more power over him than reason, that which holds first place in man to such a degree that, if it is removed, by definition he can no longer be called a man.

I am not going to write you anything more, except that the visit of your son and mine, which was most gratifying to me, would have been even more gratifying had he come empty-handed. I think I have said this to you many times, but, as I see, you do not take me at my word. I shall say it again, and I shall try to see if perchance my written word is more worthy of belief than my spoken word. My friendship is nothing to belabor yourself for, indeed it is not even a thing of great value; but even were it of the greatest value, it would not be worth the trouble. I have learned to love and to be loved for free. If friends are in need, I wish nothing withheld from any of them; when that is no longer the case, what, I ask, is the meaning of such handouts? Why such concern? Why so much trouble? Except to make me burdensome and embarrassing to friends, something I do not want. Nothing is further from my mind, since in my friendships pure trust, burning love, harmonious interests, and easy, enjoyable communication are quite enough. Whatever goes beyond these is somehow scheming, and smacks of mercenary friendship, as if a friend may be bought for a price. Nevertheless, let it go without further ado, since I feel you have concluded that I am one of the Parthian kings, and it will not do to greet me without a gift. Farewell, you and our dear Giovanni too.

Padua, October 3 [1368], at dawn.

Sen. XI, 1.

A reply to a friendly letter from Pope Urban V.*

Your Holiness deigned to honor me for years to come, O most kind Father, with your recent brief letter of praise, and for this I give such thanks to you as I can, not as I ought—great thanks, to be sure, but what I have inside, as Cicero says, is too great for tongue or pen to match in words. By your favor I reap from my studies the richest harvest of glory, but with it, worries, like darnel mixed with the grain; thus, on the one hand, the charm of your praises soothes my spirit, but on the other, a spur goads it on. You praise my letter or essay (you call it by both names) and the wisdom and eloquence in it and the zeal which, as you say, I seem to have for the common good. Of these, I recognize in myself absolutely nothing but the last. What the greatest of men approves no man will dare disapprove unless he is mad. And you say that you received that essay gratefully and kindly—I use your own adverbs—which your urbanity, whereby you fulfill the meaning of your famous name, leads me to believe. Furthermore, you mention having read it through carefully, and having learned much from it which you declare is praiseworthy for the elegance of the words and the weightiness of the ideas. I wish it were worthy, I will not say of your praises and your eyes, but only of your ears and your patience.

But you are doing what becomes you, you do not scorn anything said in good faith and in a spirit of loyalty, however uncouth and inelegant. And indeed if there is honor in being the one who honors, as Aristotle thinks, you honor yourself by elevating humble people; you are following Him whose vice-gerent you are, whose acts are examples for us; not only do you honor the worthy ones with a deserved reward, but by treating the unworthy with mercy in advance of their deserts, you make them worthy. I rejoice and I boast at being included among these by you; for although your kindness and a certain inborn love for your faithful ones bend and incline you always toward pity, you nonetheless have shown through many clear proofs how lofty, straight, unchanging, and beyond human passion is your judgment. And this gives me joy without vanity, confidence without presumption; for that which seems something to you cannot be absolutely nothing. But do not be ashamed, O blessed Father, or

* See VII, 1.

regret that you have bent your intellect and eloquence to conversations with lesser men. There are no greater men you can speak with, not even any equals; you must either be silent or converse with lesser men, a very rare but glorious predicament. Do not let the lowliness of an insignificant correspondent upset you. Caesar Augustus, who had no equal in temporal power, often exchanged the friendliest letters with humble friends, namely the poets Virgil and Horace, men of lofty talent but the humblest origin, so that to readers it is charming and wonderful to discover such a spirit and so much kindness in a man of such high station.

Therefore, what you said at the end of your letter, about being eager to see me and disposed to send me off with appropriate favors and thanks, is more than I deserve to hear from so lofty a person. Christ, who loves the humble, will repay you. But even if I, being perhaps too careful, were not to come lest my presence, which—as a fellow citizen of mine says—diminishes one's reputation, were to make you change your mind about me, yet since you wish it, and since by not commanding you command all the more (there are times when silence is more demanding than words), I have decided to obey your desire, which is no less my own. But on the one hand, summer, which has always been my natural enemy, is detaining me, and on the other, an accidental injury to my body. What is more, my age, already advanced and like a waning day, so to speak, ever more desirous of rest and fearful of exertions, is like the wayfarer tired in the evening and thinking about an inn. Nevertheless, as soon as possible I shall struggle through the obstacles and break away, so that with the hindrances removed and the difficulties overcome, I may make my way to kneel at your most holy feet as I have longed to do, and before which, even from this distance, I reverently genuflect with the knees of my soul. I seek not what the greater part of mortals seek—riches, privileges, benefices, and prelacies—but instead of all these only your blessing and good will. This will be my mound of great wealth, and the highest honors that I solicit.

Meanwhile I pray to God, who chose you, that He make your days, which I believe are truly good for the world, happy and long, and allow them to flourish with desired successes so that, under you, Italy and the world you rule enjoy restful peace and justice, and the light of the true faith illumine all the darkness of error everywhere, and the majesty of the Christian name during your reign take over and possess the entire world, and all the nations accept Christ as Lord and you as His vicar to the ends of the earth, and worship with unending adoration. Finally, I pray that after you have laudably completed your life He grant you an easy and blessed departure, or rather open the gates to a better life, and that He who infused your soul into you* and brought you into being, Christ Almighty, and the Virgin Mary welcome into their holy hands your happy soul as it leaves its earthly prison, with Peter and Paul, your friends, standing nearby, and with the host of saints surrounding it with joy, and a great throng of angels. Amen.

Padua, July 25 [1368].

* We emend *ibi* to *tibi*.

Sen. XI, 2.

To Francesco Bruni, Papal Secretary,* on the subject of the preceding letter.

Perhaps, dear friend, you will be surprised at my tardy reply; but once you know the reason, you will stop wondering. Know, then, that right before the arrival of your letter, I left here. Over and over again I was summoned by urgent requests and repeated letters from Pavia; although the summer, which is hostile to my constitution, was approaching, and on the one hand my love for rest made me hesitant, and on the other the present situation and the road, which was dangerous because of robbers, deterred me, nevertheless, the dread of seeming ungrateful was strong and the prospect of an honorable role attracted my spirit, since I felt I was being called to help with such an important peace treaty [between the Visconti of Milan and Emperor Charles IV]. So I obeyed in the hope that I could contribute in some measure to the public good; and, having departed from Padua on May 25, I arrived there on the sixth day at the third hour [midmorning].

Not to linger over particulars, I was going to return right away, notwithstanding a bruise on the shin (a part of the body with which I have had trouble since childhood), which has been bothering me for quite a few days, just as it often had before and even now keeps me in the hated hands of doctors. However, because hourly the warfare was heating up, the overland route for my return was completely blocked, nor was there any ship to be found for any price or plea that dared confront the danger. For although even the Po was afire with war, I still hoped that by taking that route I would more likely avoid my one fear, the occasional bandits, being convinced that my mission and my love of peace and hatred of war was known to both sides. And that is how it happened; while I spent a whole month and more between trying to hire a boat and various other difficulties, finally a boatman appeared who was not so frightened, and seeing my self-assurance, put aside his fear. I boarded his boat to the surprise of all—some even scolded me!—and the trip proved successful, thank God. While everywhere on the waves I found armed flotillas, and everywhere on the shore armed troops, while the sailors and servants trembled and turned pale, I alone (whether one

* See I, 6.

would call it madness or confidence) confronted it all fearless and unarmed, and not only in safety but with praise. With one voice everyone acknowledged that no one but I could have safely taken that route; and when I attributed this to my insignificance, for, as I said, small animals are apt to leap across where large ones cannot, they would answer in unison that no man, great or small, could be found who was not hated nor suspected by either side. Finally (and I know I am saying more than necessary, since I am certain that you enjoy reading all this) where all had either been captured or killed—certainly all robbed—I came away with such a boatload of wine, plump fowl, fruit, and spices that it was not soldiers' savagery but their liberality that delayed my peaceful journey. None of this do I ascribe in the least to my merits, but all to divine mercy, which gave me a spirit dedicated to peace and made this spirit widely known to all and plainly visible on my face. But let us proceed.

When I finally arrived in Padua the day before yesterday in the evening during a continuous heavy downpour, the lord of the city, your friend, a man of great power but of still greater virtue [Francesco da Carrara], expecting me earlier and happy at my return, came to meet me at the city gate. Nightfall and the rain drove him home, but he left some of his men to keep the gate open for me. I cannot tell you if I wanted to, or if I could, will you believe how much honor and love he showered upon me that evening, not only by sending his servants loaded with all kinds of gifts, but finally by coming to me in person with a few people, and sitting with me as I ate, and after dinner keeping me company in my library with conversation and storytelling on and on until bedtime. A few days later, when it was known in Venice that I had returned, our Donato [Albanzani] the grammarian, who was holding on to your letter as well as one from the Pope addressed to me, delivered both of them. Yours I received joyfully as usual, but the other not only reverently, but dazed and humbled, and from the dates of both I gathered that my subsequent letters had not arrived; nor was I surprised, for, aside from the delay due to my absence, I read in your letter that the missive from the Pope, already sealed, had been in your custody for quite a long time. You will see my answer to this letter from our most holy lord. You of course have the right to read my reply; and what I on my own promise myself, you will support with the authority of your living voice. What is clear enough in our lord's letter and is still more emphatic in yours—that in his superior judgment he approves of my trifles—I know must be attributed to divine grace and to him. While I am unworthy to hear these things, there is nothing

I could hear more willingly. There is a certain joy and pleasure in undeserved prosperity; an unlearned man does not disdain the reputation of being learned; an ugly girl rejoices that she looks beautiful to her betrothed.

Now I am awaiting the outcome of my second letter. Surely the first one could not have been luckier than to have pleased the greatest of men, to whom I beg you give my very best with all the reverence you can. To you I opened my heart regarding His Holiness, what hope and desire I had concerning him, so that you might know I was speaking about this free of any passions; I said what was on my mind, nor does it need repetition; I trust as I do that you will remember it and that you have full confidence in me. Of course, as for what I read at the beginning of your letter, that every time you sit down to write, your mind is so overwhelmed with admiration for my excellence that either you do not begin or you give up after beginning, I know you are joking with me, and you can indeed, I confess, say anything to me that you would to yourself. If anyone else said this, I would think that he was not spoofing, but mocking. There is nothing admirable about me except—amidst such a lack of virtue and knowledge—this utter casualness about my life and frankness in my speech, arising from honest simplicity, which I wish were more sophisticated.

As for your excuse for not writing, the fact that you are so busy excuses you. I beg you to give my very best to Coluccio [Salutati], whose regards you sent me. I rejoice that you have gained such a colleague in your work, and I will rejoice even more when you both get some rest, although I have no doubt that glorious work abounds in great pleasure, but I always like to wish for my friends what I wish for myself. Farewell.

Padua, July 21 [1368].

Sen. XI, 3.

To the same person,* on the same subject.

What do you want me to say or to reply? In this as in other things I am not unwilling to follow your advice; but to keep nothing from such a friend, either because I am too frank or you too cautious, I see nothing so frightful, whether the word is taken actively or passively. You will tell me the truth breeds hatred. I know, and I know from experience; yet I consider that to brave men such hatred is like love, and even desirable if they must die for their dedication to truth; but that is not the danger in the present squabble. Sometimes it is safer to do battle with many than with one; waiting for one another, they would rather have someone else avenge a wrong done to them than avenge someone else's wrong. I had a very grave contention, in writing and by name, with one of the men over there, and I survived; it involved me alone, but this involves the entire Church. However, the battles undertaken for the public good are the noblest.

"Is there nothing you fear, then?" And what is there for me to fear, I ask you, when there is nothing that can be given to me and not much that can be taken away? I speak of those things that are called contingent, for what is *mine*, no one—not just an old, unarmed priest but not even a tyrant in the prime of life or an armed robber—can snatch from me. "But if you want something, it can be denied you." Of course an episcopate could be denied me, if I thought it worth the seeking, or rather it could be given to me as a torment; and if I were out of my mind over this, an old and belated ambition could be punished with a weighty, troublesome office. Therefore, if only I did not offend the Pope (not so much because of the papacy as his rare, unparalleled virtue and the magnificent deeds that prove it, I have resolved to love and to revere him forever) who delighting in self-reproach is unlikely to get angry at others' reproaches when they are mingled with much praise of him, what do I care about the others? I know their power, I know their wealth, but I also know their character. I know who they are, and I know who I am, and I am attacking not men but men's vices.

"But meanwhile you spare your own vices." By Jove, there are none that I hate more, none that I criticize more bitterly, but I do

---

* See I, 6.

that with myself, this with another. "But it is not your business." Why not, when it is everyone's except the Saracens' and the Jews' who rejoiced and celebrated over our misfortunes? "But you struggle in vain; Crispus says that to struggle in vain and wear one's self out only to win hatred is madness at its worst" [*Jug.* 3.3]. But I do not gain nothing; on the contrary, I gain a great deal. I vent my anger, and lighten my sadness by complaining, I justify and acquit myself to posterity, I please good men, and, unless I am mistaken, God. I certainly displease evil men; and since they have no shame or conscience, I at least inflict the sting of pain on them. But I realize how many evil men there are, and how few good ones; well, I weigh them, I do not count them. Does this then seem to you a small matter? "But what harm has been done to you to make you hate thus?" None to me, but to the city of Rome, to the Church, to Peter and Paul, to Christ, in whose name I glory even if I do not fulfill his behests. Indeed I do not hate them all, not even a single one; some I even loved, and by some I seemed to be loved, and I learned nicely how much their love is worth if profit or flattery ceases. "But do you not know that often a little hatred does more harm than a great deal of love does good?" I know nothing of the sort, nor would I like to know anything to make me more cowardly. To desire nothing means to fear nothing; and just as the size of certain animals is frightening and enables them to do harm, so does the smallness and powerlessness of certain others protect them and shield them from violence. How has an eagle ever hurt a fly, or a lion an ant? I have said all this so that you may understand me and may see what is practical. You are a friend, you have been called in to deliberate; do not listen to me, do as you see fit.

As for the rest, I was saddened by the news about Stefano Colonna; and although in your letter to me you indicate some shreds of hope, still I remember that pleasing rumors are often false while the inauspicious ones are almost always true; but what can I do? My eyes are drained; so are my loins. I have run out of tears and sighs; yet I still sigh, and sighing I write this. Long ago I wept as much as I could, or more than I ought; now it is enough and more. I have not only had my fill of it, but am sorry and ashamed of my weeping. Thus, this past summer, when death, bitter indeed and quite untimely—if there were any order here—deprived me of the only sweet solace I had in this thing called life, the only joy of my old age which grows more burdensome by the day, in short the one light of my eyes, I do not say that I did not grieve, but I did not weep. Nor shall I ever weep over the death of any mortal man or my own, if

Christ wills it; and I rejoice greatly that this is also your spirit, and all the more because you say that in this you have been helped by my advice and fortified with my weapons. So you too are bearing the passing of our friend very piteously and lovingly, yet bravely and like a man, and you write of him as one unknown to me, in welcome commemoration. You do so rightly and thoughtfully, putting together a biography most worthy of you and him. However, stop speaking of him to me as though he were unknown. I met the man and observed him as much as a few hours allowed. Not only because nothing of yours can be alien to me, but because he was also mine in his own right, I want you to know that I share in your grief. Let me tell you that he came to see me last year in Venice, and with marvelous charm struck up a friendship; he made a deep impression on me, and left behind many great reminders of his good will. He was a good, modest, and sensible man, in short, just as you depict him with your pen, truly worthy of being cherished by you and all good men. May God take him from the battles of this death, and place him in the peacefulness of eternal life.

Finally, be informed that I have heard through rumor and through a letter that my good Father [Philippe de Cabassoles], the lord Patriarch of Jerusalem, has been raised to the rank of Cardinal, which I have always believed would take place, and was amazed that it has been delayed so long. And I will admit to you, as the way of the world is hard to eradicate, that I joyfully heard the first report of this, but soon, getting hold of myself, I pitied him. I do not know what undisclosed offense he committed against our lord [Francesco da Carrara] whom he loved, so to speak, more than himself, wherefore he devised this honorific kind of revenge against him; by binding him with a golden chain when he was most in need of rest and freedom, he has deprived him of any hope of rest and freedom. Perhaps I shall write him something about this, should I be blessed with spare time; for he always, to use the words of Catullus of Verona,

Has some kind thoughts about my trifles. [1.4]

Farewell.

Padua, October 4 [1368].

But alas, alas (an outcry far more habitual for me than I would like), the day after I dated this letter, I heard from the lord of this city [Francesco da Carrara] about my most loving lord Patriarch himself, something [his death] that is doubtless happy for him, but for me, grave, harsh, and lamentable—such is the spirit of us mortals. When my informant noticed how sad the story made me, he tried to put the matter in doubt. But I, as I was just saying, know that bad news is almost always true, but I have nothing more to say about it. I loved the man, and I shall not stop loving him unless I stop loving myself. I once wrote for him in my solitude, while living on his country estate, two books *De uita solitaria*; but now his change of status was prompting me to write for him two more books on the active life, and I was already mulling it over in my mind, and very unwilling, dear friend, I have been freed of this task. Farewell once again.

Sen. XI, 4.

To Coluccio [Salutati] da Stignano, another Papal Secretary.*

Some years ago, in writing to our Francesco Bruni, who was then a new friend and is now tried and true, I told him that he had struck up a friendship with an aging man. If it was true then, what do you think now? You know that age races and flies, and that we go from infancy to old age and death in the briefest moment. Such thoughts on the passage of time make me apprehensive and lazy, and with a clammy hand it pulls me back from that youthful fervor for writing; for although since then I have written many long letters to that friend and to others, yet I am finally of a different mind in these days and have changed my ways. If you ask why, it is because every step is part of the way, every hour is part of life, and, with living as with walking, you approach the end a step here, a step there. I shall henceforth be briefer in my epistolary conversations with friends, and silent with others; this is my intention, unless some compelling reason forces me to do otherwise. Old age, which usually makes men most loquacious, will make me curt.

Therefore, to you, whom I have not yet met and have recently come to know, and already cherish, I shall say nothing else for the present in return for your kind and courteous letter than that your tone and your warmth pleased my heart wonderfully. For although I am not worthy of such esteem and honor, your praise is still not a whit lower for all that, as long as you, as a connoisseur of virtue, venerate even its bare name, its vaguest shadow, and questionable traces. Perhaps you put faith in reputation, which is prone to lying; for that very reason you deserve, unless I am wrong, not to be deceived in your judgment with regard to me or anything else. I applaud your splendid character. Now what would you do, if you run into someone—whoever it might be—who has real, solid virtue? Farewell.

Padua, October 4 [1368].

---

* Early humanist and elegant writer in both Latin and the vernacular, he held high offices in the Curia and in the republic of Lucca. He became chancellor of Florence in 1375. He was considered learned in history and an expert researcher of classical antiquity. Because of his writings, Florence sought the permission of the emperor Charles IV to award him the laurel crown, but did not succeed until after his death. This is the only letter to him.

Sen. XI, 5.

To Guglielmo Maramaldo, Neapolitan knight,* that ill-founded friendships do not last.

Our Italic Orpheus [son of Floriano da Rimini, musician], who carried your letter here, did not see me, though I was close by, nor did he even inform me of his arrival. I would be surprised, except that I know that time wears away everything human. "Age bears off everything," says Maro [Ecl. 9.51].

The fleeting years rob us of everything,

says Flaccus [Ep. 2.2.55]. I would not like to resort to my own testimony for my own cause. Both in verse and in prose I have often repeated this thought in different words, because I agreed with it. To this plunder and ruination of all things, virtue is the lone exception which not only does not perish but grows with time. But I was under the impression that the friendship entered into between me and him from my prime and his boyhood, and between his father and me since my youth and his prime, was founded on virtue; and I fear that I was deceived in his case. For without question time diminishes and overturns run-of-the-mill friendships that are based on advantage or only on pleasure. For this reason the friendship I have with his father is refreshed daily, whereas my friendship with him falters and dwindles hourly and has now gone down almost to nothing. So much more dependable and solid are old men's friendships than young men's, although I enjoyed this young fellow's conversation because of that certain sweetness that I associate, I confess, with musical performances, that sometimes, thrashing out in my mind what certain philosophers have thought about the music of the spheres, and those of contrary views, I tend to agree with that side which does not begrudge the divine beings this delight of the ears, whether it is from the motion of the spheres or something else. In this matter our Orpheus, in my opinion, has far surpassed the ancient one.

Nevertheless, although I was no less delighted with his association and his conversation—for I believe that harmony is not less but more

---

* Descendant of a well-known noble family of Naples which had accompanied King Nanfred in his campaigns of the mid-thirteenth century. He fathered a son, Landolfo, who became archbishop of Bari and a cardinal under Urban VI.

in the words than in the mere sounds, and by far the most, as Tully says, in the acting—yet let him go, whatever the reason. I have learned to live most pleasantly either with friends, or, when the blame is not mine, without them, somewhat bitterly indeed, but I think I shall live. Sometimes, because life brings so many things, I almost shrink from ties and meetings with people; and because of my loathing for evil people, who are everywhere, the few good ones in a certain way make me suspicious; I suppose it is just as phenomenal to find a good man in the city as a spring of fresh water in the sea. What else need I say? Between the evil characters of the living on the one hand, and on the other the bittersweet memory of those no longer here, and the wounds of death that snatched so many good friends from me in so few years, you may view me now almost as another Bellerophon, not indeed wretched or lamenting and eating out my heart, but wandering in the fields and avoiding the footsteps of men as much as possible, and very eager, if I can, to live out what remains of this life, or rather, of this death, in the woods.

These many things especially concerning our common friend, as you see, [I relate] not without indignation so that you can inform him as soon as the occasion arises; and he will be sorry, if he has any sense of shame, that he turned his back whether through insolence or negligence, on a friendship which, although not profitable, is certainly old and perhaps creditable, and which his fine father cultivates so faithfully, as was as clear as day during my recent trip from Verona, and so often before.

Here I have written more than I thought; a certain ardor of my offended temper carried me away; from now on I shall write less than I would like. Your letter, which went through many hands on its way to me, filled me with great joy. There I read many things to make me absolutely certain that if you were as close to me as the fellow I am complaining about, you would have either come to me or let me know where to look for you. And surely if I follow this line of thought, it will be very hard to arrive at the end of this subject too. But because I am compelled by lack of time, and by necessity, to be briefer in my letters from this moment, I must be content with telling you this one thing: your love for me and your personality are not new but most welcome to me, but not so the great respect I perceive in the uniform tone of many of your letters; for while it is very well intended and certainly to your credit, still I do not in the least deserve it. Furthermore, I, whom you sought long ago with so much effort, whom you found so far away, and whom you beheld so avidly and so affectionately, I do not know whether you will ever see me again on earth. I would not say this if that great man who was our friend had lived a bit longer.

Do consider me definitely* among your friends, and make use of me if there is any need. I wish I could do something without being asked, so that the great hope you place in me might not prove useless. Without prompting, I call God to witness, that I would offer you aid and advice in your toils and in the struggles of your spirit, if I had any skill or experience in steering life's course. And since we are now and then able to do more than we think—although in most cases it is the opposite—if perchance there is anything I can do for your peace of mind and for your comfort, tell me; I am there in spirit. Here I shall stop. I am forbidden to go any further by my desire for brevity and by the fixed fule of my recent resolve. Live on and farewell, and remember me.

Padua, November 9 [1368].

---

* We emend *plenam fiduciam* to *plena me fiducia*.

Sen. XI, 6.

To Francesco Orsini,* the establishment of a new friendship.

The generous display of your noble character and the bright flame of your youthful good will has put me into a pleasant daze. Blessed be that virtue to which you are so attached that you venerate its bare name and mere shadow in me. I am grateful both for this spirit of yours and for this my lot, and, though a lover of truth, I love this most honest of errors, from which has flowed your love and this opinion you have concerning me; and I congratulate Italy and Rome, the mother of both of us, who even now gives birth to such talents. Accordingly, because I have no leisure to write much, here is the gist: I rejoice to be so dear to you before you know me, and not only do I rejoice, but I marvel; and I now begin to be yours, and shall never cease. Number me among your friends, in whatever way you wish, and be true to yourself. Farewell.

Venice, February 10 [1368].

---

* A young Roman admirer of P. This is the only letter to him.

Sen. XI, 7.

To Antonio di Donato Apenninigena [Albanzani].*

Dear son, I was happy to receive you very short letter which, if I may say so, is not any more forthright than yourself, but reflects your young age and tiny size, an essay of your intelligence and the first fruits of your pen. I beg you to continue along these lines, exercise your mind, experiment with things, strive, and rise on high. Autumn will not see the fruit of the branch if the springtime does not see its blossoms. Write, read, rehearse, learn, study so that you may become learned, but, much more important, so that you become good and every day better. And be sure not to have the evening find you without some benefit from the passing day so that soon you can be a joy to your father and a help to me who love you. For the one from whom I was expecting help, who came after me, got ahead of me, at least according to himself, a captain rather than a foot soldier, a teacher rather than a pupil. Farewell, and give my best to both your parents.

Pavia, November 19 [1368].

---

* Young son of the grammarian Donato. See V, 4.

Sen. XI, 8.

To Francesco Bruni,* a recommendation for a young student [Giovanni Malpaghini].

The bearer of this note to you was with me for three years and more, not as a servant, but as a son. I treated him as a father would, guided him, scolded him, and praised him. In short I loved him as a father would, and—this will surprise you—I hated him as a father would; he is the one I wrote you about long ago, that he had perfect handwriting: he wrote out that huge letter which, on your advice, I sent you to be delivered to our lord the Pope, which was soon delivered to him by your hand. This young man, as I was saying, always rich in talent but at first poor in learning, came to me. Now, as I can boast, using him as my witness, not through my doing but through his living with me, and observing, reading, and conversing, he goes away from here more learned than when he came; he departs with my good will, however, and my permission—not, I would add, upon my advice. What is there to say? To say it all in one word, he is young, he wishes to explore the world, which I shudder at, recalling all too vividly I once did it. He wants to see Rome, which is the one desire I dare not disapprove of, if it would stop there; for I myself, who have seen her so often, burn to see her again.

But our friend here, I surmise, wishes to fish in a larger sea, envisioning profit for himself, not a shipwreck. He wishes to try his fortune, as he says. If he finds it favorable, I shall rejoice; if adverse, as long as the ship comes through it, he will not be forbidden to seek once again this calm, though narrow, haven. It is open day and night to those who have gone away defiantly, provided they wish to return; and indeed there is an all-night lamp on the look-out, and someone waiting on the shore to receive those coming home. In this case, it is not his own impulse driving him, I believe, but just his age. He is really good, and, unless I am wrong, loves and cares for me. He is well disposed, unsettled in spirit, I admit, but modest and not unworthy of the support of good people. If his lot opens a good path for him, do not, I beg you, withhold the light of your counsel. Farewell.

[Spring 1368].

* See I, 6.

Sen. XI, 9.

To Ugo di Sanseverino,* a recommendation for the same person.

This young man that you are looking over has been for several years like a son to me, and does not cease to be so; for although he goes off in body, I trust that in spirit he does not, and I ascribe this penchant of his not so much to himself as to his age, which lacks firmness and delights in rambling. This is a habit which—not to accuse myself of it, as I often like to do—stays with many people into their old age. This young man, furthermore, is of good mind and uncommon character, but still a young man who, as usual, after entertaining many possibilities, has preferred the nobler one in the end: since he was determined to go, he chose to travel for no other motive than learning. First of all, he is thirsty for Greek letters; and while scarcely grown up, he anticipates Cato's desire in old age. Now over the space of a year, with a great deal of ingenuity and effort have I held in check this urge of his, often by begging and at times by upbraiding, pointing out, and holding before his eyes how much he still has to learn of Latin letters, also piling up the hardships and dangers, with which I thought I could temper his youthful ardor, especially since he had left one time and, as I had predicted to him, soon returned out of compelling need. And to be sure, as long as the memory of that unlucky trip was fresh, he lingered a while and gave me hope that his spirit could be controlled. Now, in the end, as happens, a rather brief respite has made him forget all he went through.

Here he is once again chomping at the bit, and no force or guile can restrain him; but with a burning desire for learning, which may or may not be wise and serious, he has left behind his country, his friends and relatives, and his aged father, and me whom he loves as a father and preferred to his father—at least he spent more time with me; and he hastens to you whom he knows only by name. And lest perhaps you marvel at it, his headlong plunge has a shadow of sense. For as soon as he had decided to set out straight for Constantinople, I explained to him that Greece is now as bereft of all learn-

---

* Influential member of the court of Naples during the reign of Joan, whom he served as general commander of the Neapolitan forces. This is the only letter of the collection to him.

ing as it was once richest in it; and he, taking my word on this one point, did not drop the proposed journey, but shifted it. He had often heard from me that a number of men expert in the Greek language live in Calabria in our day, two in particular, the monk Barlaam [da Seminara] and Leone or Leontius [Pilatus], both of them good friends of mine; the former had even been my teacher and would perhaps have accomplished something with me had death not begrudged us. So the young man decided to visit the Calabrian shores and that region of Italy once called Magna Graecia. Not unaware that while powerful everywhere you are most powerful there, he wanted a letter of recommendation from me, which he hopes will carry weight with you—and he is not mistaken.

I agreed without hesitation, thinking to give you some cheer with his intelligence and him protection through your power. For I love the fellow; and although I do not so much approve as excuse his inconstancy, I do not dare find fault with his wish to learn. Rather I am convinced that he deserves to achieve what he seeks so anxiously and so ardently that he concentrates on it alone and forgets not only difficulties or our distress, but himself and his own strength. What he despairs of finding among the Greeks, he feels certain he can find among the Calabrians. Therefore I recommend him to you. If you receive him well and help him with your means and your counsel, you will be doing something worthy of you and, I think, pleasing to God, but most pleasing to me, who have watched his departure with a touch of sadness and anxiety. Farewell.

[Spring 1368].

Sen. XI, 10.

To Lombardo da Serico [della Seta],* a note of consolation.

Dear friend, I have read your letter with a sweet bitterness, as it were, and a bitter sweetness. You bewail so gently the passing of your aged father that I sympathize with you and admire your devotion; there is nothing better that a man, and especially a son, can have, nothing more his own. Take comfort; your father has paid his debt to nature, and you yours to your father. His payment was late, and postponed long enough, your devotion is right on time. There is nothing for you to complain about, but something to rejoice over. He was born only to die and, through this brief and difficult journey, to return home to his country or, more accurately, to find his way to it. We are all born for this. There is a great variety of roads; the end of all is the same, death, or rather not the end but the passage longed for by good men. To die is certainly natural, and no more wretched than to be born, and perhaps happier. Farewell, behave manfully, and steer the rudder with your own hands now that you have lost the helmsman.

[1369].

---

* Paduan humanist and intimate friend of P. who greatly admired his frugal and continent life style. He lived with P. at Arquà after the departure of G. Malpaghini and was a beneficiary of several items in P.'s will.

Sen. XI, 11.

To the same person,* a summary description of this life.

You ask me what I think of this life, and rightfully so. Men's opinion on this score are indeed many and varied. Here is mine in a few words. To me this life seems the hardened ground of our toils, the training camp of crises, a theater of deceits, a labyrinth of errors, a troupe of mountebanks, a frightening desert, a muddy swamp, a parched tract, a rugged valley, a sheer mountain, gloomy caves, a lair for beasts, a sterile land, a rocky field, a thorny wood, a grassy meadow full of snakes, a garden of flowers but no fruit, a fountain of cares, a river of tears, a sea of miseries, troubled repose, useless labor, vain effort, welcome madness, an unlucky burden, a sweet poison, base fear, unwise carelessness, vain hope, an invented tale, false happiness, true grief, uncouth laughter, useless weeping, an empty sigh, confused order, tumultuous confusion, turbulent trepidation, perpetual uneasiness, sleepless laziness, empty abundance, rich poverty, weak power, shaky strength, ill health, constant disease, double illness, a beautiful deformity, inglorious honor, disreputable titles, silly ambition, lowliest elation, futile excellence, base loftiness, darkened light, unknown nobility, a riddled purse, a leaky jug, a bottomless cave, infinite greed, harmful desire, dropsical splendor, insatiable thirst, parched squeamishness, starved nausea, windy prosperity, ever complaining adversity, fleeting greenness, a drooping flower, a sinking charm, ephemeral beauty, sad joy, bitter sweetness, thorny pleasure, foolish wisdom, blind foresight, a hideous home, a temporary lodging, a foul prison, sailing without a rudder, old age with no staff, blindness without a guide, a slippery path, covered pits, a hidden precipice, a stealthy file, clinging birdlime, disguised traps, hidden nets, baited hooks, sharp thorns, clinging burrs, sharp thistles, stubborn crags, raging winds, rushing waves, dark whirlpools, thunderous gales, a stormy sea, wave-beaten shores, an unsafe harbor, an unrigged ship, a huge shipwreck, a workshop of crime, the scum of lust, the forge of wrath, a well of hatreds, the chains of habits, the Sirens' song, the goblets of Circe, the bonds of the world, the hooks of things, the pangs of conscience, the goads of repentance, the fires of sin, a rotting building, a crumbling foundation, gaping walls, tottering roofs, wordy brevity, broad narrowness,

* See XI, 10.

a maze of pathways, hampered steps, going around in a circle, an unsteady halt, a turning wheel, a stalled race, scruffy smoothness, prickly sweetness, flattering cruelty, treacherous caresses, false friendship, harmonious discord, a dishonest truce, inexorable war, faithless peace, simulated virtue, badness excused, fraud praised, disgrace honored, simplicity ridiculed and loyalty despised, serious trifles, brilliant insanity, talkative dullness, ignorance veiled, a swollen reputation of knowledge but in fact no knowledge, sighs of complaint, the noise of strife, the outcries of the multitude, a forgetful journey, hatred of the fatherland, love of exile, a city of goblins and ghosts, a kingdom of demons, a principality of Lucifer, for that is what the truth calls the prince of this world; in short, a lying, breathless life, a breathing death, sluggish carelessness about one's self, worry over useless things, concern for appearances, an appetite for the superfluous, a painstaking preparation for the worms, a living hell, an elaborate funeral procession of living bodies, a lingering burial, pompous vanity, an exhausting campaign, dangerous temptation, proud misery, and pitiful happiness.

That, dear friend, is how I view life, which to so many is most desirable and welcome. Nevertheless, I have not yet expressed my entire thought. For it is much worse and more wretched than can be expressed by myself or anyone in the world. But intelligent as you are, I suppose that from these few words you see inside the mind of the speaker. There is only one good thing in all the bad: unless one deserts the right path, it is the way to a good eternal life. Farewell.

In the Euganean Hills, November 29 [1370].

Sen. XI, 12.

To Urban V, Roman Pontiff,* on the innocence of the Minister General of the Order of Friars Minor.

From the outset I see many obstacles to my subject, most blessed Father: on the one hand your greatness, and on the other my small-ness, whence the difficulty of the matter about which I mean to speak. However, the first obstacle is removed by your kindness, well known to me, the second by my good faith, known—I believe—to you, and the third by my love of truth and hatred of evil. I know your greatness, but I know your gentleness too. And there comes to mind what Parius [i.e. Varius] Geminus said before Caesar: "O Caesar, those who dare speak in your presence overlook your great-ness; those who dare not, overlook your kindness" [Sen. the Elder, *Controu.*, end]. Furthermore, I know my own smallness, but I am also conscious that my heart is so sincere that when the situation seemed to demand it, I dared to speak, and not only to your face, but even against you. This you not only bore, O gentlest of men, but praised. For this is the true greatness of a man: to distinguish him-self not only in power and dignity, but in kindness. Finally, I feel the loftiness of the cause in which I join as an unsummoned witness; in ordinary litigation that would rouse suspicion, but my zeal and con-cern for supporting the truth with all my might will perhaps excuse this daring of mine.

Now, not to distract you from your holy obligations with too much talk, I come straight to the point, which you know well, and to the disagreeable story. Maestro Tommaso [da Frignano], a distin-guished man and famous professor of Holy Scripture, and Minister General of the Order Minor [of Friars]—which for many reasons, but most of all because of its founder, I am so fond of, as though I were one of the Order—is in jeopardy of his reputation and position through a conspiracy of envy by some people who are certainly not good; for just as evil men cannot love good ones, so the good ones cannot hate the good. Alas, what a foul spectacle, which is so ugly, so unworthy just to hear about that it wounds from a distance like an arrow! For, I ask, how can the eyes bear what the ears scarcely can, the name of such fine men exposed to the attacks and false ac-cusations of malevolence with no respect for virtue; the greater the

* See VII, 1.

fame, the greater the hatred and envy. Ugly, I say, and unworthy, but neither new nor surprising, except that envy ought not to be so daring under your very eyes. Otherwise the evil is common and longstanding.

I omit the more ancient examples of Socrates, Theramenes, Anaxagoras, Cicero, Seneca, Rutilius, and Metellus, whom nothing more than hatred of their virtue led to exile and death. Even in Christian times how great were the sufferings of Athanasius for his faith in Christ! How great were Ambrose's! The former, persecuted by the heretics, fleeing and wandering all over the world, withstood pains that tortured and wore out not only him as he underwent them, but even the pious reader to this day. But Ambrose, confined within the walls of his city by the Empress Justina, who raged with all the power of the empire, and by other Arians, endured what we all know. What about Augustine? Did he not escape the danger of death by luckily straying from the road when the heretics had set an ambush? What about Jerome? What about John Chrysostom? The writings of each reveal how many detractors they had. What about Boethius Severinus, also a holy and learned man, whose innocence and virtues were rewarded one way in heaven but on earth with infamy, proscription, exile, and death?

I am not including all of them, for they are endless. In truth, who ever followed the straight path of faith and virtue, and was not exposed to the attacks of persecutors, since that Apostle, writing to Timothy, says that "all who wish to live piously in Christ Jesus will suffer persecution, but evil men and seducers go from bad to worse" [2 Tim. 3:12]. Well, let them go from bad to worse, and, since they so choose, to the very worst; and may they go to their own destruction, not that of good men; indeed may they go astray until they drop, as the same Apostle says, but not lead others astray, as he goes on to say—which, as is obvious, they work at now with all the zeal of seething wickedness. If they do perchance lead someone astray with their wiles, they will not do it with you. You will remain as usual the unshaken champion of justice. That is enough for all of us who love the truth and this man's reputation. For not only I, though I be the least of all, am writing this; I take it many others have written, and many more will; there is no one who will not subscribe to this in spirit at least, unless he is inflamed by impious envy and thirsts for the ruin of good men. All good men on their knees, the entire Church, all Italy beg you, the Order and the father of the Order, blessed Francis, barefoot, poor little fellow, asks from heaven not to let his minister, so dear to Christ and to himself, be crushed by the avalanche of envy, or gnawed by the teeth of lions,* as they say.

There is one thing that astonishes me, one rumor that grieves me, if true, that a certain great and powerful man [Nicolas Cardinal Bellefaye, Protector of the Order], whose very loftiness ought to make him calm and serene, has not only befriended the accusers, and continues to do so, but has, with his urging and his advice, driven some to accuse who would never have dared otherwise. Why should I not grieve and sadly wonder by what pathway, by what blast of wind, such a cloud of anger or envy has ascended to such a lofty mind? I would indeed be even more astonished if I did not remember from history that Marcus Cato the Censor, a man of the most renowned wisdom, did one thing in his life that I deem worthy of stern rebuke: he incited against the most glorious Africanus wicked accusers who were finally mangled by the Senate and the assembly of good citizens because they sought glory for themselves by defaming so great a man. I hope and pray this will now happen in your court to these accusers about whom I am complaining, O most just surveyor of hearts, so that when you sharply chastise and chide them, they may learn to win glory not by defaming others, but by their own virtue.

To be sure, the mists of human passions invade bright minds too, but ought not to last, when the clean breeze of reason blows there. The great man whom I would not name except to praise him, would act rightly and in accordance with the demands of his dignity if he used his authority to pull back from the undertaking those whom he had roused. If, as is said, he alleges this reason for his anger, that he did not wish this man to be promoted to the governance of the Order or preferred someone else, he should blame the electors and not the one elected, who had no part in campaigning for it. Indeed, he was beyond dispute, ignorant of everything that was being done around him, when he was appointed to this honorific office. The great man, however, will moderate his anger as he sees fit, and will either tighten or loosen the reins; but you will do as befits you—you will not allow, as befits you, anyone's whim, while Christ watches over all human events and you govern the Church of Christ, to darken the reputation of fine men.

Hoping for this, I shall not weary you any longer, but shall reveal sincerely, loyally, and reverently my reason for taking up the pen; I

* We emend *theonis* to *leonis*.

can be deceived, I confess, about my own conscience—and how much more about someone else's!—since the deep abysses in the hearts of men are so many and so bottomless. Yet, insofar as either public rumor or reports worthy of belief or, in the end, conversations and those exchanges of views that open up the mind a great deal, have given me insight into this man undeservedly accused, I will say out loud what I feel. And though with proud judges the humbleness of a witness lessens the credibility of his testimony, with you, a friend of humbleness and the Vicar of the Living Truth, I present this humble but unperturbed, brief but uncorrupted testimony to the truth—I, a witness summoned not by the judge but by Christ and by my conscience. Therefore, I swear by both of them and by your head which is at once most sacred and deserving the veneration of kings, lest I be called an unsworn witness, that as far as I know and believe I will say nothing false, but the whole truth. Most blessed Father, I do know Maestro Tommaso, who is on trial, as the best and most honest of men, famous for learning, but more famous for virtues, and, what is greatest and uppermost, most famous for his outstanding devotion to the rule, his piety and the light of his Catholic faith. In sum, I wish that my soul were such as I trust his to be. I could say more. A long story could be woven about the gravity of his mind, the charm of his ways, his sobriety, his abstinence and austere life, his burning devotion, his humility and contempt for himself and the world, his sincere mercy and charity, and the other gifts of this great man. But for one of your intelligence these few things out of many, or rather even fewer, suffice; you see and understand the cause of this trouble. And just as from the accusers' hatred arise consternation and fear, not in him—for he in good conscience fears nothing—but in me and many others, so from the clemency and wisdom of the judge arise much hope and consolation. The virtue, the glory of that fine man cannot, with you presiding, be so trampled by the heel of envy that it shall not rise up all the greater from the wrongs and more beautiful, being sustained by your holy hands; and since it is solid and pure, and truly golden, it shall be all the brighter for the scraping. Finally, the hope of his innocence is in God and in you. May Christ keep you for a long time safe and sound for His Church, and, at the end of your glorious work, may He carry you over with a gentle and happy parting to His rest and to eternal glory.

Padua, January 1 [no date assigned].

Sen. XI, 13.

To the Marquis Ugo d'Este,* that he must avoid foolish sports.

Pietro Montano, your intimate and my friend, has brought me reports of you which were joyful and splendid, but not new, and they could not have made me happier. Keep up the good work. Help along your fine character with worthy studies. Strive for the heights, learn to spurn base things nobly, do not avoid any hardship until your tireless steps, advancing from one virtue to another, arrive at the highest peak of eminence. There is a new morning of life; however, the road over which we go to lasting glory and our eternal dwelling is short, though a little rough. Having started along it, follow it, and do not turn aside. Do not think that anything steep or frightening lies ahead; to expose oneself to toil and crisis for its sake and, if need be, to death—that is a man's highest duty; never shall I pull you back from this, but rather urge you on and, as much as I can, spur on your eager spirit. But to court danger on your own is not a sign of a bold spirit, but of little sense.

Therefore, to come to the point, when it is necessary, for your life, your dignity, your fatherland, fight bravely, fight like a man, and I wish you luck; but avoid these jousts that are so dangerous, harmful, and childish. I beg you, take it from me by right not of wisdom but of age. You will forgive me for counseling you impetuously perhaps, but of course loyally. Let it suffice that everyone realizes you could do very well at such sports if you felt like it; to go any further is a waste. The hazards of men are unexpected, and the wise man must take great care not to thrust himself where there is the most danger and no advantage or glory. Leave these games to those who cannot do anything greater, who do not know better, and whose life and death are despised, being equally useless. Your life is dear to your brothers, your friends, and your country; much loftier cares naturally befit your intelligence and spirit. We never read that Scipio or Caesar went in for this. I wish you a glorious and happy lot.

Padua, April 24 [1369].

---

* Brother of the Lord of Ferrara, and an active participant in equestrian military games. This is the only letter to him.

Sen. XI, 14.

To Master Bonaventura [Badoer da Padova] of the Order of Hermits, professor of Holy Scripture,* a consolatory letter on the death of his brother.

O grief, what a man, what a star we have lost [Bonsembiante Badoer]! I speak improperly and am carried away by a torrent of cheap rhetoric. We have lost nothing but a welcome, delightful intimacy and the conversation of that honeyed mouth. When he spoke, sharp darts prodded the minds of his listeners to virtue. When he taught, no one could fail to profit; the more intelligent they were, the more they profited. I do not deny that this and much else of the same sort has been snatched from us a little sooner than we would have liked; but still we could not have these things for long, in this very brief race of life, where nothing is lasting except grief and groaning. It was inevitable that either we go speedily before him or he before us. But either way the loss of such a shaky, tottering thing is not absolutely grave or lamentable. Certainly, the one whom we loved and whom we shall always love—that one, I say, we have not lost, but have sent ahead to clear the road to heaven for us with his prayers, and to wait for us there eagerly and joyfully. For where else could I imagine him to have gone if not to heaven, since even while he was on earth and weighed down by his body he enjoyed an angelic personality and a heavenly intellect. I would not do for you now what I never did for him while he was here—that is, flatter you about so fine, so peerless a brother; but human praise sounds better in the ears of anyone else than the one being praised. So help me God, in whose love is true happiness, I know perhaps a few of the living superior to him in reputation but no one in either intelligence, eloquence, or sweetness of character, which was so much a part of him that I never came away from a conversation or a meeting with him without feeling happier and calmer. Nor did I ever have a conversation with him so lengthy that it did not seem all too short to my eager ears and thirsty mind. For there were among that

---

* An Augustinian friar and theologian with a degree from Paris where he also taught for ten years. He gave the eulogy at P.'s funeral. As a result of his dedicated service to Urban VI, he was made cardinal, perhaps the first Augustinian to achieve the rank. This is the only letter to him.

man's words certain bright, winning flashes beyond the ordinary way even of those who are called teachers. There were in his speech hooks baited with sweet lessons, which caught and held fast the hearts of those who heard him, scatterbrained though they might be. Although the opportunity for such conversations was too seldom for me, since our concerns drew us apart, as well as those countless prongs and snares, those ups and downs that often separate in body and country those who are closest in spirit, nevertheless, even when away I enjoyed his wit, on the one hand recalling an absent friend, and on the other envisaging and awaiting his presence. In this I sadly feel and sadly think to myself how much of this life I have wasted in mere competition, and how often I repeat in silence, in your name and mine, that saying of Jerome: "We were not worthy of such a companion in our life." For although I said that a man must not mourn too much for the loss of a transitory thing, still the things that we mortals lose are on the whole mortal, and among them this one is certainly the gravest. But I find consolation for our loss, however great, when I contemplate our brother's happiness. For even here we would rather have had him well off without us than unhappy with us.

Therefore, we ought to rejoice instead of grieving for our brother, whom your mother gave you and love gave me; for although he has left us for a while, he has gone where the right-living and devout-thinking end up; in their ranks this brother of ours, I daresay, was either the standard-bearer or the leader. Nor indeed would I blame Nature, but rather thank the fullness of heavenly grace that he finished this tough and bumpy journey a little before his time, as one is wont to say. For it is as if a wayfarer, on a rainy winter day, were to arrive safe and sound and unwearied at the inn while the sun is still high, whereas others, exhausted, soaked, and lost, misled by rambling roads, will at last barely get there by nightfall. Perhaps we who are left behind ought to be pitied. not because we have lost him, since, as I said, he is even more ours now, but because we are aging amidst the evils of the world and dangers to ourselves, and are late for that happy, longed-for inn. Therefore, let us calm our spirits, dry our tears, smother our sighs, and let us not cast him from our memory, but call our brother back to it alive, not dead; for he truly lives with Him who is the fount of life, who had formerly revealed to him many great secrets of His Scriptures, and who now shows Himself and that face which the angels look up to with astonishment and veneration.

For a long time he was a great glory to his homeland, a great and signal honor to his order. And although you are still here, I shall nevertheless include you. Who in the world did not stare at the two of you with the eyes and the mind, fascinated especially when chance brought you together at some public gathering or on the street? Who did not love and praise and marvel at you? The very fact that you were brothers and the rarity of it added to the miracle: the two brothers had equal height, almost the same looks, nearly the same age, certainly the same profession, the same speech, dress, religion, order, and splendor as teachers. People esteemed two such brothers more than four other men, though on a par with you; they called the parents who had given birth to such a pair happy, and Padua happy since you were born and bred there. For nothing makes any country so happy as the virtue and glory of its citizens, wherefore in Virgil, Rome, no matter how mighty in wealth and empire, is called "happy" for nothing else than "for her breed of men" [*Aen.* 6.783–84]. Happy, finally, is the Order of Hermits, in which you were educated and equipped to achieve this glorious pinnacle of knowledge. I say nothing now about your parents, who I believe have long since been removed from this light; but how much the country and the order are diminished, I believe they already feel and will feel more and more each day. As for him who has departed, I have no doubt that he bears nothing ill except our grief; for he has lost nothing at all, but gained immensely, since in place of earthly corruption he has won heavenly incorruptibility, and in place of this temporal death eternal life.

What about me? I like to recall how, when he came to visit me that last afternoon while I was suffering from a long and grave illness, never again—alas—to return, and planned to set out early the next morning for the place where he was to die; as the night broke off his conversation, he finally parted from me at length most unwillingly, as though he foresaw in his heart that it would be the last conversation between us. Only then did I notice I was ill; I had not felt it during his visit. One morning a few days later, when he had reverently celebrated Mass as was his solemn and invariable custom, and was exchanging some earnest words with his friends, he suddenly realized that he was about to faint and hastened to his cell. Leaning on his bed, he began intoning that famous verse of David, "Have mercy upon me, my God" [51:3, 56:2, 57:2]. And before he could finish it, he gave up that devout and, so to speak, uniquely meritorious soul. And so to God he was restored, but from us, as Jerome says of Blaesilla, he was snatched by sudden death. About this kind of death, as Cicero says very aptly in this connection, it is difficult to speak; you see what men surmise. I would not want, nor am I allowed to say or surmise anything else, but to believe that our Savior Jesus Christ, who deemed him worthy of His table in the morning, in the evening deemed him worthy of the delights of the eternal repast and a heavenly chamber for his abode. This he deserved, this I hope for, pray for, and desire.

It is not easy to say how pained I was by that recollection because at the very time that that noble man passed away in Venice, we were in Padua; and you, as usual, had come to visit me in the evening, and had sat with me among our books, as you often do gladly but too humbly, and when I asked you whether you had any word about your brother, you replied that all was well, whereas he had expired at midday; but the shortness of the day and the rough river had delayed the report of the event. And so, on the next day, when I had learned that he had passed away and that you had left, how many times do you think I sadly cried out those words of Virgil [*Aen.* 10.501]:

Man's mind knows not his fate and future lot,

or rather, man's mind knows not his fate and present lot.

I have said much—too much, I fear! And oh, if I had the same zeal for writing that I had as a young man, how much I would tell you about the talent, the learning, the eloquence, the virtue, and the character of your brother and precursor; the subject is certainly inexhaustible. Even with what I will not call this chill of an aged mind, but this lukewarmness, I would say more, except that I would not want to bring tears to your eyes and mine, since I have resolved that I would rather lull them to rest. This is what for many days has kept me from writing, to the point where I could appear to be either slow, which I must admit of my own accord, or forgetful of you, which I would boldly deny. But my true purpose was to cause you no annoyance by addressing you at a moment that was perhaps less appropriate, nor to add to your grief rather than diminish it. I deliberately gave you time to render to your brother the brotherly tears he deserves, but beyond that, to wipe them away at the command of reason and the counsel and entreaty of a friend.

Farewell, and you who know how to console others, my good friend, console yourself, and may the consoling Spirit console you.

From your country home in the Euganean Hills, November 1 [1369–70].

Sen. XI, 15.

To Philippe [de Cabassoles], Cardinal of the Church of Saints Marcellinus and Peter,* about his own condition.

Your letter reached me when I had been suffering even more from fever and weakness for over forty days. I got up as best I could, and I received and read it with due reverence. It contained a summons from our most holy lord, the Pope, to join him; although not stated outright, I had long sensed that it was his will from his letter to me in which he deigned to insert that he wished to see me. It is too much for me anyhow, beyond any merit of mine, that so great a father and lord should care to say even a single word about me, let alone to see me. May God grant him in return a glorious and peaceful life here, and a happy and eternal one in heaven. But truly at present my excuse is well enough known, indeed too well known, and more than I would wish; and I swear by Christ, the God of Truth, that I could not go to the church next door to my house except on the arms of friends or servants, unless I were to fly. That is why out of urgent necessity I have done what** I had never before done with you: I am writing to you by another's hand, although, to confess the truth, it is the hand of such a friend as to be my own.

Well then, that is my present condition, and I shall say something more that will not be pleasant, I am sure, either to your mind or your ears. I have no hope that I will ever, from now on, regain my usual strength, or rather any strength; as you know, I am now advanced in years, and worn out and exhausted beyond measure; and just as the Apostle says, "weighed down beyond (my) strength so that (I) find even living a burden, and (I) have had the death sentence within so heavily that (I) have no confidence in (myself), but in Him who raises the dead" [2 Cor. 1:8-9]. In sum, almighty God has clearly and variously visited me in these days, although much less than I deserve. I thank Him with equal faith and reverence, both for health and sickness, and both for life and for death when it comes. But I beg you—my lord who has always procured for me, even without being asked, all good, helpful, and honorific things—to excuse me to our lord's holiness, and thank him (not, however, in

---

* See VI, 5.
** We emend *et* to *quod*.

my name, but in your own), for through this invitation he has honored me greatly with his appraisal of me. But I cannot, nor would I wish I could, do anything beyond what is pleasing to God.

Padua, October 8 [1369].

Sen. XI, 16.

A reply to the letter of Urban V* urgently calling Petrarch to Rome, and an excuse for his delay.

Amidst all the things that either Nature has bestowed upon me or Fortune, if indeed this word may be used in Catholic language , and particularly to the Vicar of Christ, I have nothing to compare to your kindness, O most blessed and holy Father. Indeed, as it is typical of a human mind always to crave something, I, while despising much that was highly prized above all things by others, was never so naïve or senseless as not to desire the attention and favor of great and illustrious men as much as a great windfall. This desire, perhaps just because it was known that I was not at all greedy or ambitious, has been fulfilled for me to the point of envy, so much have I been known or loved, or both, by almost all the Roman pontiffs of our age and by the princes, kings, and lords of the earth. Why, I myself wonder—I admit it—and I do not know unless, as I have said, the moderation of my wish deserved not being repulsed.

Nevertheless, for all this elevation, I had not yet reached the top. I felt that my honorable desire still lacked something, not because I wanted to be loved by greater men, since there were none, but by better men. There is often a big difference between two men, though they shine with equal or the same rank. What difference was there between Solomon and his son, Rehoboam, who reigned in Jerusalem? Or between Numa Pompilius and Tarquin the Proud in the city of Rome? And what between Aemilius Paullus and Terentius Varro, who were consuls at the same time? And what, finally, between Augustus Caesar and Tiberius, who if not at the same time, sat on the imperial throne consecutively? I could cite examples of pontiffs too, as I have of kings, consuls, and emperors, but I purposely abstain.

I return to the subject. Though unworthy, I have been loved at times by great men, even the greatest. But there is no truer, no surer greatness than what has been gotten not by men's fickle plaudits, but by virtue and merit. You, O greatest of fathers and best of lords, enable me to aim no longer at being loved either by greater or by better men. Thus, through that kindness and mildness of yours, you have brought my lot to fulfillment. Only one thing

---

* See VII, 1.

slightly, or to tell the truth, greatly lessens my joy arising from your esteem: that in regard to me you are relying not on yourself but perhaps on my reputation or the testimony of friends, since reputation, so to speak, is usually false, and the judgment of friends is often blind. Be that as it may, I rejoice in being so valued by the Vicar of God that I deserve to be summoned by him, whoever may have vouched for me. For although, given my health and my age, the trip may be too demanding, the invitation is beyond doubt something to boast of.

You made your wish known to me, most blessed Father, last year in your apostolic letter. It ought to have been more than enough for me that you not only wished to see me, but even thought me worthy of it. And I confess that it was enough, and more than enough, if reasons alien to me, very compelling ones in fact, had not forestalled my eagerness to hasten to you. Later you had the one, whom you felt I respected and cherished the most, summon me more directly in your name—and afterward many others who were all most dear to me and most skilled in persuasion. Most recently, when a less generous mind would long since have ascribed my delay either to laziness or to insolence, your divine benevolence summons me once again with an even sweeter letter. I could scarcely believe my eyes: first you excuse my slowness on the grounds of poor health. This excuse is indeed true and well known, but not the only one. But it alone would not be enough, for I could have come before sickness struck, had not something else stood in the way; but you further swear that you still wish to see me just as eagerly, and, though accustomed to commanding kings, ask me with touching appeals to come. I have not the strength to bear so great a display of your courtesy and geniality, since for me your requests are deservedly the strongest commands.

O gentlest Father, when I think of one thing that I read in this letter from you, joy and shame come over me in rereading it. For you say that you have been wanting to see me in person for a long time, and slip in your reason by calling me, "a person gifted with manifold virtues and knowledge." I can have no doubt as to what you say, but I am confused as to the reason. For you wish to see me because you imagine me as I have been described to you by those who deceive themselves because of their love blindfolding them with regard to me. But if you say this from your own heart, if this is what you believed, although I know to the contrary, I would still now say to you what I said then to the one whose supporting letter you requested in order to uproot me from this place, I being someone whom you alone, none of the preceding pontiffs, have known, properly honored and raised as high as you could. In writing to him, as best I could then, on the life of solitude, I said, "If you ever err in this, I rejoice, nor would I ever care to be able to free you of this error, which is an honor to me, a joy to you, and harmful to no one." Whom to believe about me is up to Your Holiness, and what they say about me is up to them; yet, given your insight—you had noticed that they were swayed by love—they ought instinctively to have been suspect.

In the midst of all this, as I seem to have written you long ago, it would be safer and wiser, whoever I may be, to lie low so as to solidify your opinion by remaining inaccessible. Yet, with reverence for you urging me on, I felt obliged, and I wanted to come more than a year ago. How I wish you could know, without my telling you, how many great obstacles stopped me! Perhaps I could have excused myself for this with a letter, were it not—to confess the truth—that, weighing my smallness and your greatness, I began to feel that such a tiny, obscure point might easily have slipped unnoticed from your capacious memory in the hurly-burly of enormous problems. Therefore, I took refuge in silence. For I do not want you to think that while you wish for the sight of this mere worm I do not wish to see the face of the father and prince of Christians, the Pontiff of Rome, and such a pontiff at that. I so love many men from history, who passed away a thousand years ago, that I would think no labor hard to see them, if allowed, no journey long to arrive at such a wished-for sight. Virtue has astonishingly long and powerful hands. She draws our minds to herself from afar, and sometimes our bodies too, as is written about many, and particularly about Livy. That statement attributed by Cicero to Laelius is quite true. He says, "There is nothing more lovely than virtue, and nothing that so draws us to cherish someone. Indeed, because of virtue and integrity we cherish in a certain sense even those we have never seen" [*Amic.* 28]. Well known are those other words with which he shows that virtue, not only in unknown people, but even in enemies, is lovely.

I do not want to speak with you about yourself, lest I begin to appear what I am not. But how would I not wish to behold him, whoever he might be, to whom Christ gave the spirit and counsel to extricate His Church, His only bride and mother of all the faithful, from that filthy and hapless prison, and lead her back to her rightful seat! Would I not venerate, love, and wholeheartedly embrace him? Would I not long for him with all my heart? I would not consider myself a Christian unless I felt that way not only toward a Roman pontiff who had served the city and me so well, but toward anyone else, including an enemy; for the admiration of great virtue has often softened, often quenched hatred. Therefore, what do I owe you if I would feel this way toward anyone? So, although at times, as I have said, I suspected you had forgotten me over a period of time, still I strove, well aware of my duty, to shake off the hindrances and rise up when, alas, O vain hopes of men, O doomed state of men, the greatest hindrance did intervene—may it be the last! An illness suddenly struck me down, one that could have crushed the strength of any young man; like a lion, it so pounded all my bones, and when at last it barely went away, it left me so frail that I can neither mount a horse nor go on foot, nor even go to church next door to my home without the support of servants or clerics. The doctors hope that spring's arrival will help. But I hope only in Him of whom it is written, "You created summer and spring" [Ps. 74:17]. If our Po flowed to the Tyrrhenian Sea as it now flows to the Adriatic, I would right now be hastening on my way and finding relief for the discomforts of my frailty in the river's gentle flow, as I often do. Now necessity, which holds even kings by the throat with nails of steel, forces me to wait, sitting or lying down amidst my books, for the solace of all my exertions, until divine aid comes whereby I could have at least some, if not the normal, use of my limbs.

To assure you that this is so, I am beginning even now hopefully to procure horses fit for the trip in the spring, knowing full well that if one horse and a retinue of three servants were enough for Cato the Censor, the grand old man, even in his high office (both points are recorded about him), one servant ought to be enough for me as a private citizen, and indeed not one horse but none. But the ways of men have become corrupt and depraved, and everything has changed for the worse. Luxury and arrogance and vanity and pleasure have overcome our minds and driven away that ancient temperance and congenial modesty. Nothing is done without being surrounded by a dusty army of horses and servants. Yet I have tried until now to resist this torrent of perverse fashion lest it completely overthrow and overwhelm me. Therefore, while I could perhaps have or at least wish for more, two horses are quite sufficient for me at home; but on a journey I need more, not because my heart is set on them, but because of the corrupt ways of our century. For somehow or other I am often better known among our people than I would like. And sometimes it is necessary, in order to avoid people's muttering, for me to conform my reluctant mind to the ways of the multitude.

I have said all this so that, since it has pleased you to bend your lofty mind down to my lowliness, you may get an inkling of my plans. Though ill, I am seeking what I shall need when I am well, but I am not waiting until I get well, lest there be some delay then; in point of fact, as soon as I begin to feel some renewed strength, I shall come at once and present myself before my lord. Since I know myself, and measure and judge myself not by the talk of the crowd but by my own conscience, I feel confident that, once you see me, a feeble old man not fit for any business, incapable of labor except what I have undertaken of my own free will, and finally good for nothing but leisure and quiet, you will quietly praise, though it is useless for you, my pious and difficult journey; and you will not deny my return but send me back at once to my retreat without taking from me what you promise to give me. All those who write me at your bidding fill me with the great hope of your beneficence, which I do not doubt is immense. But so that you may know me fully, since you by no means disdain, as is evident, information about anything so trifling, I am not one to be dragged away from my own doorstep by any hope or desire for wealth. For there is nothing in the human sphere I greatly long, strive, or hope for. Love, faith, duty, devotion, reverence, gratitude—these are the goads to move me if I am to be moved.

I have therefore never listened so earnestly, with such keen ears, to anyone's promise as I have yours when you say that you are concerned for my peace of mind. O promise worthy of you, O generous gift of a truly great mind! For what is it to me if you were to pile all the treasures under the heavens on my bosom so that, compared to me, both Crassus and Croesus would be paupers? If I lack peace of mind, would I not be very poor and wretched? Take away the wealth, leave me naked, give me only peace of mind, I shall be rich. Surely wealth is accumulated in so many different crafts and with so much struggle in order that minds may have peace. In this, as in so many other things, human diligence is greatly deceived. Riches give no one peace of mind, but rather deprive many of it.

To you, with that confidence which your kindness has allowed me, I will boast of one thing, but in the Lord. Let this be said not in praise of me but of Christ. I know, most blessed Father, very few sinners so far who are, I shall not say of calmer spirit, but of less troubled spirit than I. I do not because of this arrogate to myself the reputation of a virtuous man. For it is not a virtue, since it is not from a chosen habit, but implanted in my mind by a certain natural instinct since adolescence, to believe that riches contribute nothing to a blessed life. This peace of mind, however little it is, cannot be complete during this life's race; for who can run and be at rest? But if it will be increased for me by Your Holiness, to whom, if only for your good will, I am already indebted for a great favor, I shall then become indebted for an immense, inestimable one. Accordingly, I would accept this gift of peacefulness from no one anywhere in the world so happily as from you. For I consider no one else so worthy that I should owe my peaceful and tranquil old age to him. There is no age that needs peace as much; you would not call Cicero either opposed to this view. He says, "For old people it seems that bodily labor should be lessened and mental exercise increased" [*Off.* 1.123]. He said "exercise," not "labor." Therefore, any educated old man will embrace the former and flee the latter. For the numbness of old age is roused by exercise and made weaker by labor; and in general nothing strenuous, but everything restful, suits it.

You will take what I have said incidentally as said in my behalf and as part of my excuse. Only this morning, so to speak (for what else is a man's life than a single day, and at that a brief and troubled one?), I mean not long ago, I was complaining after a very long journey because the end had been so close; now, at evening—O incredible dizziness of events!—I find no journey short enough; any movement wearies my hollow body. You will therefore be doing something needed by me and worthy of you if, even though, as I frankly declared long ago, I seek from you nothing more than your blessing and good will, you for your part either grant or add to the tranquillity that my age needs. For a peaceful old age is the road to a peaceful death, and a peaceful death is the passage to eternal life. May Christ make this life holy and joyful for you, and the end of life distant and easy, and after these labors may He transfer you to that life without end, and to that peace about which we have been speaking at length.

Padua, December 24 [1369].

Sen. XI, 17.

To the same person,* excusing his own helplessness because of a deadly, frightening mishap en route.

We have learned, most blessed Father, that many who undertook something great either with arms or with the mind let it go because death intervened. But not to prolong this unduly, I shall make do with a few examples and skip over many. For the matter is not questionable nor lacking in documentation. To begin with some examples, in Holy Scripture, Moses, after leading the nation of Israel out of the yoke of Egyptian slavery, was overtaken by death and could not lead them into the promised land. Julius Caesar, toward the end of his life, intent on so many great projects, had so many plans for embellishing the city of Rome and for the growth and safety of the republic and the empire. [He meant]** to decorate Rome with temples and public buildings of unusual size, and with Greek and Latin libraries too; his successor, the divine Augustus, carried this out. Furthermore, he wanted to codify the civil law out of the infinite overflow of old enactments by cutting out the superfluous ones, selecting the beneficial ones, and gathering them in very few volumes to make them systematically and easily available to scholars. Justinian carried this out long afterward to the best of his ability. In addition, after Spain had been recovered for a second time following the death of Pompey the Great, he had plans to shift the armies from the west to the north and east, and to make war first upon the rebel Dacians and then the Parthians, the former a dauntless nation, the latter the most powerful next to the Romans at that time. What happened? You ask what outcome attended these and other undertakings, since I have not touched upon all of this man's last ones? Listen to Suetonius Tranquillus when he says, "Death overtook him as he was contemplating and doing such things" [*Diu. Iul.* 26.2].

Alexander the Macedonian, having overrun Asia and conquered all that part of the world, was threatening Carthage on this side, and on the other, as Lucan says, "prepared to bring his fleet into the ocean," seeking—for all I know—Taprobane [Ceylon] or the Antipodes. Hear what happened as he was making these plans, listen to what follows:

---

* See VII, 1.
** The Latin text is uncertain.

His fatal day arrived; no other way
Could nature put an end to this mad king. [10.41-42]

Cyrus, the most famous king of the Persians, having subjected Asia, was hastening with his army against Scythia. Advancing at great speed, and thinking that there could no longer be any bounds to his kingdom except those of the world, he was destroyed—a tremendous example of royal feebleness and arrogance—by a widowed, childless woman. No less ambitious were the plans of King Pyrrhus, nor was his end any happier. Aspiring to rule Italy, he upset the Roman commanders by the spectacle of his troops and the huge size of his elephants. Finally, when he was no match with the sword, he tempted his enemy with gold and gifts; but in the end, he was beaten and driven out of the Italy that he had craved. As he was starting still more wars in Greece, he too was slain by a woman's hand. Atilius Regulus, famous for many victories, and now assaulting the gates and walls of the enemy, was practically shoved out of his triumphal chariot into prison and to his death by a general's unexpected arrival and the sudden change in the fortunes of war. And as the Emperor Trajan was renewing the power and the glory of the aging empire, he was snatched away by a death ruinous to the republic. At this point I shall touch on another class of men. Virgilius Maro had begun to polish that matchless work which was to have more admirers than imitators, and was already on the verge of completing it when death entered, blocking his glorious feat, and brought the happy start to a sad ending. The same thing also happened to Lucretius and to Lucan except that their deaths were by suicide while Virgil's was natural. Some add another poet to these, one whom you may not know but he is dear to me, Papinius Statius; but they are mistaken, for he brought both his works to completion.*

I do not see how I could put myself into either category; I have about as little to contribute to one as to the other. It is not given to me to do anything at all with arms, and very little with the intellect. But there are other roads to glory. One, which was great in itself and to me the very greatest, was to come before you. What happier thing, more beyond my mean lot, could befall me, or be hoped for, than to be summoned so many times and with so many flattering letters, so kindly, so gently, to journey to the Roman Pontiff, not just any of them, but to the one Christ gave to His Church to cor-

* P. overlooks the unfinished *Achilleid.*

rect the errors of all the pontiffs of our age? What could this trip seem to be offering me if not something splendid and magnificent, inasmuch as the summons itself brought such glory that I somehow began to love myself more, and others admired me more and more, and looked up to me since so great a judge did not despise me? I was therefore coming to you with an enthusiasm that was greater than I had ever seen in any man; I am not certain whether I remembered reading about it in anyone anywhere.

But to confess the truth, that enthusiasm was only of the spirit, for the body was still weak and frail, and I had no confidence at all in my strength; all my hope was in divine assistance. Traveling thus, and hastening beyond my strength and age, but drawn by my longing for you, death unexpectedly brought me to a halt. Though incredible, why should I fear to tell the truth? It was not illness, but real death. Who would call it a poetic fiction or a tasteless hyperbole to apply the word death to a sickness or a swoon? I do not argue about unknown things; for thirty hours or more I do not remember what I was any more than what I was before I was born. There was no consciousness in my soul, no feeling in my body, to which many drastic remedies were applied, but I felt nothing whatsoever of what was being done to me and in me—no more than Polyclitus's or Phidias's marble statues would have felt. In short, everyone said and believed that I was no more.

That is the word that spread everywhere around here; in Padua and in Ferrara, where I was then, it was believed by all. Your devoted sons [Niccolò and Ugo d'Este], the ruler of this city and the ruler of the other one in whose home I stayed, and their physicians were convinced of this; and these splendid noblemen bore the news so badly that if I owed them a great deal before, now I am eternally indebted to them, and not only to them, but to both their peoples, so great was the public grief in both places at my passing. Nor did the same news travel any the less to Venice, Milan, Pavia, and other cities where I seem to have friends, so that some rushed from there to my wake or burial. Why, I imagine that this rumor has even struck your most sacred ears! What leads me to think so is not the glory of my name, which has none, but the ambition and insatiable frenzy of those who are swimming in riches, yet thirst for more; they surround you day and night, and never stop making demands on your kindness. Years ago, if you recall, when a mishap much less serious than this one struck me, they approached you one after the other, craving my benefices which, though few and small and yet more and greater than I deserve, appear to them to be many and great for this one reason—that they are mine; so great am I only because of envy. And they sought not only these two benefices, which I had at that time or have now, but those also that I had voluntarily yielded long ago to needy friends. And what might amaze me, except that greed is so rash and so blind, they sought even those I never had, with the result being, as they muddled everything, for quite a few days the entire Curia boiled over with ineffectual bulls.

Nor can I believe that they are any less active now. For avarice is always most vigilant, and while certain vices shrink with time, this one grows as it holds on and is inflamed by success. But I look down equally upon the concerns, the life, and the gossip of such people who dream of others' deaths and forget their own, who impudently anticipate what they disgustingly covet, like vultures waiting to glut themselves on others' benefices as though they were carcasses. Rather I have faith in the judgment of the others. For how could so many brilliant minds of experts, whose eyes saw me and whose hands touched me, be wrong? Therefore, since in the state I was I did not know anything and I now remember nothing about myself, why should I not believe others who bear witness that I was dead? I was dead! And here I am alive, thanks to Him who revived Lazarus; but I live to die again, and I learned at least this from dying: that what precedes or follows death could be terrifying and frightful, but death itself is scarcely more than a weak sigh, or a nice, long sleep, and, as with so many other things, what the poet says is very apt:

Sweet, deep repose, most like a gentle death.
[*Aen.* 6.522]

Now that I am once again alive, I have the same mind to come and kneel at your feet as before the mishap. Nor was I frightened by the threats of doctors who with one accord affirmed that there was no way I would reach Rome alive. While I did quite agree with them on this point—that if that violent, terrible seizure struck me in some deserted place, I was finished—I still hoped to be able to come all the way alive. I thought that whatever might happen to me there would be fine and auspicious, first because your blessing would not, I hope, fail me as I depart from this body, and then because (regardless of what your cardinals may say, and let them jeer as they please and pretend to despise the one they really hate), Rome is beyond doubt the holiest place in the world, where a true Christian must wish to live and to die. What then has held me back? Not fear, by Jove, but only weakness, which is so great that I could no more have returned to Padua than gone on to Rome, except that I did return lying prostrate in a boat, and was received by the lord of the city [Francesco da Carrara] and the entire population with amazement and much joy, staring at me as a man returning from the dead.

This is where I am, Most Holy Father, not only ill but saddened because my sincere desire failed to be realized as I hoped, and the best thing I ever undertook could not be completed. As Christ is my witness, in this whole affair I did nothing consciously, so far as it was up to me; and, often mulling it over in silence, I grieve that it so happened to me. But I am not astonished in the least, for I know the cause: I was not worthy of seeing you. Now, prostrate in body and spirit, I beg you, O Father of Christians, to spare my helplessness and to deign to number me among the least of your servants, though I be useless and unknown. And may He, who chose you to be His Vicar on earth, long keep you safe in so great an office, and receive you into His heavenly abode when you depart late from here.

Padua, May 8 [1370].

Sen. XII, 1.

To Giovanni [Dondi] da Padova, famous physician,* concerning some medical advice.

You have offered me an occasion for levity in the midst of my ills. In Cicero an excellent man jokes at the point of death. I indeed am not yet at that point, but have a grave and complicated sickness, and do not know how close I am to death; yet I will joke with you. I am not in the habit of arguing about unknown things, as many do who, in wishing to appear wise, reveal their ignorance, and, as the Comic Poet says, by understanding everything manage to understand nothing [*Andria* 17]. How could I, who never turned my eyes or my ears, not to say my mind, to medicine, indeed who until now, enjoying the best of health, disregarded—to tell the truth—that study as superfluous, and disparaged not the art itself, but its practitioners, aside from a few I cherished because they seemed to be true doctors, how could I, such as I am, I repeat, argue with the foremost doctor of this age (either the only one or one of a few) over matters regarding medicine? This is therefore not an argument but a game that I am initiating, so that for a while you may laugh at my worries and I forget my present ills and "sicknesses which line up," as the Satirist says, "to assail" [10.218–19] and beset me.

You have sent me a letter full of sincerity, concern, and professional advice, to which, in my opinion, Hippocrates could add nothing, nor remove or change anything. But how could he not agree with your advice, since he was the source from which it was drawn, while I, ignorant of it and scornful on many points, have accepted it because I was won over by your reasoning. You write that in order to get over my condition I need a partial, if not a complete, change in my life style or diet. I would certainly grant this without disagreeing, for any age has its proper nourishment both for the mind and for the body. And just as children's pursuits do not befit old people, neither do all foods. Nature so disposed this creation of hers that each part of her noble, though fragile and transitory, work is sus-

---

* A famous physician-scientist and member of the illustrious Paduan family. He built for Galeazzo Visconti a famous clock which included the movement of all the celestial bodies, and was run by a single weight that turned more than two hundred wheels. Because of the invention, the Dondi family added to its name the epithet *Dall'orologio.* He was professor of astronomy in Padua and of medicine in Florence, and was greatly esteemed by P.

tained by appropriate supports according to the changes in time. Just as a skilled architect plans in the same house rooms for summer and winter, and for every other season, so did skillful and provident nature establish several ages in the same man and assign certain appropriate attributes to each.

I call infancy and childhood the beginning of springtime; these are followed by adolescence, as the climax of springtime and closest to summer. And although no age is more frivolous, none more inconsiderate, none more prone to the stimuli of lust, still it is followed by what I would call the summertime of life—youth, which is longer blooming but still green, not indeed as flighty or inconstant, but seething with the greater fires of desire and wrath. This is succeeded by that riper season—old age, starting with the sixtieth year, according to Augustine, although it is viewed differently by others. This is like autumn, more peaceful and mild than all the others, and more fit to gather the fruits of the past, when the fires of passion have been spent by age and tamed by the pursuit of the virtues. Last is the winter of decrepitude, idle, cold, and desirous of peace and warmth, an age which certain great and flaming geniuses of the past succeeded in firing up, but this would be too long to dwell upon.

Therefore, just as I admit that these ages (of which I have already experienced three, and am guessing about the fourth) are distinguished by their concerns and activities, so do I believe that they are distinguished by food and diet, But see how I support your cause. What you have stated briefly, I am developing more fully. After interjecting one point, I shall go on with what I had in mind; and I beg you, believe that what I shall say is not to flatter you in public, but rather for the sake of the truth and our matchless friendship. Whatever I would believe from Hippocrates or Aesculapius, I would believe from you, and perhaps even more, because I consider you equal to the very greatest in art and science, and I know you are superior to them in faith and love. Therefore, if I say something differently from you, or if I contradict you, you will accept it in a friendly spirit and pretend that I am not contradicting you but those I just called the founders of medicine.

Now, first of all, I am certain that my health is as dear to your heart as your own. Nor am I any less convinced that nothing of what your predecessors have written is unknown to you, and perhaps you have even added to that with your intelligence and studies. No argument on this score, no disagreement. What is doubtful is whether every word that they let drop, as if uttered by the mouth of God, so deserves belief that it is a sin to disagree. Oh, I know that Hippocrates was indeed considered a mere man, but Aesculapius a god, not only by their people but by ours, yet a greater God struck him with lightning. And I know very well that if I allow you to use the words of your authorities, you will have no trouble proving anything you wish, but witnesses from within one's own family are suspect. I know that some men, when they argue about the truth or falseness of whatever subject, bring into their argument authorities in that same subject whose credibility was the original issue. This seems to me not a trivial flaw in disputation: for the sake of proving what you wish, to bring in what you cannot prove because it is not an established fact; and to prove what is doubtful, so to speak, by what is ambiguous. I do not accept a witness of dubious trustworthiness, even though praised by his own side.

But let me proceed; you say, and use almost as the basis of your advice, that my age and my nature have changed with the passage of time; and with a quite philosophical reminder you tell me to consider my age. In this you simply agree with me, and say in words what I am experiencing in reality. Now too it amuses me to argue your cause. Great, indeed incalculable, my friend, is the speed of life, or better, its flight; "for time flies" [*Tusc.* 1.31], says Cicero. By Jove, I would add something to the term flight, if I knew one. No swallow, no heron flies as the days of our life fly by. For we discern in them the beating of the wings and the space they cross and their onward flight, and we see them approaching their goal and reaching it momentarily; but in our case, except perhaps for very few who have been privileged with God-given talent and spirit, we see nothing at all but ourselves already there to our surprise and dumb-founded. Wherefore this flight of life cannot rightly be compared to a bird's flight, but to that of an arrow shot not by a bow, but by a cannon. If this were as well known to the young as it is to the old, life would be more honest and innocent in youth, and recollection more welcome and cheerful for the old. But now the hope for a longer life plunges blind, improvident adolescence and fleeting youth into crime and lewdness galore; old age finally wakes up when it is too late to beware of them or to undo them except with repentance and tears; it looks about and understands what purpose was served by relying on false hope.

We distinguish the ages by the changes in our opinions, as you have seen me do just now; and what we divide into bits we declare to be something great. Then we proceed to weave distant hopes and intricate webs, we lay huge foundations for complex projects, and we mentally ordain perpetual youth and happiness, we who tomorrow shall be old and wretched—not that I would call old age wretched in itself, but rather happy unless deluded by the errors of earlier ages. Nor even so is it wretched if only it rises up, and, shaking off the vanities, it gains wisdom and true opinions, albeit at the end of life, as Plato puts it. If this is what philosophers thought, what ought we to think, to whom has been granted the attainment of wisdom, virtue, and salvation without a whole lot of inquisitiveness and bother such as they went through, but with straightforward grief of spirit and pious moaning. That old age is truly wretched which is on the one hand afflicted with bodily feebleness, like mine now, and by the sickness of old age, and on the other with youthful wantonness, from which I pray God spare us, and by murky passions of the spirit.

But I return to the errors and vain hopes of the young. For I ask, what would be off limits to them whom no one opposes, everyone befriends, and not only the multitude but the whole human race? But let men deceive themselves as they please. The whole that we divide up, multiply, and stretch out is nothing; accordingly, it is that very rapid flight of our life that no one thinks about, but everyone talks about. No one, I say, gives it thought except at the end when, turning back and retracing the past, one somehow believes he has dreamed, not lived. Who does not feel that man changes with age? Or who is there who would dare deny it? I am still upholding your argument. Marble citadels yield to the years, let alone tiny earthen man, made of contrary humors; and so do the walls of the mightiest cities. Do you not see how the Babylon of yore perished, how Troy and Carthage fell, both of which were harmed not as much by years as by flames and swords and battering rams? Corinth, Syracuse, Capua, Aquileia, Chiusi, and Taranto are but small remains of ancient cities. Lacedaemon and Athens are bare names. Rome is succumbing to decrepitude, and would have succumbed by now and been reduced to ashes, were she not buttressed by the prestige of her glorious name. Innumerable others are now aging, and they too are about to meet their end quickly but unnoticed by us, inasmuch as the lifetime of cities is longer than that of men; and thus, before one city ages, many thousands of men will have aged. Nor will men alone have perished, but their fame as well, as the years and centuries silently slip by. But why marvel if cities, man-made, yield to age? Cliffs yield and mountain ranges change their appearance and nature; for example, Vesuvius has grown cold, Etna cooled, in many places the Alps have sunk, the Sicilian Peloro and the Italian Apennines, split by waves where once they stood with wooded hills, now look down upon ill-famed Charybdis bobbing in the thunderous eddies. Finally, though great men may deny this one thing—great I mean in other matters but small in this—the world, as we believe, will yield to age. Why then should I not yield? I *have* yielded; and, if I may say so, beyond the ordinary extent of those who live soberly and temperately, in whose ranks I would perhaps dare include myself, not in my own judgment, but on others' testimony.

Here I am, or more truthfully was, sixty-six years old. When I consider the years one by one, they seem to be many thousands. But when I consider them all at once, they seem a single day, and at that a short, cloudy one, toilsome and wretched. And while I know many octogenarians who are rakes and drunkards and in good health, this year has so affected me that, except for the servants' help, I have been immobile for many days now, a sad weight, burdensome to others, hateful to myself. Why is this? I can already hear you from here and the doctors on all sides agreeing that the one cause, or the main cause, for my ills is drinking water. O happy drunkenness! Others will add my eating fruit, my avoiding meat, my fasting. O pitiful abstinence! Is nothing healthy then, except drinking like a drunkard and eating like a wolf? But the issue between you and me still remains unresolved. There will perhaps be someone, not a doctor, to say that the only cause of the trouble is my sin. If we admit this, I thank my God, who cleanses the foul blemishes of many misdeeds with a light punishment.

But if anyone cites another cause, a defect in my constitution, I will produce as a live and trustworthy witness that other doctor who, if we rely on reputation at all, shares first place with you, my compatriot Tommaso [del Garbo]; I could produce others, but it is silly to call dead witnesses to court. Well, then, a year ago when we were in Pavia attending your friend, the lord of Liguria [Galeazzo Visconti], in the presence of a crowd of nobles Tommaso swore that he had never seen a stronger body than mine—I use his own word—or a healthier one, or a finer constitution. And in fact, although I remember never having had any great strength, still I had such great dexterity and agility of body that I scarcely believed anyone could outstrip me. Though these qualities in men are almost the first to fail, after the delicate and fleeting beauty of the hair, they had still accompanied me every step of the way up to the present, so that, aside from jumping and running, which I no longer need nor enjoy, I felt hardly any loss at this time in my life. But this year has made up for all the years; I have been so troubled by a lasting, indeed a year-long illness, that I am not able to stand or move around on my own feet, but only on the arms of servants. For one in trouble I rejoice, by Jove, that this is not my sixty-third year, about which I once wrote at length to the other Giovanni [Boccaccio] [*Sen.* VIII, 1 and 8], but the sixty-sixth. For although I cannot be easily swayed by outlandish and suspicious doctrines, nevertheless I could have been, if not overwhelmed, at least touched perhaps by that error of astrologers which I discussed then, if this had happened to me then.

But skipping over, at least for my part, the search for the causes, since it is inconclusive but the effects are clear, you as a physician, friend, and good man have thoroughly thought out, carefully written, and sent me remedies for this ill. If I count correctly, there are six; but I am omitting the three on which I shall not dispute with you. By a rule of your art you order me to abstain from salted meat and fish, and from raw vegetables which I usually relish; I shall certainly obey you. For my nature, looking after itself, craves this sort of food less than it used to, and is ready to give it up forever, if necessary. I hasten to those three recommendations on which I disagree with you a little, or rather a great deal. You order me to give up fasting, which I have practiced uninterruptedly from childhood to this age, and to quit the race, like a laggard, in the last lap. But this is not the first time I hear medical advice contrary to divine precepts. Nor am I unaware of what the doctors and those who condemn fasting say: it is more wholesome and becoming to divide up the food and to spread out what you are going to have for lunch into a lunch and a dinner, which is perhaps not unreasonable if the facts corresponded with the words. But those who say this (I have been with such diet-counselors) first stuff themselves in the morning and then cram in more in the evening. So they do not divide their food but double it, forgetful of those words of Plato who says, "I did not like at all being full twice in a day" [Cic., *Tusc.* 5.35.100]. Therefore, if God will deign to make me well again, I shall not drop my ingrained habit of fasting, which is second nature; nor do I skip it now except to this extent: I have modified for the time being my bread-and-water fast on Friday to the usual way of fasting until this untoward frailness lets up; but with God's help, I shall return to my former way of fasting. "But now that you are older and weaker you cannot." Indeed I can: "In Him who strengthens me I have strength for everything" [Phil. 4:13]. "But he who said this was an Apostle, you are a great sinner." But was he not also a sinner himself before he was an Apostle, or, for that matter, will Christ abandon the sinners crying out His name, for whose sake He came from heaven to earth? I am not a child of unbelief; I sorely fear for myself, but I confess I hope for much from Him though I deserve nothing, and

I doubt not that I can carry out not only these fasts, which are easy even for women and children, but any hardship with His help.

Have not many feeble old men in the desert relished coarse dark bread and run-off water, and in their constant fasting remained strong and nimble? Have you not read that Antony, almost a hundred, and Paul more than a hundred, celebrated their happy, sacred meal at Jerome's with a single loaf and the water of a tiny spring? Every time we hear this with pious ears and read it with pious eyes, we are refreshed not with food or drink but with the mere recollection of such men. Someone might say, "But God was with them." Everyone knows this, but He is with us too, otherwise we would not be. Shall I believe that God will fail me, especially when I do something good? Will He, who was with me when I scoffed and sinned, abandon me when I repent and pray? I can fast, dear friend; do not doubt it. Do not believe everything from your authorities; believe something from your friend, who was never hurt by fasting, nor will be. For why is it that palsied old women fast for months on end with harsh and meager food, but we men cannot fast for one day from large, lavish meals? This is not frailty, believe me, but gluttony. There is, therefore, no reason why I should abandon an honest, harmless habit, indeed one instituted, as Holy Church teaches, for the salvation of souls and bodies at the same time. So I hold that some have perished from hunger, more from going on a binge, but no one whatsoever from fasting.

Let us go on to the rest of your letter. Another piece of advice is not so much from you as from physicians generally, for I believe that you, knowing you deal with a contentious man, proceed all the more cautiously; but from others' opinions I judge yours, which you too launch less vigorously and in passing: you say that I should abstain from apples and every kind of fruit from trees, as though they were aconite or hemlock. But on this and on the next piece of advice I cannot refrain from repeating some of what I once wrote to that other Giovanni whom I mentioned above, with this difference: then I was angered by the memory, still fresh, of an old argument I had had in Gaul with the Pope's doctors, who for some reason or other had declared war against either my reputation or my life because I had dared write a brief but—unless I am wrong—truthful letter to the Pontiff [*Fam.* V, 19]; but now calm and oblivious of that squabble [*Inuectiue contra medicum*], I write jokingly to a friend. Good God, why this hatred or this scorn for the most beautiful things that at the same time delight the taste, the touch, the smell, and the sight? Are all men mad then, and was he alone wise who put this blot on guiltless fruits? But how could Nature so fool mankind as to hide the most danger where she put the most delight and charm? It is not the kind mother but the cruel, wicked stepmother who conceals poison with honey. If you say, "we do not condemn fruit itself, but eating too much of it," there is no longer any issue. If eating too many partridges and pheasants, whose meat I hear is the greatest delicacy for you people, does harm, why fault fruit on this score? The thing itself is not censured, but excess in all things deserves it equally. Otherwise why so much toil and effort by farmers?

What do you make of those Greeks and Latins who dealt with this subject: Hesiod, Virgil, Cato, Varro, Palladius, and many others? What, finally, of Cicero, especially in that book where he defends old age against these shortcomings and discomforts which crazy youths ascribe to that time of life? There so great a man as Cato himself, the Censor, is introduced, showering praises upon agriculture, a mechanical art, to be sure, but no doubt most useful to the world, and declaring that among many wholesome and pleasant things in life he had found nothing more ingenious than the planting and grafting of trees? And what of Cyrus, King of the Persians, who, we read in that same book, would boast of the fine looks and straight rows of trees he had planted with his own hands, or had ordered to be planted? What, finally, of those Roman generals, Appius and Decius, by whom the Appian and Decian apples seem to have been imported into Italy, the former being very sweet, the latter on the tart side, but both very tasty and bearing the names of their promoters? Since it costs nothing to disagree with the ancients, what do we make of your friend and mine, than whom there may be no better man in the world or more devoted to us? He has searched every corner of Italy for every kind of fruit trees, and has perhaps gone even beyond Italy in this quest, so as to adorn not only his own, but his friends' orchards with imported trees? Shall we then say that all contemporaries and ancients were mad except the physicians? For certainly if trees of this sort are justly condemned by physicians, it is no trifling madness to go after harmful things as diligently as it ought scarcely to have applied to beneficial things. But if neither the trees themselves nor their fruit, but unrestrained appetite alone is criticized, you already have my answer above, although I have often noticed that the most famous physicians, to excuse them at least in part, teach one thing but have something else for lunch, prescribe one way but dine differently.

There remains your last piece of advice, so alien to my nature that it checks my pen from utter astonishment: you forbid drinking pure water. Why, I ask? Is it perhaps because that great master of yours says that he had found water of no value except when taken in cases of high fever, and perhaps was right in his own case. But it can be asked whether there is really no other use for water; on the contrary, as I judge, there ought to be no argument about this either. By the saints' truth and by all men's, has one old Greekling, then, perhaps a wine-lover and a water-hater, with one brief utterance, eliminated and dried up so many sparkling springs, deep wells, lovely rivers, in short, an entire delicious element of Mother Nature? What can I say here except, oh, all those poor Alpine people, who slake their thirst at rippling springs, who not only have no wine but do not even know what it is, and yet live much more healthily than you straight-drinkers, for whom it is torture to do without wine for one day! Wretched were those poor fathers of our race before vineyards were planted, whose life span nevertheless stretched almost to a thousand years without our diseases! Those poor matrons of early Rome, for whom drinking wine was a capital crime, since when a man killed his wife for drinking he was not only unpunished, but not even reproved; nor were they therefore useless or thin-blooded women, for they bore the sons we even now admire as cultivators of virtues, scourges of vice, victorious over passions and nations, whereas our partying women bear the sons we see! Those poor Gauls of yore before they knew wine, which, as history tells you, they learned to use from Rome, which was already maturing! Or rather, these poor priests of Bacchus and Venus who, for the taste of their native wine, forsake Christ, Peter, the faith, honor, and their own souls which they consider mortal, and the Church that had been ill entrusted to them! For although here the cause may be quite hidden, this one is still alleged, as I have often said; for they would rather admit intoxication than impiety, though they can deny neither. Finally, those poor philosophers, not of India who are called Gymnosophists and Brahmins, whose leader, as he drinks spring water, boasts that he is sucking the pure breast of Mother Earth, but almost all the peoples of the Orient for whom the drinking of wine is forbidden by law!

In short, happy are we alone for having become barrels of wine; wherefore I would not like to leave out one thing against our drunkenness which I cannot decide was said more in truth or in sarcasm. Recently there arose grounds for war between the Sultan of Egyptian Babylon and ourselves, alas not for the the Christian faith nor even for empire or glory, but for commerce and greed, while Egypt and the boy Sultan were ruled by a certain man of keen mind but humble rank, reputed to have been sold as a slave a few years before but suddenly raised up by his own destiny, only to tumble down. Certain of his men wanted to persuade him to follow the example of Mithridates, and, before the Christians could invade his territory, as they were threatening to do, to punish with death all those who were in his power. But he said, "We must not recklessly decide to wipe out innocent men useful to our empire, nor does it behoove us to be upset over the threats and boasting of the Christians; for even if they are powerful and spirited, they still drink wine. Consequently, many are the things they threaten in the evening that they do not remember in the morning."

Oh, an infidel's bark, insulting, I admit, but true. For so it is, our vines dishonor our life, and with wine boiling in our veins we have become vain; and drunkenness has shut out moderation and trust in our actions and words: our friends do not believe us, nor do our enemies fear us, because our promises and our threats are mostly made at table. It is not the fault of the wine, but of those who abuse it; still, since the vice is much too widespread and deep-rooted and now can hardly be overcome except by dearth of wine, I believe, by the God of Truth, it would be good for the world if no wine were to be found anywhere, except for the Mass. You and your whole following will cry out: "Then what would our stomachs do?" They would rest, they would not gurgle, they would not bloat, not belch, not foam, not struggle; they would do what the stomachs of the ancients did before wine was used, and what today the stomachs do of those who have yet to use it. But we blame our stomach for what is the gullet's fault, we try to flush with wine sicknesses brought on by wine, as though fighting fire with fire. I know a man who is still living not far from here, and is a fit witness of his condition; I knew him when I was young and he was in the prime of life, but so afflicted with the gout in his hands and feet that he could hardly do anything. Ten years later I saw him again, rid of the gout and any vestiges of his old ills, and enjoying the free, unimpaired use of his limbs; I was astonished, and he, understanding the reason for my astonishment, said, "Wine had broken and shackled me; water restored me and freed me." The other day, when I heard from his son that the gout had recurred after so long a time, I wrote him to be careful lest his enemy, the gout, had returned with his friend, wine. He replied that it had happened not from drinking wine, but just from eating bread dunked in wine. Go now and deny that wine is a fine thing, since it produces the gout, maintains it, and makes it recur by the mere smell of it, so to speak.

Wine certainly deceived its own inventor, and he who had planted the first vine was the first to be tripped up by the vine. Wine plunged Lot, by divine judgment the only righteous man out of so many thousands, into a horrible incest.* Wine kept Nabal of Carmel at the banquet, forgetful on the one hand of his weakness and of the insult to King David,** and, on the other, of the king's power, as death stood very close to striking the drunkard, had not his wife's foresight met the danger to her husband. Absalom, who was angered by the wrong done to his violated sister, decided to kill his first-born brother, Amnon, and ordered him to be killed while heavy with wine, although he could have done it in other ways—but wine does so easily expose its addicts to destruction. And to intermingle secular with sacred letters, because of wine that young son of the Scythian Queen was tricked by Cyrus, King of the Persians, and destroyed with his entire army. The Istrians who had conquered the Romans while sober were in turn conquered when drunk. Alexander the Macedonian, unconquered by the sword, was conquered by wine, and driven to a premature death. The triumvir, Antony, was changed from a Roman to a barbarian by wine, with the scandalous loss of his life and reputation. Cato says that all those who tried to overthrow the republic were intoxicated by wine, with the sole exception of Julius Caesar. Finally, Cato's own reputation was jeopardized by wine; but, being firmly rooted, it remained unshaken. And what memory or what pen would not fall short in enumerating the sad, dismal events caused by wine?

But, to summarize, many ills come to mortals because of wine. And you doctors forbid drinking water to a man who from infancy and boyhood to the end of adolescence was brought up exclusively on water; after the habit had become second nature—something that your profession especially, as I hear, says must be taken into consideration—I barely joined the ranks of wine-drinkers later on, and I love the well even now somewhat more than the barrel. I realize the passage of the Apostle, in writing to Timothy, stands against me. He says, "Drink water no longer" [1 Tim. 5:23]. Now does he not seem to be on your side talking to me? But maybe he had a different habit or nature, not in harmony with mine, and, having been used to wine since youth, he was shifting over to water when he was older, which is the opposite of me. Therefore, Paul realized that this

* P. confuses Noah (Gen. 9:19–22) and Lot (19:30–37).
** 1 Sam. 25:36–38; David was not yet king.

change, which perhaps arose from being devout, was harmful to Timothy, and forbids him to do what it would be harmful to forbid me to do. For had not Paul himself said otherwise for people in general that in wine lies wantonness, and that it is good not to eat meat or drink wine? He prescribed wine not as wine but as medicine. For he says, "Use wine moderately for your stomach and for your recurring infirmities" [1 Tim. 5:23]. Lastly this year has brought me something new and unusual, namely frequent illnesses, but when I am well, I am not aware of my stomach, whereas many complain of it each and every day.

But if now and then some indisposition strikes me, I find nothing more beneficial than drinking good fresh water. I know I am saying something new and incredible to doctors; but, if I am worthy of it, something I say about myself can be believed, for I affirm this after experiencing it a thousand times. "But your age has changed." Who does not know that? While we speak, it changes, and will change until it cannot change any longer; only death will bring that about. But am I so senseless and dull that I do not feel what is good or bad for me? I have grown cooler, but not cold; and though colder than I used to be, I am still somewhat warmer than many of my contemporaries and juniors, and yet I use water more sparingly than I used to. What more do you want? That I abstain from water altogether? You would get nowhere wanting that. I suspect that with your advice and that of your friends you have brought it about that I have come to these hills that are fertile and charming in other things, but waterless, where I cannot drink pure water, though I crave it; in fact, between the spring and this house the water becomes so warm from the sun's rays that it ceases to be palatable. But if I return to that brand-new well in my town house, remembering this awful one, I shall see how much credence I shall give to the advice of doctors.

Still, relying upon your learning and intelligence, you construct this powerful argument against me. You say, "Even if you will not believe the doctors, will you not at least believe in yourself and in experience, mother of the arts? Consider how many sicknesses this year has brought you beyond the usual because of your contempt for medical remedies. Drinking water, eating fruit, and fasting are the causes of these ills." As you see, I willingly grant you the first part, that many sicknesses have attacked me at one time. But who will prove the second, that those causes which the doctors are pushing have brought me these sufferings before their time, and not rather that perhaps they have long deferred them? Hidden and very deep are the workings of nature, which is the hardest to judge rightly. However, let truth stand its ground; but my opinion, firmly based on much experience, will not be shaken either by that one Greekling, nor by all the Greeks put together, not if Ulysses were to return armed with his wiles, Achilles with his sword, Ajax with his onrush, Nestor with his authority, Agamemnon with his scepter.

Nor am I unaware of what you are about to say, which is the usual: "Do as you please. But know that by not believing in doctors you will not live as long." I have lived enough, my friend, and if the play is over, I do not refuse to quit, or even if it is unfinished and the Stage Manager decides to halt it; for I am tired by now, and, were I to die today, it would not be fair for me to complain about the brevity of life. For if everyone were to reach my age, the world would be too small for the human race; and I am so far from wanting to live long as to fear that I have lived too long, when I recall what friends, what fine men I have sent on ahead of me, and how very little is here except the same today as yesterday, and something worse every day. How many dangers from all sides, how many threats from fortune! How many mockeries of our ways rain down upon us from the north, the eternal root of our ills, and how receptive our Italy shows itself to barbarism—which I would easily endure in other countries but not in this one—and finally what a lack of virtues, what a monopoly of vices, what bores the people and events are! And you think that, in the midst of this, life is joyful or sweet to me? It is harsh and bitter, but all harshness and all bitterness must be soothed by equanimity and patience. I therefore live tolerant of life, not eager for it. But whatever sort of life could be prolonged if I obey the doctors, I certainly do not worry about this at all, nor do I know. Indeed it is one of those things, I confess, I do not know in the least; for whether it is because one cannot safely believe in you altogether, or because it is hard for us to believe everything (and for one who believes a few things it is dangerous not to believe them all), I have known many who have obeyed doctors, and even doctors themselves, to have brief, sickly lives while others, defying them, live longer and healthier. Furthermore, neither my life nor that of any mortal is long; but mine can no longer be considered short, according to the ordinary measure of the normal lifetime.

One must close one's ears to the multitude, shake off the clouds and darkness of error, and cast off the desire for life and the fear of death. Otherwise there will be no end: always subtracting something from our age, always deceiving ourselves will be fun. We shall always wish to be young and to appear young; death will elicit a true confession. I do not now complain that life is short; I wish rather it were not bad and useless. Maro lived fourteen years less than I, Cicero three, Aristotle three, Caesar ten, and Scipio ten, one the conqueror of the world, the other the destroyer of Carthage and Numantia [in northern Spain]. I skip over Alexander, Achilles, and the doomed family of Priam, and, among our own, Drusus, Germanicus, Marcellinus, and the other illustrious men who perished in the very bloom of life. Is it not enough for me to have surpassed such great men in length of life, even though Augustus and Augustine outdid me by ten years, Horatius Flaccus by one year more than that, Plato by fifteen years, Simonides and Chrysippus by as much, Cato by twenty and more, Hiero of Syracuse by twenty-five, Carneades by twenty-five, Massinissa by thirty-five, Valerius Corvinus by thirty-five, as well as Metellus and Fabius? Isocrates and Sophocles approached this number, as did Sophocles, Cleanthes, and Varro, or even reached it; and Gorgias of Leontini exceeded it by seven years. And so? There are times when to hanker for what is highest is a virtue. But in transitory things let us be satisfied with mediocrity.

Therefore, although not the pleasure of living, which (as I have said) is, I admit, none as I look at the ways of our era, but my plans for my studies would require a little more of life, I still feel that, were I to live another hundred years, there would always be something or other missing. And so I say once again: I have lived enough; but I shall live on as long as it pleases Him of whom it is written, "You have established his limits which cannot be surpassed" [Job 14:5], and I thank God for all things and am ready either way, whether He bids me to live or to die. Nor shall I wish for a long life from Him, something I never did even when I could have more becomingly, but for a good departure from life, hoping not in my own merits but in His mercy that the end of this life will be the beginning of a better one.

I have joked with you at a distance, dear friend, as I like to do when present. And although, watching the flight of time, I had long since made up my mind to be briefer from now on, especially in my letters, you have made me forget this resolution, so pleasant was it for me to weave with you a long discourse about nothing, until daylight came and the edge of the paper—in spite of squeezing my handwriting for lack of space. Stay healthy and happy, and remember me.

Among the Euganean Hills, July 13 [1370].

Sen. XII, 2.

To the same person,* on the same subject.

I see your strategy, my friend; you have descended into the fray with all your troops. Who would not fear such a stout warrior, so heavily armed, deploying all his forces with such energy? I understand: you seek a victory, for while Plato says that it was the universal style of the Spartans to be fired by the thirst for victory, today it is the universal style of everyone here. We have all become Spartans. But tell me, O good sir, I beg you, if perchance you overcome me because of your strength or my weakness, will you at the same time overcome the truth and your conscience? I believe, by heaven, and I base my hope on your fine sense of decency, that although you may outdo your debater in speech, still you will confess in silence that you have been overcome by the truth.

Many things, to be sure, dissuade me and pull me back from this duel and war of words, so to speak, besides the vigor of your mind and your skill in doing battle: first, that weakness of body which my sickness, as it went away, left behind, and I know not whether this will linger forever or be the bane of my life; and then my time is not free but taken up not only, as always, with endless studying that begins anew each day and which I guess you know about, but also with practical things, which you do not know. I am much involved in farming and in architecture; and so that you may know how well I have been restored by physicians' advice, I now seek everywhere all kinds of trees, since this is the most propitious season for grafting. I do this all the more confidently now that you declare you are not an enemy of fruit, as I feared, but a well-wisher. I shall pray to the heavenly Farmer that He plant and water in my mind with His own hands that moderation which is beneficial, or rather essential, to fruit no more than to all things; without it nothing is done rightly. Yet although the same season is beginning to be unsuitable for my other present interest, namely building, I still do not cease or slow down, but am instead hastening the construction of a bedroom for you, which you would not call rustic except for its silence and peacefulness. There, whenever you retire from the annoyance of city life, we shall continually argue only about food, since we are wholeheartedly in agreement on everything that lies beneath the heavens or above them.

* See XII, 1.

Besides these reasons, I am held back by a third and more powerful one: I fear you, for my naïve fear is as great as my true love. I know, of course, that if I express freely what is on my mind, I shall offend your ears and, what I especially would not like, offend your mind. But on the other hand, if I were to keep still, I am afraid you would think that I look down on you. That is far from the case; so you see the quandary I am in. I shall try to take the middle of the road so as to avoid, if possible, both extremes equally, and if the subject forces me to slip into either extreme, I would rather offend you for a moment than in any way look down on you; for with friends, an affront is made up by an apology that cancels it, but contempt cuts the nerves of friendship, and so in a friendship there is no such thing. But affronts are frequent; or rather, rare are the friendships without them, as Annaeus says in speaking about a friend, "I do not love him if I never offend him" [*Ep.* 25.1]. Perhaps I shall offend you; but my preference will be to avoid it, if I can. If I wished to use the untrammeled right of friendship to the full, that is, to pretend nothing, to hide nothing, but to say everything to you as though to myself, I figure it would be very difficult, nearly impossible not to offend you; and so, considering the matter from all sides and anticipating with friendly fear in case I do offend you, I now seek forgiveness in advance and shall assume from your kindness that you will gladly grant it to me at this time.

There is one more thing I would preface before beginning. I see you in a twofold role, the friend and the doctor. With a friend I so agree on everything that there can be nothing you think or like that I do not think and like immediately. For I know friendship in no other terms than two minds becoming one. However, with the doctors my feud on many important matters is old and unresolved, and do not suppose it arose from nothing. It has sprung from prolonged experience and close observation, since—to confess the truth—I have seen how rarely the effects of their art live up to their promises; and that is no less offensive to the nature of my mind than poison is to the nature of the body. I have not prefaced all this lest your mind be upset by the sting of my words; for although you are one person and cannot really be divided in two, nevertheless, even individual things are divided by the intellect. Consequently, if you read anything pleasant and soothing in this letter, take it as something said to a friend; if anything is a little on the bitter side, consider it said against the doctor, and curb your anger or surprise, and say, "This is being said not to Giovanni but to a doctor."

Now I come to the matter at hand, in which I do not so much

hope but want to be briefer, first because I have discussed it so often with friends and with doctors (and it is beginning to verge upon boredom), and then, if I cannot avoid offending you because of the nature of the subject, I can at any rate lessen the offense with brevity. But I am not hopeful because of the very complexity of the matter and the vehemence of the argument with which you so ardently take the side of medicine—and not without warrant. For it was surely not through choice but through destiny that you followed in your father's footsteps, as so often happens in one's youth, though your intelligence deserved to be given over to better pursuits and to follow a far different path—bypassing the doubtful and ineffective remedies for this dark, filthy, doomed dungeon, to pursue remedies for the spirit, that immortal and noble part of us. How I wish that had been done, not only for your glory and salvation, but for the great comfort of my life as well! But I drop this, since you have already been for a long time what you ought to have been, and this is, I believe, not the place for changing direction, even though we know of not a few illustrious men who, even at an advanced age, changed their goal in life and their studies; but I pass over this, lest I seem to accost with suggestions the man with whom I must do battle, and to urge him to defect and join my side.

At the outset then, you took up arms (pious ones under the circumstances) for your authors, whom I appear not to have revered enough; and in order to seek the support of others for them, you brought into the fray Priscian and Cicero as authorities, adding Virgil, Homer, and others, but last of all Ptolemy. He, admittedly, is appropriate; for in my court his cause is the same as the doctors', not indeed always, but where there is talk of prognostications—which the astrologers do most eagerly and boldly, not to say shamelessly—and where men's fate is inferred from the stars, which is contrary not only to the true faith and our religion, but to all who properly philosophize. But you ask, in more words to be sure, what amounts to this: "If I am to believe Priscian about the parts of speech and how they are joined together, or generally about agreement, and if I am to believe Cicero about embellishment, and Homer and Virgil about storytelling, why not, for the same reason, the doctors about bodily health?" You introduce other famous names that are trustworthy each in his field. But when many of them are headed for me by the same path, by facing one or a few I have faced them all.

But now where shall I turn? I realize I am in great danger, and I confess I would rather have kept still, but could not. Your reputation urges me on, as well as a saying of Titus Livy, your townsman, or rather of Hanno the Carthaginian in Livy's pages. As I would to a doctor, he says to a senator questioning him, "If I were to remain silent, I would appear either arrogant or browbeaten, of which the first befits a man careless of others' freedom, the second a man careless of his own freedom" [23.12.9]. Therefore, I must reply. Nor ought I to say anything but what I truly feel. For often silence is a good thing; lying is always bad. This is why I ask, what has any of these in common with the doctors? The grammarian's subject, or goal, if we prefer to call it so, is correctness; the rhetorician's is ornamentation of speech, and, as they themselves say, the orator's function is to speak fittingly for the sake of persuasion; his goal is to persuade with speech. Concerning the first, I see that Priscian and certain others deal with what is proper to the Latin language, although, being arbitrary, it could have been otherwise; but it is well presented, as we use it, by* the author you name, having collected the testimony of those who devised it, "when the tongue of Cato and Ennius," as Flaccus says—and no less that of Tully and Maro and several others—"enriched the language of the fathers" [*Ars P.* 56-57] of yore. Comparing their usage with Priscian's teachings, I cannot deny that grammar has been well transmitted by him, and any error is not his, but theirs. For all the blame falls upon the originator, if there is any blame; the one who cites him is free of blame and often shares in the praise.

This is also my opinion of Cicero; my ears and my mind drive me to the conviction that nothing can be said more sweetly, more splendidly, or with greater power of persuasion by any man. Now the poet's function, about which it is customary to theorize, is not to invent, that is, to lie, as certain ignorant people believe. If this were so, the Muses would be everywhere, and there would be too many poets on every corner; but surely they have been such a rare breed that only the orators are fewer. And so? Their function is to invent, that is, to compose and adorn, and to sketch with artful colors the truth of things, whether mortal or natural or whatever else, and to cover it with a veil of neat fiction; once removed, truth will shine forth all the more welcome in the finding the more difficult the quest for it. For who does not know that this was done by Homer and Virgil more elegantly than anyone else?

But go on and prepare yourself to be patient. I believe the goal of medicine is healing, not literary ornamentation, and the job of a

* We emend *ad* to *ab.*

physician is not to make speeches, in my opinion, but to cure. How good were the cures of Hippocrates and the rest we do not know, unless perchance we must needs put faith in Galen, who boasted about himself a great deal, or believe that Aesculapius revived Hippolytus, and that through him a reply was given to the royal prophet, who asked, "Will doctors revive the dead" [Ps. 88:11]? But whatever our opinion about things ancient (which because of the distance in time and place, can be invented at will), speaking of physicians who live at the same time and in the same place with us, laying aside the lies of the Arabs, I can assert that I know some who know what they are talking about; as for the rest, it would be polite not to say anything. For I know not through what luck or guilty choice they learn everything better than the one thing they profess; and no one better than you, I am certain, knows the extent of their success in curing sick people, and no one would more gladly show them up. For no one hates ignorance more than a man of science. Unless I believed this of you, I would not love you so much, nor make so much of you. Nevertheless you keep quiet, and not so much out of generosity as self-interest, lest you turn your colleagues against you, although it would certainly be most fitting for you in the name of justice to take on not only the hatred of a few men, but the enmity of the whole world without flinching, and to reproach, refute, and cry out against them: "Why do you deceive the human race, and, taking advantage of the credulity and ignorance of the wretched, peddle fatal lies in place of the truth; and why is it that for murder, for which everyone deserves punishment, and no one impunity, you alone go after unearned rewards?" How beautifully, how powerfully that would sound coming from your mouth! But you shun hatred; fear or ignorance makes the rest mute. I alone cry out and am not heard; the multitude has gone deaf, learned men along with you shrink from arguing. Those I accuse say I am suspect, as though it were a question of the consulship or other civil office, or inheritance, or any kind of offense or partisanship, or in short about anything but truth alone. And so with you silent, and me beginning to feel hoarse, and the others dozing or certainly shutting their eyes and dissembling, the deadly error has gotten very deep roots, planted in rich soil, aided by the hoe of the mass folly, fattened by the moisture of age-old license, and reveling in the ordained fees, not to mention impunity.

Why should I be afraid to speak openly to a friend rather than to a physician? Hearing on the one side the doctors' words, and on the other observing their cures, I often recall the idea stated in Cicero's books on rhetoric that it is easy to speak about an art, but difficult to go by its rules. That this is so is borne out nowhere more clearly than in this art. With words they cure all over the place; in fact they kill, so that in their actions they seem quite other than they seemed in speech. And yet, O foul monstrosity, the public's faith in them, speaking thus, doing thus, is no less; and besides the many things you mention, medicine has this over the other arts: it is the safest. One barbarism or a simple solecism exposes the grammarian; one slight offense to the ear disgraces the orator or poet. A doctor kills and is not blamed; nor is he satisfied with killing unless he blames something else: a chill carried off this one, fasting that one, the eating of apples that one, drinking water that other. No one dies except by his own grave fault. No one is cured without great praise for the doctor.

Although these things are not pleasing to the ears or flattering or agreeable, you nevertheless know that I am speaking the truth. I am not unaware of what it means to attack doctors in a doctor's presence, but this is a rare and noble doctor and there are hordes of those ignoble doctors; nor would I do so at all, unless I knew that this doctor differs from the common herd—hence, your title "the Illustrious"—and unless I had learned that often the disrepute of many redounds to the praise of one. Therefore I know to whom I speak and what I speak, nor did I come unknowingly upon these rocks: I speak something harsh, unpleasant to the ears, but not unwelcome to a mind dedicated to the truth, not to any party-line, and eager for what is so in fact, not in people's fancies. I will be found never to have said anything against medicine, if there is such a thing, yet oftentimes a great deal against those who want to be called doctors. And I swear to God I do it unwillingly. Compelled by the facts, I wish I could say the opposite, believe the opposite. For it is perfectly easy to understand that this would be much more welcome to me, first because I know of no other profession where I have more friends (but every friendship must yield to the truth), and second for my own sake. Am I too not a man mortal and fragile, and, if incapable of bodily immortality, certainly seeking good health? For this I would now need, and over the years I would often have needed, the advice of doctors. While the need was often present, the remedies were always absent—not fine promises, however, and comforting words, as though what I needed was a comforter and a moral philosopher, not a doctor. But since verbal elegance and fluency are not for a doctor, but actual effectiveness (for just as no medicine makes one eloquent, so no eloquence makes one well), it was not without reason that the poet [*Aen.* 12.397], in tune with nature—and I feel I must repeat this in all such disputations—called medicine the silent art, which today is not only talkative but clamorous. So I have always found in my infirmities as many words as I wanted, and a few more, but no results. Yet I have gotten by up to now; and why do you think, except that my time had not yet come?

From these experiences and a thousand like them, which I pass over lest the joke slip into satire, I think you see why I do not believe your doctors on health in the same way I believe Priscian on grammar, Cicero on oratory, Virgil and Homer on poetry. Nor should you ascribe this, as you profess, to my rudeness or presumption. For I feel certain that any doctor who is not stubborn (and the greater he is, the more he will do it), when he comes home and retires to his bedroom with the door closed, and begins mulling these things over, however grievous to hear, will perhaps contradict them outwardly, but unless he wants to deceive himself, he will inwardly confess that they are true, repeating to himself how often he has duped the hopes of others, and been duped by his own craft. I have entered upon this course not by some chance without many experiences, but under the guidance of the greatest authorities. I have no doubt you know what that most learned man, Plinius Secundus [Pliny the Elder], wrote about you doctors, and what the wisest of the Romans, Cato the Censor, predicted, so much before you all came from Greece to Italy. But I do not care to belabor the obvious. To the entire first part of your letter and to what you asked of me with many words I have replied with still more.

Before proceeding further, I recognize that I have said something objectionable that can be attacked by those who delight in the art of setting snares with words, as though I had placed in doubt the very existence of medicine, which of course would never have been named by so many great minds unless it were something. But I do not doubt that medicine exists and is a great thing, inasmuch as in Scripture it was created by God and in profane literature it was attributed to the immortal gods' invention. This was said with reference to Apollo and his son Aesculapius. I know that if no mortal were to survive, medicine and the other arts would still exist in themselves. But existing in the abstract or in the mind of God alone, what good would they do to the health of so-and-so's body or the embellishment of so-and-so's mind? That the arts exist is not enough to make them of any avail to men; they must also be known to men. But listen briefly to how I believe medicine is known to the doctors themselves. It is not I, dear friend, but the facts that speak when, besides the deadly outcomes of slight illnesses, we see how doctors themselves in general live so that we must suspect that either this thing called medicine, whatever it may be in itself, among men is still some kind of deceptive art thought up to the vast peril and loss of mortals, whereby a few become rich but many are imperiled, or that it is a true art, usefully devised but least understood by our fellow men and least applicable to the natures of men, of which the variety is inestimable. For what other conclusion remains when out of a thousand remedies not one helps us, many do harm and often kill? I speak of those who glory in the renowned—and I wish it were true—title of Doctor of Physic! As for those others whom they call surgeons, upon whom alone they stamp the dirty, disreputable name of mechanics, I have experienced excellent cures at their hands both in myself and in others, and often have seen them either cure quickly or ease grave wounds and ugly sores by applying poultices; anyhow, they see what they are doing, and what they find useless they change. But once thé blind remedies of the others stick in the vitals within, it is all over; and about these what can I suspect or say further? Nothing, perhaps, except that I see the upshot: that the art is divine, if you will, embellished and exalted above the stars with praises however great, which you bestow most attentively. With this I would more readily agree if you were to praise it with deeds rather than words; but the doctors have doubts about the art itself, and what they praise in words they despise in their conduct.

If we say this, what certitude about this art is left for me or others when doctors have none (for to say that they knowingly and willingly harm themselves lacks the ring of truth); what else remains probable, I mean at this age? Perhaps I would have felt otherwise about the ancients if only the story is true that there was a doctor and, unless my memory tricks me, an Asclepiad, who dared say that if any sickness came to him throughout his life, aside from the final one in his decrepitude, he did not want to be called a doctor, and that because of his constant health until the very end, he deserved to be called a doctor; indeed whether by his own impulse or some fate, he did something more than he had promised, since he met death not through disease but by a fall from a height at a very advanced age. When today I see young and healthy doctors falling ill and dying everywhere, what do you tell others to hope for? Listen so that the subject may not lack a contemporary example, although there are plenty everywhere: that countryman of mine [Tommaso del Garbo] was alive the day before yesterday, but now—O shifting wheel of fortune, O hazardous and feeble art of medicine!—from such wealth and such a high reputation that he too was believed able to raise the dead (not by me of course but by many), he is suddenly gone from this light. My earlier letter mentioned him as a witness of my robust constitution; and he died while still in his prime, and with the body not just of a very strong man but of a bull. What will you say now? Never would you say that he did not know medicine, lest either his reputation or the truth contradict you. So either medicine does not help sicknesses, or he whom medicine had made rich despised it. And often, I admit, I observed him putting away figs, apples, and cherries, not as men eat them, but as cattle like to chomp hay. I have noticed the same thing in many others too who disagree with me in word, but agree with me in practice and thought, and especially in that those dark and hellish potions, which they characteristically hold out to others they cast away when held out to them. On the latter point, they are no dummies* if only they were not so eager on the former. Therefore, whichever of these positions you choose, I believe you will not find a reason why we ought to revere medicine, as if without it there is no deliverance, when we see its experts either deserted by it in times of highest need, or deserting it.

O man of learning, are you marveling at my outlook? Do you consider me so naturally silly or senseless from age that when I am so in need of advice I reject sound advice? But knowing not how to discern, amidst so many ambiguities, anything positive which not even the practitioners of the profession know, and uncertain what to follow, what to avoid, what to accept, what to cling to, I shudder at the whole wavering, shaky, confused business and remain within the confines of my nature, or rather of heavenly assistance. Do you take issue with this: if on the shore of a dangerous river, not knowing the ford, with one calling me hither and another yon, and meanwhile watching my guides sink, I halt, either waiting for a boat or looking for a bridge or, for that matter, another way, will you laugh at me and not rather praise me? Or is my hesitation unjustified? Is the torrent of this life unambiguous? Are the shipwrecks of rulers and leaders too infrequent? What else can I conclude about them except that either they deceive willfully or rather are deceived and do not know what they advise, when I see those who had made a fortune on medical advice either using their own advice less than anybody else does, or dying from their own advice? In order to convince me

* We emend *insule* to *insulsi* (Laurentian: *insulse*).

to believe in doctors, two things are necessary: neither persuasion nor argument, for either one is quite in vain, but first let them, above all others, obey their own advice, and next, when they have followed their own advice, let it turn out well. If any of this is missing, words are wasted. So what if I am not swayed by words to believe either one, not moved by syllogisms? If a rhetorician or dialectician were to prove that I have horns, do you think that for the sake of exploring the truth of his conclusion, I should touch my forehead with my hands?

Here I see you reading through all this with unfurrowed brow; for you cannot be angry at anything that is spoken by a friend or in behalf of your friend, the truth, even though the thing itself being said were unpleasant and even false, as long as to the speaker it seemed really true, as it now seems to me that nothing truer can be said. So I believe facts and not words. But it is not so with those friends of yours, who hold on to their opinion with their teeth, however damaging to anyone, provided it is profitable to themselves, and who become implacably angry when it is pulled out of their grip. Thus, many years ago when I happened to be living in Gaul, this same quarrel arose with the Pope's doctors, who were supported by the cardinals' doctors.* After much had been thrashed out in talk and in writing, and finally the issue was laid aside, they broke into insults; perhaps because they did not realize how many things could be said against me, they began to attack bitterly the art of poetry. I said with a smile that I wondered why, if they were offended by me, they took it out on the innocent Virgil, for although I had once found youthful pleasure in writing poetry, I was now intent on quite different pursuits. Seething with anger, they asked what art I professed, saying they would speak against it; as a result it appeared clear as day that they were not searching for the truth but for vengeance. I, remembering Paulinus, Bishop of Nola, answered that I knew no art, but was a gardener. I never could have said it more truly than now, for I am exclusively a gardener, and you sin against the goddess Pomona by taking me with all this talk away from grafting trees and growing herbs.

Now, laying aside the jokes, if someone were to ask seriously what art I have, I would not reply as Pythagoras did. When asked, like me, he blushed to call himself *sophos*—that is, wise, an epithet the first Seven Sages had used—and replied that he was a philosopher,

---

* This led to P.'s writing the *Inuectiue contra medicum*.

being the first of all to coin the word—that is, not yet wise but a lover of wisdom, a name at that time most humble, but one that shortly thereafter swelled up fiercely, and today is boastful and empty. To those who profess it, not lovers of wisdom but of showing off and of frivolous squabbles, I have only this to say: that I am certainly not a practitioner of that art but a lover who does not have it, yet longs for whatever art is going to make me better. And if anyone wants to speak against it, he will be declaring war not against me but against virtue and truth.

But now I shall return to the thread of your discourse: to what you say, such as it is, to win trust for doctors, namely, that they have worked very hard. In truth, I neither deny nor admit this, nor do I know. But let it be so: if you say that everything glorious takes work, I will admit it. If you turn the argument around, I shall deny it. Work always precedes glory, but not always does glory follow work. Is not the work of a sailor or of a farmer any greater than of a general or a philosopher? Therefore, while all glory takes work, nevertheless, work is often without glory. As for the point that follows, that there can be no arguing with a doctor when one is in such a state, I agree with that too; and if I remember, I had said first off that I was not arguing with a doctor but joking with a friend.

But you mount your attack closer and tighter. Therefore, since medicine's authority does not impress me, my own confession seems to you to hold me captive; and, hemmed in by your weapons, I am taken by storm with my own. The idea is not new; many have perished with their own weapons. Thus, in the mountains of Gilboa, after King Saul vainly begged his squire to kill him with a sword, he perished by falling on his own sword. Similarly, in the valley of the terebinth, after David felled Goliath, he used Goliath's sword to cut his head off since he did not have his own. So in Troy, on that last night, Coroebus dressed up with enemy arms and urged his fellows to do the same; and thus armed they dispatched many of the Greeks to Orcus. In short, how, I ask, have you, with my weapons, won a victory over me? Evidently because I confessed what I cannot deny, even if I wanted to, that my age as well as my nature is changing daily and has changed. What do you prove from this? That once my nature changes, my way of living must also change? Who would deny this, except one who forgets his mortality and frailty? But I said that it has taken place in me, and I ask again whether this seems to you a small change: that whereas in my prime I used to drink my fill of pure water morning, noon, and night, now I sip it moderately just once in the evening—and that on the advice not of the medical art but of Nature. Whoever I am, she herself understands what is good for me, unless I am wrong. And if today she desired what she once did (I mean in those things not contrary to honor and salvation), I would humor her, recalling the words of Cato in Tully's book: "We follow Nature, the best leader, like a god, and we obey her" [*Sen*. 5]. I have obeyed Nature and would always unless the command of a greater one stopped me—I mean not Hippocrates, but God.

What more is there to say? If at that age I saw unripe or sour plums or something of the sort, roused by a fire inside of me, I would run and pluck them from the branches to eat them; now when I pass them, I scarcely glance at them, and, recalling what I used to do, I smile and silently say to myself: "O changing human quirks!" Why is it that what sometimes I used to do all day long, eat nothing but apples, pears, figs, and peaches, I now simply take one of them before or after a meal, constantly tightening the reins of moderation upon the enjoyment of taste, not because it is Galen who suggests it to me, but my consultant, my nature, which, as long as she stays sane, knows better than to crave anything harmful.

From this same source too comes what you attacked me with, like a deadly shaft: namely, that I patiently and obediently take only three of the six pieces of advice you offer most loyally, I am sure. With all due respect to such a great friend and physician, I do it not so much through your advice, or anyone's, but hers; for she does not change without cause, especially in a man freed from youthful passions. Now when the doctors agree with that inner infallible consultant, I gladly do as they say, but not otherwise. And therefore I refuse with unfettered obstinacy the other three pieces of advice, like unfair conditions of peace. And I will rather do eternal battle with the doctors than take that yoke on my neck.

How could I throw away good, ripe fruit baked by the sun? Perhaps because Hippocrates did not like them? I have known some like that, some of them utterly dissolute, others sober and temperate, but they could not bear either the smell or the sight of fruit. I saw a cardinal of the Roman Church, a worthy and aged man, who so detested quinces that whenever he saw even one his face would break out into an anguished sweat and turn ghastly pale, and it was the responsibility of his attendants not to let him be upset by such an encounter. I saw, in the palace of the Roman Pontiff, Clement VI, another whom his fellow youths would chase throughout the huge building with a single rose, filling the halls with laughter and noise. The smell of a rose was so hateful to him it was rumored that when several times there was no other escape from it, he jumped through the window or whatever, at grave risk to his life. And yet it would not be easy for me to say whether the smell of anything else is more pleasant than the smell of that fruit or flower.

What else can we suppose but that if those two had been authorities on medicine, they would have condemned quinces and roses in their books, and they would have demanded that everyone take their word for it. These, however, dear friend, are not judgments but weaknesses of nature and flaws, not to be able to endure what everyone else has a perfect right to enjoy. On the other hand, there are some who recommend and extol everything they enjoy; for them, taste takes the place of reason. I knew one like that and, if I am not wrong, so did you—Giovanni da Parma, who was my fellow canon, my brother in that church; aside from his other qualities, he had built up a great medical reputation, not only in his own country but in the Roman Curia among all those satraps and that motley rabble of doctors, so that he was considered the first or among the first of them. In the universal way of doctors, he ranted against all fruit; but figs alone he not only allowed but praised. And you know the reason: the other fruits disagreed with him, but he was a glutton for figs. If we go by that, we will have to live by someone else's taste. But I can perhaps hope for some agreement, both with you on this, and with Hippocrates on another matter, since you do not condemn fruit, and he praises the drinking of water—so you write. Nevertheless, in both you require moderation, which I so require and praise in these as in everything that without it I do not grant that anything, however good, is well done. So, what are we arguing about? I wonder why you believed that this had to be repeated since I had addressed them sufficiently, I think, in my previous letter: namely, that this bad reputation belongs not to fruit or water, but to excess. We are still going back and forth over our original ground, and—what an old proverb forbids—we are redoing what is already done. See how the lance and the sword you took from my armory do not penetrate either my shield or my breast-plate? For you to win you must take up arms from somewhere else, and sharpen them on other whetstones.

But here new reasons for argument arise crosswise. Since I was prepared to go on forever without three of the things you call harmful, you ask why I will not do without the other three, as though believing one thing that somebody says entailed believing everything. But if I followed the doctors in those things I abstain from, perhaps you would not be wrong to ask, since the same argument, as you believe, holds for the rest and the consultant is the same. But since, as I have said, it is Nature that prompts me, if I am asked why I stick to something else, I reply: do not ask me this, ask her who up to now has counseled me one way for these things, another way for those. If perchance—although I doubt it—she starts giving me the same advice or command about these other things, I shall obey, recalling that memorable saying of Cicero, "What else is it to make war like the giants against the gods, if not to fight against Nature" [*Sen.* 5]?

There remains something I hardly expected to happen, namely, to argue or to jest once more about fasting: as though you were making light of what I said about being able to do anything through Him who comforts me, you say—whether as a doctor or because you believe that God can do all things—that He not only can make healthy the one who fasts and the one who goes without any food, but can make him immortal; but you add that you speak according to the rules of medicine, by which you judge it impossible that I could fast and be healthy. Therefore, dear friend, see how widely our opinions differ: without fasting I would scarcely hope for health. Indeed I believe that nothing can be done well without God's help, and this is why I said what I would say in any matter, however small. But in this one I do not call for any unusual miracle from God, as if He made someone live long without food or made him in some way immortal; but simply according to the laws, if not of medicine, then of nature and my own practice, I can fast and have always fasted from boyhood, and shall fast as long as I can, and I shall be able to as long as I live. But I do not add as long as I am healthy. Every time I cease being healthy, I shall not only be able to fast, but be compelled to. In that state I take no food. The sickness itself feeds me—with unappetizing food, to be sure.

You deal with me about fasting and food and other things as if I were one of that crowd who, as we say in the vernacular, do not know they have eaten enough until their belly aches. You are still dwelling upon the classification of foods. I knew that this is the idea not only of doctors but of all epicures; I certainly did not know it was yours. Now, as I see and regret, it is yours. But I said what I felt about this too in my other letter. Whatever doctors may determine, I believe that frequent meals are neither wholesome to the body nor good for our character. One must not stimulate the gullet too often, nor struggle with one's appetite too often. Such a struggle is risky, tricky, and, as Cicero says, greasy; and Augustine when he was already old admitted that he was often overcome by food, while, to use his own words, "the unhappy soul gaily disguised the trafficking in pleasure with the pretext of health." It is enough to attend to this slave, the soul's beast of burden, once a day, although a large part of mankind, or rather I must sadly say almost all men, with all their might stuff and fatten this unruly, kicking ass while the soul, which it was assigned to obey, starves and is even considered an alien by men, and either it is not recognized or is hated, as though man were nothing more than a body, even though it was written: each man's mind is the man, not that figure that can be pointed to with a finger. You have Aristotle who must be followed as a teacher when he speaks of the soul, as Cicero himself says. But neither he nor you seem to be seeking anything but what the soul is, or what are its passions; and, satisfied with your definitions, you force it to go hungry, concentrating your entire effort on this frail, rotten body, a most noble subject, so you say; but what it really is, everyone recognizes in himself, unless he is mad or oblivious of himself. Would that you did even this well! I would say that nothing more should be required of a doctor. But how well it is done I have said today and many times in the past—perhaps too much for my own peace and quiet, but not more than befits a concern for the truth.

As for what you wish to conclude from the practical example that like a small fire one must not commit to an old stomach too many things to absorb and digest at once, but bit by bit (I use medical terms as the subject requires), this hardly needs any proving. But what is the point? Your argument places great stress on my age; for I openly and truthfully admit it, unlike the majority that hides or denies it. We read about them and see them among the people struggling stubbornly to minimize their age as though death could be put off by lying about it. But do you not know that some people at forty are older than others at sixty? Old age is not the same for all, just as life is not. I could flood you with examples of commoners, but I prefer famous ones. Have you not read how frail and terribly weak the adolescent son of Africanus was, whereas at almost the same time old Cato and King Massinissa in his ninetieth year had undiminished strength and a great capacity for work? You number my years, you do not ponder my condition, but whoever wishes to render a balanced judgment must consider many things. Please forgive me: this has diverted you a bit from the right path with respect to me. For there is no doubt that you want, or rather yearn, to heal me. Nor is that saying of Cicero ambiguous, that once doctors have found the cause of a disease they think they have found the cure. But "this is the rub, this is the point" [*Aen.* 6.129].

What else delays the effect of your sincere advice if not your applying hot remedies to my age and treating my years, not me, whereas all my bodily ills come from too much heat? I had often understood this, but never more clearly than in the present year when the report of my condition on the one hand and the warmth of your devoted love brought you to these mountains, and with you came that fine gentleman like you in spirit, in profession, and in name, whom I got to know first through you, and who is now my friend. How great was your astonishment when you entered my room and such heat burst from me as would scarcely be credible in a young man, so that nearly the whole room was burning hot. Though I could hardly say anything, overcome by fever and drowsiness, I could hear the exclamations of astonishment without being astonished myself, since to me nothing new had happened, and familiarity removes the miraculous from everything. In most people, to be sure, old age is cold and frail; still certain old men are warm-blooded and robust. I like to recall famous examples from antiquity and from recent times. In Rome I saw Stefano Colonna, a remarkable man at any age, who around his eightieth year happened to watch some stalwart young men engaged in equestrian games; there was a jinxed spear nearby that no one to that day had been able to bend, let alone break. Jokingly he accused the young men of slackness, and his first-born son, a well-trained man-at-arms, answered, "It is easy, father, for one at leisure to pass judgment from the window on those who are struggling, and to ridicule the present while admiring times past, as old people do." With a noble impulse Stefano dashed downstairs shouting to himself, "So you think you are men?" And mounting a horse that stood nearby, he spurred it on; and, seizing that spear in a strong grip, he broke it in many pieces, to the dismay of the spectators, especially his son.

I have never mixed with really robust types even in my robust years; now I mix with weaklings. Until now I used to mix with the healthy, and not even now, at the times when I am in tolerable health, do I feel any weakness of the stomach; I wish I could say the same of my other parts. Now I say what I can truthfully: while healthy, as God is my witness, I have never judged that any food or drink harmed me, at least that I remember; if even once I had judged the opposite, my mental cast is such that I would have abstained from them forever. But perhaps they harmed me without my feeling it; this can happen, and so can the opposite; by myself I do not know this, nor would I have anyone worth believing, since I hear daily others' complaints, "Today's lunch, yesterday's dinner did me harm; this wine, that water upset me." I suffer from nothing at all like this, unless Avicenna perhaps feels my cramps better than I do. If I were to believe it, I would, by Jove, wish I had no feeling and no stomach. Many think they are handsome when they are ugly, because they cannot see their own face, and willingly fool themselves, and wish to be fooled by others, and are fooled by the mirror. But who would not feel that he is sick unless he were numb through and through, or bloodless, especially when the sickness is serious, as those who suffer from a sick stomach declare? I have heard of a man who lost an eye and was asked teasingly how he was; he replied, "The doctor says I can see, but it seems to me I cannot." But just as when I believe no one who says I am well when I am ill, so when I am well I believe no one who maintains that I am ill.

The little flame inside of me can digest what is put into it, and something more if necessary. "But it used to do more at times." I do not question this, but I would feed it more because I was hungrier. But my appetite for almost everything has long since diminished; and I, along with Cato, am very thankful to old age which, as you see, increased my greed for conversation, but removed it for food and drink. Neither then nor today do I put into my stomach more than it can bear; I always put in somewhat less. And while there is no certain rule for this, since the same food is too much for one but too little for another, as you know Aristotle says in the *Ethics*—using the example of the athlete, Milo of Croton, whose daily food is reported to have been a whole big ox which he ate all by himself in the evening without feeling any discomfort—nevertheless my meal, though perhaps too much for many frailer people, when measured against the average custom of men, tended naturally to be light; and I tried always to lessen rather than increase it. And, if I dare glory in the Lord to a friend, since reaching manhood, I have seldom arisen from my frugal, modest table or from a banquet with friends or princes without being hungry, nor did I ever indulge more freely on the pretext of having fasted that day, although perhaps I would eat somewhat more heartily the next day since it was spiced by hunger from the previous day. Therefore, while the religious, even when they fast, are wont to eat a double snack, as they themselves call it, God forbid that I should do so; I have never had more than a single light meal. And who would ever believe that I would have so much to say about food and the stomach? But my words are addressed to a doctor, although he deserves to say and hear something more important; however, I say these things confidently because I know I speak the truth. Nor am I saying what I would much rather not have said for the sake of empty boasting, but in the name of truth, and I choose to appear boastful rather than to allow you any suspicion that I was up to something dishonest under the guise of honesty—making it gluttony not fasting. For although it may be less harmful to go beyond the limit, still either way is bad.

But you insist, against fasting and other parts of my idea, that I ought to agree with the doctors, at least in what Nature herself urges, and that the human body, consisting of contrary elements, and being variable and sensitive, is undergoing incessant changes. Who has ever doubted this? I do not need anyone to persuade me, but in this I believe not the doctors but nature, or rather I do not believe, I know it. You remember how much I said about this when I wrote you before, and you realize how much more could be said if something that is by itself, alas, too obvious to everyone, needed proof. In thinking about this and as if holding the document in my handwriting, and already exulting as the winner, you hurl a syllogism against me, clearly a mature, scientific one, not a childish exercise, such as* those bawlers use who fill all our streets and squares and do not know how to speak without arguing; they cannot argue because they do not know how, nor—which would have been best— have they learned to keep still, and so, what is worst, they cry out, they get angry, and they go crazy. You say, "As nature changes either with the years or from other causes, one's way of life must change." I do not deny this. "Now your nature has been changed both by your age and by sickness." Even if I wanted to deny this, I cannot deny what I have admitted. But you act politely and gravely not by bringing in that ill-tempered "ergo" from Paris and Oxford, which has undone a thousand minds; instead what do you say? "From these premises, since, as I know, you are no stranger to the form of syllogistic argumentation, what is necessarily inferred you see as clearly as the noon-day light." I see plainly; I clearly see. But don't you see that you needlessly want to extort what is conceded voluntarily? This is Caesar's way, of whom it is said:

I'm ashamed to go where I am unopposed. [Luc. 2.446]

If you reread my first letter, and if you read this one, you will certainly discover that I have changed my way of life, but primarily that part of it which Nature suggests should be changed. Why then do I not do the same in the rest of it? I have already said why; and hav-

* We emend *qualibet* to *quali*.

ing been so often bombarded by the same snippy questions, I repeat one thing. Make it so that she suggests it, and I shall absolutely do it. And let this reply also serve for your other argument, which comes down to the same thing; you wish to prove that if a change is made in one part, it must be made in all. You say this as if all were equal instead of there being a huge difference in things all around— one more harmful or more beneficial than the other.

Now then, would you too like to hear a rough-and-ready syllogism? In accord with natural change, as I had admitted from the beginning, one's life also ought to be changed. But my nature has changed, and to that degree my life has changed. You do not expect me to infer that one must therefore obey the commands whether of nature, as I say, or of medicine, as you assert. Besides, my nature has changed in degree rather than kind; I used to be very hot, now I am not very hot, but I am still warm. Water is a cold element, and fruits are icy. The voice of the doctor has it, so I hear, that opposites are cured with opposites; wherefore as one sometimes has been lavish in the use of these things, one ought to be more sparing now. But I have done both these things—you know what follows.

I noted that in your letter I seem to you very stubborn in defense of water and fruit, whereas a large part of doctors seem more stubborn in accusing them, and without any reason or basis at all, which upsets me even more. I want no other witness but you. For after discussing the matter at length, what do you find in these that is bad, what that is not very good except excess? How are water or fruit at fault here? Why do doctors hate them so? Why do these things deserve any more blame than pheasants? But pheasants are the doctors' friends, and they do not want to call them names. This is all right, provided the innocent are not called names. For we owe our friends love just as we owe everyone justice. I often wonder and ask people what has caused such friendship between you people and those birds. But perhaps, transported from the shores of the river Phasis in Colchis, whence they got their name, to Greece on Jason's ship, as it is reported, and being more precious because of the distance (since difficulty raises the price of things), they began to be valued and praised from one nation to the next; and because of their fame they reached distant lands and the doctors of the following centuries. But no partiality changes the truth, although it often fights against it. However dear and cherished your pheasants are, however good in themselves, once you add excess, they will be bad; or rather not they but the excess is bad—and so with fruit, so with water, so with other things.

But since you have made more of a fuss about water, what else can I write except what I have written? For we say almost the same thing even though we appear to say the opposite. I know that drinking water, when it exceeds the mean, is harmful to the body. But what of drinking wine, you do not deny that it is still more harmful? And justly so; for while water can be a drag on the body, wine often does harm to the body and the soul, although, surprisingly, among your praises of wine (in which I wish you were not so zealous), you said that it increases the heat, which I say I do not need, but to no avail. I think I have abundantly shown how many people in the better centuries lived well on pure water without wine, and would today, since nature discovered water and gluttony wine; but you, my expert disputant, skip this topic as if inadvertently, as if ignorant of what is the majesty, so to speak, of water when compared to the few good points of wine, its many evils and terrible effects. But as I said, I shall go easy on this also, and not unwillingly—go easy, I say, not give up, except when I stop living and drinking these earthly drinks, which at times sharpen thirst and at times soothe it, but never get rid of it, and, heaven willing, I shall go not to the fabulous nectar of the gods but to that spring of water gushing to eternal life; he who drinks it shall thirst no more.

Meanwhile, I shall drink water moderately from these springs, and take wine moderately, not because it is wholesome, but because I have to in the midst of drunkards for whom their wine, not their blood, is the ebb and flow of life; otherwise, they will shun me as a wild man, a churl. But take it from me: if our King and our God, Jesus Christ, whose whole life is a shining model of the good, and who condescended to take unto Himself all our infirmities except sin, had not made use of these things, I would never, in my present resolve—and I call His godhead to witness—drink wine or eat meat, that dangerous drink and that heavy food that I would give up because of my devotion not to Pythagoras, but to Christ. Nor would I listen to doctors who praise both those things; their obstinate stubbornness surprises me. Why so? If the pursuit of the mean, but at the least a sense of shame, does not dissuade educated men from these unworthy praises, and if the gods are willing, they ought to listen to the Arabs too on this matter. Now I do indeed drink and eat like the others; however, I do not praise it, and am compelled by custom to do what I do not approve.

Before closing, I ask a special favor of you: that you keep your Arab authorities in banishment from any advice to me; I hate the entire race. I know that the Greeks were once the most ingenious and eloquent men; they produced many philosophers, the greatest poets and outstanding orators and mathematicians. That part of the world gave birth to the chief physicians; but you know what kind of physicians the Arabs are, I know what kind of poets they are. There is nothing more charming, softer, more lax, in a word, more base. And although the minds of different races are suitable for different things, yet, as you like to say, intelligence shines forth generally. But why say more? I shall scarcely be persuaded that anything good can come from Arabia; but you learned men, through some strange mental weakness, so celebrate them with great and, unless I am mistaken, undeserved trumpeting, that I remember hearing that man I recently mentioned, Giovanni da Parma, tell an audience of doctors, who upheld his words, that if there were any Latins on a par with Hippocrates, he could speak, to be sure, but unless he were Greek or Arab, he would not dare write, and if he did, he would be scorned. These words not only scorched my heart like a nettle, but stuck there like an awl; and how much more deeply it would have struck if I had happened to be a student of medicine! Surely the pain would have had enough force to make me throw away my books. As it is, I hurt for the sake of the Latins, and especially those of our people for whom, if the truth be told, the road to glory has by shameful diffidence been shut off and that saying of Laberius, "Praise is open to all" [*Sat.* 2.7.9], has been eliminated.

Thus, after Plato and Aristotle, Varro and Cicero dared to write on matters dealing with every area of philosophy; after Demosthenes, Cicero did the same with things pertaining to eloquence, and after Homer, Maro dared to write poetry; and each Latin writer equaled or surpassed the one he followed. After Herodotus and Thucydides, Titus Livy and Sallustius Crispus wrote histories, and left their predecessors far, far behind. After Lycurgus and Solon and the laws of the Twelve Tables, our jurisconsults—from so few seeds sparingly sprinkled in the furrows of Greek minds—gathered such a rich harvest of civil laws into the storehouses of the Roman Republic that they easily showed themselves the victors in that field. After the mathematicians of the Greeks, our own Severinus did not fear to write. After their four theologians, our four wrote in such a way that they surpassed them by common consent. It is only after the Arabs that no one will be allowed to write. In short, we frequently overcame the Greeks in talent and style, and we frequently equaled them; or rather, if we trust Cicero, we always won whenever we competed; if such a great man has truthfully said this about us in comparison with the Greeks, it can be said with much greater confidence in comparison with other peoples, that is, except those measly Arabs as you would have it. O infamous exception, O marvelous dizziness of things, O Italian intellects benumbed or quenched! I singularly weep over your talent, hemmed in by such narrowness.

I must have flooded you, I think, with these burdensome and bitter words, foreign to my purpose, and so I hasten to conclude. I follow impulse too much; and if you knew how many and diverse are the cares that meanwhile press upon me, you would be dazed. But stop confronting me with the experience of the past and of the future, as you are wont to do, and trying to prove that water, fruit, fasting either have been or will be the causes of my illnesses. Certainly, if you prove this, I am defeated, I hold my hands up, I surrender. But so far you have neither proven this nor will you, I hope; just as I cannot prove so much as believe the opposite, that those things have not harmed but benefitted me. I am not unaware that excess, not just of these but of anything, has harmed and will harm all men. So, in sum, if, as you say, Hippocrates praises water, and you—a second Hippocrates to me, or [something greater] if there is among doctors anything greater than Hippocrates—are a friend to apples and fruit, I say what I often repeat, so that for once I may be heard: excess in all things is reprehensible. Wherever you turn, there remains between us only the argument over fasting; so persuade yourself: there can be no end to it unless you give in, which you would do without any disgrace, for it is more praiseworthy to surrender to truth than to win with a lie. And whichever side may be truer, certainly mine is at least more worthy.

But here I have returned step by step to my point of departure. Fasting is in any case a holy thing, useful and healthy for both soul and body, necessary—I will confidently say—for scholars and for those engaged in anything good, whether it be the pursuit of devoutness or a literary career. For we are not talking about athletes or miners, or of those who crush the Sicyonian olive with their feet [Virgil, G. 2.517]. But certainly it is unbecoming a sober, chaste man who honorably keeps his body pure, or the magnanimous man who launches vast projects, or the learned man contemplating sublime things, to sit at table often and long, and to share this brief, fleeting time in equal measure with sensuality, and devote what is left over from the banqueting either to business or to prayer or to philosophy. Far be it from our ways; rather let the opposite hold: what is left over from serious pursuits should be allotted to the refreshment of the body. For this body is not for lordship but for service; we are souls by birth, and just as a servant must feed upon the master's leavings and be content, so the body upon the leavings of the soul. This is the place to include one thing more. How many times do you think I have participated in conversations of transalpine rulers, especially prelates, where the talk turned to our ways? I felt that, among other things, they were astonished, and some of them even railed at the dinners of the Italians, about whom they had otherwise formed a high opinion. And it pained me all the more because I realized that their criticism was justified and in agreement with Plato's idea. For he too, in a certain letter to Archytas of Tarentum, disapproves of the Italian dinner table.

I could easily bear the censure of so great a philosopher. But with what spirit, with what pain do you think I hear that we are surpassed by the barbarians in sobriety? Nor does it escape me that once our forefathers, I mean the ancient Romans, did not have the custom of lunching, whence that poetic saying,

He goes after the same meal at close of day.
[*Aen.* 4.77]

Let the doctors argue over what is more wholesome for the body. For I have heard that, as in so many things, they are also at odds on this question; surely, for getting things done, which the Romans above all went in for, I should think it is more conducive to put off meals until evening, since the daytime is suitable for action while the night is inclement and idle, more fit for refreshment and rest. Nor am I against dinner unless it is piled on top of lunch, but the doctors pass on wondrous, wild ideas, and with the support of gluttony and the multitude, they teach one another that nothing is worse than fasting. And you marvel, saying that you do not know nor ever heard that doctors' advice is opposed to divine counsel, or contrary to divine precept. But I marvel no less that a man like you has not heard what is known to the bleary-eyed and to barbers, because what displeases is always received by sluggish ears. I do not want to show you where to search for something that you will then be sorry to have found. But if you seek, you will find it.

You doctors do disagree with divine counsel in many things, as when you think about the body, that great enemy and prison of the soul, especially when it comes to fasting. Now let whoever has tough nails go and dig out the error that has so many roots. And oh, how I wish that by talking I could convert you to fasting, you who try to turn me away from fasting, and that you were willing to unlearn medicine, at least on this point! Believe me, you would be glad to have given in; for besides the many hidden benefits to body and soul, you would surely see one with your own eyes before the year slipped away: take the mirror in hand and you would see your color much improved.

To resume and summarize, then, the three points over which we are at war, I shall try to gain the middle ground of sobriety; if I must stray into one extreme or the other, I would rather grow pale with water than flushed with wine. I would rather put up with fruit than meat, and perish exhausted with fasting than swollen with debauchery; at the least my corpse will be cleaner and nobler. But now we have battled enough, and more, over an unusual and quite alien subject. I would never have thought of doing this with anyone else who is a doctor and nothing more, now that I have come to loathe arguments and disagreements even more than I used to. Who could calmly see all his possessions plundered and himself left naked, robbed of his only garment? Who would not spring to arms, to wrath and hatred? This is what obviously happened to me before with those papal doctors I recalled above. But I fear nothing like that from you, for whom medicine is a slight addition to your wealth of knowledge, although you did long ago make it the profession of your youth, as often many profess other arts; yet, without it you would almost be greater and richer by whatever standard of mine. Therefore, I nonchalantly step in and trample, as it were, the estate of a very wealthy landowner and friend, the barren corner of a broad field; and I cut down with my scythe the pesky brambles, almost wishing that you may be freed of them, since you are so entangled in them that they impede and turn you away from tilling a richer field.

However the matter may come out, while you in the meantime renew the war, I shall come there. Often the coming together of warriors face to face has been the means of peace and conciliation. Perhaps peace will be easy while both sides draw up their ranks; for we both have wanted the same thing, however differently, you from doctors and I from God, namely that whatever remains of life I spend in good health, so that life itself be happier and longer—even though when we defer it for long, if anything here is long, we must still die. Farewell. I have written this while feverish in my Euganean villa to forget the fever for a short while.

November 17 [1370].

Sen. XIII, 1.

To the magnificent Marquis Niccolò d'Este, Lord of Ferrara,* condolences for the death of his brother [Ugo].

Alas, I am too hardy and long-lived! That is why I, born unhappy under an unlucky star, have been kept for so long in this wretched, fleeting life in order to feel nothing joyful or sweet, but endure everything sad and bitter; I live only for this: to hear daily of the deaths of friends and dear ones, and, as the Satirist says [based on Juv. 10.244–45],

> bewailing many,
> In endless grief and black garb I grow old,

exhausted from weeping thoughout my life. I had determined henceforth not to weep over the death of any man, and I considered that my duty both to my profession and to my age, but the pain, all too much, has touched me to the quick. Alas, O most distinguished man! We have lost, or rather have sent on ahead, you the most loving, excellent brother, I the kindest of lords in rank, the most obedient son in love, who through no merit of mine whatsoever but only his nobility of mind, had begun to love me for some time, as you know—and not just to love but to worship so that I enjoyed it very deeply and marveled no less whence such great affection and veneration with such inequality in age and position. Usually that age either shuns or shudders at this age of mine, but with him it was not so.

I remember, and shall never forget nor must I forget, that in this very year, while on my way to Rome, I was delayed by that terrible mishap in your home where my lot, at least merciful in this, had carried me; and you cared for me, not as if I were a petty foreigner, but as some great man of your own blood. I struggled with a grave, harsh, and—as the public believed—final illness; and that happy, blessed soul came to visit me three or four times each day with such conversation, such compassion, such an expression! What constant solace he brought me, what gifts, what easing of my pain with his meek, gentle voice, so that for joy and admiration of his goodness I scarcely felt my own discomfort! I will not speak of how he would

---

* Lord of Ferrara and brother of Ugo. This is the only letter to him.

come from abroad to call on me in the friendliest ways, or the messengers he sent with gifts and deeply touching, heart-warming letters that surpassed any gift: in sum, I say, he was a young man in his prime attending upon a half-dead crank. Alas, I could not believe, nor was it believable, that he was to die before me; nor could it have happened, were there any order to human affairs. But it did happen because there is no order here, no constancy, no stable or lasting joy, but confusion and toil and pain and groaning, from which no destiny, no wealth, no lofty rank exempts any man. I neither ignore nor diminish with words your loss and that of us all who have loved you and him. We have certainly lost for a time a great, rare, fine adornment and comfort of life, which we cannot help weeping over even for a while, and missing. Nevertheless, remedies have been found even for great afflictions; to deal with them would require not a brief letter, but a huge book.

Let this one suffice because of the shortness of time. If we grieve for ourselves, that saying of Cicero comes to mind which is worth repeating in these situations: "to be deeply distressed over one's own loss shows that one loves not the friend but himself" [*Amic.* 59]. But if the grief is for the friend's sake, it is in vain; not only because the event cannot be undone, but also because it is a happy event, at least for him. For I daresay what I believe to be true, that nothing bad has happened to your brother, or rather much that is good. Even though our eyes search for him anxiously, beyond doubt he is well; his mind was so noble, his life so kind and innocent, that nothing else can be expected to happen to him. He lives, though to men's eyes he appeared to die; or rather he is now beginning to live. As wise men like to say, this thing called life is death; he lives, I say, and with his Creator, with His angels and the blessed spirits of holy men he is enjoying a blessed eternity, snatched from the dangers of the world and the sport of fortune. If the way back were open, he would not want to come. He is happy to have changed toil for rest, fear for carefreeness, misery for happiness. And although he seemed also to be happy when he was with us, no one is truly happy here, as the most learned agree; he is happy, then, and we are wretched while we are here. "Wherefore I fear to grieve over what has become of him," as Cicero has Laelius say, "lest it bespeak envy rather than friendship" [*Amic.* 14]. And now he, in my opinion, is remembering us and all his dear ones, among whom, because he so wished, I count myself, but above all his great, fine brother whom he always loved as no other, and now loves all the more warmly, the closer he is to the eternal love.

For we are not, thank God, of that herd that thinks souls perish with bodies. The immortality of the soul and the resurrection of the body console us about our death and that of our dear ones; the first of these was a consolation for the philosophers, the other for us alone. About all this I will go on and on, if I choose to follow the thrust and ardor of my mind, but I cannot, for I have no bodily strength. For since I parted from you, and, alas, for the last time from him, not a day has passed for me without grave ills. So I have barely written this much. But I trust the wisdom and greatness of your mind that you will bear both this calamity—none more bitter could have happened to you!—and all human sufferings with a lofty, unyielding mind; and, assuaging the sadness that assails your feelings with your natural virtue, you will submit in all things to the divine will, and silently consider how divine providence, from which you have received so much that is great, has bestowed upon you this strange good which, though bitter now to the taste, is perhaps wholesome and desirable, given the evils of the world.

I have written you this with trembling hand and weeping eyes as soon as the sad news reached me this very hour; so, though ill, saddened, desolate, I am trying to console others. Therefore, you must dry your tears, hold back your sighs, and crush your grief; this befits your preeminence which, if it is real, finds nothing difficult. You, O princes and masters of the earth, have been placed on high to be examples to others; all eyes observe you, all ears hear you, all tongues speak of you, and all your acts and words are carefully weighed. You must try with all your might not to say something plebeian or vulgar, not to feel anything ignoble and lowly, but everything lordly and lofty, lest Fortune with some blows knock you down or even bend you; the greater you are, the more heavily armed she often is against you. You hold this rank among men in vain, unless you have spirits more serene and lofty than other men—a burden, I admit, but true glory and great honor are not acquired without much industry and great toil.

Here I make an end of speaking—would that it were of grieving too. I hope you will willingly do what you are asked to; and so that this will be so, I beg you as a suppliant, as do all of us who love your name. May Christ, the great Consoler, comfort you and keep you in His grace.

Arquà, August 5 [1370], in the morning.

Sen. XIII, 2.

To Philippe de Mézières, Knight and Chancellor of Cyprus,* a similar consolation and lament over the death of a friend of theirs.

The fount of tears that gushed from the depths of my grieving spirit through these eyes was both stirred and checked by your letter. You moved my heart in so many ways, however you happened to feel, that you made clear what we have been told by learned men—that eloquence is, as it were, omnipotent. You placed so vividly before my eyes the grave, irreparable harm done to me and to all of Italy that, had your learned hand not immediately applied the gentlest medicine to my harsh wound, the pain piled upon pain would have promptly extinguished my weak spirit, pierced by hidden stings. For who—not only one bound to him by great friendship and family ties and obliged to him for so many favors, but anyone at all except a misanthrope—would not cry his eyes out over the passing of our Giacomo [de' Rossi]? A friend of the virtues has been snatched from earth, one of the very few who survive to our day, the pride of our soldiery and the image of an ancient warrior, wiped out in the very bloom of youth. In truth, though I love him fondly, love does not deceive me; his death has extinguished the light of valor in a sad eclipse. For who more than he was a true soldier, who more upright, more blameless, more fair, or braver and kinder as circumstances required: his magnanimity joined to humility, and his humility joined to magnanimity amazed everyone, a rare combination indeed.

By his character he gave luster to the renown of his blood; while nature had made him noble, his valor made him truly fine, flawless, and utterly courteous, so that he would not lack any of the praises of knighthood, nor would our century, so void of valor, as Seneca says about his Demetrius, lack either a model or a reproach. He was one whom many wished to follow in the steep pathway to glory through deeds; few could, but even his enemies respected his heroic

---

* Born in Picardy, he served as chancellor of the Kingdom of Cyprus. He participated in the campaigns of Peter I, King of Cyprus, against the Saracens. He also served Peter II, after whose death he was appointed state counselor by Charles V, who entrusted him with the education of his son who was to become Charles VI. This is the only letter to him.

valor. Those who hated him could not hate it. Good men loved it,* evil men admired it; for valor has this rooted in it: it draws good men to love it and evil men to be astonished by it. That is the kind of man he was. He missed out on nothing whatsoever—except a longer life, someone may say. But I call no life short that has fulfilled the exercise of the virtues. It makes no difference how much space you take to display your jewels; a huge chest does not increase the value of your treasure, nor a small one diminish it. Time added to his life would have profited us and all those to whom he was dear or for whom he served as an example; but what would it have been for him except more danger and toil? He accomplished all those things leading to true glory; he could have done more but not greater things. In his youth there was such maturity, in his maturity such winsomeness, in his winsomeness such discipline, in his discipline such mildness! Such finally was his virtue in spirit, constancy in purpose, keenness in counsel, circumspection in the present, foresight into the future, politeness in conversation, faithfulness to his word, diligence in his dealings and actions, devotion to friends, mild, short-lived hatred toward his enemies, respect for his superiors, kindness to his subjects, and a sense of justice for all mankind. There was no one nimbler than he when unarmed, no one tougher when armed, no one slower to anger, no one quicker to forgive, as one who never undertook warfare except for the sake of peace.

It is both sweet and bitter for me to speak at length with you about him, about the one we loved—or rather, love. And if some people have woven long stories about some lazy but powerful men because they admired their wealth, how great a book could be woven about this man, especially by one who knows everything about him! But on the one hand grief stops my pen, on the other you deprived me of the wherewithal, by so touching upon his praises that perhaps someone could be praised more copiously, but certainly no better or more truthfully; happy he to have such a pen and so fine a man praising him with such style, and happy your pen to have such a subject! Famed for his virtue, and helped by your eloquence, he will live a long time, indeed he will undoubtedly live forever with Him who is the Fount of Life, and here as well through his renown; in a word, the just man will live eternally in memory; thus you have earned an illustrious name for yourselves in turn, he from your testimony, and you as his herald. For who would not be

* We emend *illam* to *illum*.

honored by your pen, and what pen would not be made eloquent in praise of him? Thanks be to you not only in my name but in the name of all good men; for you have tilled with the sharp, shining ploughshare of your wit the fertile field of his praises, something neither I nor, I believe, anyone else could have done. And you have watered with the devoted outpouring of your great love the blooming meadows of his virtues.

Passing over many great things magnificently written by you and faithfully recounted, I would not want to overlook one that soothed my ears and spirit with wonderful charm as you spoke; and so I would like now to recapture the sweetness again by a welcome repetition. O your happy eyes, which saw that man's deeds not long ago in Alexandria; happy he too, although it would have been advantageous to be set free and to be with Christ, as from his youth he longed to be, yet the measure of his life was extended until he performed deeds pleasing to the Lord of Heaven who looks down upon human events, and disseminated through all the lands, lending him great fame for our age to recall and for posterity to commend, and finally for you to write about tearfully and for me to read weeping. Happy too are your ears for having heard his brave, wholesome, and glorious counsels; had they been heeded, the noble King Peter of Cyprus, who suffered an unworthy end, but whose memory is sacred, would be alive—as far as I can judge; nor would he have fallen into the impious hands of a gang of scoundrels. And now perhaps our brother Giacomo, serving under the same King Peter, having yet to fulfill his fate (as one whom pious labor nourishes and holy training invigorates, or rather both of them equally serving the eternal King), would be spreading the name of Christ throughout the east and south, extending the boundaries and power of Christendom, and by now not only Alexandria, but Memphis, Antioch, Damascus, and Babylon would belong to the Christians. For everything belongs to Christ; and our God needs none of our possessions. It was being conquered for us; and whatever it amounted to, the conquest was ours, and now the loss is ours. For nothing can be given to Christ or taken away besides the human heart, which is all He desires. To us, I say, that noble city had been given through the courage of a few, with whom you too took part. It has been taken away from us through either the cowardice or the treachery of many; it brings me no less shame now that it is lost than it brought honor when it was captured. Yet so go the affairs of mortals as a rule. Seldom has sound counsel lacked an opponent.

Thus, while each pursued his own lust, and not the common

good—which is a daily evil in councils—the better side was overcome by the larger, and the truth by mere numbers. Greedy barbarity won out, and the despicable love of plunder, the fear of interrupting pleasure briefly; virtue succumbed, naked and deserted. And so, laden with booty, which is the only thing they had come for under the pretense of religion, but weighed down and overwhelmed with disgrace, they departed, dropping and ignoring their crusades—I doubt whether anything more glorious has been contemplated within our grandfathers' memory. But enough of this.

Before I stop, there is one thing to be touched upon, to give testimony of your incomparable loyalty. You indeed, noble sir, honor with touching kindness a friend who has been taken from our midst; not only do your speech and pen testify to the affection of your spirit, but you also embrace with constant love his surviving children. You are doing a good thing, certainly worthy of you. Neither I nor anyone in his family has any doubt that you would consider yours the children of such a friend. For whomever the roots belong to must also own the branches; that man was yours until the end, nor, as I sense, was he ever yours more than he is now—I mean now that he has been poured forth from the inexhaustible fount of the highest love, and is all charity. Certainly King David was indulgent to the son of Jonathan, who he remembered had loved him even though he had suffered great persecution from Jonathan's father. And King Massinissa of Numidia, because of his recollection of Africanus, treated all the descendants of the Scipios with amazing love until the end of his very long life.

But now this is enough: I shall control the urge to go on, otherwise there will be no end to my weeping. You have taught me, when my eyes were moist with weeping, to weep more copiously, and, when drained of tears, to check them. I obeyed you in grief; why should I not obey you in solace? I shall be consoled because you bid me and because I must. For longer mourning is foolish, both harmful to the one who mourns, and useless for the one who is being mourned. I shall not let my manifold misery, due to his death, disturb that happy and joyful soul any more with my groans, since it is crowned in the heavenly vault with the laurel of its virtues and triumphs over vices and invisible enemies. You live on, and remember both the departed one and [me] his survivor. Farewell.

Padua, November 4 [1369].

Sen. XIII, 3.

To Giovanni [Fei] d'Arezzo,* on the writer's birthplace.

I read with pleasure the letter of a man I did not know except by name; there was also another Giovanni d'Arezzo [Aghinolfi, Chancellor of the Gonzaga] with whom I enjoyed a long and faithful friendship until the end of his life. Therefore, at the name of Giovanni d'Arezzo, which often used to sound sweetly in my ears long ago, I perked up my head and my mind, as though awakened from a lengthy sleep, and the grateful memory of that dear man was renewed in me. What has delighted me in this new Giovanni, I admit, is the noble character and the maturity of style in a young man, like an old graybeard; but especially this affection and this love for a man whom I doubt you have ever seen and certainly have not met. It could never have been so great unless some notion of my merit had deceived you—an enormous error—but honest and praiseworthy, especially at your age. Sometimes the sound and splendor of a false name has stirred certain men to leave behind those they were following, and has led them to true glory.

You wish, and not only wish, but beg that I honor you with my friendship—a sterile thing—and a letter, if only one, which you promise to save like a treasure or a sacred relic, for the lasting glory not only of yourself, as you say, but of your posterity as well. I am not, dear friend, the one to turn to for this; as you know, it befalls only a few to bestow fame on those to whom they write; I am not among them. For how could I give to others what I have not yet achieved for myself with so much effort? Nonetheless I am not writing to glorify you, nor to scorn you. And I write in difficult straits, surrounded by a great crowd of responsibilities; for, to gratify you all the more, lack of time makes me chary. But this will not stop me from replying to what you ask so urgently, namely, whether I was born in Arezzo. I imagine you have heard this, and you ask as though seeking great honors for your native town—and certainly, being the birthplace of famous men, enhances, I admit, and dignifies the lands which in themselves were obscure. The doubt about Homer is longstanding and remains an unsettled dispute among many peoples, as each claims him for itself and pulls in glory from

---

* Staunch admirer of P. from Arezzo, which was P.'s birthplace, and avid collector of his works.

so great a native son. It is well known that, by being born, Pythagoras raised Samos to prominence, and Bias Priene, Thales Miletus, Democritus Abdera, Anaxagoras Clazomenae, Xenocrates Chalcedon, Zeno Elea, Aristotle Stagira, Theophrastus Lesbos, and, among our own, Cicero Arpinum, and Virgil the poor, cramped village of Mantua, then called Andes, Augustine Thagaste and Jerome Stridon. But I repeat, I am not of their number, nor does your fatherland need the help of any particular person to be noble, since we read that it was numbered among the three principal cities of Etruria from the very beginning of the Roman Empire.

But since you ask so earnestly, I shall reply even a little more than you ask. Well, this withered flower and tasteless fruit was not only born and bred in Arezzo, but in an interior street of that town commonly called Garden Lane, of Florentine parents driven into exile, at the very time when it was the practice in our cities to expel the better faction; Bologna took some survivors of our shipwreck into her kind bosom, Arezzo others. Let me add to this a story that I hope you will read with no reluctance. In the Jubilee year, as I was returning from Rome and passing through Arezzo, certain noble townsmen of yours, judged me worthy to be escorted by them. Before leading me beyond the city walls, they took me unawares through that street, and to my amazement and ignorance pointed out the house where I was born, certainly not large or fancy, but befitting an exile. And among other things they said something that, to use Livy's words, filled me with more wonder than credence [1.1], that at one time the owner of that house had wanted to enlarge it, but was publicly forbidden to do so, lest anything be changed from how it looked when this insignificant little man and great sinner entered this wretched, toilsome life across that threshold. So your townsmen point to it with pride, and Arezzo thus accords to an outsider more than Florence does to her own citizen. But I realize that these and other weightier things must be borne bravely, and the bitter must be weighed against the sweet, although the bitter outweighs it. And just as I do for many other things, so I do for this one: I expressly thank God, who gave me this heart and this mind.

Now you have what you sought, the efficacy of your appeal has overcome my distractions and my slowness. One thing more: if you wish my friendship, henceforth you must not shower me with praises that are undeserved and not for me. Treat me as I deserve. Do not flatter me, but needle me, tear me apart, chafe me, insult me. That is not my due at this age, but the evidence of my past life invites it; no one can help but be eloquent on this subject. You have heard my name; you must also have heard of my vices. To praise someone unworthy is a heavy and vain labor; finally, if you care for me, say what you will when speaking with others about me, but with me do as I insist, and as is worthy of you and me equally. While I am alive, do not sing me a panegyric, but a satire. Farewell.

Arquà, in the Euganean Hills, September 9 [1370].

Sen. XIII, 4.

To the same person.*

I note that you have a deep-seated longing for my trifles. I do not consider myself learned for this, but you loyal, fond of me, and eager to know me. You say you have many of my letters; I should like you to have all of them, particularly in a corrected text, but it will never be up to me, and I should like the same about other things too. Besides, you hope you have collected all my vernacular writings and my poetry, but that is hard for me to believe. You realize, however, that they more than other writings require the most exact corrections, since I suppose you have begged them from various people who did not even understand them. Furthermore, there are a number of short books which perhaps you will enjoy. I certainly shall be happy to have your talent and scholarship helped by my productions, if luck is with us; but enough for now. I left your letter behind as I was leaving my country home, nor do I remember very well whether it contained anything else needing a reply. Farewell, and please give my very best to that fine rhetorician and gentleman, our Pietro [da Muglio].

Padua, January 2 [1370–74].

* See XIII, 3.

Sen. XIII, 5.

To Donato Apenninigena [Albanzani], grammarian,* along with a certain short work addressed to him.

You now have, dear friend, the long-awaited and long-promised little book [*De ignorantia*] on a vast topic, namely, my ignorance and that of many others. Had I been free to stretch the topic with the hammer of study on the anvil of the mind, believe me, it would have swollen to the size of a camel's load or an elephant's. What wider subject ifor discussion, what greater field than a treatise on human ignorance, and especially my own? You will now read this just as you used to listen to me telling stories on winter nights before the fire, and digressing wherever my inspiration led. It is, to be sure, called a book, but it is a conversation; aside from its name, it has nothing of a book, neither the size nor the arrangment nor the style, nor finally the seriousness—as though it were hurriedly written by someone hastening on a journey. But it was my idea to call it a book so that I might win you over with a small gift but a big name; though I trust that you like everything of mine, still I thought to trick you in this way. Among friends it is common to play such tricks when we are going to send a little fruit or a bit of dessert: we set it inside a silver dish and wrap it in a white napkin. For what is sent is neither more nor better, but it is more welcome to the receiver and more becoming to the sender. So I have ennobled a small thing within a beautiful cover. And while I could call it a letter, I have called it a book, which will be no cheaper in your eyes because it is interwoven with ever so many erasures and additions, and loaded with a full margin on all sides. For if the eyes have been cheated of any beauty, still it ought to be clear that just as much charm has been added for the mind, because you in particular understand from this that you are to me a very close friend, to whom I write thus for you to view the additions and erasures as so many tokens of friendship and pledges of love. And besides, you cannot doubt that it is mine, since it is in my handwriting (very well known to you from the past) and comes to you disfigured, as if purposely, by so many scars. Recall that Suetonius Tranquillus wrote something similar about the emperor Nero, saying, "There have come into my hands notebooks and papers with some well-known verses of his, written in his own

* See V, 4.

hand so that it is easy to see that they were not copied or taken down from dictation, but laboriously traced as if by one thinking and composing; so much was erased or inserted or written above the lines" [*Nero* 52]. Thus Suetonius; now I have nothing more to write to you. Live on, remember me, and farewell.

Padua, January 13 [1371], in my sickbed at eleven o'clock at night.

Sen. XIII, 6.

To Antonio, son of the above-mentioned Donato [Albanzani], on avoiding the wrong choice of a profession.***

I have received your brief letter, son, and the treat along with it, I mean the pears whose like cannot be found anywhere on earth—I think—except in Italy, "the great mother of fruit," as Maro calls it [G. 2.173]; both were most welcome to me. But I would not like you to take on this trouble hereafter: perhaps you wish to follow your father's footsteps, who would most willingly lavish on me what he has and what he does not have. You would do well to follow him in everything. With him leading you, you will never stray from the straight path of virtue. For you have a father whom, perhaps because of your age, you still do not know, but others do know him, and I am one of them. Therefore, follow him, court him, keep your eyes on him, believe him; he will steer you to a safe harbor. Do not look down upon him because he is not a doctor or a chattering dialectician. There are no true philosophers anywhere, but many dialecticians all over. He is certainly one to heal the emotions of your youth and to prune with the scythe of true conclusions the false notions that burgeon at your age, and to plant true ideas in your tender heart. Believe me, your father is a good man, learned and sensible, and, to put it briefly, he is what Flaccus calls "a man up to standard" [*Serm.* 1.5.32–33], who loves you immensely, even beyond a father's love, though at times it may seem otherwise to you. Flattery does not become a father or benefit a son. But though I would like you to follow him in everything else, I would not in this one thing. Those gifts are not expected of you, your resources, or your age. Just study and do your best, and soar on the wings of intelligence and study, and in this do not just follow your father but rise beyond him, for he wishes to be outdone by you. You are about to undertake a great journey. As the Comic says, "There is no room for sloth or foolishnes" [*Andria* 206]; from the arts to which you have applied yourself, choose what will serve you and what you find wholesome for your soul and your character. Cast off the rest like poison.

---

* See XI, 7.
** We emend *atrium* to *artium*.

I do not speak without reason. Love for you and for your father forces me to speak. I have known professors of those arts from infancy to this day. Your age is tender and flexible, altogether impressionable; there are many thorns, many snares, many hooks that can easily grab a simple, defenseless soul and turn it away from religion under the pretext of knowledge. Many are the blind alleys, many the labyrinths in which is written: this is the road to the knowledge of all kinds of things. Those who pursue that road achieve ignorance of the Creator of all. The destination of the alluring way is horrifying, and leads from the promised light to darkness. Often the inadvertent young soul enters this path credulous and desirous of everything. There is in our souls, I cannot deny it—and especially in those endowed with a noble intelligence—an implanted charm of learning and knowing, but one that must be governed by reason. For there are many things which it is the height of knowledge not to know. Almost every art has something good, but requires the faculty of discretion. Beware, then, dear son, while there is still time before you become involved and arrive at a point from which you cannot return. From your character I have hopes that you will know beyond your age how to reject vain appearances and how to cull what is real and lasting, so that you may become not a windy arguer but a real master, and—in a word—a man such as your father and I and all who love you expect you to be.

Try to become learned and, if you can, a philosopher, which you cannot be unless you love true wisdom. You wish to be wise and learned; be devout, a lover of knowledge but even more of virtue, a friend of Aristotle but more a friend of Christ, without whose support whatever you build will undoubtedly crumble. But be an enemy of Averroes, the enemy of Christ, and read that passage from the psalm: "Their judges have been sucked in, enveloped by the rock" [141:6]; and believe what the divine Augustine says about that passage and store it as deep as you can within your breast, for unless I truly loved you and truly feared for you, I would not be saying these things. And I give you these warnings not because I am more learned but because I am older than you. Nevertheless, you will report these things as soon as you can to your father, my friend, and if he approves of my advice, it must be good. Otherwise do what he who begot you tells you. Farewell.

[1368–70].

Sen. XIII, 7.

To Francesco [da Fiano],* a Roman youth and student of rhetoric.

Your earlier letter, which has reached me later, has made me love you all the more; I was delighted with your intelligence, your style, and—something unusual for me—your boyish flatteries and such an outburst of affection, not from any merit of an unknown man but solely from an admirer's devotion. Love of an elder is an excellent sign in a young one. Finally, I was delighted with your Roman descent; nothing more glorious under the heavens either has been, or, unless I miss my guess, ever will be. Furthermore, what should in no way be buried in silence, the letter is the work of the one who inspired it, the magnanimous, incomparable Pandolfo [Malatesta]—no one on earth is dearer to me. But your other letter had aroused in me enormous fear and sorrow over the grave and critical illness of our Pietro [da Muglio], your teacher of rhetoric and my best friend. Who but an enemy of knowledge and virtue would not be moved to tears by the collapse of so great a man? I am so convinced that there is no mortal who loves him more than I and who is more deeply touched by his trouble. With a heart dismayed and saddened, and with tearful eyes, I read your letter; and, at once, as you and my fear urged, raising my thoughts, my face, my voice, and both hands to heaven, I prayed to the Author of all good not to take that man who is still serving the world, and not to deprive me of this comfort of my life, and not to decree by the eternal law of destiny that I outlive him, but that he outlive me.

I sadly remember that I have often prayed thus for other friends; but, alas, that my prayers were often to no avail. Yet in this case, though I be an unworthy suppliant, because the prayers are in themselves worthy, I hope to be heard, especially because many days have passed and I hear nothing new. The passing of such a man could not have escaped public notice; nor could that elude my ears, intent as they are on nothing else. Therefore, as I sense, my Pietro is alive; and I pray to Christ that he may long live happily here, and at last happily in heaven forever. But cheer him with my words, and kindly encourage him to prick up his weary hopes and to learn to bear this human lot; and lastly bid him to be well and remember me. Farewell.

[Arquà, October 16, 1370 or 1371].

---

* Unknown personally to P. but so highly regarded by Pandolfo Malatesta that he once urged P. to take him into his household. This is the only letter to him.

Sen. XIII, 8.

To Matteo Longo,* Archdeacon of Liège,** on their respective condition.

It happened to be a solemn feast day, which the sudden arrival of your letter made even more solemn and joyful; I mean the day which once brought the kings from the East to worship at the Savior's feet has now brought to me from the far west the nicest letter of such a friend with its lovely greetings. As Christ, who sees all things, is my witness, hardly anything could have been more joyful for me to hear. For many years now, I had heard nothing definite about you, though your face always remained fixed in my heart, and was never allowed nor will be allowed to be torn away either by distance or time or fortune. But I was doubtful and, as is common for the human mind, fearful, especially after I left Milan and a certain trusty friend of mine from Bergamo [probably Enrico Capra] passed away, who, aware of my devotion, often kept me informed of your life and health, at times orally and at times by letter. Although nature has brought us forth mortal so that we should neither expect immortality nor fear death, nevertheless, reflecting on the fact that—aside from you and the most reverend Philippe [de Cabassoles], Bishop of Cavaillon while we were together in what is called the Roman Curia, and now Cardinal Bishop of Sabina—no one I have loved since youth still survives, I could not, I confess, help but fear, worrying about both of you, but all the more about you because I had less news. And, reckoning up my losses, and sighing on and on, I would say silently to myself: "Oh, what can that dear Father and friend of yours be doing now? Oh, if only he is alive and feels the fair breeze about him! Oh, if only things are going well with him! Oh, how I wish that he would live and be well and not leave me alone in this vale of tears!" Thank God, instead of what I formerly feared, I can rejoice and exult over the one I feared for, hearing that he is not only alive but safe and sound. You have done the very best, as you always do, when by your brief letter you freed me from long anxiety.

---

* Friend of P. since his university days in Bologna. He was of an ancient and noble family, and served as archdeacon of Liège. He often visited P. at Vaucluse. This is the only letter of the collection to him.

** We emend *Lacodiensem* to *Leodiensem*.

Since in part of your letter you ask that I write you about my own state, if one can call a "state" what is steadily slipping, here it is in brief: through Christ's grace, my mind is tranquil and at rest, and, unless I am mistaken, I have long since been freed of my youthful passions. As one who, along with you, is amazed at the human race—which we know all too well—I despise everybody; but I "boast in the Lord" [2 Cor. 10:17], wherefore I hope that I am allowed to. I was sound of body for a long time, but I have been ill for these two years, and often taken for dead; yet, I am still alive, and, however little I may be, I am as usual all yours. In almost everything else I am the same as I was when you last saw me, which, if I figure it correctly, was twenty-four years ago, almost a lifetime, not to say a long enough time to be apart. I could indeed have climbed higher, but I did not wish to; all heights are suspect to me. Thus I remained in my humility, believing it more advantageous and agreeable; in short, I am hardly richer than I was in anything except in years and some books, but I would rather be rich in knowledge and virtue. In nothing am I less well off, except good health and friends, of whom grim death snatched away so very many in a few years, wreaking havoc upon my patience. For a time I lived on and off in Venice. I am now residing at my church in Padua. Without my knowing it, God made me leave there just in time, as the war, which is now raging between these cities, was imminent. There I would have been suspect, here I am welcome; but I spend a large part of my time in the country, and even now, as ever, I am desirous of solitude and quiet; I read, I write, I think; this is my life, this my joy, which has been with me since youth. It amazes me that I have learned so little in so long a time from such constant study. As for the rest, I envy no man, I hate no one; and, whereas I wrote quite a long time ago, "I despise no one except myself," now I despise many, myself first. Thus my early age was scornful of everyone except itself because of my youthful conceit and illusion; but my middle age was scornful of itself alone with manly seriousness; this most advanced age, with the freedom of an old man, is scornful of itself more than all others, and of almost everyone except those whom an outstanding virtue redeems from scorn—a rare breed.

Besides, I fear no one greatly unless I greatly love him; I desire nothing greatly except a good end. I shun a throng of servants as if they were my enemies; I would shun them all if I were allowed to. But my age and weakness do not allow me. I am unable to shun visitors in any retreat or hideout, being, as they are, the respectful bores and strains of my life. I have built for myself in the Euganean

Hills a small house, but handsome and decent. There I am spending in peace the remainder of the life that is granted me, and with clinging memory and the mind's arms I embrace my deceased and absent friends ever more tightly. I especially remember you and long to see you if some circumstance would let me. To hide nothing about me from you, often in these years I have been summoned by the Roman Pontiff, by the Emperor, even by the King of France and other princes, with great urgency and confidence; indeed I know not why or for what merit, but—as I rather think—by some obscure destiny. But so far I have turned a deaf ear to all of them; for against the advice of many, I judge this to be better for my freedom. But I am keeping you too long; excuse me, I beg you, and farewell.

Padua, on the eve of Epiphany [1371-72].

Sen. XIII, 9.

To Pandolfo Malatesta,* a friendly letter.

Not many days ago, honored sir, I received your letter full of that old-fashioned kindness which the world knows so well; for various reasons and to reply more promptly I left my country home, where I like to live much more than in town, and returned to Padua. There, being certain that it would please you because of your concern, I planned to write you about my health, that from a long illness I was nearly restored to good health; but so that you should hear the sad truth, I believe, rather than a cheerful falsehood, heaven caused my usual fever to recur unexpectedly and most violently on the eighth of May. The doctors assembled, some urged on by our lord's bidding and others drawn by the friendship they bore me. After many arguments back and forth (you know their ways), they determined that I would die in the middle of the night; and it already was the first watch of that night. You see how little time was left to my life, if the chatter of these Hippocrateses were true, but daily they confirm more and more the opinion I have always had of them; they said that the only way for me to live a little longer was to interrupt my sleep by tying me up with some kind of cords; that way perhaps I would last until dawn—a few hours at the price of discomfort. Since, however, to deprive me of sleep in that state would undoubtedly have led to death, the instructions were not carried out. I begged my friends and ordered my servants not to give my body any treatment the doctors ordered; if anything absolutely had to be done, it should be just the opposite. And so I spent that night "in a deep, sweet sleep, most like a placid death," as Maro says [*Aen.* 6.522].

But why detain you with words? When they returned in the morning, perhaps to attend the funeral, they found me, who was to have died in the middle of the night, writing, and astonished, they could say nothing except that I was an amazing man. After being so often disappointed and unmasked in my case, they do not cease to assert impudently over and over again what they know nothing about, but

---

* Lord of Pesaro, skilled condottiere, and admirer of letters. Upon hearing of P.'s fame, he commissioned his portrait in order to know him more intimately (see *Sen.* I, 6). He fought for the Visconti of Milan and for the Republic of Florence, and often sought P.'s advice.

they find no other shield to cover their ignorance. If perhaps I am amazing, how much more are they, and those who believe them are not just amazing but benumbing. So here I am, Your Excellency; my destiny turns me round and round, and though I may appear healthy, still, in my opinion, I am always ill. Otherwise why should so many fevers burst out so suddenly, and constantly recur? But really, whether I had died in the middle of that night or were to die tonight, what is it to me? I was on my way there. And what harm is there in falling, if I am bound to fall soon, or what good is it to get up only to collapse immediately? Nevertheless, since such a small concern so touches your generous heart as to yearn to know how it goes with me, be informed that I am quite insecure about my physical state—not I alone but all of us mortals who live down here. I, however, am all the more insecure, the more visibly I fight with Death every day; whether she will speedily strike me down, as she has already threatened four times in the space of a year, or hold off for a little while, she will not hold off for long. I thank Christ, my God, equally for all things. He knows what is best for me, and He will do it. As the dying Socrates says in Cicero, "Whether it is better to die or to live, God knows; but I believe that no man does."* As for me, I sum it up thus. Neither you, the worthiest of men, nor any of those who hold me dear should have any other thought or wish than that of a good end for me. Surely it is high time. There is no use in living to the point of disgust; it is enough to have one's fill of it. Live happily, remember me, and farewell.

In the Euganean Hills, June 8 [1371–72].

---

* Quoted from Plato, *Apology* 42a; Socrates said this at his trial, considerably before the death sentence was carried out.

Sen. XIII, 10.

To the same person* who invites him to a healthful place during the plague.

Your brief and charming letter—nothing lovelier can be imagined!—brought me immense joy and comfort in adversity, even though it really contained nothing new. For I have long known how you feel toward me; but what was dulled and past in my mind this present note from you has renewed. Thus in reading it, I was so joyful that, forgetting my present woes, I concentrated entirely upon you; and I relaxed and breathed deeply for your presence that I yearn for, and suddenly such a great urge to write seized me that if I went along with it I would weary these fingers that are long since exhausted, and your ears that are busy with greater things. But time is lacking for what I wish, and my bad health does not allow it; I barely write out these few words.

Therefore let one point suffice: I reverently embrace your offers and express what thanks I can; and I swear by Christ, the God of Truth, that I do not expect any more from any man than from you; and if any misfortune, such as besets and tramples even the crowns of kings, should force me into indigence, there is no one whose home or coffers or farmhouse I would turn to more confidently than yours. For experience has taught me that yours is mine. I would—I admit—come eagerly where you invite me, not driven by fear of death, but drawn by the longing for you, if I were not stopped by my bodily condition. But your love for me is truly noble and most appreciated; it is unconcerned for itself but fearful for me, who fear nothing. I beg you, therefore, lay aside this fear; for I am neither in Padua nor in Venice, the cities where the plague now holds sway, but in the Euganean Hills, a very pleasant, healthful place that this messenger of yours has seen with his own eyes since I showed him around. The lord of these parts [Francesco da Carrara], your friend, often comes here, taken with love for me and the looks of the place, to spend a little time with me. I want you to know, besides, that the passing of your wife, who was very dear to me though we never met, has saddened me, not so much for herself, who has left behind these miseries and is now doubtless enjoying a happy life (such was the splendor of her Roman chastity, like

---

* See XIII, 9.

her noble birth), but for your mental state, which I felt was frantic with sighs and overflowing with tears. Who can remain unmoved by such a loss? Many things can be said here—the subject is vast, but the time is limited. This is the gist of it all: let your great virtue, so often recognized in great undertakings, overcome this great sorrow. This befits your greatness; so do it, and may Christ, the best comforter, give you solace. Farewell.

Arquà, September 1 [1371-72].

Sen. XIII, 11.

To the same person,* who invites him to a safe place during the war.

Your kindness toward me never ceases nor slows down; I feel as much gratitude as could ever be expected from a grateful man's heart. Two years ago, in order to rescue me from the jaws of a plague, raging far and wide, you called me with coaxing letters and messengers to come to a safe place. Now you invite me to peaceful surroundings, to rescue me from the threat of war. So in every crisis and in every upheaval, whether of the elements or of men, you embrace me with fond memory; you, who could be my son in age, have assumed the role of father in your love and caring; you urge me on with letters capable of tearing rocks from stubborn cliffs. You further mention escorts and horses; you omit nothing at all, even though I have enough horses and escorts and an boundless desire to come. But I lack bodily strength and vigor, and I have far too much to keep me busy here. As my spirit hastens to you, these things hold me back. Add to this the inclement weather, the impassable road, and above all the shame of leaving in this state of things. I would not like to appear fearful now, something I have never been. But if these things were to improve, it might be that with the arrival of spring I might actually visit you and at last humor your desire and mine no less, by staying a while with you. There is no need to tempt me with the loveliness of those places. I know them to be as you write and as I myself once saw some as a boy; and, besides, any place where you may be cannot seem to my mind as other than lovely and delightful.

My vernacular trifles come to you as a gesture of friendship by means of this messenger of yours; I wish they were worthy of your hands, your eyes, and your judgment. You will view them not only with patience, but—I have no doubt—gladly and eagerly, and will deem them worthy of some section of your library, perhaps the furthest one. You will find in them much that needs to be excused, but they do not despair of forgiveness as they will undergo the judgment of a friendly critic. Let the rambling madness of lovers, which is the subject right at the outset, above all excuse the variety of the work; and let my age excuse the crudeness of the style, for I was a

* See XIII, 9.

boy when I wrote what you will be reading most. If that excuse does
not suffice, let the sanction of a request coming from you, to whom
I can deny nothing, be my excuse. At this age, I confess, I observe
with reluctance the youthful trifles that I would like to be unknown
to all, including me, if it were possible. For while the talent of that
age may emerge in any style whatsoever, still the subject matter does
not become the gravity of old age. But what can I do? Now they
have all circulated among the multitude, and are being read more
willingly than what I later wrote seriously for sounder minds. How
then could I deny you, so great a man and so kind to me and pressing for them with such eagerness, what the multitude has and
mangles against my wishes? Therefore, however they may be, you
have no right to complain; for you have what you sought.

> Remember, Roman father, 'twas you bade me;
> Where I'm at fault, you have yourself to pardon,

as the great Ausonius says to Theodosius the Emperor [*Prof. Burd.*
4.21–22]. Let the poor, inelegant lettering be excused by the scarcity
of scribes; for this once famous university, strange to say, has hardly
any. Let the scribe's laziness and the outbreak of wars excuse my
tardiness; I would have sent them long ago had not Mars, who
thunders on all sides, forbidden it. If you come across any errors, let
my involvements excuse me, since they so overwhelm me that I had
others check them over. Finally, let my absence excuse the poverty
of their outer garment; for of course, had I been present when it
was bound in book form, it would have had a silk cover and at least
silver clasps.

Now many things present themselves to my pen about your grave
illness, which frightened and saddened me terribly, and many things
about the calamities of your dear ones, which call for my heartfelt
laments. But now my weary pen demurs. I do not want you to believe that I read without sighing—let alone without tears—that part of
your letter which has forever renewed for me the bittersweet memory of your august and peerless wife as well as your noble brother.
For she loved me as if I were her father, even though she had never
seen me herself, but only through your eyes, and she in turn was deserving of my pure love. He knew me most intimately, loved me,
and attended me not only in words, as is the custom nowadays, but
with many real and significant services, and, in conclusion, had become for me exactly like another Pandolfo. I therefore affirm before
Christ that scarcely any other two people could have died and dealt

my heart such a cruel blow. But what are we to do? There is no other remedy than patience. It is useless to try to persuade you of this, not only because it has often been treated by the greatest men and by little me; but because even on this point whatever is usually said or can be said must already be well known to you, a most wise man, most abreast of human circumstances. The highest consolation of all is that both must be believed to have traveled a straight path to heaven, such was their life, such the faith, devotion, and chastity of that outstanding lady, such the excellence of that famous man. Thus one cause for mourning ceases. For if something bad has happened, it has happened to us. This must be overcome by our strength of mind, lest we appear to love ourselves too much or to bear our adversities too weakly. Farewell.

Padua, January 4, [1372], with frozen fingers and war raging.

Sen. XIII, 12.

To Philippe [de Cabassoles], Bishop of Sabina, legate of the Apostolic See.*

Not many days ago I heard news of your illness from a letter of that renowned knight, who is my most loving son and so devoted to you; concerned about your health, and aware of my state of mind, he had written me that you had been gravely ill but that things were beginning to look better. I was not impressed so much by the news of your convalescence as of your illness. For while all men easily believe what they wish, I alone believe what I fear. Considering, then, the difficulty of the journey, the time of year, and the adverse factor of age, I was in constant fear until finally, in my state of anxiety and suspense, I received your letter. Then, learning about your recovery and laying aside my fear, I turned wholly to joy and pious vows and due thanksgiving, and spent the day rejoicing. The peoples of Greece were no happier when they heard the herald's voice declaring the edict of the Roman general** that they had been restored to freedom than I was at the testimony of your letter declaring that you had been freed by order of the King of Heaven. Why not? Of all those I have cherished you are almost the only one still surviving, and I pray that you will survive for a long time, and when it is time for departing, you may depart well and happily after me; for surely the condition of one who lives a long time is hard, sending ahead all his loved ones and "growing old dressed in black," as the Satirist says [based on 10.245].

I am glad to hear of your arrival in these parts, which I hope will prove glorious for you and useful and happy for Italy; such news of your integrity and virtue has preceded you and already attracted everyone's minds. I rejoice particularly on my own account since your presence in a nearby place gives rise to a hope—may it be true!—which is all I desire: to see your face at least once more before I die. For almost twenty whole years, I have been deprived of the sight of you—O my hateful lot!—for almost twenty whole years. Two years ago the then glorious Pontiff, Urban V, and yourself, vying with each other, invited me to Rome, where under his auspices and leadership Christ's Church, which had wandered too long,

* See VI, 5.
** P. Quinctius Flamininus at the Isthmian games in 196 B.C. (Livy 33.32).

had then lately returned but not for long enough; and I hastily set out. But in the midst of the journey I was overcome by a grave illness or, to speak more truly, a temporary death, and was compelled to return. Consequently, I did not see him or see you again. You were in a position to hear all that happened, from my letter to him and from the oral reports of many of his prelates. I have no doubt it grieved you; now, unless my lot to the very end begrudges it to me, I shall hold you and kiss that right hand from which have come forth so many sweet letters, pious condolences, and wholesome warnings. And although during this time, when we have not been visiting each other, I have always remained fixed in the same station, although at times I was invited to climb, you have risen not as much as you deserved, but much anyhow, even against your will, at all times an illustrious man.

You were then a humble bishop, now you are a full-fledged cardinal; but I shall still embrace you with that old familiarity as a most indulgent father of mine, and recall in memory the past times and those trips and outings we once took in the woods at your country estate at the source of the Sorgue all day long until evening, forgetful of food, and those vigils we spent, often with wondrous delight, at the same place among the books, forgetul of sleep all night long until dawn. All these things never slip from my memory, nor can they slip, though not only the Alps or a narrow strait, but even the entire ocean, or even Lethe itself were thrust in between. I would dictate to you with youthful enthusiasm something new every day, among many other things the two books of *De uita solitaria*. You took them up with such joy and eagerness that, as you indicated to me in a subsequent letter, you threw away almost all other books and had mine read to you constantly, even during meals, which was contrary to your custom. But with your great esteem you incessantly spurred me on to other works. Therefore, consider with what great joy I await this coming day—you who know my mind. But may God spare those who wished to impose upon your shoulders, tired from long and devoted labor, such a heavy, though honorific, weight, and persuaded the Pope to do so. I know their ways; as long as it goes well with them they care not how it is for others. They consider not others' toil or danger, but only their own pleasures. Among them are some to whom the presence of any good men is hateful, and they not only wish them to be elsewhere but not to be altogether, so that they may sin the more freely without opposition or authoritative witnesses. But may God turn their schemes of whatever kind to the good. And He will do it, I hope.

But nothing further about all this for now, except to recommend to you, as though he were another me, that young man I mentioned in my opening words [Donato, son of Giovanni Aghinolfi]; he has a rare and most excellent character, loves you with utmost reverence and affection, and, taken with your qualities, has chosen you for his only father, and is totally devoted to serving and honoring you. I would not do this so confidently unless I judged him most worthy of your favor and that of any good man, even though for his own sake I owe him much and for the sake of the memory of his fine father I owe him* everything.

There remains for me to reply to what I read in one portion of your letter, that at the moment of your departure you spoke to the Pontiff about me and my affairs; and I learned from the letters of those present at the meeting that you honored my name with many praises, and that he received your words with kindness and replied generously. Neither part of it surprises me. When he was still a Roman Cardinal [Pierre Roger, later Gregory XI], I received great tokens of his good will, first from messengers and later in person as he followed Urban to Rome and looked me up in Pavia, and finally with a very kind letter when he attained the supreme human office. You have done as you always do; I would thank you except that I have thanked you once and for all, and then because one does not thank those who do well what they themselves care about.

Finally, you say that your heart exulted with immense joy when you heard manly reports about me, that I kept up my courage despite my grave sickness and manifold discomforts. Let it be said not to my praise but to Christ's, O most excellent Father, so that your joy may be fuller and you may on my behalf render thanks unto Him who has given me this courage. When, during my illness—if it may be called that—my friends gathered around me daily and left weeping, upon seeing me, I never uttered a sigh nor shed a single tear, but remained so fearless and serene that often I bewildered the doctors as they probed me with their hands. And I would have been bewildered myself, except that I felt that my patience was not from me but from heaven which, though always present, was most present for me during this time, so that frequently I recalled the Apostle's saying to the Corinthians, "But God is faithful, who will not allow you to be tempted beyond your powers, but will afford along with temptation success as well, so that you may hold

* We emend *et* to *ei*.

firm" [1 Cor. 10:13]. That temptation was certainly fierce; it led me almost to a hatred of life, and if it did much harm to this poor mortal body, I hope it did my soul good. I recognize my own frailty. I recognize God's mercy, who rewarded my patience with unexpected healing. I would say more properly that He heaped one mercy upon another. For it is written, "I shall pity him that I pity, and I shall use pity with him that I shall pity" [Exod. 33:19]; to these two mercies may He add, if it please Him, a third; may He order to be credited to my account these great sufferings, with which He has disciplined me. And may He be willing to be liberal on the rest of my debt and prone to forgiveness, recalling His blood which outweighs on the balance of justice not only my sins but all men's.

Heaping on these three a fourth mercy as well, may He restore along with my health at least as much strength that I can finally make my way to see you, which I have always wished for, and hoped for too at the first report of your arrival. But in this and in all things, may God's will be done. If I cannot do this, I shall under His guidance see you in our fatherland, and may You, O Christ, not deny me this last request. May You not part me from him after death, whom I held dearest in this life. I, a humble sinner, ask only for my one friend what holy Ambrose asked for his two, Gratian and Valentinian, with the difference that by his prayer he was doing it for their good, that they should be with him, but I am doing it for my good, that I should be with you, most loving Father. Farewell.

Arquà, June 26 [1372-73].

Sen. XIII, 13.

To Francesco Bruni, Papal Secretary,* expressing some of his concerns confidentially.

Leaving money matters aside (you have composed a huge letter but I would not even deign to put my pen to such a task—this is not the place to deal with that), I come to what disturbs me and what I laughed to read in your letter. Philippe [de Cabassoles], Bishop of Sabina, a very fine man and an asset to the Church and the world, and to me an overindulgent father, came to see the Pope late on the night before he was to set out for Italy on official business. After he was given leave, he then, in order to impress my name more firmly on the Pope's mind, recommended me to him most insistently. And when the Pope received this with a look of approval and kind words, the Bishop put a lot into a few words, for the hour was late, and said, "I beg you, O Most Holy Father, to hold this man in your good graces both for my sake, since I love him more than words can say, and still more for his own sake. For believe me, he is truly the one and only phoenix on earth." After saying this over and over, he left.

However, once he had left, one of the reverend fathers who with their fingers sway the heavens, took up the talk about me, and sarcastically mocking the praiser and the one praised, he twisted the term "phoenix" in various ways. And although you, with your ingrained propriety, withheld from me both who he was and what he said, still I seem to know as though I were present. Proud by nature and by fortune, he can say openly whatever comes into his big mouth about me, whom he once was very fond of and now loathes; he too was once dear to me, but is now deservedly hateful. If you ask me why the change in both of us, I shall explain briefly. He hates me because my truthfulness is his enemy, and because my frankness is always the adversary of pride. I hate him for many reasons, but among the first, because the lie is his friend; to put it in one word, he himself along with the devil is the father of the lie. That is enough said about him, indeed too much, although I could say a great deal more if I felt like it; I fear no one except those I love, and, as you have heard, I do not love him. And how I wish he and I had the same station in life, not that I would be great as he is—Christ knows I would not like that—but that he would be small as

* See I, 6.

I am, and that we might be living somewhere under fair judges. Unless I miss my guess, soon I would not be a phoenix, as my admirer asserted, his love blunting his otherwise lynxlike eyes, but he would be a screech-owl. I have vented all this from a wrathful stomach; for they have the idea that because of their wealth, ill-gotten and bound for a bad end, they are free to do anything. But there are times when poverty, no less than riches, gives courage to speak out, and wealth imposes silence on many.

This too was in your letter: that you believe the Pope is very well disposed toward me, but because of the crowd of ravenous cardinals, whom he had recently raised from the lowest to the highest state, his will is not to be translated into action, and that, as a result, you do not expect anything magnificent for me. Well, let him quench their thirst if he can, which neither the Tagus nor the Hermus nor the Pactolus nor, finally, the entire ocean, if it were made of gold, will satisfy; but let him not worry about me. For I thirst for nothing, hunger for nothing, except that, for what little remains of my life, if it be granted, I may live well and die well; that does not require great wealth anyhow. Of course, once this twelve fold quagmire has been filled or, speaking more precisely, stirred up all the more, if then God brings my name back into the Pope's memory, he will dispose of me as he sees fit. I shall not make any great distinction as to whether anything great is done for me, or modest, or nothing. My mind is equally prepared for anything: it has learned to endure both honors and snubs.

But if by chance, since this can come into question, I were asked what I desire or what I would like, I shall reply to the first that I desire nothing of the things that man can give; to the second I shall say that I do not know, as one who has not spent even one hour of his entire life on such things. Yet I shall add what Cotta says in Cicero: "In almost all things I would more readily say what it is not than what it is" [*Nat. D.* 1.160], and so I want no prelacy, indeed I have never wanted one, nor anything else, however plush, to which any worry is attached. My soul alone is worry enough for me, and I wish I were up to its care. As for the rest, let him do as he pleases, but I would sound one warning in particular: do not let any hope push you to do anything on my account that would prove embarrassing on yours. I would rather be nearly anything than an embarrassment; I would endure from either friend or foe nearly any reproach, provided it be not for treachery or for currying favor. But to whom am I saying this? Why, to one who, though he may not know my face, certainly knows my mind, my ways, and all my smallest affairs and hopes. Know this as well. If anything should by chance be bestowed upon me, I believe it can soon be bestowed on someone else. For I am already being worn away, and feel that the hour of my dissolution is at hand. Alas for poor me, who cannot say what follows. Surely, dear brother, besides the natural law of life, which is nothing more than a brief, slippery race toward death, every day I see myself almost visibly being rushed to the end, even beyond the exigencies of age, and dramatically shrunk and fading like a shadow. It surprises me, since I do not think I have so lived that this should have happened to me. But Christ bears witness that I do not grieve; rather, if it is happening to me because of my sins, I even rejoice greatly. For I recall that I have long since begged from the Lord, both with my voice and my pen, that He make me pay my debts as much as possible while in this life and with my limbs, before the time of haplessness comes. It is all right if I obtain once what I have so often sought. Farewell.

[1371-72].

Sen. XIII, 14.

To the same person,* more explicitly on the same subjects.

Strange to say, dear friend, though I have never actually seen you, I know you better than many with whom I have spent long years. The reason for this is manifest. I have fastened more deeply upon you those eyes with which we discern more. You hold your peace, and I know why. You do not write because you cannot write what you wished. Do not, I beg you, do not add insult to injury. I speak incorrectly. An injury to which another can be added is no injury. The injury to me is no trifle—being without the usual comfort of a letter from you. Do you too not know me? Indeed I say and write it often, and all the more confidently the more surely I know it is true. There is nothing whatsoever I desire or hope for except a good departure from this life. I have read and verified that the greedy appetite is infinite unless it is curbed by reason; this I seem to have long since done. If I did so in the bloom of youth, what do you think I do now? Greed in elderly people is foolish, and none the less for being ordinary; on the contrary, the more common, the more foolish. What, I ask, is madder than to want more money for the journey as the journey grows shorter? And when you have safely covered a long stretch of the road, to tremble within sight of the inn? Therefore, write something, I beg you, if not of great profit to me, at least of great delight. Write that you are safe and sound, and that you remember me. That is enough; although for greed nothing is enough, for friendship the safety and well-being of a friend is enough. Write what you decide on for yourself, whether to die in that foul exile or at last to return to your flourishing country. In short, write whatever you wish, as long as you write something, and by seeing your well-known handwriting, I will know that you are alive and well.

Perhaps you believe that because the matter before the Pontiff [Gregory XI] proceeds slowly, I am overwhelmed with shame or sorrow. May I never suffer from such paltry weakness! May you never suffer from such obtuse credulity. It takes more than that to upset me, let alone to discourage me. Yes, after I heard the rumor of his election, I said to myself, "This man is constantly saying he loves you, you could hope for something, were you one of those who

* See I, 6.

eagerly stretch their hand out when there is hope from any quarter"; this alone, nothing more, until I received his charming letter such as I would scarcely expect from my peers. And although it was full of great hopes and many promises, it still did not push me any further than to thank him in a letter, and, seeking absolutely nothing, I deferred everything to His Holiness. Was it not enough and more than enough for me that the Father of Christians himself wrote me first, as no one knows* better than you who dictated the apostolic letter, in which I recognized your personality and the penmanship of your son who is a son to me. I am preserving it like a treasure along with his predecessor's letter; and whenever I want to boast in private with my friends, I produce both letters at the same time, and I say, "See what two Vicars of Jesus Christ in a row have written me!" If you think that I wish for anything further, or else that I resent anything, you are mistaken.

I believe in the Pontiff's good will toward me. Nor do I seek anything more than from my ordinary friends. For those who seek only favors from friends are trafficking in friendship, not nurturing it. But were his will to change and cool down by inertia—as happens in almost everything—why should I be surprised or angry? I am not so untried in human nature. Is the Pontiff not a man, and does the Holy Spirit not say through David's mouth, "Every man is a liar" [Ps. 116:11], not even one is excepted? And did the first of all pontiffs, Peter, lie when he denied under oath, "I do not know the man" [Matt. 26:72]? And is our present Pontiff not free either to have once said what he did not mean, or not to want now what he wanted then? I do not, however, believe either. For I and the truth have great enemies there, who with all their might block any emolument or honor for me. If they knew what I think of them and how much better off I am with my limited means than they are with all their pomp and empty greatness, perhaps they would stop opposing me; or perhaps, goaded by the pricks of envy, they would oppose me much more ardently still, the more good and prominent men pay honor to me. I say "to me," for what they think is done for them is not done for them but for their ribbons and medals. And how many are there who, while doing them homage, despise and hate them! And why, I ask, have useless wealth, and all its worries and pleasures? Why the empty, inglorious honors, with all their heavy, silly medals, with which the fools are puffed up and haughty

* We emend *sit* to *scit*.

and pleased with themselves while they displease God and the world? What help, I say, will these things give to their unhappy soul in its very last hour, or to their body fed sumptuously for so long and soon to be cheap food for worms, hideous to see and foul-smelling? They imagine that hour will arrive for them late; for they know that it will come anyhow. To the majority of them, because of their extreme age, it is close, and because of the weakness of mortals and the brevity of life and variety of events, it is near for everyone, and cannot be far off.

Not to hide anything from you contrary to the law of friendship, this is really why I would be angry with you if I could, that through fear of these men and bewilderment you have been silent about it. It would never have occurred to me to believe it; but you look up to my enemies so much because they wear purple, men whom for this very reason I look down upon just as much. I have been the greatest despiser of the idle rich since my teens; do you think that I admire in my old age those I despised in my youth? The opposite is true, that many things I admired when young I despise now that I am old, and you will begin to despise them as soon as you rein in the untamed cupidity that seizes you. Please forgive me, it is indignation that speaks out, not myself. For I am astonished that you stick in that rotten filth, now that you are wealthy and already old; just as I was in favor of your going there, given your age and your financial straits, now that the reasons no longer apply, I am* in favor of your leaving there. As Annaeus says, "What will be the result? Why are you waiting until you no longer have anything left to hunger for? That time will never be." Read what follows, and figure that it is being said to you, not to another. He was talking to Lucilius, he is talking to you, or rather to all those who labor under the same disease of the mind. Unless my memory fails me, it is the nineteenth letter [19.6]. I have said what I had to. You will do what you wish, as long as you bear in mind that beautiful Florence awaits you while smelly Avignon disgusts you. Choose where you would rather die, and, whatever you choose, consider my zeal well meant. Love and fear force me to speak. Otherwise I am not in the habit of assuming for myself the office of critic or adviser. I have enough to criticize in myself.

But let us once and for all leave this matter behind, which I believe is disagreeable to both you and me. In sum, I have a right to

---

* We emend *sim* to *sum*.

insist on this: that when you are with the Pontiff you should not be worried about me more than I wish or than does some good. For nothing could be more unwelcome to me. Leave the matter itself to his will and to my luck; or rather, I leave everything to Divine Providence; and since I seem not yet sufficiently known to one who I thought knew me very well, I shall in good faith reveal to you all the recesses of my heart. Know, then, and take it from me, that I will not enjoy great wealth any more than honest poverty. Did a modest livelihood not satisfy a spirit that poverty would satisfy? Such a livelihood has always been with me so that* until the present I have lived comfortably enough to envy no one, while many have always envied me; were my wealth to increase, the harm that I fear from it is somewhat more than the good I hope for. Mulling this over in my mind, I am changing what I said in my previous letter to you, that if God were to recall my name to the Pontiff's memory, he should do whatever he pleased about me; and in this regard I pray He may not remind him. And thus I feel that it would be more to my advantage to become poorer than richer. Those who attack me, though they think to hurt me, are nevertheless doing me good; and, for all their hostile spirit, in effect they feel as I do. But you, as though let down by your great hope and overcome in a great battle, keep silent simply because you failed to make me rich; instead take courage and "dare to despise riches," as Maro says [Aen. 8.364], not only for yourself but for your friends too. And if anyone perchance wished to make me rich, resist and stop him with all your might. I am writing nothing to the Pontiff lest I remind him of me and of his promise. If by chance he should remember it by himself, tell him outright how I feel, which I believe you are beginning to understand, so that he may realize how much happier Anarcharsis was than Hanno, Diogenes than Alexander. But I do not wish to rely on these examples as much as on that of the most level-headed Xenocrates: when the same Alexander sent him fifty talents, he, rather than appearing to scorn the royal gift and saddening the messengers, accepted only thirty minae, which was a tiny part of the magnificent present [one percent]. I shall follow his example, and of all the things the Roman Pontiff may either wish or be able to give, I embrace and hold on to his letter, with which he greatly honored my name, and the apostolic blessing inserted into the letter. I want nothing else whatsoever.

* We emend *ita* to *ut*.

What then? Someone may say, "Are you so stubborn as to want nothing?" I do indeed want and crave everything good, whether public or private, with this specification, that I count among good things none of those that the multitude calls good, even though they appear delightful and are often helpful for human needs; but often they are destructive and deadly. If then I am asked what I crave, I crave that good that is always good and can never be changed into evil. It occurs to me now to repeat to you something I once wrote to him who raised in me a great hope of seeing the world changed, Urban V of happiest memory: I wish human affairs to go well so that those things I saw in their worst state during my life I may leave behind in the best state when I die. He indeed went off, and—I am sorry to say—what he began nobly he forsook as a result of the most prejudiced, underhanded counsel, so that he showed how difficult it is, not to undertake great things, but to persevere. He went off, I say, and soon passed away; and I know not what to suspect—not only I but the world—about those who feared that his intention was to return [to Rome], and who are determined to detain Christ's Church in exile as long as they can. Well, if he had stayed a little longer in this life (for no one stays very long here), doubtless he would have received my more recent letter, which I had already started, and he would have read my opinion of his departure expressed with the great frankness of a little man. And if he read the first one with pleasure—where I had reproached him sharply for having settled in that prison the See of Peter that had been entrusted to him—and sent me a reply full of praises, which to me was the surest sign* of a well-trained mind, this one too I believe he would have greeted even more enthusiastically. For I was arming myself with even sharper barbs of reproach, since the blame for abandoning a glorious undertaking is heavier than for not starting it. But he, as I have said, deserted his bride while the wedding chamber was being made ready, and removed himself from curses and insults by dying so soon.**

But do you think I have stopped wishing that things on earth go well? By Pollux, I have not stopped wishing, but hoping. For me he seemed the one man most capable of accomplishing what I wished, someone whom neither ignorance nor its sister, inexperience, ought

---

* We emend *iudicium* to *indicium*.

** A gingerly allusion to the troubles that beset the Pope, his cardinals, and their retinue in Italy after they left Avignon in 1367.

to have blinded, nor shameful indulgence and unmanly attachments discouraged, as I wrote to him at length. He was truly an excellent man, and most adept at every good work if he were allowed to do it. But perseverance in a noble cause is a great and rare quality. What else is it to hold a steady counsel amidst so many deceitful, crafty counsels, so many dissident voices, so many conflicting winds, than to navigate successfully against the wind? For a man to accomplish it alone is difficult, or impossible, to tell the truth; sometimes it is done with the aid of many, with the sweat of many rowers, but he whom I name had none. Everyone was straining in the opposite direction, everyone was eager to follow the wind, everyone to go on to the rocks and to shipwreck. What could he alone have done amidst so many obstacles?

But what am I saying? While I excuse the guilt of another, I am nearly stumbling myself into my own guilt. He could have done it all despite all his opponents, had he really wanted to; he wanted to, all right—I do not deny it—but more sluggishly than the weight of so great a matter demanded. So he allowed himself to be turned toward the worst side, and to please evil men he displeased Christ and Peter and all good men. And, good God, what men did he wish to please? Those indeed who did not like him and whom he did not like anyway, because of the natural hatred between virtue and vice. O happy man, had he despised and, with the authority that was especially his, squelched his impious advisers, and stuck to his noble objective! He would have been numbered forever among the most famous if, as I recently wrote dolefully and will now repeat more dolefully, if in the grip of death, which was very close to him, indeed upon him—and he must have known it because, whereas it is great folly not to contemplate death at all ages, it is the greatest madness and insanity in old age—if, as I was saying, in the grip of death he had ordered his cot carried before the altar of Peter the Apostle, whose guest and successor he was, and there yielded up his soul tranquilly and gladly, making God and men his witnesses that if ever the Holy See were to depart from there, it would be not his fault but theirs who were the perpetrators of so shameful a flight. He did not know how to do this or was unable to or, as they say, did not want to; for of course he was able and he did know how. So he took upon himself the guilt of many villains, through whose advice he undid badly what he had done well. Forgive him, O merciful Jesus Christ, this softness and weakness of mind, both this fault and all the other faults and misdeeds of his youth, and do not remember his senile ignorance because, as men now go, in my judgment he was a good man.

As I recall, I never actually saw him, even though he was often sent to Milan by his predecessor while I was living there, frequenting either the courts of the rulers or public places, but keeping within the cloister of my blessed host, Ambrose. And yet I saw him with my mind and studied him most diligently, and, as we have heard all around, his reputation for holiness is now at its height, and he is famous for miracles, something that happened to none of his recent predecessors. Yet this holy man is still being slurred by those very ones to whom I, a sinner, am hateful, as I have said, for no other reason than their hatred of the truth; so I take heart. But he, surprisingly, is hated for this reason alone: he led the Roman cardinals, sullen wanderers, back to Rome, that is, to their own home, and they feared he would do it again. He will be forever hated not by all the cardinals, I believe, but by the worst of them all, which is the same as though a blind man, having been saved from a dangerous pit by a helping hand and guided back to the door of his home, forever hated his guide. And so, since they cannot hurt him otherwise, they strike him with their serpentine tongues. But their poison sticks to their evil jaws, and they fail to harm the one they strike; I wish they had likewise done no harm with another poison, but then too they failed to do harm when they excluded the best of men from the college of the worst, something that could not have been more pleasing to him or more acceptable. For hardly any punishment is harsher than to abide with those who are unlike you in character. Now happy and secure, he despises from on high the curses of those he scorned when they were with him. No virtue has ever been so outstanding as to lack detractors. Christ himself had detractors, so did Mary; what can others hope for?

But I return to my subject. Since he has forsaken so suddenly my hope, which was then flourishing the most, and since our pontiffs or rulers have no concern for this, if then God Himself, who has the power, would restore it to me so that I may leave things on earth in a good or at least a tolerable state, how gladly do you suppose I would die? He indeed can do all things, but offended—I believe—by our sins, He would not do this one thing, and deservedly so. Certainly when I view the youth of our time, deformed both by vices of the soul and by the treatment of the body, I lose whatever hope I might have. And though this century of ours was not good at its inception, it was somehow bearable, but past the middle, it has so fallen into all kinds of disgrace and crime that it seems to me to have reached the depth of wretchedness. What do you want me to say? The end of this generation is the beginning of the next, which is given over to no honorable pursuit and buried under so many infamies and vanities that it seems destined to make our age pardonable, so far as one can guess the fruit from the blossom. I am sorry and ashamed that by living on I have fallen into this time when I see what I wish I did not see; but I prefer either to have met my end, far removed from all this in time or in place, thirty years ago, or to have finished this racecourse in China or India.

To quit this pompous talk at last (since I am a nobody), I for one am growing old with unbearable distaste for this century and no hope of any improvement in the next; and clearly I am approaching the end any day, so that I feel I know for certain that it cannot be postponed. My very age persuades me of this now, and I feel besieged and attacked beyond the usual. But why should I not wish to be freed from it, and, if heaven grants, to be with Christ, since I could wish to be anywhere except in hell, to get away from here? But enough about the public good; the private good I desired was peace of mind, which that most holy Pontiff promised me in his letter and through his messengers, not only as Pope but as a father. I have no doubt he would have kept his promise as best he could, even though keeping it is not up to a man but up to God. Therefore, I seek it from Him.

Now that you are fully informed of what to fear and what to want for your friend, never ask anything for me from any man; but instead, I beg you, pray to Christ that, since I no longer hope to see the condition of the world as I wanted it, I may see the condition of my wretched soul settled and peaceful so as to depart confidently and happily from this death to the true life. Farewell and be happy.

Among the Euganean Hills, where I now dwell unless the wars drive me away. June 28 [1371-72].

Sen. XIII, 15.

To Giovanni Dondi, Paduan physician.*

The joy and sincere pleasure that you derive from my recovery, most excellent sir, is no surprise to me, nor is it open to doubt. Still you should not rejoice too much at it; this recovery of mine is not firm but weak, shaky and unsteady, just as any mortal's, but mine more than most. While I seem perfectly well, suddenly an attack comes from somewhere or other in my nature or my luck. Wherefore I shall not consider myself recovered until I depart from all the evils of life; and may it be soon, provided I depart with Christ's approval. Yet, in these evils, this at least is good, that I give thanks to God for everything, and blessed is He who bestows this attitude upon me, and though I would rejoice more in some other condition, still this one is perhaps better. Bitter things are not always bad for us, nor sweet things always good. Writing that you are always refreshed by my conversation, and therefore can hardly bear my absence, does not surprise me. This is love's own eternal power. But when you add that you are also perfected by it, I confess that I cannot but be surprised. Since you said it, you will have to determine how an imperfect person may perfect anyone. But this too is no ignoble error of lovers: to imagine that someone they love is as they desire them. Be that as it may, I enjoy and exult in this opinion of yours, and I repeat what in writing *De uita solitaria* I remember saying to Philippe [de Cabassoles], who was then Bishop of Cavaillon. If indeed you are mistaken in this, I rejoice, nor would I want ever to see you able to surmount this error, since it is glorious for me, joyful for you, harmful to no one. But enough of this. There is no need for me even to say that I, in turn, am happy for your good health, and all the more so since we who live in the country hear graver news every day from the city. For rest is more welcome in the midst of labors, safety in the midst of dangers, and prosperity in the midst of adversity. Farewell.

Arquà, August 28 [1371–72].

* See XII, 1.

Sen. XIII, 16.

To the same person.*

Your safety is my joy; but your discontent, the sickness and deaths in your family are wounds to my mind. But you need no reminders: a man must bear everything human with patience. We were born for this. What you write about the imperfection of mortals I quite approve. Nothing is truer. But when you add that you draw from me not that ultimate perfection, which is given to few men or to no one, but still no meager perfection, and that therefore you are eager for my presence, I do rejoice, by Jove, that it is so; if not, I repeat what I have said previously: I am happy to seem so to you. I would write more, but I shall soon be there myself. Farewell, and remember me.

Arquà, October 30 [1372].

* See XII, 1.

Sen. XIII, 17.

To Gasparo [Squaro dei Broaspini] di Verona,* about himself.

Your concern for me, your anxiety and fear, which are the companions of love, are not new or unknown, but once were very well known not only to me but to everyone else; but now I find them again in your most touching letter. I would thank you except that we are one, and no one thanks himself. I returned to the city the day before yesterday, and today or tomorrow at the latest I expect my little retinue, left behind in the country. The books I had there I have taken with me. Christ will watch over the house and the rest, since He has cared for me and watched over me from childhood, or rather from my mother's womb, though I am unworthy and undeserving. If nonetheless it is destined to be burned, God's will be done; besides, the grave, my final home, is enough for me. What love dictates and what you write about inscribing my name on the very threshold of the house shows devotion rather than adjustment to the circumstances and the times. Mars does not respect the names of scholars. My name, dear friend, is not as dear or respected by others as it is by you. Nor do I rate myself so high as to hope that my name will profit me much, not even in peace, let alone in war. Therefore, as I said before, I commit everything to God who, with his peaceful dew, is able either to assuage or to quench the flames of the enemy's hatred. One matter I would not like to overlook, though I am in a great hurry: with such anxious solicitude you have brought about what I thought was impossible, namely, that I now love my Gasparo even more than I always did. Farewell, and pray to God for me.

Padua, November 17 [1372].

---

* A close friend of P. during his last years. Originally introduced to P. by Salutati, P. often employed him to transcribe the final books of the *Familiares* and to deliver letters to friends.

Sen. XIII, 18.

To the same person,* on the war situation.

I have read your short letter, which was not different from its sisters in being full of worry, love, and fear; and I am as grateful as I ought to be. But I would not want you to be upset over such things and to interrupt your noble occupations. My servants, for whom I feared far more than for myself, have escaped the thunders of Mars, and, thank God, are here with me. I intended to write nothing more to you now; but in order to fill the rest of the little sheet, something new, in part comical, comes to mind to put here, namely, a certain fool's words that are not at all foolish.

Once upon a time, when great conflicts broke out between the Florentines and the Pisans—which we have seen too often, almost every year, through the fault of both sides—the Florentine army was already marching out of the gates when a certain fool who used to go naked through the city, struck by the looks of the maneuver, asked what it was all about. He was told by some bystander: "You idiot, don't you know that war has been declared against the Pisans?" To this the fool replied, "Will there not be a peace after this war?" The bystander said, "How can you think of peace, you madman? The war is just now beginning." "Nevertheless," said the fool, "I am asking whether there will be peace sometime after this war." And the other replied, "No war is everlasting; there will be a peace at some time anyhow, but now there is war." The fool said, "But then would it not be better to make peace now before the war starts or goes further?" What can I say, except that, if one might say so, that fool with this remark would seem to me to have been the wise one? Would that these warriors of ours would now ponder this more seriously! Perhaps it would mean that the war would not have begun or would be over before we were crushed by harm to both sides and by disastrous battles, after which there will be peace anyhow. It will be a good thing, even if late, though it would be wonderful if it were sooner; but their ears are closed to sane advice, and, as he said, they are going ahead with the war, or rather they are going to ruin, going mad. Truly the causes of all evils are men's sins. Enough for now; we shall see what happens, and we shall await the will of the Lord of Heaven. Farewell.

Padua, November 22 [1372].

* See XIII, 17.

Sen. XIV, 1.

To the magnificent Francesco da Carrara, Lord of Padua,* on the qualities of one who rules a state.

For a long time, O distinguished gentleman, I have been thinking of writing you something. Meanwhile you, in your usual way, gently reprove me, and I too see that your name does not deserve to be passed over among so many names of men high and low, and that I owe so much to your good deeds and your father's that this name could not slip from my memory without enormous ingratitude, and certainly never has to this day. I therefore mean to write, but look for a starting point, and find none. For there is not just one approach to the subject, and the many approaches make my mind hesitate like a wayfarer at a crossroads. On the one hand, your too frequent liberality toward me calls my pen to give thanks, and of course it is a very common practice to give thanks for the favors received from friends and especially from princes; I myself have adhered to it with you for quite a while until, weighed down by your unending kindness, more bountiful every day, and kept by an inborn sense of shame from sending back words in return for real things, I decided to encompass with my mind the greatness of your gifts, which I cannot grasp with language, and to measure them with grateful silence rather than empty words.

Debarred from this subject, I turn to the vast and easy task of singing your praises. For this too is the practice of some, to praise princes, which I myself have sometimes done, deferring not to the favor of the one praised as much as to the truth, and arousing virtue with the spur of praises, for nothing is more powerful to stimulate a noble spirit. In the first place, the eulogist's flattery in this offends me, and even more his fickleness. For there are those who praise unworthy men, and others who with amazing flightiness soon attack those whom they have praised—nothing is more unbecoming than this, nothing more base. Indeed, in this I rate Cicero the worst, so much that, while admiring and loving him above all pagan writers,

---

* Great admirer of P., as had been his father. P.'s last diplomatic mission was in his behalf in late 1373 when, despite his many ills, he accompanied Francesco's son to Venice where the younger Carrara [Francesco Novello] was compelled to apologize to the Venetian Senate. He displayed his love for P. not only through favors, but by attending and actively participating in P.'s funeral.

in this alone I almost hate him: he either burdens or (shall I say?) honors quite a few people, but especially Julius Caesar, with what might be called either a bundle of praises or a blazoning, and then subjects him to insults and abuse. Read his letters to his brother Quintus; there everything in them about Caesar is put respectfully and favorably. Then go through his letters to Atticus; there first you will see mixed feelings, and finally everything hateful and nasty. Read his orations addressed either to Caesar himself or to the Senate in his presence; there the praises of Caesar are so great that they seem undeserved by any mortal nor within the capacity of a mortal mind to compose. But proceed further, read his books *De officiis* and his *Philippic Orations*: you will find hatred no less than love, and reproaches no less than praises, and, to make this great shift still more unworthy, all the praise is lavished on the living man, all the vituperation on him when he is gone. This I could bear more calmly had he found fault with the live man and praised the departed one. For death usually extinguishes or softens envy and hatred; Caesar, however, has his destiny to comfort him, a partner greater than anyone else, his nephew and adopted son, Caesar Augustus, who while lesser in military prowess was surely greater in his ability to rule. And the same Cicero praised him boundlessly but was more daring in that he abused him boundlessly while alive and wrote to him directly. With reluctance I say these things about a very great man whom I cherish; but truth is greater and more cherished. I am sorry that it is so, but it is. I have no doubt that were he here he would easily respond with his all-powerful eloquence to all of this, but the truth is not altered by words. I think it will never happen that because of some mental sickness I will censure what I had praised.

But to return to the point where I left off—as I was about to initiate my discussion with you, this thought occured to me at the outset. While true virtue does not reject deserved glory, and glory likes to follow it, as a shadow follows the body, even when virtue does not want it, still this gentleman, as you could make out from many signs, would rather be criticized to his face than praised, and it would be much easier to serve him with honest complaints than with praises, even if true. What, then, shall I do? Where shall I turn? A man I feared to praise I would not fear to criticize if the matter for criticizing were as broad as that for praising. There is, I admit, this condition of mortals—that no one is completely beyond criticism. He can be called perfect and excellent whose weaknesses are few and small. Therefore, give thanks unto God for having made you as you are, so that if your critic and eulogist were of equal talent, your eulogist would be much more eloquent, just as of two farmers who are equal in skill and strength, the one to whom the luck of the draw has assigned more fertile land will appear more noteworthy; or just as of two sailors equal in very way, the one will be more prosperous whose sailing is done with more propitious winds and calmer seas. But after I had decided to criticize you and to use such matter for my epistolary conversation, I found nothing in you worthy of criticism, except that one thing about which some time ago I spoke to you at length in private. If in this you deign to listen to my humble and sincere advice, you will without doubt do something most wholesome for your body, your soul, your present fame, and your future glory; and so, to speak to you just as Crastinus spoke to Caesar on the battlefield in Thessaly: "You will thank me either alive or dead" [*Civ.* 3.91.3]. But enough of this; what need is there for words with one who knows and understands all things? You know what I mean, and that I ought not to wish and cannot wish anything but your good; and I have no doubt that you know this. But I pass over this as well, knowing that flattery is neither becoming for me nor pleasing to you.

Since this is so, I see I am now spared the job of telling a long story which, as I have said, would hardly be pleasing to you and is well known to everyone: namely, how in the very flower of youth you were deprived of your worthy and magnanimous father, under whom you were able to learn both by instruction and by example all that is most noble and magnificent; and how, at the very time when you still seemed very much in need of guidance, you rose to command everyone else and ruled over the state that had been entrusted to you while not yet full-grown—and with energy that went beyond your years, and with such maturity and ripe judgment that at first no unrest, no disturbances flared up within the state in spite of the great shift. Subsequently, from the great deficit, which the burden of debt made all the heavier, you soon gained great wealth; and later, as you grew little by little in age and experience, you showed yourself not only an outstanding prince to your own people but a model for princes of other cities, to the point where I have often heard neighboring people wishing to be subject to you and envying your subjects. Meanwhile, you have never been given to presumptuous arrogance or idle pleasure; with the utmost zeal you have concentrated on this one thing: that everyone should know that you are peaceful without laziness, glorious without being proud, so that in you modesty vies with magnanimity.

Thus, among your many great distinctions, with unbelievable kindness you made yourself available even to the humblest on almost an equal footing, yet you arranged the most advantageous marriages for your daughters, who were courted from the ends of the earth. And at the same time, while desiring peace for the commonwealth more than anyone else, you alone built many strong fortresses at suitable points along your country's borders, something that had never occurred either to the people when the state had a republican government, or to anyone of your dynasty when they held the reins of office so long. In sum, you so conducted yourself in everything that the citizens were free and secure under your leadership, and no innocent blood was shed; and you pacified all your neighbors either through fear or love or admiration for your valor. And for many years you kept your fatherland prosperous with serene tranquillity and continuous peace, until finally the adversary of the human race and enemy of peace suddenly stirred up a most grievous war from a quarter where you feared nothing of the sort [Venice]; though a great lover of peace, you undertook that war fearlessly and waged it for a long time with great determination, in spite of being deprived of the aid you had hoped for. When it seemed to you more advantageous, you diplomatically restored the former peace and with one stroke achieved double praise for your bravery and prudence. All this I say, and much else like it I omit, wherein you have vastly surpassed all the princes of your state and of many others, not so much in your own opinion as in everyone else's.

But if, therefore, to praise you more minutely is flattery, since your deeds speak for themselves, and I consider criticizing you utterly absurd and silence unbecoming, with my train of thought incomplete after I have begun to speak, what then have I in mind? I shall tell you: to elaborate something I believe is well known to you without any elaboration. But sometimes a reminder helps even one who knows; for the mind, however well informed, is led back, when someone else reminds it, to the memory of what it knows thoroughly and has often applied; and where it was going at its own pace, it is hustled along by the promptings of another's tongue. I shall describe, then, something which almost everyone knows but pretends not to: what sort of man should he be to whom the care of his country is entrusted? I am aware that one could fill books with this, but I will be satisfied with having filled a letter; for a single word on certain people has had more effect than a very long speech on others, and there is greater potency in the mind of the listener than in the eloquence of the speaker, whoever he may be. Indeed, to repeat what I often have said, there has to be an inner spark for you to kindle by blowing on it and to coax into flame. Otherwise, you will blow in vain upon dead ashes. I hope, or rather, I know, that within you there are not only faint embers but bright, blazing coals, and besides, a peerless flame of virtue and a mind fit for everything good, which never forgets anything it hears or sees.

I recognize how much a single letter, a famous one indeed, produced by a great talent, from Marcus Brutus to Marcus Tullius Cicero, inspired your spirit with virtue, so that for a long time you could scarcely speak of anything else, and I often said to myself, "Unless he were a friend of virtue, he would never have been moved so strongly by so brief an encomium, however masterly" [in Cic., *Ad Brut.* 1.4a]. Often I was pleased with myself too for having procured that letter for you, and for having rescued it when it was buried in hoary oblivion.

Before getting into the subject I have undertaken, I shall insert one passage from Cicero himself which I believe is not unknown to you, whereby you may hear with greater delight what the ruler of a state ought to be, when you have first heard how dear he is to God, and how dear the state itself is to God. Here then is a passage from the sixth book of the *Republic.* "Africanus said, 'So that you may be more eager to protect the republic, know that all those who have upheld, aided, and increased the fatherland have a special place reserved for them in heaven, where they may enjoy blessedness forever. For there is nothing done on earth more pleasing to that supreme God who rules over the entire world, than the councils and gatherings of men united by law, which are called states; the rulers and guardians of these have set out from up here and will return here'" [6.1.13]. This conversation, however, was imagined to be in the vault of heaven. Who, therefore, except the utterly heartless, who hate virtue and scorn happiness, would not seek such exertions and such rewards? For although it is a pagan who speaks, still the thought is not contrary to Christian truth and religion, even if our way of speaking is different from theirs on the creation of men and of the soul. Now I shall do what I promised, and show what the ruler of a country should be, so that, by looking at this as though looking at yourself in the mirror, whenever you see yourself in what I describe, as you will very often, you may enjoy it and daily become more faithful and more obedient to the Dispenser of all virtue and good, and with a huge effort rise through the barriers of hardship to that level where you cannot rise any further. But if at times you feel you lack anything, rub your face, as it were, and with the hand that works wipe the brow that basks in fame, and see to it that you become handsomer than you yourself were, or surely purer.

First of all, this ruler must be friendly and not frightening to good people, for it is necessary to frighten the evil ones if he is the friend of justice. "For he carries a sword not without reason since he is the minister of God," as the Apostle says [Rom. 13:4]. But nothing is more foolish, nothing more removed from the stability of a principality, than to wish to be feared by everyone, although certain princes, both ancient and modern, have wished for nothing more than to be feared, and have believed that nothing but fear and cruelty keeps them in power; we have read this explicitly about the barbaric Emperor Maximinus. Nothing is further from the truth than that opinion; it is wise to be loved, not feared, except perhaps in the way that a devoted son fears a good father; any other fear is contrary to their purpose. For they wish to rule a long time and to lead an unworried life; to be feared is contrary to both goals, to be cherished is consistent with both. Fear takes away both longevity and security, good will brings both; and to make the statement more convincing, listen to Cicero, or rather listen to the truth speaking through Cicero's mouth. He says, "Of all things, none is more conducive to securing power and retaining it than to be loved, nothing more alien than to be feared" [*Off.* 2.7.23], and not much later, "Fear is a bad guardian of longevity, contrariwise affection is trustworthy, even to eternity" [ibid.]; and so that you may know the subject was very close to his heart, he says the same thing elsewhere, "To be a respected citizen, to be worthy of the state, to be praised, cherished and loved is glorious; but to be feared and hated is invidious, detestable, feeble, foredoomed" [*Phil.* 1.4.33].

To speak now of security is pointless, since there is no one so uncouth and ignorant as not to know that it is taken away and wiped out by fear. At this point some people come up with the claim that this fear is in the subjects and not in the ruler, so that not his security but theirs is shaken. In response to these I cite the very famous words of Laberius, a Roman knight, a wise and learned man, which he aimed at Julius Caesar, "He who is feared by many must fear many" [Macrob., *Sat.* 2.7.24]; but so that this saying may have even more power, it should be reinforced by another similar saying and by the authority of Cicero himself, whom I often mention. He says, "Indeed, those who wish to be feared must themselves fear the same ones who fear them" [*Off.* 2.7.24]. He borrows the essence of this idea—lest we be ashamed to imitate—from Ennius. For Ennius says brilliantly, "Whomever they fear they hate; each seeks the end of the one he hates" [Cic., *Off.* 2.7.23]. I add that whoever longs for something strives to bring it about. What many people are pushed toward by strong passions can scarcely be postponed.

Although all this is so, there have been and still are those even today who say, "Let them hate, as long as they fear" [Suet., *Calig.* 30]. This was the saying, as told by Euripides, of that cruel tyrant, Atreus. Gaius Caligula, who was no gentler than Atreus, through daily use made the saying his own, which proved of no benefit either to the originator of it nor to his followers. Some have seen fit to believe and to say that even Julius Caesar used to repeat this—certainly surprising if true. For apart from his appetite for glory and power, which was great, not to say excessive, he did everything to be liked rather than feared, on the one hand through a certain mildness and kindness, and on the other, through admirable munificence and liberality, so that from the whole empire and from all his victories, as great authorities attest, he kept nothing for himself except the power to dispense such things to others. He was so prone to mercy that even Cicero wrote of him that he used to forget nothing except past injuries. To forgive is indeed a noble kind of revenge, to forget is most noble, so that the man who was now his friend, now his enemy, attributed this to him as the greatest boon of nature. What else is there to say? He so abounded in these virtues, not to mention others, as no one ever before, although he got no fit reward for them, inasmuch as he was cut down by those very men whom he had loaded with the highest honors and riches, and to whom he, the victor, had yielded every right of victory, all enmity, all their wrongdoing; nor did his liberality or clemency help him, wherefore it was for good reason that at his funeral those words of Pacuvius were sung, "To think I saved them to be killed by them" [Suet., *Jul.* 84]. Since this is so, one may ask whatever cause stirred up hatred against him; for that conspiracy was not exempt from hatred. I find no cause, except a certain insolence and haughtiness of spirit that raised him above the traditional rules; for he enjoyed honors too much and usurped dignities beyond his due. Rome was not yet used to putting up with imperial pomp such as it later tolerated from far inferior rulers, so that by comparison his could appear to be wonderful humility.

If then no power, no wealth protected such a man from the hatred of many, there remains to ask what skills are needed to seek love, since, just as hatred is the cause of ruin, so love is the cause of its opposite; the former casts one down, the latter gives support. What am I to say here, except that the nature of love in the public sphere is one and the same as in the private. Annaeus Seneca says, "I shall show you a love charm with no drug, no herb, no witch's spell: if you wish to be loved, love" [Ep. 9.6]. That is it, I swear. And while any number of things may be said here, this still sums it all up. What is the need for magical arts? For money or toil? Love is a free thing, it is won by love alone. Who is so hard-hearted as to shrink from returning an honorable love? For a dishonorable love is not love, but hatred hidden under an honorable name, and to be repaid not with love but with hatred. To return love to someone who loves basely is no more than to coddle one misdeed with another, and to want to be a partner in another's wrongdoing.

Therefore, leaving this aside, let us return to that other honorable love, from which a great and honorable joy ought to arise for you, since you must at all events feel so beloved by your people that it is as though you were not the lord of the citizens but the father of the fatherland. This was the title of nearly all the ancient emperors, but while for some it was quite deserved, for others it was so undeserved that nothing could be more so. Caesar Augustus was called the father of the fatherland, and Nero was called the father of the fatherland. The former was a true father, the latter was a true enemy both of his fatherland and of family love.* To you this true title will apply. There is no citizen, I mean of those to whom the peace and tranquillity of their country is welcome, who looks upon you otherwise or who thinks of you as anything other than a father. You must strive to make this deserved by your deeds and everlasting in time, and you will do it, I hope, you will do at my urging and begging what you have done all along on your own. But know that only justice and the love of your citizens can bestow this upon you; if you wish to be a true father to your citizens, you must wish for them what you wish for your own son. I am not telling you to love each one of the citizens as much as your son, but like a son. God Himself, the supreme lawgiver, did not say, "You must love your neighbor as much as yourself," but rather "like yourself" [Lev. 19:18, Matt. 22:39], that is, sincerely, without pretense, without advantage or reward, with unadorned, spontaneous love. Nevertheless, I daresay, without prejudice to any truer opinion, that you must love if not each of the citizens, yet all the citizens together and the entire republic not only as much as a son or your parents, but as much as yourself.

---

* Nero murdered his mother and his wife.

In the case of individual dear ones, we have a special feeling for each; but in the state you must love all: your citizens, then, are like your children, or rather, to put it another way, like the limbs of your own body or the parts of your own soul, for the state is but one body of which you are the head. But this love is displayed by kind words and much more by loyal deeds, and particularly, as I was saying, by deeds of justice and piety. For who would not love one who he believes is devoted, just, harmless, and loves him? But if to love are added the kind deeds that such good princes do for their subjects, then an incredible amount of good flares up; no finer, no tighter bond than that can be woven for an unending reign. So let weapons be put aside, along with hired bodyguards, bugles, trumpets; let such things be turned against the enemy; to deal with the citizens all you need is good will. As Cicero says, "You ought to be surrounded by the love and good will of your citizens, not by arms" [*Phil.* 2.4.112]. But I understand citizens to be those who love the constitution of the state, not those who seek daily changes. For these should be considered, not citizens, but rebels and public enemies. The subject itself often reminds me of Augustus: this is his most famous saying, "Whoever does not want the present constitution to be changed is both a good citizen and a good man" [Macrob., *Sat.* 2.4.18]. Consequently, whoever wants the opposite is undoubtedly an evil man unworthy of the name and fellowship of good citizens and men. But your nature has abundantly taught you these skills by which love and good will can be gained. They are not only a ladder to glory, but to heaven, wherefore that good father, in speaking to the best of sons, said, "Cherish justice and loyalty, which is important with regard to parents and relatives, but most of all to your fatherland; and that life is the road to heaven" [Cic., *Rep.* 6.16]. What lover of heaven would not love the road that leads to heaven?

There are countless examples of how badly arms have defended evil and unjust princes from oppressed citizens, but it will suffice to touch on the most powerful and the worst. What did his German bodyguards avail Gaius [Caligula], even though they rushed to his defense? In the utmost danger Nero discovered that his garrison of soldiers and his guards had fled. But no cohorts of soldiers were necessary for Augustus or for Vespasian and Titus. Read about the passing of Augustus. You will not find armed sentinels, but friendly citizens standing around him in the midst of his friends' conversation—finally amidst his beloved wife's kisses as though he were not breathing his last or gone, but somehow lulled to sleep; and the body of the deceased was interred with more than human honors, his memory hallowed. Since Vespasian would say that an emperor ought to die standing, he breathed his last in the arms of people raising him to his feet. His son Titus was honored after his decease by a hasty gathering of the Senate and by a boundless expression of gratitude; he was overtaken by an untimely but peaceful death; as it is written of him "mankind's loss was greater than his own" [Suet., *Tit.* 10]. Unless I am mistaken, this saying ought to be pondered and committed to memory by all those who spend their lives in any ruling position, namely, that their death may be tranquil and happy for them, but for their subjects fearful and hurtful; many rulers strive for the opposite. Why, in Rome, where these I have mentioned and many others passed away unarmed, peacefully, and happily, and left behind the noblest monuments and the most glorious memories of their names, in that same city, Domitian, Titus's brother, was killed, and the Senate itself, as I see it written, "mangled him with the most bitter and most insulting shouts; his statues were taken down and dashed to the ground; finally it was decreed that his inscriptions be erased, and his memory abolished" [Suet., *Dom.* 23]. And Galba's head was displayed to the enemy and affixed to a spear, and carried about by camp followers and orderlies throughout the camp, a spectacle and mockery for all. And Vitellius was butchered with the tiniest strokes on the Gemonian stairs and chopped up, and dragged on a hook from there to the Tiber. Numerous others have suffered a similar fate.

But why such a difference in those deaths? Did it result from anything other than the difference in their lives? It is thus appropriate that the most learned of princes, Marcus Aurelius Antoni[n]us, who at the height of power acquired the name and learning of a philosopher, after discussing the downfall of several rulers who had preceded him in that position, concluded by saying that the death of almost everyone was consistent with his life, and predicted that he accordingly would be among those who would die peacefully—and he was not wrong. But if that great and wise man said it, and any wise man knows it to be so, who can have any doubt at all that one must live a good and harmless life not only to enjoy the many other benefits of life, but particularly for this one reason—that we also die well; surely that very last hour is worth matching with the course of all the preceding years, although to right thinkers that moment is but a crossing to eternity. Nor indeed is it surprising that, since we enter a large city through a narrow gateway, and sail the vast seas on a tiny bark, similarly through the narrowest doorway of death we enter into the infinity of time; for as the spirit was when death took it from here, so will it be when death gives it back to all the ages.

The outstanding and by far the broadest function of justice, of which I speak, is to give each his due, to harm no one without extraordinary cause, and, even if there has been cause, to incline toward mercy, imitating the manner of the Heavenly Judge and Eternal King. Since everyone needs mercy because no one is altogether immune from sin, and mercy is owed to virtually everyone because of our weak nature, it follows that one who wishes to be truly just must also be merciful. Therefore, while mercy and justice seem to be opposites at first sight, they are inseparably joined by sound judgment; or rather, it is evident that "justice is mercy and mercy is justice," as Saint Ambrose beautifully says in his book *On the Passing of the Emperor Theodosius* [PL 16:1456], so that the two are not only joined but are one. Yet, this does not require that impunity be granted to assassins, traitors, poisoners, and others of that kind lest, while seeming merciful to a few, you be cruel to many more, but rather that mercy should not be denied those who have slipped through a thoughtless mistake, if this can be done without setting a bad precedent. Otherwise, it can happen that too much mercy and indiscriminate leniency may lead to greater cruelty.

Furthermore, another effective way to earn the love of the citizens is for the ruler not only to be just, but also generous to his people; if he cannot to each one, then at least to all together, for hardly anybody cherishes one from whom he hopes for nothing good in either the public or the private sphere. I am speaking of that love that people have for princes, for love between friends is something else, self-contained and neither asking nor expecting anything. Under this heading is the restoration of temples and public buildings, for which Augustus Caesar above all was praised, so that Titus Livy [4.20] deservedly called him "the builder or the restorer of all the temples," and, as Tranquillus says, he himself "rightfully boasted that he had taken over a city of brick and was leaving it marble" [*Aug.* 28]. To that may be added the building of city walls, which conferred a singularly glorious name upon Aurelian, who was otherwise a harsh and bloody emperor. Although he ruled no more than six years, and not six full years at that, "he so enhanced in that short time the walls of the city of Rome" which we see today that, as the historian Flavius Vopiscus, following I believe the measurements of those times, says, "the circumference of his walls cover nearly fifty miles" [*Hist. Aug.* 26.39.2]. In this matter be grateful to your predecessors' industry, which freed you from anxiety on this score; indeed

I know of no other city anywhere, either abroad or in our country, ringed with better walls than yours.

But the ancients, I believe, were no less concerned with roads than with walls; for if walls are a safe protection in war, roads are the most welcome trappings of peace. The difference is that walls stand by their own weight for a long time, while roads get torn up because of the continuous traffic of men and especially of horses, and, above all, our infernal carriages; I admit I wish with all my heart that Erichthonius had never invented them. They damage not only the roads but the foundations of houses and the hearts of those who live in them and have some good purpose in mind. Therefore, bring help now to these roads, torn up over the years, which demand your aid by their mute disfigurement. You must not make yourself intractable to them, for you are in debt not only to the country and your citizens, and should be concerned about your country's appearance and the citizens' precious comfort—which I am certain you are—but you owe yourself the same thing as well. For I do not think I have ever seen anyone, not only princes but men of any rank, save only for your own father of glorious memory, who would travel for so long and so often on horseback throughout the country. Nor am I criticizing this habit of your family, whose only enthusiasm and only care was for the commonwealth; indeed, the sight of a good prince is most pleasing to loyal citizens. Therefore, you ought to take care that what you do most eagerly you do most safely, so that by removing danger and hardship, you may enjoy an easy and noble recreation in horseback riding. Entrust this business to some good man, who is zealous for you and the state. Do not fear that you may appear to be inflicting on some well-known nobleman the outrage of a demeaning task. To a well-informed mind and to a citizen above the average nothing will appear demeaning that is commanded for the service of his country.

At this juncture an anecdote is in order. There was in Thebes a very brave and at the same time learned man, Epaminondas, whom, if we overlook his luck, which often raises up unworthy men, and attend only to his virtue, I would not scruple to call either the leading man of Greece or one of the very few. To this great man, with whom it is clear the glory of his fatherland was born and died (as is most truthfully written about him), his fellow citizens in their wrath, a frequent evil in free cities, assigned the job of paving the streets, which was considered by them the most demeaning, in order to cloud the glory of so admired a man. He did not avenge the insult either with the sword or even with words, but taking on the assigned task readily, he said, "I shall take care that the unworthiness of the duty handed to me harms me less than my worthiness benefits it, so that in my hands, instead of being base and ignoble it may become the noblest" [V. Max. 3.7.ext.5]. Indeed, by splendid management he soon made it so that a job which had been despised even by the lower classes became, after him, desirable even for the illustrious. Therefore, to whichever industrious and trustworthy man you now assign this work, I hope the same will happen: that many will vie for it afterward, and so your ancient fatherland will slowly grow young again through the love of its citizens.

One rather silly thing occurs to me now to write. It is what I spoke to you about in person lately in my library when you came to visit me that time, an honor that your esteem confers on me, who am unworthy of it. Before our eyes was the thing that afforded the subject for conversation. Your country is indeed such: venerable for the nobility of its citizens, the fertility of its site, and its antiquity, being even older by many centuries than the city of Rome itself, and graced thereafter with a university and famous for its clergy, cults, and holy places—climaxed by Prosdocimus the Pontiff, Anthony the Younger, and the virgin Justina; and something I consider not to be scorned, nor should you: it is ennobled by you, its lord and governor, and finally by Virgil's poem. This city, I say, so radiant with so many splendors, with you looking on and not interfering when you could, is being spoiled as if it were an overgrown, worthless pasture by herds of pigs which you can hear everywhere, grunting wherever you turn, and you can see them digging up the ground—a filthy sight, a disgusting sound, both of which we have been tolerating through long habit, but it is the visitors who criticize us and marvel. While it is deservedly hateful to everyone, to no one must it be more hateful than to men on horseback, for whom it is always a nuisance, often a danger too, when the horses are thrown into a daze and sometimes into a tumble by the charge of that filthy, unruly creature.

Well, when I discussed this with you, you said that there was an old public statute forbidding this on pain of anyone who so wished being allowed to seize pigs found in public places. But do you not know that everything human grows old, as men do? The Roman laws have grown pretty old; and were they not studied constantly in the schools, beyond doubt they would have decayed by now. What do you think will happen to municipal statutes? So, to enforce that old statute, it must be renewed and proclaimed by the town crier with either the same or heavier penalties set. Furthermore, some men should be dispatched to catch the pigs on the loose so that these urban herdsmen will understand, if only when their own loss teaches them, that they are not allowed to do what is forbidden to all by the public laws. Let those who own the pigs feed them in the country; let those who have no farm keep them penned in their house; but let those who have no house not spoil the citizens' houses nor the looks of the honorable fatherland, nor believe that they are allowed to turn their famous city of Padua into a pigsty because they feel like it. Perhaps someone would say that all this is trivial; I contend it is neither trivial nor to be disdained. The majesty of the noble and ancient city must be restored not only in major things but in small ones, not only in those that relate to the core of the constitution, but also its outward decorum so that the eyes may also get their share of the common happiness, and citizens may enjoy and be proud of the improved looks of the city, and strangers feel that they have not entered a farmstead but a city. This is what you owe your fatherland, this I consider worthy of you, this above all is yours to do. But enough has been said about this subject.

From all of this there now arises something else, that after you have repaired the public roads within and around the city, you ought to undertake with special care the project of draining the marshes lying all around it. There is no other way you can so improve the looks of the lovely region, and change the Euganean Hills that are besieged by these marshes and so widely known and ennobled by Minerva's branches and the richest vine of famed Bacchus, into a veritable showpiece of the best land, and even to restore to banished Ceres the rich fields that surplus water now covers. Thus on all sides the utility will be no less than the beauty, and you will gain manifold praises through a single effort.

I beg you, grasp this portion of glory too, which all your forebears either did not see or disdained or feared to undertake. God will be there with you in the labor of love. For nature is there already, since almost all the marshes are at the higher altitudes, making it very easy to drain them to a lower level, either into the nearest rivers or the neighboring sea. So the present generation will enjoy the fertile land, the beautiful countryside, the clear sky, and wholesome climate, and future generations will remember your name forever just because of this one thing. But although to those lovers of unproductive idleness the project seems impossible, as I often hear with indignation, nevertheless, as common sense itself tells me and as the inhabitants assure me, it is not only possible but simple. Only put your hand to it, O generous lord; a happy outcome will attend your loyal effort. Do not consider unworthy of you a project which Julius Caesar considered worthy of him; it is written that toward the end, along with much else, he planned to drain the Pomptine Marshes and to dig through the Isthmus, the mountain on which Corinth is located, so that the route for those sailing to the east or to the north would be shortened. I could wish that you were so great as to tackle that project. As it is, I call upon you, while you have life and health, and your age is fit for it, to have only the marshes in your country—not distant ones as the Pomptine Marshes were but close by and under your very eyes—cleaned out and drained by your order and encouragement. And to make you laugh, so that I may not be said to put nothing down toward this business but words, I, a foreigner, offer my own little savings to cover a small part of the expense. What do I owe the citizens? What do I owe the lord?* If perchance the amount of the outsider's contribution must be specified, you will know in due time. For now I shall reply what a freedman of his once said to Augustus Caesar: "What I contribute, sir, toward the cost of the new project, remains to be seen" [Macrob., *Sat.* 2.4.24].

But of course, regarding the care of the roads, which I discussed earlier, the more creditable this effort is, and at the same time easier, the prompter you ought to be. For as I hear, public funds have long since been assigned so that, as the matter requires, it could be done without burdening the citizens, and without loss to you or to the treasury. Neither do I deny nor am I unaware that one to whom the care of a state has been entrusted must use the utmost foresight to abstain from incurring useless, unneeded expenses so as not to exhaust the treasury on needless things and to be insufficient for needed ones; therefore, he must waste nothing, do nothing whatsoever unless it contributes to the beauty or welfare of the state or the realm over which he presides. In short, let him do all things as a caretaker, not as a lord. Indeed, it is philosophical advice exposed at greater length in books on politics and shown to be both useful and in accord with equity. The rest are not rulers and saviors of cities, but robbers. Therefore let him always remember what the Emperor Hadrian said—whether it was more creditable to his honesty or to his unpretentiousness, I do not know—as Aelius Spartianus wrote, "He often said both in the assembly and in the Senate that he would so handle the public business as never to forget that it was

* The exact meaning of the Latin is uncertain.

the people's not his own" [*Hist. Aug.* 1.8.3]. So I say a ruler should do everything as one who will give an account of everything; he must do it, anyhow, if not to men, then to God. It is very well known that Augustus Caesar, ill as he was, rendered an account of his rule to the Senate. And whoever has determined to live a good and honest life, regardless of station, so behaves and looks after everything that, though beholden to no one, he can still give an account and a plausible explanation to everyone; for this, as Cicero puts it, is nearly the definition of duty—which, "if neglected, must signify the neglect of virtue itself" [*Off.* 1.29.101]. But what does it matter not to be beholden to another when the spirit is beholden to itself and its conscience, which, unless it is satisfied, makes life sad and disturbed? Therefore, one rightfully praises those words spoken to the Senate; although not by the best prince, still it was the best saying, and full of noble trustworthiness. Tiberius said, "I shall devote myself so as to give an account of my deeds and words" [Suet., *Tib.* 28]. Note that this was something more than we were seeking: an account not only of deeds but of words.

Concerning thrift in public expenditures, it is well to consider the words of the Emperor Vespasian. Although he had liberally made many public improvements, still, to an inventor who promised to transport huge columns to the Capitoline at little cost, he gave a payment worthy of such cleverness but did not allow him on the job, saying, "Let me feed my poor little people on bread" [Suet., *Vesp.* 18], an utterly kind and praiseworthy concern for a good prince, to ward off at any cost the common peoples's hunger, and at the same time to procure plenty of plain food and what goes with it—innocent enjoyment. In point of fact, that saying of the Emperor Aurelian, that "there can be nothing more joyful than the Roman people when they are full" [*Hist. Aug.* 26.47.4], can be applied equally to all peoples—they are saddened more by the lack of food than of virtue; thus is the happiness of all peoples located in the body rather than in the spirit. From this concern evidently emerges not only the happiness of ordinary people, but also the safety of those who govern; for there is nothing more terrible than a famished populace, about whom it is said,

A starving rabble knows no fear. [Luc. 3.58]

This has come to light not only in ancient writings, but often in recent examples, and especially in Rome lately. In this regard the diligence of Julius Caesar is praised the most, inasmuch as in both the Gallic and the German wars he was always most attentive to this problem. And upon returning to Rome, he was no slower to get hold of grain in order to meet the people's needs; he sent ships to all the fertile islands with this unremitting purpose. No less was the diligence of Augustus Caesar, about whom it is written that in times of food shortage he often distributed grain to the people at a very low price, and free—so much to each man.

This is after all the true praise of a ruler if it is done not in the spirit of flattery, since many are used to appeasing the people to make them more easygoing and to skin them alive all the more readily, but through real fatherly devotion, as was evident in Augustus. Although he had relieved the people suffering from hunger—sometimes by selling grain cheap, as I have said, sometimes by dispensing it free—he refuted their complaints about the lack of wine with a staid and pointed speech, in which he established that he was not a condescending prince, but a wholesome one who loved his people. He said that the city of Rome had plenty of aqueducts to meet the people's thirst, and that this had been done by his son-in-law Marcus Agrippa [Suet., *Aug.* 42]. He left unmentioned the Tiber flowing within the city walls; and in fact grain and wine are not on a par, since the one is always necessary for life whereas the other is often harmful, but would not have been any the less attractive to the people, who love what is pleasurable more than what is necessary; but that good and wise prince did not give heed to what they enjoyed but to what benefited them. Now this concern over the grain supply is so vital to princes that I find it was shared even by evil and lazy ones, whence it is easy to note how much it should mean to the good ones. From this, God and the nature of the regions that you govern largely free you, by the fertility that enables you to come to the aid of others more often than you beg from them. It makes sense nevertheless in good times for the mind to be prepared for adversity, and, as though from a look-out, to scan with watchful forethought not only what is now but what could be, lest any unanticipated change of things upset it.

Thus far I have touched upon things that are necessary—whether in more words than I had to or less, I do not know. This indulgence in banquets and circus games, and in the exhibition of strange animals, which is of no use and feeds the eyes on mere pleasure, which is a brief, coarse delight, unworthy of refined eyes—this must be utterly rejected even though welcome to the crazy multitude, the worst judge of things. Here I cannot quite bring myself to admire the wisdom of the ancient Romans who, knowing the vanity of it all, just to curry favor with the people, were not afraid to deplete for this madness the treasury that should have been put to other uses; but if I chose to speak about this, and about which leaders in their day slipped into this pitfall, and to detail each one's folly, it will be too long a history and remote from our purpose. Therefore I return to our point.

When a ruler, then, has decided to impose some burden on his people, which he ought never to wish to do unless pressed by public need, he should so do it that all understand he is struggling with necessity and is doing it unwillingly, and would be only too glad to hold back if the situation did not force him. It will also be an immense glory to him if he contributes something of his own to the general levy, and, as the people's moderator, proves by his conscientious moderation that he is one of the people, as is recorded that the Roman Senate did during the Second Punic War by the advice and persuasion of the consul Valerius Laevinus, with much praise on all sides. Then, whatever is levied, let it always bend toward the milder, lighter side; and let that excellent saying never be forgotten, though it was—as I have said—not by a very good prince, who, when officials urged a burdensome tribute upon the provinces, is reported to have written back to them "that it is the business of a good shepherd to shear the flock, not to flay them" [Suet., *Tib.* 32]. If the saying about the provinces is rightly praised, what is one to think about the homeland? Accordingly, since I would like to compare you only to the good and illustrious, I beg you, imitate them and follow the examples of those who by deeds and words have earned loud praise for justice. Therefore, when the hope of some great revenue is presented by the tax collectors, set mentally before you Antoninus Pius, of whom it is written that he was never happy over any revenue which oppressed a provincial. How much less, then, a citizen? Likewise Constantius, whose saying is praiseworthy: "The public wealth is better held by private persons than kept inside one vault" [Eutrop. 11.2]; and his saying has double justification. For safekeeping by many is stricter than by one, and at the same time more useful, because private parties gain profits from the money through their industry, whereas in one place what is it but an idle, useless weight piled up by greediness? Who does not see that the wealth of the people is the prince's wealth, just as, vice-versa, the poet says,

> Poverty, forced to serve, weighs heavy, not
> Upon herself but on her master's back. [Luc. 3.152]

There are also other simpler ways that effectively win love; they are hard, I admit, for haughty princes but, when the mind is disposed toward courtesy, they are easy and pleasant. They are of this type: sympathizing, consoling, making calls, conversing. You have a paragon of this in Hadrian about whom it is written, "He visited the sick two or three times a day, including some untitled gentlemen and freedmen; he cheered them up, helped them with advice, and always had some as his dinner guests" [Hist. Aug. 1.9.7]; this is what he did. And what mind, I ask, is so sour as not to be sweetened by such great gentleness, especially from his lord? And no one is better endowed with these qualities than you. Use them; follow your nature; everything that you wish will come to you. Sympathize with those who are down and out and with those who are suffering either from sickness or some other calamity, and, if you can, bring them help; and beyond doubt you owe it to them: they are your own. Who but a villain and a monster must be begged to love and help his own? But just as the love of the people is won by nothing more easily than by kindness and liberality, so on the other hand nothing is more able to arouse hatred than cruelty and greed. Were they to be compared, cruelty is harsher but greed more common; cruelty rages more harshly but against a few, greed more mildly but against everyone. These two vices have ruined innumerable tyrants and princes, and rendered them hateful and notorious down through the centuries. It is pointless to speak with you any longer about cruelty; not only are you free of it but you so loathe it that for no one is it harder to struggle against his nature than it is for you even to think, let alone to do, anything cruel. Cruelty belongs to an ignoble, petty spirit with no self-respect: to leave nothing unavenged, when offered the possibility of vengeance, is a vice alien to the nature of man and especially of a prince, to whom the power of vengeance is vengeance enough. That is why that brief saying of Hadrian will be praised long into the future. To one who had been his mortal enemy when he was in private life, and who had a right to tremble, and feared the worst when he succeeded to power, Hadrian said with untroubled brow, "You are safe from me" [Hist. Aug. 1.17.1]. But no more on this, except that the highest good of nature is, in my opinion, human feeling, without which not only can one not be called good, but not even a man.

But it is more difficult to uproot greed from the mind. What man is there who does not hanker for something? I urge and beseech you, since an honorable, lordly living has been provided for you by a bountiful God, do not pursue a lustful appetite; for it is always thirsty, insatiable, unending, and whoever yields to it, loses what is his while reaching for another's. You wonder perhaps? It is so, by heaven: whoever intensely craves something, and does not yet have it, forgets even what he does have. Thus is the gullible will led astray, and while imagining profits, they do not see their losses; I do not know whether mortal life has any more vexing evil. And do not say to yourself or to others what many say: "Things are well for me now, I admit, but what shall I do many years from now?" This is indeed a futile concern for us, uncertain as we are not only about years but about one hour of life. Cast away this anxiety altogether. It is written, "Cast your care upon the Lord and He will nourish you and will never let the righteous be shaken" [Ps. 55:23]. Why do you shake? Why distress yourself? Why are you so worried? Do you not know that the Lord is worried about you? You have a good Guardian; He will not fail you or desert you. Again, it is written, "Disclose your way to the Lord and hope in Him, and He will do it" [Ps. 37:5]. Someone may say, "Such advice is for monks, not princes." Whoever says so does not understand that princes are all the more bound to love God and hope in Him, the more things, and the greater, they have received from Him. For it is a kind of ingratitude not to hope for lesser things from the One from whom you have received greater things. He who fed you from infancy will feed you until the end, nor will He desert you while you hope in Him, since He did not desert you when you did not yet know enough to hope in Him, and indeed when you were hidden in your mother's womb.

If greed, which is difficult to root out, keeps jabbing you, I will show you an irreproachable, noble greed: lust after the treasures of virtue and the grandiose furnishing of glory, which neither moths nor rust nor thieves can harm. However, in the event of a war, as happened to you recently, or of some unavoidable problem, those who direct their lord's eye to gain at his people's expense—which is the common habit of nearly every courtier—should be viewed as enemies of his life and his fame. They incite their lords to steal and pillage, reaping the hatred of their subjects, they are the most iniquitous breed of men, tormenting nations and deceiving their lords, and ruining others and themselves at the same time. About them there is a true and memorable saying of Marius Maximus, whom Aelius Lampridius mentions in his history of the Emperor Alexander; I give you his exact words: "That state in which the prince is evil is better and you might say more secure than one in which the prince's friends are evil, inasmuch as one evil man can be checked by many good ones, whereas many evil men cannot be overcome in any way by one, however good" [*Hist. Aug.* 18.65.4]. That is why this Alexander was a good prince; for, besides the virtue implanted in his spirit, he had, as is written in the same place, "friends who were scrupulous and august, not malicious or thieving or hypocritical or cunning or conspiring for evil or enemies of the good or lustful or cruel or cheating him or mocking or leading him around like a fool; but scrupulous, august, temperate, religious, loving their prince, who neither would laugh at him themselves, nor wanted him to be a laughing stock, who sold nothing, told no lies, made nothing up, and never duped their prince's judgment to make him love them" [*Hist. Aug.* 18.66.2]. So these are his words; such are the friends for princes to want and seek.

But others, like a plague for the princes and the people, should be shut out and avoided as if enemies, masters of evil arts, inasmuch as they do not know the good arts and hate them. In the first place they teach their lord the same greed with which they themselves seethe, so that if they persuade him, they make their pupil worse than they are. For while the avarice of private persons is evil, that of princes is by far the worst; the more license he has to do harm and the handsomer it is for a prince to despise evil things, the uglier it is to admire them and lust for them. Not without reason did that wisest prince mentioned above, Marcus Antoni[n]us, used to say that avarice in an emperor is the bitterest evil. For this, Pertinax and Galba deserved the kind of death that others deserved for cruelty. Therefore, let those who love virtue and crave a good reputation, hate and flee this evil, but princes above all because they are the leaders of men and to them has been entrusted the state itself, a huge gain and an ample reward; if they run the state properly, they will be the richest of all mortals and have imperishable riches—a happy, clear conscience, the love of God and of men. But to those who want to follow their appetite, everything will come out the opposite. They will not satisfy their insatiable hearts, and will suffer from the hatred of God and men. Thus have wise men seen it, thus has experience, the surest teacher, taught that greed is not quenched by wealth, but kindled; and the best advice is that of Epicurus, that to become rich, one need not add to his riches, but subtract from his desires, although if what are called riches were truly riches, they would surely make poeple rich; but that is not so.

Therefore, all the treasures under the sun would not make one man rich; one brief and modest thought will do so, turning him away from avarice and looking back to nature. In the *Economics* Aristotle discusses many, many ways of making money, to which the courtiers of princes of our age have added innumerable others, so that great philosopher seems to be less learned in this regard. A good prince, however, must put all of them out of his mind and despise whatever arts seem to have been instituted to gain an advantage against justice, since it has been determined by the most learned and wisest men that nothing can be advantageous that is not also just and honorable.

About courtiers—when they are good there is nothing better (this is rare), but when they are evil there is nothing worse (and this is usual)—about these last, I say, you have my opinion, or rather not mine but Diocletian's who, if he had not been so impious against our religion, could be ranked with some justice among the outstanding princes. About these courtiers, then, these are his memorable words, unless I am mistaken, written down verbatim in the book on the life of Aurelian. He says, "Four or five team up and devise one plot to deceive the emperor; they tell him what he must approve. The emperor, who is shut up in his palace, does not know the truth; he is bound to know only what they tell him; he appoints judges who ought not to be appointed, and he removes from public office those he should retain" [*Hist. Aug.* 26.43.4]. Why say more? As Diocletian himself would say, "They sell out a good, prudent, righteous emperor" [*Hist. Aug.* 26.43.2]. Even after this and other things led him to abdicate, he concluded that there is nothing harder than to rule well. And this is indeed true. Princes should not think that happiness has come to them along with ease; they have achieved some kind of happiness, but certainly the hardest kind. Whoever does not believe me, let him at least believe an experienced prince.

While on this subject, I can scarcely warn and urge you enough about one thing: you must not put anyone of that kind in charge of the state entrusted to you so that someone else besides you is lord. There have been many in power who, while eager to exalt their followers, debased themselves and became contemptible and hated by their people; they were sold out and mocked because of those very ones they had promoted. The outstanding example, Claudius, who preceded Nero as emperor, was cheapened when he so exalted his good-for-nothing freedmen, Posides, Felix, Narcissus, and Pallas, that they ruled the provinces and despoiled him and the empire, and he, unhappily, had to beg from his affluent slaves; "being bound to them and his wives," as Tranquillus says, "he behaved not like a prince but like a servant" [*Claud.* 28], and, through their advice and prompting, acted very foolishly and cruelly. Heliogabalus was censured on the same count because he had around him those who could control everything, to everyone's sorrow, and put everything up for sale, while unprincipled friends "made him," as Lampridius says, "even more of a fool than he was" [*Hist. Aug.* 27.15.1–2]. Didius Julianus was blamed for the same thing, because those over whom he should have ruled with imperial authority he put in charge of ruling the empire. Nevertheless, under stupid or mediocre princes such things are somehow tolerable. But from you I accept nothing mediocre, nothing that is not superior and unique; you would not satisfy my hope, and that of many, unless you either match or surpass any and all the good and famous men; if perchance anything falls short of this, I would not attribute it to nature, but to you. But why linger over lesser men when it is well known that under Marcus Antoni[n]us, so great a man and prince, freedmen also had great power? Both you and everyone who intends to be preeminent and do good ought to see to it more carefully that, under the pretext of benevolence, in which you abound, you not let yourself slip into this vice, even as famous princes have done. For although all famous men deserve imitation, still one must not embrace everything they do. There is no one who does not err in some way and fall short of himself.

But you will say, and perhaps are already saying, "This fellow is teaching me ingratitude; how could I allow those who deserve it not to share in my prosperity? Is that what you tell me to do?" Far from it. Nothing is less worthy of a prince or of a man than ingratitude. Every virtue has some detractors, every vice has some defenders. Ingratitude alone has never pleased anyone, while gratitude has never displeased anyone. But there are many other great things with which to reward those who deserve it: horses, clothing, arms, plates, money, houses, farms, and the like. See that you do not, as it is written, "give outsiders your honor" [Prov. 5:9]—if not for your own sake (for, as I know you, you would be ready to share cheerfully not only your power but your life with your followers) at any rate for the sake of your country itself, which God gave you to rule. Keep this in mind: nothing is sadder and nothing more bothersome to a people than to see many over them, especially unworthy ones; so let all know that you alone are their lord, let them attend you alone, love you alone, lastly let them fear you alone. Let them regard the others, not as having any power, but as sent by you who, once they have done your bidding, are private persons endowed with no dignity or power. I am not speaking without cause; I myself have seen and observed in great nations amazing patience toward their lord, however harsh and pitiless, but no less amazing resentment and impatience when they were forced to fear and look up to more than one lord. I believe I have discussed this very subject with you too, unless I am mistaken, when you deigned to visit me last year in my country retreat.

To speak about other friends, who love not your wealth, but you and your honor, whatever anyone tells you, the most faithful and upright cultivator of friendships, may seem superfluous, especially since this subject is examined by Marcus Tullius in his elegant volume. Here is a general summary of it all. Nothing in human life is sweeter than friendship, nothing, after virtue, more sacred; and those who excel the most in power and virtue need friends the most to share prosperity and adversity. One must seek nothing disgraceful from a friend, do nothing disgraceful for a friend, deny nothing honorable to a friend. By these basic principles, everything belonging to friends must be shared, one spirit, one will, not to be sundered by any hope or fear or danger; one must love a friend as another self, even despite any unequal rank; in short, one must do everything as Pythagoras tells us, to make the two into one. Is not the same expressed once for all in Sacred Scripture, where it is written in the Acts of the Apostles, "The multitude of believers had one heart, one soul, nor did any one of them, whatever he possessed, say that anything was his, but they had everything in common" [4:32]? And if anyone were to say that was the friendship of people who believed and loved each other in Christ, I speak of no other friendship, and believe there is neither stable friendship nor anything solid unless Christ is the foundation. But neither did the philosophers of the Gentiles believe that there can be true friendship without true wisdom and virtue; but this must not be construed to mean, as some have said with ridiculous fussiness, that there is not and never was any wise man. We are not seeking one that does not exist; we are satisfied with what the human condition affords, and between such men we define the friendship I speak of, that consummate, perfect friendship; and if very few pairs of friends can be counted, among whom the younger Africanus and Laelius have the most illustrious reputation, still there is this sweet and gentle friendship shared by good men, in which there is no room for flattery or nastiness or disdain or discord or quarreling, except over the friend's welfare or honor, but only peace, consolation, and good fellowship. In short, nothing false in it, nothing dissembling or hidden, but everything pure and simple and open; with such a friend I would say that everything must be shared: advice, acts, honors, riches, and finally the breath, the blood, life itself, as we know many have done gladly, and have been justly praised. But to go into this now would take too long, for quite enough has been said about false and true friendship for the time being.

So I shall proceed without following any order except what chance offers; as the thoughts come to mind, so I put them down on paper. Since, then, I have said something about loyalty and generosity toward friends, I shall add one point to what has already been said. Even though what the poet says is especially true today, "Now money's given only to the rich" [Mart. 5.81.2], and many cunning, crafty men do this, and to use Tully's words, "lend out kindness at interest" [Amic. 9.31], being most generous with those who are most able to repay the favor, still, you who seek from your good deeds nothing but to do good and the happines which comes from that—a mind at peace with itself—do take the opposite course. To those more in need, be more generous not only with your own money, but by receiving from the rich without harm to them and donating it to the poor. You have an example of this in Alexander himself, the exceptional youth and ruler about whom I have spoken; for he would do thus. I am aware that what I say can be used against me; though not rich enough to be envied, still I, because of your gift and your father's am in need of nothing. In my judgment this is the pinnacle of wealth! But in this discussion I am not looking at myself nor at others, but only at you.

There is one other matter now on my mind that should prove pleasing to you. I realize that usually magnanimity is praised in a prince, not humility. But each to his own opinion. As for me, I consider both praiseworthy and not contradictory, as fools believe. For in this, as in much else—in practically everything—the multitude is mistaken. There are those who call a haughty man noble and a timid one humble; both are equally false. I want a prince who is humble in his circle and in prosperity, magnanimous against the enemy and in adversity, never timid or haughty. It seems to me that humility is the first step to every virtue. Still, certain blind and faint-hearted men do not believe themselves lords unless they put on airs and are puffed up beyond all bounds; hence those follies of stupid princes. Gaius Caligula, the vilest of princes, discontented with his utterly undeserved human honors, wanted divine honors, and, putting statues of himself in the temples, he wished to be adored and worshipped as a god, he who was not fit for a routine greeting. Why, he even set up his own temple to his divinity and sacrifices and priests and a golden effigy—much besides, which is tedious to pursue; for he evidently thought of enhancing his honor by that which betrayed his stupidity. Was anyone more uncommodious than Commodus, or uglier? Yet to this most evil son of the best father sacrifices were offered as to a god, and statues were raised in the guise of Hercules to him who not only was not a god, and not even a man, but rather an utterly foul, savage beast. Even Heliogabalus himself, not only the filthiest of rulers, but of men, came to be worshipped. All of them deserved to be butchered on the spot and thrown into the Tiber and the sewers. I speak about them against my will, I admit, and am ashamed and grieved that such men were our emperors because, as I believe, our sins so demanded. But not what I might wish, but what the facts show, must so be said, so that our transalpine barbarians should be less angry with me if at times I say about them too what I feel; I am moved by the truth, not by hatred. For I do not hate men, but vices, and I hate them not less but much more in our own people than in others, just like burrs, tares, and thistles in my own field than in another's. But I confess I can in no way stand the vain boasting of a people who are good for nothing and so quick to brag about themselves and to lie.

Lest I get into a new argument with faraway people, I shall return to my topic. After those emperors then, Diocletian wanted to be worshipped; and by attaching gems not only to his clothing but even to his shoes, he changed the Roman and the imperial dress, an enormous novelty for a man otherwise earnest and not ill-mannered, and one who finally abdicated his power for love of peace and quiet. In sum, I believe that haughtiness and pomp proceed not from magnanimity but from mental weakness; for it seems to base minds, as soon as they have reached some level of excellence, that they have ascended to heaven, so that, at once forgetting what they are, they lose themselves in fancies; but to the truly magnanimous nothing is great, nothing can unsettle them. Thus, Caesar Augustus, the greatest and the best of princes, not only did not wish for divine honors or want to be worshipped, but he did not even want to be called "lord" either by his children or grandchildren, or rather, as Tranquillus says, "he always shuddered at the title of 'lord' as a curse and an insult" [*Aug.* 53], and forbade its use by edict, and gravely rebuked with a gesture, a look, or a word those who acted otherwise. Alexander did likewise, not that King of Macedonia who exceeded all in haughtiness and vanity, and who, as conqueror of the Persians, was conquered by the Persians' manners and being worshipped in the Persian manner, with relentless madness wished to appear a god and a god's son, to the great outrage of religious ears; but I refer to that other Alexander, the Roman Emperor, whom we have had occasion to mention often today, and who not only forbade the worship of himself, but wished to be greeted simply by his own name, in this fashion: "Hail, Alexander." But if anyone were to greet him with words of flattery or a bow of his head, he would either put him out or mock him caustically with scoffing laughter.

If I know you and your ways, which I have come to know over so many years, and think I do know, I do not doubt that you bear the title of "lord" more with patience than with pleasure. More than once I heard you saying, and insisting under oath, that being the lord did not please you, and that you were prepared to lay it aside voluntarily, except that you feared someone else would invade the state and perhaps place it under a heavier yoke, and you would be forced to live under a lord—which you would not like; otherwise you would much rather be free than a lord, since you would have more than enough wealth and power on your own, and would rather spend your prime of life relieved of so many cares and tranquil, and your old age honored when it came. From all this I can plainly guess and am convinced from what pleases you so little that consequently you do not glory in the title either. But since it is difficult to correct a people and to abolish a longstanding custom, you allow them to speak as they please, and you speak as is right and proper. For you do not style yourself "lord" either in writing or in speaking; and, looking down with a lofty spirit upon the fashion that the princes of our time and the lords of the earth use, you sign just your name to letters without any fancy additions. And you never use the plural form, but always the singular, not only with superiors, but with equals and inferiors as well. And even with me—there is no one more humble—you do not say "we," as the others do, but "I wish this," "I beg this," "I bid this."

Whenever I read this, I am delighted, and silently say to myself, "If this man had a swelled head, his words would be swollen too, just as those who want to appear more than one are not even one, in fact they are nothing." It is good of you, and noble, to do this, and you imitate the greatest men, although you do so not in imitation but through your own instinct. Examine the letters of Julius and Augustus Caesar, of which you will find many in Josephus, and some in Suetonius, and in them never is "we" written or "we wish" or "we command," but "I wish," and "I command," and the like. Indeed, as you like to joke, our contempeoraries speak of themselves in the plural and seem to include themselves, their wives, their children, and their servants; you designate no one else but you alone, you alone bid and direct whatever it is. I like this spirit, the modesty, the style which not only those two just named, but many, many of the princes of old used, all of whom are attested by letters extant in various books. I mention this so that you may rejoice in your style, and others may be ashamed of theirs, which they think is a sign of a great spirit whereas it clearly betrays an inferior and arrogant one. But this modesty of yours in language reminds me of another, namely, that which is manifest in your dress and commends you to the eyes of onlookers, as the other does to the ears; wherefore on all sides, by the judgment of reason and the senses, you are esteemed a perfect and most modest gentleman. For while the other lords of the earth flit before their subjects' faces, laden and adorned with gold and finery, not unlike altars on feast days, and consider themselves all the greater, the costlier the cloth they are wrapped in, you go about content with modest dress so that it is not dress or display that proves you the lord, but your dignified manners and your authoritative bearing—a double good, just as the opposite is a double evil: ostentation, hateful in itself, and the dangerous contagion of imitation, for the people strive to imitate all the actions and mannerisms of their prince. It is thus very true that no one harms the state more than those who harm by example, for what the poet says is true, "The whole world follows the example of the king" [Claud., *De IV Cons. Hon.* 299–300]. So it is, by heaven: the bad habits of rulers are harmful not only to themselves but to everyone.

There is an appropriate and relevant passage on this in Marcus Tullius's third book *On the Laws*. He says, "For it is not so evil for princes to do wrong, although evil in itself is evil, as that there are so many imitators of princes. For if you review history, you will notice that whatever the character of the most prominent men, such was the state, and whatever change occurred in the princes, the same followed among the people. And this is no less true than the opinion of our beloved Plato, who says that when the musicians' songs are changed the constitution of a state is changed. But I believe that when the life and style of the nobles are changed, the character of the state is changed—wherefore vicious rulers are the more harmful to the state; for not only do they contract vices themselves, but they infuse them into the state, and they are a hindrance not only because they are corrupt but because they corrupt others, and do more harm by their example than by their wrongdoing" [3.14.31]. So says Cicero. But, every time I see you, I always say to myself and to others, "No one will learn arrogance while he is our leader; no one will put on fancy clothes"; and often what is written about Hannibal in Livy occurs to me: "His dress was not at all outstanding among his comtemporaries, his arms and horses were admired" [21.4.8], although this is not so praiseworthy in time of war and in a warrior since all indulgences are ruled out. You display modesty in time of peace and prosperity, which are the mothers of immoderation and insolence. Therefore, considering everything, this dress of yours brings to mind not so much that Hannibal, of whom I have spoken, but Augustus Caesar, about whom it is written that as lord of all kings and people at a time of universal peace, he did not lightly put on any other clothes but those made at home by his wife, his sister, his daughter, and his granddaughters.

Many other things now come to mind if I, who perhaps bored you with this, was not afraid of wearing you out by pursuing it all. One thing I believe can in no way be passed over, which does most to make princes glorious and august (in this you need no one to urge you on): that you should honor outstanding men and make them your closest friends. You are already so inclined to it on your own that your very nature keeps you from doing the opposite if you wanted to; nothing is done better than what is done under the lead of nature. Habit is effective, learning too; nature is more so, and if all three are joined, they are most effective. But I call outstanding those whom some excellence has distinguished from the common herd, whom unusual justice and holiness, alas, rare in our age, or experience and training in strategy, or resourcefulness in literature, and knowledge of things has made unique. But although "many consider strategy greater than civic business, this opinion must still be toned down," as Cicero says in the first book of De officiis [1.22.74]. He gives Greek and Latin examples, Themistocles and Solon, Lysander and Lycurgus, and of our people, Gaius Marius and Marcus Scaurus, Gnaeus Pompey and Quintus Catulus, the younger Africanus and Publius Nasica; and finally, being a man most anxious for glory, he included himself among these examples. And not unjustly at that, for doubtless Antonius accomplished no more when he crushed Catiline with his army in battle array than Cicero when he exposed the foul conspiracy by high statesmanship, and threw the conspirators into prison. In this study of civic business, men of letters excel. But among these, jurists occupy a prominent place, being always most useful to the state if to their knowledge of law is added love and devotion to justics, and, to use Cicero's words, "they are experts in law no more than in justice" [Phil. 9.5.10]. For there are those who strike at the law and the justice they profess, who are quite unworthy of the title of their profession. For it is not enough to know it, unless you want it too; good will attends right knowledge. Many princes adorned their reign with such men: Hadrian with Julius Celsus, Salvius Julianus, and Neratius Priscus; Antoni[n]us with Scaevola; Severus with Papinian; Alexander with Domitius Ulpian, Fabius Sabinus, Julius Paullus, and many, many others. You too, as much as this age allows, have always honored the university of your country with jurists. There are also other kinds of learned men from whom one can expect timely advice, learned conversation, and, as Alexander used to say, literary talk. Thus we read that Julius Caesar would bestow citizenship on physicians and teachers of the liberal arts.

Above all we ought, no doubt, to prefer those who profess the sacred science that they call theology, provided that they keep it uncorrupted by empty sophistries. That most prudent prince's purpose was for learned men to live more willingly in Rome and to invite others to study in the hope of such a great reward; for Roman citizenship was an extremely precious thing then. Hence, when Paul the Apostle claimed that he was a Roman citizen, the tribune who held him remarked, "I obtained this citizenship at a high price" [Acts 22:28]. You, noble sir, who cannot give anything so great, will at least offer this: to rank learned men, distinguished in liberal studies, among your citizens and treat them with courtesy, so as to renew and adorn the city and the university, now so old, with the presence of illustrious men. For nothing attracts learned men as much as the company and the respect of princes. Indeed, Augustus Caesar gathered around him that renowned retinue not so much through his power as through his hospitality and his courteous ways; therefore, he had in his company Marcus Tullius Cicero first, later Asinius Pollio, Valerius Messala, and Parius [i.e. Varius] Geminus, the finest orators; he also had Publius Virgilius and Horatius Flaccus, incomparable poets, to whom there are familiar letters from the prince himself in which that greatest of men and lord of the world not only made himself equal to those villagers who came from Mantua and Venusia, but in a sense subordinated himself, so that no one should ever be ashamed of his friendship with commoners whom genius and learning ennoble. For who, I ask, would be ashamed of what Augustus was not? Besides, he had Tucca and Var[i]us of Cremona, and Ovid of Sulmona, although he judged this last one unworthy of his company, and banished him. He also had Marcus Varro, generally considered the most learned of the Romans, and Titus Livy of Padua, the father of history who, were he alive today, would be a fellow citizen of yours; he had many others too, and was made glorious by the company of learned men no less than by all the Roman legions. For what could the thirty-five tribes of the Roman people or the forty-four legions of warriors (that is how many I find that he had) have bestowed upon him, compared to what Virgil alone contributed to his eternal fame? That at least lives on; the other things have perished.

The fame of Caesar's graciousness came not only from Italy but some from Greece. What, I ask you, can be more attractive to deserving, exceptional men than to spend their lives under a just and kind prince who is also a favorable judge of merit? That is why I believe that many of these men would from time to time depart from your country if you did not hold on to them with the bonds of your well-known kindness. I certainly applaud and approve this; for while men at arms can be useful to you at the moment, and perform timely services, men of letters can provide timely advice and a lasting name, as well as show you the straight path to heaven and raise you on the wings of their tongues as you ascend, and bring you back to the straight path should you digress.

But I have already said enough, and, I fear, too much. At first I had intended to exhort you at the end to reform your people's ways; now, in reflecting that what I attempt is utterly impossible and could never be done by force of laws or of kings, I have changed my mind. To deliberate over the impossible is certainly useless. Yet, there is one custom of your people I cannot overlook, and I not only urge you but adjure you to apply your corrective hand to this public evil and not to say, "What you call upon me to correct is not restricted to my country, but is common to many cities." It pertains to your own dignity, so that just as you have received many unique gifts which have made you excel among your contemporaries, your country should receive something unique from you to excel the neighboring states. You certainly know, O best of men, that in the Old Testament it is written, "We all die" [2 Kings 13:14], but in the New Testament it is written, "it is ordained for men to die once" [Heb. 9:27]. Finally, in pagan authors it is said that "having to die is certain, and that what is uncertain is whether it will occur on this very day" [Cic., *Tusc.* 1.48.115]. Even though this were written nowhere, it would be no less certain, since nature tells us so over and over. Now whether it happens to us through nature or from custom turned into second nature, we can scarcely bear the death of our dear ones without grief and sobbing, and we attend their funerals often with sad lamentations, a custom which I have hardly anywhere seen so deeply rooted as in your country. Someone dies, whether he is a commoner or a noble—for that matter, it makes no difference because the spirits of commoners are stricken by emotions no less, but often even more than those of nobles, and they see less what is proper. No sooner has he breathed his last than uncontrolled grief and a torrent of tears burst forth. I am not asking you to forbid this; for it would be futile and perhaps impossible for a man [not to grieve], although the prophet Jeremiah says, "Do not bemoan the dead, nor mourn over them with tears" [22:10], while the great poet Euripides wrote in *Cresphontes*, "Considering the evils of the present life, it is proper that we grieve at the birth of our dear ones and rejoice in their passing" [quoted by Cic., *Tusc.* 1.48.115]; but this opinion, being too philosophical, is known to very few, and quite unheard of and unthinkable among the multitude.

What then am I asking? I shall tell you. A coffin is carried out, a crowd of women bursts forth, filling the streets and squares with loud and uncontrolled shrieks, so that if anyone who does not know what is happening were to come on the scene, he could easily suspect either that they had gone mad or that the city had been captured by the enemy. Then when they have arrived at the church door, the horrible outburst doubles; and where hymns ought to be sung to Christ or devout prayers poured out for the soul of the departed in a subdued voice or in silence, there sad complaints echo and the sacred altars shake with the wailing of women, all because a mortal has died. This custom, because I consider it contrary to a decent, honorable society, and unworthy of your government, I not only advise you to reform, but if I may, I beg you. Order that no woman should set foot outside her house on this account. If weeping is sweet for those in misery, let her weep at home to her heart's content, and not sadden the public places.

Well, then, I have perhaps said more than I ought, but less than I wished. If I have erred on either side, forgive me, illustrious sir, and take it as well intentioned, and rule your state long and happily, and farewell.

Arquà, November 28 [1373].

Sen. XIV, 2.

To the same person,* that human events are and are not surprising.

When I was weighed down and almost put to sleep by the boredom of present events, a saying of yours, eminent sir, very brief but at the same time very wise, roused me. It went like this: you both marvel and do not marvel at all that is done or happens in the world, be it good or bad; and you leave me to judge this like an expert (I am using your words) and a teacher. In all this I recognize your wit, once very well known to me, and I am weighing the point of your noble riddle, which has something in common with Heraclitus. He once said: "We go down and do not go down into the same river twice" [Sen., *Ep.* 58.23]. You maintain that you marvel and do not marvel at this same thing. These seem to be contradictory, but they are not; both have their reasons for a wise man to marvel and not to marvel, and neither should thus be considered marvelous. There once was someone who asked: "If there is a God, whence evil? But if there is no God, whence the good?" [Boethius, *De cons.* 1.4]. Perhaps the question was muddled for him; for us and for all who are not out of their minds, there is absolutely no doubt that God exists. While "the fool says in his heart, 'There is no God'" [Ps. 14:1], yet about this same God, not only innumerable foreign nations, but, sad to say, many of our own people either through ignorance or pride feel and did feel wrongly. Indeed, not only theologians of the Christian religion, but even the philosophers of the pagan superstition, have complained of this, the latter wrongfully since they err not on one point or another, but on everything they say or feel inasmuch as they praise gods, not God.

But not to stray any further from the subject, there is no doubt that whatever good anywhere is from this one God, while whatever evil exists is either from demonic suggestion or the perversity of men who were created with free will and incline toward what is worse. Therefore, when you see in a man either unusual piety or charity or faith, this, I admit, is something to marvel at. Why, I ask? Only because of the extreme rarity; for rarity has made many things marvelous that nature had not; but the satirical poet says that good men are rare, and holds that they are barely seven in number, and

---

* See XIV, 1.

they in turn are reduced to one by the royal prophet [David]. But let us follow what the two have in common: whatever the number, it is certain that the good are very few, as everyone knows; this is the reason for marveling, whence the same Satirist says,

> If now a friend does not welsh on a pledge,
> Or gives an old purse back with verdigris,
> 'Tis untoward honesty; it must be writ
> In Tuscan records and then expiated
> With garlanded ewe-lamb [13.60–63]

and all that follows along these lines. But contrariwise, when you begin to consider that every virtue is from no one other than Him who is the Lord of Virtues, you will not marvel that, from Him who is omnipotent and wills the good, the virtue that at first sight surprised you was infused not only into a rational soul, but into a brute animal or an unfeeling stone. On the other hand, if at times a son rises against a father, a brother against a brother, a wife against a husband, a servant against a master, and someone who has forgotten a benefit rises against his benefactor, trampling on gratitude and loyalty, who would not grieve and marvel that the number of evil ones is much greater than the good? Yet when the mind turns back to the cause I have spoken of and especially to everyday custom, it will instantly stop being surprised. For who can be surprised at something that is always before his eyes and whose opposite he hardly ever sees?

This, my lord, is the sense that my little intelligence has extracted from your little maxim. If this is right, if that is your point, good; if not, I shall be happy to hear your point from you and shall accept it. But I urge and beseech you that, as befits your greatness and wisdom, marveling at nothing human but considering everything to be lower than virtue, and fastening the anchor of hope in Christ and His mercy, you vigilantly and earnestly beware of those who thirst so greedily for your blood. Be unafraid and unflinching before all things, fearing nothing, but being circumspect and watchful in all that you do, trusting yourself not randomly to those who smile at you, but only to the most proven faith of your own people—a difficult skill, I confess, to discern the pure mind from the counterfeit. But I have great faith in your ability and in your experience with things, in which you yield to no one. Above all, I hope in the protection of Jesus Christ, about whom it is written, "If I have perceived iniquity in my heart, the Lord will not listen to me" [Ps. 66:18], words which, if scrutinized seriously, ought to have greatly frightened those who seek your ruin without any just cause. But it is all right; you are safe, and the sharp tip of the conspiracy has been broken off now that so many plots have been exposed.[*]

As for the rest, they will be more cautious in their plotting, and you more adept at foiling them; and Christ Himself, your guardian from the beginning, will not desert you at the end. For if Valerius during a similar conspiracy wrote that the eyes of the gods watched over the safety of Tiberius, and if that most learned of princes, Marcus Antoni[n]us, in a like danger, comforted his wife Faustina in his letter, and wrote thus about the false gods, "Do rest assured, the gods are fearsome, and my piety is dear to them" [*Hist. Aug.* 6.11], what can you say and hope about the true God? I, however much a sinner, humbly recommend you and your life and safety to Him. Furthermore, I wish that besides prayers and vows I could furnish you with some help or sound advice. I have never done anything more willingly.

[1373–74].

---

[*] The reference is to a second failed plot against the life of Francesco da Carrara by his brother in late 1373.

Sen. XV, 1.

To Stefano Colonna, Papal Prothonotary.*

Lately I have written you many letters, but have not been favored with a single reply. I am surprised, not indeed in view of their writer nor the handwriting, but in view of the subject they dealt with, something important to your family and mine, your kin and my lords; for their tender age is no bar to the love and esteem deeply implanted in me. Any scion of that root, which I have cherished and will cherish as long as I cherish myself, will always be my lord and at the same time my son; not death nor the waters of the Lethean whirlpool shall deprive me of that love. As you know, I have here the books that once belonged to the elder Agapito Colonna of glorious memory, and now to our youngsters. Three or four times during these two years I have wrestled with death; if it had laid me low, those books could easily have been lost, to the vast detriment of those young people and to the anguish of my spirit. And how many times did I write to you, how many times to their most noble mother to relieve me of this burden; but you have dragged out the matter so long, either with no answer or an ambiguous one, that I am again compelled to write and to beg you by all the saints in heaven that you relieve me of this heavy load as soon as possible! If nowadays it is marvelous, as the Satirist thinks, not to repudiate an obligation that one has been entrusted with, how much more marvelous is it not to want it back, and not to listen to one begging to return it. Believe me, if the books were not on civil and canon law, but by Cicero and Varro, perhaps I would not be asking you so many times. Therefore, you do as it seems best to you, for, although weary of the business, I shall keep my word and, as long as I can, keep my eye on them; if it is up to you—the ones directly involved—whatever happens is not my fault. Let the truth itself and this letter excuse me. I beseech you to answer this in the name of whatever love you ever felt for me, and if you still hold dear the memory of our departed ones, who I hope live forever in heaven, and certainly still live in my memory. Please allow, or rather bring it about, that henceforth I may speak to you about something besides housekeeping. Live on, think of me, and farewell.

[1370–73].

---

* A younger member of the large Colonna family, which had befriended P. for so many years, Stefano was the grandson of Stefano Colonna the Elder. He served the Church in many capacities and was later made cardinal by Urban VI. He often acted as intermediary between P. and the pope.

Sen. XV, 2.

To the same person,* a reply to a summons from the Roman Pontiff, Gregory XI.

Among the many things you write, to which I reply either in a separate letter or orally through your messenger, you say that the Supreme Pontiff [Gregory XI] desires my presence neither to put me to work nor to make use of me, but for this one purpose, as he says: that my presence should grace his court. I confess I too wish first of all that I were such that it could fairly be expected of me. For the less I am that, the more honor the august Father does me. But second, I wish he desired my presence in those places where I, a sinner and—unless I am mistaken—Christ and Peter desire his. For if I could not go, I would try my best to be carried, as I once did when Urban [V] called me, although at that time the means failed my loyal will, perhaps in order that I not see very sadly with my eyes what I sadly heard with my ears—the Pontiff himself returning to that awful prison. But what shall I now reply to so great a summoner? What do you think? Even though the place is hateful to me, still I would willingly come to so lovable a master, had not old age and an army of diseases conspired against me and so beset me that I can scarcely set out to the nearby church. For I am not entitled to anything from him, but I hope for much and have indeed very many signs of his love for me—those very kind words which, aside from the many others he often sent through messengers, he personally addressed to me in Pavia while on his way to Rome in his predecessor's retinue. But now my bodily condition is such that I can in no way come; why, even if I were there, I would be of no use to him, but an encumbrance instead, for then, among other things, I would have to be provided with doctors. But I joke with you, honored sir; I have never believed in doctors nor ever will. Farewell.

Arquà, December 1 [1371-73].

---

* See XV, 1.

Sen. XV, 3.

To Lombardo della Seta,* on living in the country and in the city.

Nothing I could have heard is more welcome than what you have written me. The point is not that you say you feel a great desire to see me. I am sure that it is so, or rather, that it cannot be otherwise; well known is your loyalty to me, your affection, your love, not through empty words or smiles, which are the weak links of passing friendships, but through the infallible proofs of facts, which are the strong, tight bond between minds. And although I delight and rejoice in this desire of yours, amazingly, almost incredibly, I delight even more in the obstacle. Who has ever heard this: someone likes some one thing intensely, but likes the opposite much more? Yet it is so. I rejoice, by heaven, that you are eager to see me, for I too am eager to see you. [As I will soon explain], I wish we would not see each other; for although in spirit you always see me and I you, still the sight, the presence, and the conversations of friends have something of live pleasure, or rather as much as one can imagine. In this I quite agree with Annaeus, but I do not equally agree when he says, "There comes to us from those we love, even though they are far off, a joy, but it is slight and vanishing" [Ep. 35.3]. I agree more with what the same author says elsewhere: "A friend must be kept in the mind; for it is never apart from us, and whatever it wants it sees daily" [Ep. 55.11]. The privilege of honest friendship must be no less than that of mad love, about which it is written, "The absent lover hears and sees his absent love" [ibid.]. What is written in Seneca to an absent friend, "Study with me, dine with me, walk with me" [ibid.], is no less natural than what we find written in Virgil about one in love,

His face, his words cling fast within her heart.
[Aen. 4.4–5]

So what he says about the joy of those who are apart may also be true of those who have lightly painted within their minds the images of friends. But those who have carved them there, as though made of solid marble, have a joy that is not slight and vanishing, but

* See XI, 10.

sound; such an image is felt not only when a friend is separated by a short distance, but even when he is dead and buried.

As I have said, therefore, I rejoice that you are eager to see me with your eyes as you do with your mind; but I rejoice more and more that your desire is curbed by fear of seeing once again the city that I now inhabit not from choice but sad necessity [Padua]; and although I would be most happy to see you, I am even happier not to see you—that is, when I consider the reason rather than the fact itself. I beg you, then, to stand firm and not let our love sway you from this holy and prudent intention. I would prefer you not come to me than come to the city at the same time, only to find that you cannot have all of me. You would scarcely find anything of such great value that it cannot be shrugged off and wisely done without because of the danger of going after it: you were right, Flaccus, when you said,

> You, tireless merchant, rush to the furthest
> Indies. [*Ep.* 1.1.45]

From there, of course, precious stones and spices are brought to us—a long journey, great exertion, and no little danger, but such are the ways of men that avarice deems nothing too arduous, gluttony nothing too difficult; and, to express this, the poet adds [1.1.46],

> Fleeing o'er seas, o'er rocks, through fires from poverty.

That is, through storms and crags and the inclement weather and extreme heat. But imagine that the journey then went through real fire, and that what is sought from there had to be snatched from the midst of flames; no one will then run to the Indies.

Yet in cities not only does actual fire burn, but something much graver and more dismal, namely, the invisible flames of the heart and the blaze of all the vices. In short, there are as many sinks of lust and factories of crime as there are cities; for where, I ask, except in cities, do foul pleasures dwell? Where do we find pandering, and chastity laid low everywhere, decency trampled upon, and propriety driven out? Where finally do we find lewdness, adultery, incest, and every kind of corruption? Where fraud, tricks, false contracts, babies smuggled in or left to die, and wills faked to please the heirs? Where thefts and robberies? Where perjuries and dangerous lies and corrupt judges, faithless notaries, false witnesses, and justice crushed between the dispensers of justice? Where, after all, do we find false joy, true grief, empty glory, real disgrace? Where insatiable luxury and gluttony, sad poverty, worrisome and overworked wealth, voracious usury, and noisy displays? Where do we find a mountain of arrogance, a valley of fears, a swamp of lusts, a forest of troubles, a sea of miseries, a tempest of lawsuits, clouds of error, and a well of hatred? Where do we find a constant shower of tears, equally uncouth laughter and mourning, complaints and outcries, bitter quarrels and squabbles, honeyed and poisoned flattery, slanderous whispers, unsuspected backbiting, and party strife constantly enflamed, and, to summarize it all at once, where do we find the flight of virtue and the dominance of every sin? Enmities both hidden and open, the snares of fraud, mortal plots, poisonings, slaughters, and whatever evil is perpetrated by man against man? Look, I have said much, but still not yet everything. Whoever wishes to see or hear things of this type does not have far to go: let him seek out the next city whichever it may be, however small, however large, and he will find it full and bloated with such things; a city is surely the source of these and of all evils, to the point that what was founded for the protection of the human race has been turned to its destruction.

Therefore, you are right and wise to fear returning to a place where no one who has ever lived there without being the worse for it, and whence no one ever departed except to become better or went into exile without being the better for it. Leave it to its own citizens; you belong to another state; live in the country. That is the sweet, harmless, and peaceful dwelling place, befitting your ways, to pursue not pleasure but virtue, or rather a sober and modest pleasure; for there is no more certain or delightful pleasure than that which is gotten by innocence and virtue from the good things of the spirit. Live there to cultivate not the body but the intellect, or rather the body too, which is stifled by excess but thrives on thrift and frugality—in short, a place to please not the world but God, and not to heed what blind men and madmen from the outside, but what your conscience within you and the heavenly Watcher above, think about you. In everything that you would do honestly, devoutly, religiously, usefully, you must flee as far as possible from the multitude's advice and opinions; and I am in favor of closing your ears to them as though they were the Sirens' songs, and likewise averting your eyes as though from some basilisk; this advice I give to you and me, and to all those aspiring to the same goal. But since I think I spoke about this copiously in books addressed to my dear Philippe [de Cabassoles], always a great man anyhow, but then an obscure bishop, now an illustrious cardinal of the Roman Church in rank but not behavior, I am now happy to refer you to those books, and to continue what I began.

I was delighted by the dialogue at the end of your letter that you had with your guests who wondered at your tenor of life and praised a life of pleasure. Why would it not please and delight me? Nothing is more meaningful, nothing more terse, from which I feel like excerpting a few things so that you may understand the flavor I relish from your piece, whose trim, witty brevity made me laugh, and whose balanced truthfulness amazed me. When one of that herd enslaved to the vilest part of the filthy body, the belly, laughingly asked what you ate, you replied bread and barley-groats; and when he asked what you drank, you pointed to the well. Very well done; for what else, if she were asked, would Nature herself reply, and not only Nature—the wisest of all—but Annaeus, a keen Stoic, of a manly sect in agreement with nature, and even that famous advocate of pleasure, Epicurus, who said, "Nature desires bread and water. No one is poor in these, and whoever limits his desires to them vies with Jupiter himself for the title of the Happy" [*Frag.* 467–68]. What else can we say here than what the leaders of both ways of life say in agreement on this point? Just as Annaeus follows Epicurus in this, so does his nephew follow Annaeus when he says,

A river and Ceres are all that people need. [Luc. 4.381]

And lest this wound the multitude's palate, I interpret it in a way that Seneca himself, in another place, says: "Water and barley-groats or a small piece of dark bread are not attractive things, but it is the height of pleasure to be able to get pleasure even from them, and to limit oneself to what no foul blow of fortune could take away" [*Ep.* 18.10].

And elsewhere, Attalus, not that wealthy king of Pergamum, who doubtless would have felt differently, but that poor friend of Seneca, says, "Turn to true riches; learn to be satisfied with little, and, as a great and proud man, cry out 'let us have water, let us have barley-groats, let us challenge Jupiter himself to match our happiness'" [ibid., 110.18]. To your reply, however, you added vegetables at times, and pulse, and cow's milk. Once again this was sensible, since Epicurus himself, though the author and defender of an unmanly opinion, is still reported to have lived

Happy on produce from his tiny garden. [Juv. 13.123]

And Curius, the bravest Roman general, who conquered the strongest nation in Italy and the richest king of Greece, is described thus,

The vegetables picked from his small garden
Himself would set upon a little hearth. [ibid.]

The same holds for pulse, which you heard were served to the Emperor Severus, among all those luxuries, and to the philosopher Pythagoras, who shunned meats. The same holds finally for milk; we read that Caesar Augustus liked it milked not only from cows, but from buffalo. Who in the world would scorn or spit out food that he hears was not only tolerated but sought by the lord of the world? But shameful gluttony, together with swollen pride, has made us squeamish of everything except what cost or rarity recommends. Man, a lazy, unsteady, and at the same time a stubborn, butting animal, so eager for pleasures and foods, is himself destined soon to be food for worms. But let us move on.

Who would not be delighted by that other reply of yours when, to someone who asked whether you ate meat too, you said that you were not a wolf; this also was well done. But add, "neither am I a lion or a bear or a vulture, or any other savage beast." We too eat meat sometimes, like the rest, but were it not that Christ, our King and our God—to repeat what I recently wrote to a friend we share—not indeed because He gave way to gluttony, nor yielded to necessity (although He as a man was at times hungry and thirsty), but rather condescending to our weakness, as I believe, is said to have partaken of meat, I too would venture, with Virgil, to call it the food of the wicked. In describing that Golden Age before Jove, the prince of many evils and errors, he says [G. 2.536–38],

Before the rule of the Dictaean king,
Before our wicked race dined on slain bullocks,
Saturn the golden led this life on earth,

namely, a sparing, modest life, contented with the fruits of the earth and abstaining from the slaughter of animals, especially land animals. Things changed first under Jove, and it has gradually come down so far that not only bullocks but no animal is spared—even foul, loathsome ones, poisonous ones, too, are tried; and man, who is a land animal himself, has come to believe that he can scarcely live without the killing of land animals. Why, there are even, according to many great authors, the Anthropophagi, a northern race around the river Borysthenes, who quiet their hunger more greedily with human flesh than any other food, and so have caused a dismal, unpeopled emptiness all around them, far and wide, and likewise a fearful abundance of beasts. On the opposite side of the world, in the south, there are reports of another people with the same food and the same name, but less famous. Both races are more savage than the Ophiophagi, who feed on serpents, since that food is dangerous in itself, whereas the other is horrible and heartless toward one's fellow man.

Therefore, I ask, when will those who do not abstain from man and snakes abstain from cattle? Believe me, dear friend, wherever you turn, man is the most ferocious animal, and at the same time the weakest and softest, and, to put it briefly, the most wretched. This is why every day I agree more readily with what many authors write about man. Read the seventh book of the *Natural History*, where Pliny, a meticulously learned man, seems to me at the beginning to have put into a nutshell the sum of human misery, complex and varied—and none the less so for being squeezed into a narrow space. I thought it not inconsistent with my purpose to extract one small part for you today and insert it in this letter. "Of all the animals," he says, "to man alone was grief given, to him alone was given lust, innumerable kinds at that, and through each and every part of the body; to him alone, ambition, avarice, an immense eagerness to live, superstition, and concern for burial, and even for what will be after him. But no animal has a more fragile life, none a greater hankering for everything, a more jumbled fear, and a wilder rage" [7.5]. These are Pliny's words. To these one can add what also pertains to our subject: that no animal's gluttony is more troubled or more restless; consequently, while for all the animals one food suffices, for man alone all foods do not suffice.

But to continue where I left off, since man has so great a variety of food unworthy either of human consumption or of such relentless pursuit, Apuleius Madaurensis, at the end of his book entitled *Asclepius*, is right to say, as if boasting, "We have turned to a pure, vegetarian dinner; nowadays no dinner is vegetarian, and it is considered an insult to serve plain food" [41.33]. I do not place this last among human miseries, about which much has been written in books, but nothing, to my knowledge, more briefly than what Job says: "Man, born of woman, living a short while, is burdened with many miseries" [14:1]. Alas, how many and weighty, and how unavoidable! Because of them some are driven to maintain that it is best for man not to be born, and next best to die as soon as possible. Yet, among such miseries, blind and wretched mortals, ignorant

of the facts and forgetful of their condition, exult. Gorged with wine
and meat as the ultimate in happiness, they gloat and laugh at or
even hate us for condemning their madness by too free a word or
raised eyebrow, nor do they listen to David who says, "The food was
still in their mouths, and the wrath of God came down* upon
them" [Ps. 78:30–31], nor do they hear that popular saying, "The
extremes of joy are followed by lament." What can you expect? Because of these and other things, but especially because of my observation of things on earth, I agree more each day with the poet who,
since we have come to this point in our discourse, must not be overlooked. In the eighteenth book of the *Odyssey*, then, Homer says,

The earth nourishes nothing more wretched than man.
[18.130]

But let that be enough; my hatred for the subject I have been talking about has carried me further than I intended.

What about when you were asked for your Corinthian ware and
you produced Samian—or as we call it—earthenware? Really, that fire
in Corinth, which first produced the Corinthian alloy, did not just
destroy the houses of one city, but the manners and minds of
mortals far and wide; the boundless appetite for it has smeared the
stain of greed on the most glorious reputation of the greatest men,
whence, as is known, Augustus Caesar was called a Corinthiarian by
his detractors. But that Curius, whom I mentioned above, resisted
vanities with such constancy of mind that he, so great a man, so
great a conqueror—we read—would roast turnips over a fire, and
serve them on earthenware; and we marvel when, as he was busy
with that, not his friends but the very enemy, out of sheer admiration for his virtue, brought him not Corinthian bronze but a great
weight of gold, which he most nobly declined because he preferred
earthenware.

To the one who asked you who your cook was, you replied "fire,"
and that too was very appropriate. To our ancestors the cook was
the cheapest of all slaves; now he is the head of the family. You ask
the reason? You will find none except gluttony; this was not the only
evil brought upon us by conquered Asia, exposing the conquerors,
disarmed and enervated, to be conquered by the enemy's licentious-
ness; how much better it would have been not to conquer Asia! But

* We emend *ascendit* to *descendit*.

to your persistent questioner who wanted to know whether you had either a manservant or a maidservant, you said that first you did not want to have an enemy; second, that Satan lives in hell; and I say that both replies were no less fitting. For servants are real enemies, whatever compliment Seneca may pay them, while woman for the most part is a real devil, an enemy of peace, a fountain of impatience, a subject for quarrels—to be without her is certain tranquillity.

What is more, the one who asked you about a wife seems to me not quite to know your way of life, nor to have quite understood how badly, how discordantly the study of philosophy goes with marriage, wherefore here too your reply was truly praiseworthy both for content and brevity, when you said you were not Orpheus—that is, so taken with a wife that you would eagerly descend into Tartarus, with the help of your lyre-strings, to seek out Eurydice. And even if you were Orpheus, and wild beasts and trees followed your playing on the Thracian lyre, you would never go down there upon my urging. Let wives be for those who enjoy endless female company, nightly embraces and squabbles, babies' wailing, and sleepless bother, and in this way above all are building up the glory of their name and the continuation of the family—there is nothing more uncertain than that! Let us, if it is granted, propagate our name, not through marriage but through talent, not through children but through books, with the help not of a woman but of virtue. He who seeks a wife's aid for the sake of posterity and for glory, trusts too little in himself and in God. A wife will bear you sons and in turn—by their fecundity—grandsons, and cares and labors; you will not have a famous and long-lasting name unless you produce it for yourself. Amidst so many births to women, this one is for men.

How great would Plato's or Aristotle's or Homer's and Virgil's name be today, if they had thought it was to be gotten through matrimony and offspring? These are not the paths to glory, as they are said to be, but sidetracks and roamings; they do not lead to the splendor of fame, but often to dangers, and more often to disgrace, and almost always to disgust; and certainly the examples of dangers and disgrace are countless. Ask the Atridae and the Argive soothsayer [Amphiaraus], and among our generals, Africanus the Younger and the great Pompey and his colleague Crassus, and Agrippa, and among the emperors Julius Caesar, and Tiberius and Severus—two husbands among the thousand adulteries of the two Julias—and Domitian with his Domitia, who had the same name and character, and above all Claudius who, between his Messalinas and Agrippinas, will confess on the one hand that he was defiled with [Messalina's] filthy, promiscuous lust, and on the other ambushed and killed by [Agrippina's] disguised poison. I pass over King Mark and King Arthur and the tales of Britain and Philip of Macedon, falsely believed to be Alexander's father. Also I say nothing about our own contemporaries lest the truth be too annoying, as it often is for the living. For bedrooms are full of couples who cannot stand each other; so are all beds, houses, streets, palaces, squares, and we could go on and on dealing with this. It is not necessary to page through volumes; just step into the street, you will be bombarded on all sides by family squabbles and shouting. A great witness of this is Socrates in particular, unless a greater one is Hadrian and the greatest one Augustus.

What shall I say about children, for whose sake a wife is wanted? How risky a bargain both of them are—wives and children—cannot be told. But leaving out what is endless, since enough has been said about wives, and turning to children, let witnesses come forth to give a summary taste of things: Marcus Aurelius Antoni[n]us, and the one I just mentioned, Severus Septimius. The historian Julius Capitolinus writes about the first in this fashion: "This great and good man, linked to the gods in life and death, left behind his son, Commodus; but if he had been happy, he would have left no son" [*M. Aur.* 18.4]. About the two of them, Aelius Spartianus says, "Let us come to their children. Who would have been happier than Marcus had he not left Commodus as his heir? Who more than Septimius Severus, had he not begotten Bassianus" [*Seu.* 21.4-6]? But where are we heading, and where do we leave Cicero, for whom alone, as the same historian says, "It would have been better for him alone not to have children" [*Seu.* 21.2]. I do not take this to mean that it would have been better only for him, since the same has been said about others, and can be said about still more, but rather that it would have been best for him to have been alone—that is, solitary, unattended by children and by a wife besides, which was not the case. For he would be either unknown or disreputable, were it not that by writing and reading books he had gained more glory than by taking a wife and begetting children. Being outlived by his loathsome son Marcus—whom he praised, alas, so many times—he seems to have been unhappy after death, as some like to say. But what he was able to do was to avoid his vexatious wife by an opportune divorce, nor could he ever be induced to bend his neck once again to that yoke, having once experienced and condemned it.* But we,

---

* P. was surprisingly uninformed about Cicero's second marriage to Publilia, after divorcing Terentia.

from whom that remedy has been taken away even if it were necessary, must see to it—thank God!—while we have our freedom and no shackles; and we have seen to it that we do not fall into this trap. So I congratulate our foresight or our good fortune that you have constantly acted thus until now, although people in general are against you, and that I, who in my youth was fickle in many things but always single-minded on this point, have reached this age. I have said so much about taking a wife that our conduct, which often displeases the wise, may at least in this regard please us.

Two things are still left before I let you return to your leisure: the first is that to the one who marveled that you had left the city, you said that you had left cares, worries, and annoyances; what could you have said that was truer or briefer? You might have added crimes as well, and all those things mentioned above, or by David in the psalm: iniquity and contradiction and struggle and injustice and usury and fraud and, finally, inhumanity and forgetfulness of the best things, and the practice of the worst ones. And since today we began to use Seneca as a witness, let us not bother to pester any other. What then does he say? "The conversation of man is harmful," and soon afterward he adds, "in fact the more people we mingle with, the greater the danger," and speaking of himself he says, "I return more avaricious, more ambitious, more lustful, indeed more cruel and inhuman because I have been among men" [*Ep.* 7.2–3]. And again, after saying that he learned from his dear Attalus many good and wholesome things, he added, "And then, having returned to city life, I kept little of what had been a good start" [ibid., 108.15]. If that happened to such a stalwart man as Seneca, so stern and constant, what do we believe would happen to frail men? A perfectly beautiful environment, and desirable for wise men, where avarice, ambition, lust, even cruelty and inhumanity are learned, but where good and wholesome things are unlearned! Because you so eagerly flee the city, your friends must wonder and marvel, along with the multitude, who in their wretched blindness have placed their happiness in taverns and baths, in brothels and shambles.

The same holds for their other astonishment because you disdain the association of live people and so willingly enjoy the tombs and the company of the dead. The ignorant laugh at this; but the wise, if there are any, would praise it; for from those whom they call alive you can learn hardly anything good, either in word or in example. On the contrary, you can hardly learn anything evil from the dead, but many good things every day, inasmuch as the former are most annoying, while the latter are always affable and modest. Although they may have been difficult and stubborn while they lived on earth (something that is nearly beyond our frailty to avoid altogether), still, in their conversations which they wrote down and left behind, the flower and fruit of their intellect is undiluted and abounding in much that is honest, useful, and enjoyable, whereas from our contemporaries, whether living (to say it more truthfully, breathing) or dead (more correctly, dead and buried), nothing good appears, not even a hope of it. Who, therefore, is so blind and so stupid as to prefer to be among them? It takes a long time to go through your individual points, but I have enjoyed mentioning these so that you may know your ideas have my approval, and that once I had finished reading them, I said to myself, "This gentleman is treading the right path, and is now sailing within the harbor with Terence's old man [*An.* 845], and is entitled to hate the multitude's ways and time spent in the city." Farewell.

[1373].

Sen. XV, 4.

To Guglielmo Maramaldo, Neapolitan knight.*

As you are wont to do in everything, dear friend, you wanted me to share, through your letter, in the recent events in Naples; for you did not just describe or depict the sequence of that—to my mind—most delightful history, something that, duly done, would befit an outstanding writer or a consummate painter, but you have set me down in the midst of the events, which is the mark of a superhuman intellect. I did not read, nor hear them, but I saw them and was present at everything with you, a rare accomplishment for few men; I feel no ordinary gratitude to you. The joys and honors of the one you describe, a son to me, in case you do not know, are mine; I glory and celebrate as he does well and prospers. The gracious queen has kept her ways, and has learned to do nothing paltry; the Parthenopean [Neapolitan] noblemen likewise, although I seemed sometimes to speak otherwise in this regard when appalled by that hellish game, which—for all I know—is still played in your country; but I reflected that no city is so civilized that it has not something deserving of criticism; and now those noblemen come forth, worthy of unstinting praise and applause for everything else—they are always liberal, bountiful, and faithful friends. Rome herself will testify that it is so; for during the Second Punic War, when the strength of the empire was laid low and she was deserted by almost all of Italy, or rather worn down and overwhelmed by all, betrayed by your neighbors, the Capuans, more than anyone else (from whom she deserved much better since she had waged many great wars in their behalf, but in turn endured the gravest wrongs from them), she still felt in her darkest hour the unparalleled generosity and faithfulness of the Neapolitans. Therefore I am persuaded by both ancient and modern proofs to conclude that whoever knows Parthenope and does not love her, either does not know virtue or does not love it. Therefore, those most noble citizens, as usual, did a fine thing when they escorted with magnificent honors, as you write, a fine young nobleman dedicated to every good deed, hailing from another part of Italy, to be sure, and at his side their fair ward, born—I believe— and reared among them to be united in splendid wedlock. In this one act the Neapolitans maintained their tradition, bestowing due

* See XI, 5.

honor on those who well deserved it. But let us go on.

The report on my condition that you request is a little too long, and so I forgo it. The gist of it is that for a sinner whose spirit is not in despair, I am well; I have never concentrated more on worthwhile studies, I have never derived greater pleasure from them than I do today. I shall tell you something amazing but true: while I am growing too old for everything else, for this alone I grow younger every day. What is called Fortune behaves in her usual way with me. I have neither too little nor too much; or rather I have too much, since many envy me, which I once did not believe but now I know is so; and there is nothing under the heavens I really crave, except a good end. With such a spirit, do I seem to you not rich enough? It seems that only this pathetic body wants to break faith with me. I am speaking out of turn; this was the stipulation between us in the first place, and now we have been together long enough. Live on well and happy, and remember me.

[After 1368].

Sen. XV, 5.

To his brother Gherardo, Carthusian friar.*

It is a long time—if I am not mistaken, this is the fourth year—since I had any news of you; quite a long lapse for two who were born of one womb, although, thank God, I hope that from now on nothing will be reported about you but blessedness and prosperity, inasmuch as you have ascended to a place where everything is safe. What you pressed for in your last letter to me has been carried out quickly, and the same will be done for everything you may want; for I have long known the modesty of your desires which I have no doubt I can fulfill as surely as I want to. My health, which I know you are anxious to learn about, is so changeable and uncertain that I could scarcely describe it in words; I would like** to be able to set it forth as best I may. I have been ill for a full three years, whether it is my age or my sins or, as I rather believe, both. Look at what once I wrote to Giovanni Colonna, of pious memory, cardinal, lord, and my patron: that few brothers reach old age together. Lo and behold, I say, we have reached it and we are among those few, I first and you second. We have both reached the goal we sought; it is high time that in return for the bodily health we have enjoyed to the point of being envied, we taste our share of human misery, or rather not misery but human nature. Although I have heard that you are still not showing your age too much, I did not either until that time; but you know that all the time I was a few steps ahead of you, so to speak, in age, you were ahead of me in strength; therefore wait, and be prepared in spirit. You will not avoid the discomforts of old age for long without the help of death, which we should desire although we fear it. Often through these years, the doctors, from whom I believe nothing, and my friends, from whom I believe everything, have despaired of me and of my life. I am not upset at all about this; for what does it matter in what part of this tiring journey I stop? Rest anywhere is welcome for the weary; therefore, whether I be healthy or ill, whether I live or die, let it be as the

---

* He was three years P.'s junior, and was also educated at Bologna. After a carefree youth in Avignon, he entered the Carthusian Order in 1343 and remained at the monastery of Montrieux for his entire life. His decision had a profound influence upon P. both personally and in his writings. This is the only letter in the collection to him.

** We emend *queam* to *aueam*.

Lord pleases, blessed be the name of the Lord.

Otherwise, I stand, though unworthy, in great favor and repute with men, not only the populace, but princes (would that it were so with the Lord Jesus Christ!), not to mention the emperor and other kings. Not only does the present Pontiff [Gregory XI] summon me, but the late Pontiff [Urban V] waited for me until his passing, and more than once summoned me with the kindest letters, or rather, to speak accurately, begged me to come; and I was gladly doing it, especially because I was being called to a holy and venerable place, but a nearly mortal illness, which had already come upon me without my realizing it, stopped me in my tracks. If you were to ask why I am being summoned, I do not know, and I wonder. I have never been good at close quarters with lords, and if I ever were, I have now stopped being so; in any event, I am not now. Furthermore, my age and my health, as you have heard, are not fit for journeys, of which (how time does change things!) you saw how I could never get enough not so many years ago. Finally, considering the entire situation, I made up my mind to leave behind all the grand projects, such as everyone would pray for, and limit myself to a modest, solitary life. Therefore, not to go too far from a church, I built a small but decent, delightful house in these Euganean Hills, not more than ten miles from the city of Padua; and I have bought olive groves and some vines, which more than suffice for my modest little household. Though sick in body, here, dear brother, I live with no commotion, no alarms, no anxieties, always reading and writing and praising God, and thanking God both for the good things and for my ills which, if I am not mistaken, are not punishments but workouts, and furthermore praying incessantly to Christ for a good end of life and for His mercy and forgiveness, as well as for amnesty for my youthful sins, whence there is nothing that sounds sweeter on my lips than those words of David, "Do not remember the sins of my youth and my follies" [Ps. 25:7]. Meanwhile, I sigh only for you, my one and only brother, and often say silently to myself: "Oh, how I wish there were some Carthusian monastery in these hills, which would really be an ideal place for my brother to complete his service, well known to Christ, that he has performed most faithfully for over thirty years; then would I finally have the full comfort that can be had on earth." For all the other dear ones are here with me, and would be happy if my illness did not upset their spirits. There is a greater abundance of friends here than anywhere else; although we had many friends in different lands, death has stripped us of almost all of them—a common affliction for all who grow old. What is more, the lord of these places, a man of vast wisdom, loves and honors me as though he were my son, not my lord, and he feels this way both for himself and in memory of his magnanimous father who loved me as a brother.

I am describing all of this for you in detail, to make sure you know all that I imagine you want to know. Those ordinary, homely things that I considered worthy of notice but not of writing down, I have entrusted to the messenger's oral report. Among the things not to be overlooked I would include the fact that in my present condition I have neither great wealth nor troublesome poverty—which seems to me the best state of affairs, and which I rate as the utmost riches. Being content with my situation, I do not much miss anything else. I know hardly any man with whom I would like to exchange my condition—I mean my external condition. The internal state of my soul I would very gladly change with all good and holy men. Indeed, what are great riches to me, or in what would it be better for me, or rather, in what way would it not be worse if I were to own much more land or gold? This is not the place for me to discuss the dangers and toils of great wealth; they are all known and familiar. Who has not heard this saying of Horace:

> Those who seek much lack much; he is well-off
> Whom God has given what suffices with
> A sparing hand. [*Carm.* 3.16.42–44]

Indeed, is it not enough to have plenty of what is necessary, without being weighed down with what is superfluous? In my case, I not only abound in those things that are necessary for me, but for all my dear ones, and you above anyone else. Just write what you want done; I shall not disappoint your desire or delay it. Nor indeed would I wait for you to ask, but would gladly attend to it, if I had not learned that the small amount I sent you several times did not reach you; your religious order, I suppose, strictly bars it. Meanwhile, you have written that should I die before you—which, if it happens, will be according to the natural order and to my desire—I should bequeath a certain sum of money to you in my will that would come to you in tiny payments as the need arises. Please know that I did it long ago, and I made the bequest three times as much as you requested. Still, there is no point in waiting for death to ratify the will. Just tell me; it shall be done, and it will be more pleasing to you and to me that I do it myself rather than my heir. I have said all this to you, my loving brother, and why not, though your memory alone will suffice to think of me.

But since I have begun to speak of my threefold condition, and you see how I feel about my soul and worldly goods, and your love for me compels you to believe it, listen now to my opinion on what remains. I believe that these bodily ills, so frequent and so severe, have been given me for the salvation of my soul, and are as beneficial as they are painful. This is what I hope for from God, just let Him along with my sufferings vouchsafe patience too, so that what He has done until now, I hope He will do to the end. Yet, if He, who alone can do so, offers me bodily health (which I neither seek nor will ever seek)—not the health I had long ago in my youth, but lately while already growing old—though I have no doubt that perhaps it would be useless for the soul, still I would not refuse it, so that in what little is left of my life I may complete without anguish or hindrance my studies which, I must admit, are being seriously hampered. Such is this love of one's body that nature has instilled in miserable mortals! But if He were ready to do something He has never done for anyone but could do for all, namely, restore my adolescence or my youth and bring back the past—if I were to agree—I swear by Christ Himself, about whom we are speaking, that I would not agree; for nothing is more miserable than either of those times of life with their inevitable train of vices. This will surprise our old men, who try to appear what they cannot be, since there is certainly nothing sillier, nothing more unsightly than an old man who wants to appear young. I shall say something that will make them marvel even more. If immortality were offered me, I would refuse to live forever among these goings-on, for it is hardest to take a long journey with fools for companions. And that servant is not faithful who does not miss his lord's countenance, no matter what delights surround him. Farewell, O brother in Christ.

[1371–73].

Sen. XV, 6.

To Fra Luigi Marsili of the Order of St. Augustine,* words of encouragement.

You offer great and abundant reason to your dear ones for rejoicing and hoping, and above all others to me; perhaps no one else has kept his eyes on you more earnestly than I have. God gave you the clear light of intellect; and He added the spurs of noble energy, and hence knowledge of various things that is extraordinary for your age. For it is He, no one else, who gives generously to all and does not reproach them. To Him alone befits what Persius jokingly applied to something quite different—"a teacher of art and bestower of talent" [*Prol.* 10]. And just as your intellect helps you to understand things, so your tongue does to express them; failure of the tongue has often tarnished great minds and made them appear no match for lesser ones. Endowed with all this and bolstered by the favor of God and men, you at break of morn entered upon the high road of a demanding religion, led by one behind whom nobody has ever gone astray, unless by his own choice. I mean Augustine; clinging to his footsteps is, without fail, the way to heaven and to glory. You were scarcely past boyhood when you were brought to me at the insistence of that relative of yours, a good man and a friend of mine. For a while I refused because of your tender age at that time; but you instantly filled me with good hope, so that, contrary to my custom and intent, I embraced a very inequal friendship with you. Later, when you would often return to see me, I would view you each time with more delight, wondering how at your age you could have such great desire for my friendship, and I would often repeat to myself, and later to friends too, those words of Father Ambrose, "If that boy lives, he will be something great."

Meanwhile, many years passed, for nothing passes so silently and so quickly; and long after your return to your country I missed seeing you. See now how my boy has returned to me, but as Naso says [*Met.* 10.523],

Already a youth, already a man, already
Handsomer than himself,

* An Augustinian monk from Florence whom P. had met while Marsili was still a boy. Very learned in theology and science, he was highly respected by the citizens of Florence and by P.

that is, with a beauty which neither age will diminish, nor disease nor death snatch away. Therefore, I no longer just hope for you; I hope and rejoice at the same time. For joy is the word used for the present good; hope is for the future. Here I am already holding you equal to great men, soon it will be to the greatest. Just go, hasten on the journey you have undertaken, rouse yourself. Add to your intellect a double spur, of honor on the one hand, of shame on the other. You have started in the morning, do not slacken at noon. Lazy travelers, when they look up at the sun in the middle of the sky, reckoning that there is a lot of daylight left, are wont to seek the shade and give themselves over to sleep or rest; at length they awaken late and realize that night is falling and that they have been tricked. I certainly do not fear this from you. This is not what the warmth of your spirit assures me, nor what your brow, your eyes, your words declare; but the fact remains that such an error has detained and turned away many about to come to the top, when, relying on the authority of some madman or other, they imagine for themselves with vain conviction some age or other that stands still. It never stands still at any point, but is always moving and sliding and running and rushing and, as Cicero says, flying.

Perhaps the inertia of old age is excused somehow by weakness, and the host of sicknesses that press upon it on all sides; still if there is any remnant of engrained virtue, and the flight of years has not bereft it of everything, with great energy it drives away from its realm the numbness of age and brings back by the hand the youthful vigor for noble deeds. You remember that Martius Portius Cato studied Latin literature while already growing old, and Greek when already old; and that Socrates, after literature, turned to the lyre at the same age; that Carneades, intent on philosophy, kept forgetting dinner; that Plato, to his dying day was traveling nearly all over the world, either keeping under his pillow Sophron's *Mimes*, according to Valerius, or writing, according to Cicero; that Simonides in his eighties entered a poetry contest; that Chrysippus at that same age, and Isocrates and Sophocles at nearly a hundred, published their finest works; and that Solon in his old age, after codifying the laws for his fellow citizens, always aspired to poetry and finally thirsted after letters, and was learning even near death. I could add examples of the old men who in their last years handled military or civil affairs with great flair.

But my discourse is to one eager for a different way of life. All this, and the like, is absolutely admirable and glorious in old age, but in youth they are so obligatory and appropriate that nothing is more shameful, more inexcusable, and finally more hopeless than a lazy young man. For certain vices yield to the years and diminish; others worsen and increase; among these is sloth. And so, when you see a lazy young man, how can you expect a concerned old man? Aware of this, you will take care so that no part of your time slides past you wasted, and you never be flattered by any hope of a longer or slower life. For it is very short and likewise very fleeting, and, whether it is shorter or more fleeting is hard to say, so evenly matched is its speed with its shortness. In truth, this life, for which we suffer so much pain and torment, is nothing, and this selfsame nothing never stands still. But while it is being sought after, it vanishes like smoke. Young people must not wait until they are slow at doing what they now do quickly, but during youth must hasten so as to rejoice in old age, be remembered when dead, live on after being buried, and, as Ennius says, "fly on the tongues of learned men" [Cic., *Tusc.* 1.15.34]. This, dear friend, is the age to learn; what it studiously gathers, learned old age will distribute, and what it has gotten from many it will disburse to still more. In seeking for things, it is madness to wait for a later age that can hardly hold on to what it has gotten.

But I would not mention only scholars, for whom there is no other age except the one you are in, that is strongest in body and mind, and free of obstacles, except those which it makes for itself or with which it narrows its own road as do many people who, forgetful of the knowledge and virtue to which they were destined, pursue their lusts, and do not turn away from their willfulness until they become a disgrace and a grief to their loved ones, a joy to their enemies, a mockery to the multitude; and useless from any point of view, unfit for letters or lusts, they arrive at their dotage. But I should also touch upon a few of another kind of men whose example may rouse you, and who, although they could have waited for a later age, chose this one and no other for doing brave deeds; they did not postpone it even a little, and if they had, it would not have come out right, as it did. Certainly at this age Achilles was already attacking Troy, Alexander India, Scipio Africanus had crushed the west and was crushing the south, Pompey the Great had pacified Spain and all the seas, overcoming the pirates. At this age Drusus Nero was harrying Germany and had already arrived at the forks of the Rhine, laying waste and conquering everything with such valor and youthful prowess that he made himself forever venerable, even to the enemy—something that to this day the Germans neither deny nor try to hide; sometimes when I happened to be in that part of the world, I have assessed this, and I know it by the frank admission of this new emperor and his court. I could cite many examples, but hardly more illustrious ones.

Rouse yourself with these goads; in their company rise up. It is sweet to follow in the footsteps of the great and to compare one's self with those great spirits. Do not say, "I am young, I still have a lot of time," for whereas this is doubtful, that other saying is very true, that a day never returns. Seize it, therefore, lest it pass you by fruitlessly, and, as happens to the majority of men, or rather to almost all men, lest it flow through your fingers like water. But indeed, suppose you had a lot of time assured, which no one has ever had, yet it is well to be chary of this and of everything while it is plentiful; for when it runs out, there is no use guarding what is lost. I therefore warn and beseech you again and again that you let no day slip by out of laziness, but each evening take stock of yourself like a thrifty head of a family with an untrustworthy steward, "This I did today, this I began, this I learned, in this I have become the wiser, in that better." For I exhort you no less to virtue than to knowledge, but all the more easier it is to acquire and the more worthwhile to find. They say this was the way of the Pythagoreans; but whoever it was, let it be yours.

Rouse yourself and examine your days one by one; and any day that you find to have gone by you with no benefit, consider that you have not even lived that day. Titus Caesar said, "Friends, I have lost a day" [Suet., *Tit.* 8.1]. If he is praised for saying that he had been of no use to others on that day, what do you think one who was of no use to himself would say? We cannot, I admit, constantly bend over a book, nor always be by ourselves and calm; we are frail and the world is stormy, and things are all mixed up. This we can do: see to it that no day pass without our sifting through it and reflecting upon ourselves. For how shall we see to other people's business if we neglect our own? Well, whether sitting or standing or walking, one can think about himself and his concerns—in council, at a gathering, and, although Cicero thinks otherwise, even at a banquet, though less seriously. There is hardly a field so barren, a mind so stubborn that constant, careful tending does not make soft and fertile. What then should I hope for your mind, which Nature herself made fertile and tractable? As Cato says in Tully's book, follow Nature, the best guide, as though she were a god [*Sen.* 5], or rather follow God Himself, the Father of Nature and of all things, who calls out to you, and to all whom He created and redeemed, in a loud voice not only from heaven where He reigns eternally, but even from that roughest pole which He climbed for us in triumph, naked and crowned with thorns. He calls everyone, I say; few hear Him. Be one of the few; otherwise it would be better to be nothing. Listen and heed Him from whom you received body and soul and mind, through whom you are as we rejoice that you are, through whom you will be, unless you spurn Him, as we wish and hope you will be. I shall not bother you today with anything further, being certain that this—much less for that matter—is enough for you, since you understand, even though I were to say nothing, what I desire from you, or what others do who love you.

Yet there is one thing I shall not pass over so that you will not give ear to those who, under pretext of theological studies, try to discourage you from any knowledge of secular letters. Had Lactantius and Augustine done without them, not to mention others, Lactantius would not have undermined the superstitions of the pagans so easily, and Augustine would not have built the *City of God* with such great craftsmanship and mighty ramparts. It is well for a theologian to know many things besides theology, or rather, if possible, to know nearly everything, so as to be equipped against the insults of carnal men. Certainly there is one God to whom all things are subject; so the knowledge of God is one, which all other knowledge subserves well; but the same Augustine discusses these things in the second book of *On Christian Doctrine*. Therefore read about his advice, which you can do without prejudice to our main goal; and learn all you can, provided you do not weaken your talent or your memory, and always remember that you are a theologian, not a poet or a philosopher, except insofar as a true philosopher is a lover of true wisdom, and the true wisdom of God the Father is Christ.

To this I would add that in all learning your particular concern should not be how hidden or obscure is what you are concentrating on, but how true and clear. For there are those who vainly boast especially of what neither they themselves nor others understand; they are a foolish lot. Just as truth is the goal of the intellect, so clarity is its happiness, unless I am mistaken. In all holiness and virtue, however, never abandon Socrates' easy shortcut to glory, namely, that you try to be what you want to appear to others. For there are some of the worst men who want to appear the best, as though they were fooling God and their own conscience as they fool other people. You have many guides along this twofold path. For both, Augustine alone will suffice, your personal leader whom you see struggling most magnificently with noble passion at your very age against his errors and vices. If ever there was in him any error in his life or in his doctrine, the first was taken away by an antithetical way of life; the second was rooted out by his own hand in that finest of books, so that nothing is safer than to follow at the same time both the life and the doctrine of that man.

Lest this ever slip from your memory, I beg you lastly that as soon as you arrive where you are longing to be, which I trust will be soon, you write one short book against that mad dog, Averroes, who, moved by unspeakable madness, barks against his Lord, Christ, and the Catholic faith. Collect his blasphemies from all over. This was something, as you know, I once started; but always, enormous responsibilities—now more than usual—and the lack of time, no less than of knowledge, forestalled me. So apply all the power and energy of your intellect to a task sinfully neglected by many great men; and dedicate it to me, whether I am alive then, or have departed in the meantime. For it is always time for everyone, and myself among others, to think about departing. Have no doubts about lacking either intellect or writing ability, although these are often lacking in some of your brethren; Christ will be with you as you handle His business, just as He was there even at your birth. Farewell.

[1373].

Sen. XV, 7.

To the same person,* with a copy of St. Augustine's Confessions.

My kindnesses toward you, dear friend, which you enumerate at length, I would say without offending you, are nothing at all, except that I have loved you ever since your childhood when I already had some sort of premonition about you, and now I love you more and more each day, hoping soon to see in you the kind of man I am eager to see. I willingly give you the book you request, and I would give it more willingly if it were as it was when given to me in my teens by Dionigi [di Borgo S. Sepolcro], that preeminent professor of sacred literature in your order, an outstanding man in every respect, and a most indulgent father to me. But, being unsettled both by nature perhaps and then because of my age, I found it charming for its subject and author and handy to carry because of its small size; so I often took it throughout Italy practically, and France, and Germany, to the point that my hands and the book seemed to be one, so inseparable had they become from endless holding. Not to speak of the many tumbles we took into rivers and on land, I shall tell you something marvelous: once near Nice, on the Var, it went with me under the sea. Doubtless it would have been the end, had Christ not snatched both of us from the imminent danger. Thus, it has grown old with me in my comings and goings, so that now, being old, it cannot be read by an old man without enormous difficulty; and now at length, after having left Augustine's house, it returns home, and now again, I suspect, it will travel with you. Take it such as it is, and take good care of it, and start using my belongings in your own right and abstaining from unnecessary verbiage; whatever you like, do not ask for it, but take it. Farewell, be happy, and every time you approach His table, pray to Christ for me.

Arquà, January 8 [1374].

* See XV, 6.

Sen. XV, 8.

To Giovanni Boccaccio,* an excuse for his silence.

You can marvel but, I hope, not be offended too because, though I either could not or would not write you anything else, I did not at least give some reply to your letter. As often happens to those who are the busiest, while I mull over many things, I accomplish nothing. To be sure, my friend, if I go into the story of my concerns, however inane, the concern itself will bring forth and add to my concern. In short, what I had often undertaken I was never able to finish; but lest you perhaps suspect something else, since this is old news and has long been well known to you, I add another more powerful, more recent reason for my silence, which I would be happier to have kept quiet in order not to prick your ears and your spirit with the sting of odious talk, except that you have doubtless heard it from others, or are about to. Well, then, health left me along with you; I was never well after that, and I have a feeling I shall never again be well. While my age helps my sickness along, nothing helps my health, unless perchance you think that I either consult doctors or have more faith in them that I used to. But more and more every day, I dread those monsters and keep them from my door like enemies, except sometimes those whom the force of friendship, not of medicine, bids me to let in on condition that I shall not do anything or take anything they may prescribe.

Now at length I write nothing about what I had decided last year, but just one thing: your apologia, which at the behest of noble wrath you poured out upon my critics, pleased me very much, and I was delighted by your sympathy, your style, and ideas, and I know those fellows deserved all this and even more; but I would not like your fine intellect to heat up as much as they deserve—they are not worth your consideration or your wrath. Leave them to their own devices, but do not betray your character, nor let their madness sting you more keenly than me, who am the primary target, although I cannot be either touched or offended without your feeling it. Accordingly, rest assured that what was at the beginning of your letter—that some Lorenzo or other, a learned man, you say, but actually quite ignorant of my nature and my circumstances, said that I, upon hearing the opinion they had expressed about me, was at once enraged and

---

* See I, 5.

grabbed a pen and replied to them—is far from the truth, with all due respect to him; perhaps he heard it, but whoever said this first either was mistaken, I swear, or else lied. The opinion of my judges drove me not to rage but to laughter; for however true it was, they themselves were the silliest. I did not take pen in hand to reply immediately, but after a full year had elapsed, when I was sailing up the Po and feeling bored; I had nothing else to do then nor would I ever have done it or thought of doing it, if the unending resentment and constant complaints of our Donato had not prompted me. I have, dear friend, become hardened since adolescence against such bites of envy. Know that what I did not believe for a while is quite true, for I have been besieged by these pests, and the contrary is false. I must add that, as I was saddened and put out with you for sneaking away, and reproaching myself and perhaps weeping too, I congratulate you upon returning safe and sound. Farewell.

[1369–73].

Sen. XV, 9.

To Donato Apenninigena [Albanzani],* that one must not seek any gain from friendship.

How many times have I warned and pleaded? How often coaxing, how often losing my temper, have I argued with you, now with my tongue, now with my pen, lest your liberality sully me with the suspicion of greed? You persist; and while you concentrate on your own reputation, you do not realize the damage to mine. Since when have I deserved this from you, I ask, that you make me appear either so greedy or so proud that my friendship cannot be gained without a high price that goes on forever? Thus, you not only repeat this munificence of yours, but in your last letter, promise to make it annual and perpetual—which is the very thing that I would never want done, but you threaten** never to stop doing it. I would almost call your word more offensive and rude than the action itself, and yet I believe there lives no one on earth whose friendship is easier to gain [than mine] if only the personalities are compatible; never have I wanted from a friend anything except what no friendship can be without, namely, being loved. What place have gifts in this? Perhaps that custom goes with loving a woman, and not honorably at that, but for pay. I do not want your gifts but your heart; I have it. When a thing reaches its perfection, there is enough of it. Whatever is added on top of that tends to spoil it. What good is it to seek out those things and overwhelm me with what I do not need and you do not have in abundance. If I do not want them, I wonder why you do it; but if I do want them, I wonder why you want to be either my friend or anyone else's who expects from you anything but yourself, unless perhaps in time of great need when everything is scarce and the law of faithful friendship demands that nothing be withheld but everything shared and nothing private. Indeed that law, which pounds adamantine nails even in the skulls of the loftiest kings, to use the words of Flaccus, has the power to grip both of us, but for now it is closer to you than me; for, as you know, I am about to perish richer in worldly goods than you; I have no present need. My Donato is more than enough for me, given [donatus] I say, not bought. Why then should you buy me, to whom you did not sell but

---

* See V, 4.
** We emend *imitari* to *minitaris* (Laurentian: *minitari*).

gave yourself? It is no equal friendship when one is given and the other bought, or rather no friendship when everything is not free on both sides.

So what is it that you are doing? None of your letters comes without something, none of your messengers comes to me empty-handed; while I get ready either to read the letter or to listen to your messengers, your gifts jump out sideways. But why, I ask, unless perhaps you want always to follow that saying of Terence [*Phorm*. 41–42] which I admit is common but

> unfair—that those who have less
> Must always give more to the richer ones.

I beg you, do not make me feel bad and bitter so that you may be good and liberal. Though often with words, men are sometimes defamed by deeds; I reject your promise for the future, I complain about the past and I entreat you to change your ways. If you do the opposite, you will upset me and force me to what I have not done so far in order not to upset you—namely, to choose to appear rude rather than greedy. Whatever you send, I shall send back; that is how I shall avenge myself, and what entreaties were unable to do, perhaps an insult will accomplish, that you should stop troubling me with your largesse. In all things there is a certain limit you cannot overstep without offending decency. We have not divided the inheritance of Crassus so that his avarice has come to me and his wealth to you. Lastly, I am not one of the Parthian kings whom no one was allowed to greet without a gift. Farewell.

[1368–70].

Sen. XV, 10.

To Pietro Bolognese [da Muglio], rhetorician,* that mortal things are to be scorned.

That short letter from you has given me enormous comfort. Although nothing anywhere on earth is dearer to me than friendship, I would except virtue alone, on Cicero's advice, if I had any virtue; likewise, I hear nothing more willingly about friends than that they are as I wish myself to be, despising everything the multitude either admires or fears. Take this plague, without equal in all the centuries, which now for twenty-five years has been wearing down not only our continent, but the entire world with successive blows. It has again, with its annual fury, attacked that lovely city where you were born, where you now reside, and which was once, when I was in my teens, a temple of every honorable delight. What then do I think you are doing in the midst of such a great upheaval, except what you yourself say? Even if you do not say it, I know. Many are fleeing, everyone is fearful, you are neither—splendid, magnificent! For what is more foolish than to fear what you cannot avoid by any strategy, and what you aggravate by fearing? What is more useless than to flee what will always confront you wherever you may flee? Let the timid flee across the mountains and seas, cunningly perhaps if the people who live across the mountains and seas were not also dying.

You say you have a spirit that you learned from me; that is your love and your kindness speaking, not you. For you could not have learned anything from me, but I could learn much from you, had I not lacked either the intelligence or the diligence. You write that to you it is a dreadful burden not to have been with me longer, and not to have culled my mannerisms or my words, which used to bring you delight and profit (I use your own words to the letter). I swear I wish it were so, but I am no more elated by the praises of friends than downcast by the slurs of rivals; I am perfectly aware of my situation. Be that as it may, I rejoice that you think of me thus; nevertheless, I do not therefore feel that I am wiser, but that you are kinder. I too cannot stand such a prolonged separation, and I wish for your presence, especially among these Euganean Hills where, amidst so many ills in the world, my household and I have cheerful tasks and, as it seems, the most wholesome air—no matter

* See IV, 3.

that it is a treacherous, unstable element. You are always present to me in spirit, and you will be as long as I live. I am not going to write you more for now except to praise your attitude and urge you to be true to your brave spirit; and as for those who fear death and are struggling to get away, tell them for me that they torture themselves in vain. For neither can the human condition be put aside except by putting aside one's humanity, nor is there any other escape from death except to die. Farewell.

[Arquà, 1374].

Sen. XV, 11.

To Benvenuto da Imola, rhetorician,* on poets.

Neither my bodily health nor my leisure time avails to reply to your letter; therefore, in a few words, if I can, I shall dispose of things that deserved many; if this satisfies you, I will be happy. In any event, I would be more ready to listen than to speak, to learn than to teach. You justifiaby inquire whether this art [poetry], which certain people attribute to me and which I confess I loved from a tender age, is one of the liberal arts. I say that it has hardly been counted among the liberal arts, but is beyond all the liberal arts and takes them all in; although this can be shown in many ways, Felix Capella suffices, who, as you know, dealt poetically with all seven. Do not be troubled because it is not listed among the liberal arts, among which we know that neither theology nor philosophy is included; it is a great thing to be included among the greats, but sometimes it is greater to be left out, just as the prince is left out of the number of great citizens. The liberal arts begin the experience of knowledge in the human mind; the other unnamed ones among them finish and adorn what has been begun.

For the rest, I do not change the opinion I expressed in my *Invectives*. Whatever is said justly against poets applies to dramatists. For what you say about Boethius, who is cited as a witness against poets, that he was not a dramatist, I admit; and the man's authority forces us to. Well then, the philosophical rebuke is directed not against the writer, but against the style. For the elegiac style was more fitting for dramatic and amatory subjects; it is imagined to have stirred Philosophy, as though she were unaware of what she meant, so that she poured forth those words; had she condemned everything poetic without exception, that man, who was not only learned but holy, would by no means have retained until the end of the work the style he had begun and its association with prostitutes on stage. For throughout the book many things are said poetically.

On the other hand, one must not be surprised that great men have sometimes used a style that is not only silly, but even obscene, such as the Platonic passages in the *Saturnalia*, which I would rather

---

* A widely respected teacher, scholar, and disciple of Boccaccio, he lectured on Dante publicly in Bologna, and wrote commentaries on various writers, including one on P.'s *Bucolics*. This is the only letter to him.

that such a great philosopher had never said. Sometimes a sort of waywardness, sometimes an enthusiasm of the spirit carries it where it does not belong, and although the contents are bad, the style is still good, and the art irreproachable if turned to a happier subject. In this way, then, I believe that whatever is said against poets should be said against dramatists, not only by saints, but even by Cicero himself; for no other nonpoet has said more in favor of poets. Still I do not deny that others too have said some absurd things, indeed many, to which what you say Jerome wrote can apply—namely, that poetic language is the food of demons; for they were men, subject to errors, and not only men but pagans. Otherwise, if we take it simply, Jerome himself grazed a lot on such food; in all his writings he reeks of a poetic style which he himself realizes; he excuses himself somewhere, not superfluously, for this very thing. Quite often—I admit—the language of poets is bad; why would it not be, since their life too is the worst?

What then am I to say here? And what do you think? Only what I feel and what I believe: the poets, not the poetry, must be blamed for it. For it is a fact that some people make the worst use of the best things, and we have heard of famous theologians who were great heretics, and moral philosophers with the worst morals; this is not the fault of the arts, but of those who use the arts badly. I daresay that if poetry were to befall a good, pious intellect, it can be directed to the praise of Christ and the adornment of true religion. If you approve of this, all well and good. But if not, I too have left this pursuit behind me; and if I hear a better argument, I will gladly yield not only to your opinion, but to that of any learned man. Farewell.

Padua, in my sickbed, February 9 [1373].

Sen. XV, 12.

To a certain very fickle and restless man [Giovanni Malpaghini].*

I congratulate you for having arrived in a safe port after so many trials and storms of the spirit. You are dearer to fortune, or rather to God, than to yourself; you flitter about and wear yourself out for nothing. He provides you with rest, even if you do not want it. You want to wander over a hard path; He directs you with His hand on the road of peace. There you are now, through His guidance, with an excellent man [Francesco Bruni] who is so dear to me that I scarcely know whether I have anyone dearer on earth; whoever cannot live with him, can live with no one I know. I advise you to get to know him, and learn finally to stay still for a while. A healthy man does not keep tossing around in bed, a decent woman does not marry over and over; being a man, learn to behave like one; being a man, learn how to put up with men, whom you are commanded not only to put up with, but to love, and do not disdain those by whom you should not wish to be disdained. Do not flee all men; wherever you come, you will find men; you must live either with men or with beasts. I would recommend solitude if I did not know that you cannot bear either solitude or company. It is a disease of the spirit, and a very grave one at that; it can only be restrained by the virtue of the spirit. There are certain things which are, at the same time, both the causes and remedies of sicknesses. Your mind drives you. Let it stop you; if it will not do this, all my warnings through the years will have been in vain, scattered to the winds. I also congratulate you for having seen the city of Rome; in all your wanderings, though you go throughout the world, you will not see anything like it. You have seen the capital of the world, dirty, I admit, and unkempt; that it is the capital would not be denied even by its enemies—those who wish to be called Roman emperors and Roman pontiffs even now, and boast of these titles though they are anything but Romans. Why this is so, meditate on your own, and know that you have not seen Rome, but the hills where Rome used to be.

[September 1370].

---

* A brilliant pupil and protégé of Donato Albanzani, he helped P. with his work, especially with the transcription of the *Familiares*. After four years in P.'s service, he unexpectedly decided to leave, to P.'s consternation. P. never found a satisfactory replacement. This is the only letter to him. [See *Sen*. V, 5–6].

Sen. XV, 13.

To Gasparo di Verona [Squaro dei Broaspini].*

I was happy to see your note, dearest friend, like anything from you. Concerning what you ask, I have nothing certain to write back; for nothing is more uncertain to me than the condition of this wreck of a body. I will say the one thing I can; I left my country home not only unwillingly, but under duress, with dire necessity compelling me. It drove me away, it is keeping me here; yet, as far as I can guess, I shall be returning before Easter. For often that saying of Horace [*Serm.* 2.6.60] rings out in my heart's ear:

O dear farm, when shall I see you again?

But although I know—not now for the first time—that you have always desired to see me and be with me, which I confess is not my just desert but your indulgence, still I dare not urge you to come; for I am aware of your busy schedule. If you decide to come to your friend's, or rather your own home then, even though you hasten, I believe you will find me in the country, where not only my eyes and those of my dear ones, but the walls themselves in their own way will be most happy to see you, exulting at the arrival of so dear a guest. When your friend comes, I shall greet him, for he is now living on his farm, dedicated both to agriculture and philosophy, an altogether good and loyal man who cares for us.

[Padua, 1373].

---

* See XIII, 17.

Sen. XV, 14.

To Philippe [de Cabassoles], Cardinal Bishop of Sabina,* on the state of his health.

You may be surprised and perturbed, were it not that the lofti-ness of your perceptive intelligence, anticipating everything, curbed your surprise, and your gentleness, incapable of anger, curbed your turmoil. Otherwise, who would not be upset because after being summoned so many times by such a man with such kind letters that ought to tear loose the rocks from the most solid mountains, I still do not budge from here. However, what am I being invited to, I ask, and what was it previously? Then it was to the three things which, of all that is under the heavens, were singularly desired by me: to the city of Rome, which I have seen so many times, but never without the very sight of it making me all the more eager to see it again; to the Roman Pontiff [Gregory XI] who, tired of inviting me, laid upon you, whose voice is better known to me, the burden of inviting me that you would willingly take on—the Pontiff whom I had never seen with my eyes, but seeing him just once would have been for me a huge share of earthly happiness, not because he was such a great lord, but because he was such a fine man; and finally to you and your face, awesome to me and always lovable more than any other—which Christ and I know indeed how badly I wanted to see, and you (I suppose) feel by infallible divination—your face to which I was so comfortably accustomed since youth, and from which I was later separated for so long by my cruel fortune. What wonder, then, if I am racked and squeezed by boundless longing? I say, then, that the other dear ones whom death has still left me, I often saw during these years; I seem not to have seen you for centuries.

Why then do I hesitate so much? Do you think, shall I say, be-cause those three desirable things have been reduced to one, since you have left Rome and the Pope has departed from the human sphere? I do not say this; my longing for you alone is enough. What then? There is indeed, dear Father, a real excuse, but a difficult one. My situation, in short, is quite unbelievable to those who do not know, monstrous to those who do know and are perceptive; but I will say what the situation is and the truth itself will merit the cred-ibility which I suppose *I* may not merit. Well, then, often when I ap-

---

* See VI, 5.

pear healthy, I am so seized by a powerful surge and sudden fevers that I suddenly seem lifeless; and I drive everyone to despair of my life, except a few who know me more intimately. At the end of barely one day, suddenly, beyond anyone's hope, I rise up as if revived and, as though I had not been in that condition, I return to my pen and books, and go about my business as usual. I have suffered from this not once or twice, but more than ten times in the last two years, to the point where these ups and downs, this fluctuation has tricked even the doctors, several of whom are friends of mine here. It is doubtful whether they trick more often than they are tricked; for in the middle of the night they have said publicly that I was about to die, yet upon returning the next morning to escort me, I suppose, to the grave, they find me writing. So they are dazed and have nothing to say except that I am an amazing man; suppose I am amazing in this and in other things perhaps, how much more amazing are they themselves! They are called doctors and are literate men; they read everything, Aristotle, Tully, Seneca, Virgil. Why, they even gape at dialectic, rhetoric, poetry, and astrology, and, what is worse, alchemy; only medicine do they neglect. Strange to say, while they strive to know so many things, they ignore the one thing above all that they profess. But this is an old argument I have with them, an old issue.

I had decided to come to you and to your superior [the Pope] who summons me, undertaking the journey at the beginning of spring and by water as far as possible, the rest by land at a slow pace. But I shall tell you something to astonish you: here we had no springtime. The hottest summer followed the harshest winter without anything in between. Yet I stuck to what I had started and was preparing my baggage when, alas, at dusk on the seventh day of this month, my usual fever struck me; when the news spread, all the doctors gathered round, even though they had been fooled about me so many times. One of them, distinguished by the great title of philosopher (O title once venerable, now prostituted to vanity and ignorance!) confidently observed that I would not live to see the next day. Thank God, I saw that day and some others since; and if the eyes and the color of a man forecast the truth, I can now see even more of them, although I am older than that most inept trafficker of human life; for he has made such a habit of saying that anyone who is sick will pass away the next night, and he so fears to lie now and then in promising a recovery that he lies incessantly in threatening the opposite. But both I, worn out by age, and he, wasted away, will doubtless be short-lived, unless I am mistaken; and there will be no loss to philosophy from my death, but a huge loss from his, as certain people will perhaps think. But I would confidently swear that he does not know in the least either what a philosopher does or what the word philosophy itself really means.

But enough about this man, whose name I have consciously concealed. For I usually withhold the names of those against whom I speak, lest I bring them either fame or infamy; so I come back from him to myself. Therefore, not as he saw fit, who, relying on the mere title of physician, places boundaries on the life of mortals and on the death of the living and pays no attention to how he himself is more like a dead man than a live one, but rather as He saw fit who has all my years and months and days numbered under His watchful eyes, I recovered and rose up healthy, as it appears, but so weak that for the present I do not think about travel, although I have not changed my mind for the future, provided no such setback recurs. Otherwise, what good will it have done me to get back on my feet if I have to fall ill again right away? I do not really know where I get this mockery of a life; I admit my sins would deserve this and even much heavier punishment, but my way of life and sobriety deserved something else, if I am not mistaken. But if I am suffering these things for my sins, I rejoice and thank God; just let it all be credited to my account, and may my Creator be more prompt and willing to forgive me because of it. I now write nothing further about my coming, for I would not like to deceive you with my promises too often. Nevertheless, I am giving it much thought, and I find comfort in these thoughts, not unaware that men's thoughts are vain, and bearing in mind my mortality and frailty. I can only wish; all the rest is in the hands of God. To be sure, I am hoping and striving to see you before I die; but whether indeed I see you or not, I always do see you and shall go on seeing you, as God who sees all is my witness.

Besides I would not want to overlook one thing that I think you are thinking of, for it is especially necessary for both of us, and indeed for everyone. You, I believe, are asking me silently, and I am replying to you at the end of this letter: what do I do in this condition and amidst the tribulations of this life, amidst such frequent conflicts between the body and sicknesses; what strategy do I adopt for myself and commend to you, who are now also troubled with your own problems? I wish for you the same as I conclude for my own benefit; therefore, do listen. There is really no external remedy, unless perhaps we now for the first time place faith in doctors that they bring the help to weak old men that they were never able to bring to young and strong ones. You know how our doctors have always been God and nature; either we had no others, or they did nothing or really hurt us. Consequently the strategy concerning them remains unalterable for me, and the same, I believe for you; for we both have had one and the same teacher, experience; we have learned one and the same lesson. After all, our true Doctor is in heaven above and within our soul. This is where we must seek aid, and where we must pin our hope; meanwhile we must strive with all our might so that with divine help and our own exertion we may escape to safety. Surely, if you wanted to cross a rather wide ditch in one leap, you would start running from a distance so as to reach the jumping-off place, fresh and nimble from the added momentum. Now that we are to cross the horrible pit of death, which no one avoids, and which we either know or believe is the most dangerous of all, we shall not come to it unwarily, shall we? May this be far from our minds throughout life, believe me! Or if we have neglected this through disastrous postponement, at least at this stage of our life we must prepare our spirit, rouse our mind, collect our strength, throw off whatever presses upon us, and grasp whatever helps. With this support we may face that hour unhindered and fearless, and cross that pit of no return which, if perchance we fail in our first leap, leaves no hope of ever leaping again. Nevertheless there is nothing at all that we must provide for and be worried about as much as grasping faithfully and humbly the right hand of God, which is both necessary and ready for the wretched everywhere, but especially there. It alone can overcome death and lead us to immortality. Farewell.

[1371–72].

Sen. XV, 15.

To the same person,* with a short poem requested by him.

You ask, and by asking you command (for me there is no difference between your entreaties and your commands, since there would be none between your commands and your silence so long as I knew what you wanted); you ask, I say, that I send you through this messenger of yours some verses I once composed in that very famous cave [near Marseille] where, as they say, that blessed sinner, Mary Magdalen, did her penance for thirty years or more. It so happened that I went there with that man who had much more luck than wisdom [Umberto Delfini]. After resisting for a long time, I was finally overcome and dragged off not so much by his appeals as by those of Giovanni Cardinal Colonna of sacred memory, to whom I could refuse nothing. Thus, in that holy but dreadful cave I lived three days and three nights without respite, and often I would wander through the forest; and, not much charmed by the company that I was with, I turned to my usual solace which I have improvised for myself to drive away boredom, namely, feigning in my mind the presence of absent friends, and turning my thoughts from those who are present to converse with those who are absent. As I was going about it, you were the first there with me; at that time, my acquaintance with you, a minor bishop, but always a great gentleman, was recent. Thus, when we sat down on one side of the cave, I fancied you urging me to say something brief in honor of that most holy lady. I obeyed you all the more readily because, just as the minds of pious men are inclined toward every devotion but more so to a particular one, I had already realized that you had picked her out among the sainted women, like Martin among the sainted men.

I did it extemporaneously and rapidy, as one who could brook no delay in any matter then because of my enthusiasm and youthful daring, as Maro says. For, in case you have forgotten—since we gladly forget the disgusting and worrisome things that depress us—it is now thirty-four years since this was done (see if that is long enough for us to have grown old!), a whole decade before I dedicated my book De uita solitaria to you while residing in your country home. Upon my return, I read to you these unrevised verses which had been written in your name and mine, inasmuch as I had composed

* See VI, 5.

them with you as an imaginary witness and prompter; after that I threw them on the mounds of my writing, and did not think of them any more. Now you are requesting them, and it was difficult to find them among my other writings, still more so to find them in my memory. For they had perished there, and I had totally forgotten that I had done anything of the kind; eventually, by means of the datings that I habitually use in filing them away, with toil and dust I found them, and they now come to you as they were, half mangled and dirty; nor am I changing anything in them, although I could change much, so that you may see not what I am but what I was, and so with a certain delight you may recall the first essays of our youth.

Dear friend of God, look kindly on our tears,
And heed our humble prayers; for our salvation
Take thought. Indeed thou canst; for not in vain
Wast thou allowed to touch and bathe His holy
Feet with thy weeping and to wipe them dry
With thy sleek tresses and to kiss His soles,
And on thy Lord's head sprinkle precious scents.
Nor vainly when He rose up from the dead
Met He thee first: Christ, King of heavenly
Olympus, vouchsafed thee to hear His voice
And see His limbs; so shalt thou ever have
Undying glory and eternal light.
He had seen thee cling to His cross without
Shrinking from dire torments at Jewish hands,
And taunts and insults of the furious crowd,
Their tongues as cruel as strokes of the whip.
But thou, grieved and at the same time intrepid,
Didst pass thy fingers o'er the gory spikes,
Thy tears soaking His wounds, thy savage fists
Beating thy breast, and hands relentlessly
Tearing thine hair. This, I say, had He seen
While His stout-hearted men fled far and wide,
Driven by fear. Remembering this, therefore,
He came back first to thee, ere any other,
To thee alone presented first Himself.
And then, on leaving earth and to the stars
Returning, He fed thee for thirty years
Beneath this cliff, ne'er needing mortal food

For such a long time, since thou wast content
With naught but God-sent feasts and wholesome dew.
This cave thine home, damp from the dripping rocks,
Gloomy with frightful slime, had yet surpassed
The golden roofs of kings and every comfort
And opulent lands. Here willingly shut in,
Clad in thy long hair, reft of other garb,
'Tis said thou didst endure thrice ten Decembers,
Not broken by the frost nor whelmed with dread,
Since hunger, cold, and the hard bed of stone
Were sweetened by the love and hope implanted
Deep in thy breast. Here, to the eyes of men
Unseen, surrounded by angelic hosts,
From thy bodily prison wast thou worthy,
For seven hours of the day upward borne,
To hear responsive hymns of heavenly choirs.

Live on and be well; remember me.

[1369-72].

Supreme Pontiff [Gregory XI], who made me his by his high esteem and his kind words and letters—although by universal duty everyone is his who is Christ's. Nevertheless, I replied to your request then not what I wished but what I could: that I had no books of Cicero other than the ones in general circulation and those which our lord himself has—and not even all of those, I think. I added one thing, and it was really true, that I had owned others but had lost them, a matter requiring a long explanation that I shortened for lack of time. You say that letter did not reach you, and you ask me to repeat what I wrote, not only so that you may know, but so that you may enjoy my letter, things which, I hope, your love and generous esteem force you to say. I shall obey; and although for a busy and feeble old age writing is not only hard work, as you say, but a punishment, still I shall write. You decide on the pleasure it gives you, I am talking about the weariness. Certainly, if I follow my intention, today I shall be wearying you.

This then is the situation. From early childhood, when everyone else was poring over Prosperus or Aesop, I brooded over Cicero's books, whether through natural instinct or the urgings of my father, a great admirer of that author, who would easily have risen high had not concern for the family distracted his noble mind and forced him, an exile burdened with a family, to turn to other business. At that age of course I could understand nothing; only a certain sweetness and tunefulness of the words so held me that anything else I either read or heard seemed to me coarse and extremely unmusical. On this, I confess, a child's judgment was not childish, if what is not based on any reason ought to be called reason. But it was marvelous that, while I understood nothing, I felt what I feel so much later, now that I understand something, however little. Daily my longing grew, and my father's admiration and devotion encouraged my immature propensity for a time; and in this alone I was not lazy. When I had scarcely broken the shell, I relished the kernel's sweetness, and I never let anything that happened interfere, being prepared willingly to deprive myself of every indulgence in order to collect books by Cicero from all over. Thus, without the need for any external prodding, I continued in this study until greed got the better of spunk and shoved me toward the study of civil law so that, God willing, I might learn what was the law of borrowing and lending, wills and codicils, rural and urban real estate, and forget Cicero, who describes the most wholesome laws that are most salutary for life.

A full seven years I spent in that study; it would be more truthful

Sen. XVI, 1.

To Luca da Penna, Papal Secretary, * *on Cicero's books.*

Honored gentleman, you will forgive my style for perhaps appea
ing disrespectful to some people, but I call God to witness that it
not in the least, for I know not how to use any other style. I spea
to you in the singular since you are one person, and in this I follo
nature and ancestral custom, not modern flattery; and I am su
prised that a man such as you speaks to me in any other way sin
I too am one person—I wish I were a whole one and not split in
many shreds of vices. Furthermore, this is how I ordinarily addre
the Roman Emperor and other kings, as well as Roman Pontiffs;
I did otherwise I would seem to myself to be lying. But why n
when we do not speak otherwise to Jesus Christ Himself, the Ki
of kings, and the Lord of lords, not to mention many others
much lesser rank, though very great? And to do now what I or
did with an old friend, I shall boast to my new friend that I thin
am not the originator, of course, but the restorer of this st
throughout Italy. When I began to use it in my teens, I was laugl
at by my contemporaries, who later vied with one another to fol
me in this very thing.**

Now I can begin. Your most recent letter spent many days
route, inasmuch as it was sent from the left bank of the Rhone
February 5, and quite late on March 23, at dusk, it reached
Euganean Hills, by the inmost recess of the Adriatic Sea, where,
and infirm, I lead the solitary life I have enjoyed since youth, lo
the country, hating the cities. You had asked me to help you, a
certain work you have lately begun, with some books of Cicerd
had any unusual ones, any from abroad—of course at your exp
to make the request fairer. You hoped, I suppose, and justly, t
would not be intractable to a sincere request, even from one
had never met me, whether out of respect for your reputation w
reaches far and wide, or especially out of the reverence owed to
at whose command you had taken on that work, our lord

---

* Papal secretary and expert in jurisprudence, he often served as legal ad\
the Pope. This is the only letter in the collection to him.

** P went back to the classical Latin rule of using the singular *tu* to any
spondent regardless of rank. This was contrary to the medieval custom of us
to a superior or through courtesy to an equal.

to say I wasted them! And to tell you something that will practically make you laugh and cry, it once happened to me that—for God knows what purpose, hardly a noble one—all of Cicero's works that I had been able to acquire, along with those of several poets, as though enemies of lucrative studies, were pulled in my presence from the hiding places where I had put them, fearing what did soon happen; and they were cast on the flames like heretical books, a sight at which I groaned just as if I myself had been tossed on the same fire. I recall that my father, seeing me so sad, thereupon quickly grabbed two books, already nearly burned by the fire, and, holding a Virgil in his right hand and Cicero's *Rhetoric* in his left, handed both to me, and smiled at my tears. "Take this one," he said, "as an occasional recreation for your spirit, and this one as a prop for your law studies." Comforting my heart with so few companions, but such great ones, I dried my tears. Later, on the threshold of adulthood, when I came of age and renounced the law books, I returned to my old studies all the more fervently because an interrupted pleasure comes back all the keener.

Not long after, when I was about twenty-two, I became an intimate of the Colonna lords, a very noble but, alas, doomed family, which to me will always be venerable and pitiable; under them I spent almost all of my young manhood and my verdant years; my mentor was that incomparable gentleman, Giacomo Colonna, then Bishop of Lombez, whose remembrance is equally sweet and bitter for me. The world was not worthy of him; Christ wanted him for Himself and quickly carried him off from earth and gave him back to heaven. And since an old man has pestered an old man to write this, an old man will pester an old man to read it. Well, then, he had seen me in Bologna long before, when I was scarcely more than a boy; and as he would say afterward, he had been charmed by my appearance, without knowing yet who I was or where from, except that he recognized a student from a student's gown; for he continued at that university, which I quit—as you have heard—until he graduated with honors, and soon advanced into an episcopate due not to his years but to his merits. For this reason, after setting out for what is called the Roman Curia, he saw me again there, destined as I was to that accursed prison. I barely had a stubble on my cheeks; and after checking into my circumstances more thoroughly, at last he summoned me to his presence. Nothing, I believe, was ever sweeter and more delightful than that, no one more dignified, livelier, wiser, better than that gentleman, no one more modest in prosperity or braver and more contant in adversity.

I speak not of things heard, but of things seen with my own eyes; already he had no peer in eloquence; he held men's hearts in his hands, whether addressing the clergy or the people. Wherever it suited him to speak, he would sway the minds of his audience. Already in his letters and in his daily conversations he was so clear that, whether you read him or heard him, you would look into his heart and need no one to explain what he said, so closely did his words match his thoughts. His love for his family was without equal, his liberality toward his friends untiring, his sympathy for the poor inexhaustible, his friendliness toward all constant; this was so great a man that, to use Flaccus's words, "he was a man down to his toe-nails" [Serm. 1.5.32–33]. His majesty of countenance and character was such that, just seeing him in a crown, you would rank him a prince. When he had seen me only twice, he held me fast in the grip of his brilliant conversation, so that he alone dwelt in the very citadel of my mind—which he has never left since, nor ever will. By chance he was then about to leave for his diocese in Gascony and did not realize—I think—how enthralled I was by him; he begged of me what he could have bidden, that I accompny him on that journey. Whether he was pleased by my loyalty (which however he could not yet know but which that keen-eyed man read on my brow) or by my talent or my style in the vernacular, which engrossed me in the flush of youth, I obeyed him and went along.

O how time flies, O fleeting life! Forty-four years have passed since then; never, I believe, was a summer happier. Upon his return he made me an intimate of his most reverend brother, Giovanni, a very worthy and upright gentleman, beyond the wont of cardinals and of all his brothers, and finally of the grand old man, his father Stefano, about whom, as Crispus says of Carthage, "I think it better to say nothing than to say too little" [Jug. 19.2]. Please indulge me just in this, if in my self-absorption I bore you while humoring myself, for it has been bitter-sweet for me to recall to mind Giacomo Colonna by speaking of him, my first lord and greatest glory of my youth. As I have said, never will he leave my memory who, alas all too soon, dashed my hopes and those of all his friends, not to mention his father's and brothers' who all perished at almost the same time. This is exactly the thirty-third year since his death, as Cato says of Africanus in Tully's book; but if either my pen had any power or men's reputations followed their deserts, I would confidently say what he says in that same place: "All the years to come will carry on that man's memory" [Sen. 19]. But I have reopened my wounds and my pains enough.

Now I return to Cicero. Thus, being known for some sort of reputation, however false, as a man of genius, but much more for the favor of such eminent lords, I had formed various friendships here and there, because I was in a place where people assembled from every part of the world. When these friends would at length depart, and, as it happens, ask me whether I wanted anything from their country, I would reply "nothing besides books, Cicero's above all." I would give them lists; I kept after them in writing and through messengers. You have no idea how often I begged them and how often I sent money, not only throughout Italy, where I was better known, but throughout Gaul and Germany, and even to Spain and Britain; you will be surprised to hear that I even sent to Greece; I was expecting Cicero, but got Homer. He came to me in Greek, but was put into Latin through my procurement and at my expense, and now he lives happily with me among the Latins. What do you expect?

> Effort overcomes everything,
> Unabashed,

says Maro [*G*. 1.145–46]. With much concentration and pains I again collected many little volumes from everywhere, but often they were duplicates, rarely any of those I wanted the most, so that, as often happens in human experience, I lacked many, but I had more than enough of many. I had of course not yet touched the holy books, being blinded by error and puffed up with the stamp of youth. I had, in effect, no taste for anything but Cicero, especially after I read Quintilian's *Oratorical Institutions*, where his point in a certain passage is plainly this—the book is not here, and I forget the words—that whoever really likes Cicero should have good hopes for himself; he says this in that book where he treats of eloquence and orators, and with untrammeled judgment condemns the style of that great man, Annaeus Seneca, who was then universally popular. I was confirmed more and more in my opinion by these words of so great a guarantor that whenever, in my desire to travel (which I would often do at that time), I set off for faraway places, if I happened to see a monastery in the distance, I would immediately turn aside and say, "Who knows if there is something I want here?"

When I was about twenty-five, I was hurrying through Belgium and Switzerland; but when I reached Liège, hearing that there was a good supply of books, I stopped and kept my companions waiting until I could copy one of Cicero's orations by a friend's hand, and another by my own, which I circulated afterward throughout Italy. To make you laugh, in that fine uncivilized town it was a real chore to find ink, and at that nearly the color of saffron. By that time, despairing of the books of the *Republic,* I eagerly sought the book *On Consolation,* but did not find it. I looked for the book *In Praise of Philosophy,* because its very title excited me, and also because in Augustine's books, which I had begun to read by then, I had found that the book had greatly helped him to change his life and seek the truth; thus, on every count it seemed worthy of a most diligent search. To be sure, I believed it would be no trouble, for it was on hand right away—not the book but a false frontispiece of the actual book; this I tell you from experience lest sometime the same mistake that fooled me deceive you—although I imagine that would be impossible. I kept reading and finding nothing that was promised by the title, and I was shocked and ascribed someone else's error to my own stupidity. Later, while reading (nature has made me an insatiable reader), I came across Augustine's books *On the Trinity,* a divine work, and I found reference there to the book, not the one I had, but the one I thought I had; and he took from that book something I find most delightful. I was dumbstruck; and, figuring it was an opportunity for me to check through it, feverishly, most intently I read the whole book on a certain day. Of course, I found nothing at all of what Augustine had quoted, and ashamed to have been so long in error, I concluded that the book was not *In Praise of Philosophy,* but was uncertain of what it was. The style was a sign that it was Cicero's, for the eloquence of that divine writer is inimitable. After this, on my last visit to Naples, my fine friend Barbato da Sulmona (whom perhaps you know at least by name), being aware of my wish, gave me a little book of Cicero's, at the end of which was only the beginning of his book, the *Academics,* which I read through; and, comparing it with the one entitled *In Praise of Philosophy,* I discovered, plain as day, that the latter was two books—for that is how many there are—the third and fourth, or the second and third, of the *Academics,* a work that is more subtle than it is practical or useful. Thus, I was freed from a long-continuing error.

Long before I had chanced to know a certain venerable old man whose name, I imagine, is still remembered in the Curia, Raimondo Superano, to whom I addressed a youthful letter these forty years ago which still exists. He had the richest collection of books; and, as a jurist, in which profession he was eminent, he looked down upon everything else except Livy in whom he took amazing delight; but his intellect, however great, was unaccustomed to history and would come to a standstill. Finding me useful to him in that study, as he used to say, he embraced me with so much love that you would have thought him my father rather than my friend. He proved generous to me beyond ordinary measure, both in lending and in giving books; I received from him some by Varro and by Cicero. One volume of Cicero contained the usual works, but along with those very ones were the books *On the Orator* and *On the Laws*—incomplete, as they almost always appear, and, in addition, two rare books *On Glory*, which made me feel very rich by just seeing them. It would take a long time to go through the ones I went after and how and where, except for one most elegant volume whose equal would be hard to find. It was found among my father's effects, and had been a favorite of his; it had escaped his executors' clutches, not because they wanted it to be safe with me, but because, intent on finding booty of greater value, as they thought, in the estate, they had overlooked it as something worthless. In all this there was nothing new, as I have said, aside from those two books *On Glory* and a number of orations and letters. But, not to struggle against fortune in vain, I, like a thirsty traveler at a mere trickle of a brook, cheered up as best I could with the well-known works.

But am I not the odd one, and do I not give you cause to wonder, since I have been asked for one story and am telling another? You asked me to say how I lost some books; I am saying how I acquired them, so that by knowing how toilsome it was to acquire them you may realize how painful it was to lose them. Now I shall dispatch with your question. Almost from infancy I had a teacher [Convenevole da Prato] who taught me my first letters; under him I later picked up grammar and rhetoric, for he was a professor and preceptor of both. I do not know his equal in the field of theory, but in practice, he was not quite like Horace's whetstone, which can sharpen iron but not cut it. He ran a school, according to reports, for a full sixty years, and how many pupils this famous man had in so long a time can be more easily imagined than stated. Among them were many men great in knowledge and rank—namely professors of law and teachers of sacred literature, and bishops and abbots besides, and finally one cardinal [Nicola da Prato], to whom I was dear as a boy because of his regard for my father; he was a man no greater for his rank and fortune—since he was Bishop of Ostia—than for his wisdom and culture. And that teacher, incredible to say, loved me—who was the least of all—above so many great ones, as was known to all. Nor did he himself try to hide it, wherefore Cardinal Giovanni Colonna of blessed memory, whom I mention above, any time he wanted to joke with him (for he enjoyed conversations with that very simple old man and excellent grammarian), used to question him thus as he came for a visit: "Tell me, professor, among all these great pupils of yours whom—as I know—you love, is there any place for our Francesco?" With tears instantly welling up, he would either say nothing or sometimes withdraw; or if he could speak, he would swear by all that is holy that he had never, out of them all, loved any one so much. As long as my father lived, he helped this poor fellow quite generously. For poverty and old age, those relentless, intractable companions, had pressed upon him; after my father's passing, he put all his hope in me. Although it was too much for me, I felt bound to him by loyalty and obedience, and stood by him with all the assistance I could; and when I lacked money, which was often, I would relieve his needs by resorting to my friends, at times with my guarantees, at times with my entreaties, and by pawning things with the moneylenders. A thousand times he carried off my books and other possessions for this purpose, and returned them, until poverty overcame honesty. At one point, pressed by an emergency, he pretended that for a certain work of his he needed those two volumes of Cicero, one my father's, the other my friend's, and other books; I handed them over, and he took them away. For every day he would start books with a wonderful title-page; and once the preface was finished, which is first in the book but usually composed last, he would shift his restless fancy to another work.

But why do I take all day to tell it to you? When the stalling began to seem suspicious, because the books had not been lent for relief of poverty but for study, I began to investigate more seriously what he had been done with them; and when I learned of the pawnbrokers, I asked him to tell me who had them so that I should have a chance to redeem them. Filled with shame and tears, he refused to do so because it would disgrace him if another were to do what he ought to be doing; I should wait a short while; he would soon do what was his responsibility. I offered him as much money as he wanted for the transaction, and he refused it, begging me not to brand him with such infamy. Although I had no confidence in his word, I said nothing, being unwilling to upset one whom I loved. Meanwhile, driven by poverty, he went to Tuscany, where he was born, while I, as usual, was in seclusion at the source of the Sorgue, in my transalpine solitude; I heard the news that he had moved on no sooner than that he had passed away. His fellow townsmen, who had crowned him with laurel belatedly at his funeral, begged me to compose some honorific inscription to his memory. Afterward, in spite of diligent searching, I was never able to find the slightest trace of the lost Cicero; for I would not have taken the trouble for the other books. So I lost both the books and the teacher at the same time. There you have the story you requested, a little too long, I admit, but it has been pleasant for me both to recall old friends, and to have a long talk with a new one, who, though unknown, is commended by his own letter and vouched for by a man whose word I would take for anything. But now I feel how fitting it would be to rewrite this letter because of the additions and erasures, but your courtesy will make allowance for my being busy and tired, and will look upon whatever offends your eyes as so many tokens of familiarity. Farewell.

Arquà, April 27 [1374].

Sen. XVI, 2.

To Francesco da Siena, physician,* the pledging of a new friendship.

Your unexpected letter, out of the blue, full of your sincere affection and praises of me (would that they were as true as they are friendly), reached me at a late hour when I was packed for a journey and about to leave on the morrow. The usual does not cause suffering, as you doctors say. Traveling is nothing new for me, but quite familiar and almost second nature; the present state of affairs, however, makes the journey questionable and worrisome. Yet I will go, drawn on the one side by love, and driven on the other by duty. In the midst of this, though tempted not to reply because I am so busy, your fervent desire for friendship has nonetheless won and prompted me to write you back this brief, makeshift reply, rather than nothing; perhaps I shall answer at greater length, if I happen to have a free day, which I can scarcely hope for. I should like to be what you, my friend, make me, but I am not; whatever I may be, I do not refuse to be yours, since that is what you want. I will say this for now, lest you complain of being slighted. Farewell.

Padua, March 22 [after 1362].

* A teacher of logic and philosophy at the University of Florence, and of medicine at Perugia, he became a famous physician. He served many popes, and wrote a number of medical treatises.

Sen. XVI, 3.

To the same person, * *about his own book,* De uita solitaria.

A letter from you just reached me. With perfect justification it was praised by a most upright judge of everything except where I am concerned, and it brought along the testimony of the one who praised it [Philippe de Cabassoles]. Yet it would perhaps have remained unanswered, were it not that, as Cicero says, you treat me to an authentic document; for you inserted one short letter I wrote many years ago in response to you [preceding letter]. This you presented like a promissory note at a trial, as though what I did once I must do always; but judge how fair it is. Here I am, beset on the one hand by endless duties that exceed my strength, and, on the other, by declining age which some people call a sickness in itself, and, by an army of other grave sicknesses. Perhaps I would have been excused, had I chosen the easy course of silence; but when I saw that letter of mine in the very heart of yours, I laughed to myself over the artful, friendly craftiness, and silently I said, "There is no way out; I must write, since I have written." Thus, with marvelous skill you are forcing me to write, though I am already tired not only of writing, but of living.

Indeed, to skip over many things, I have included in two quite large volumes four hundred or more letters, for the most part not brief but immense, which issued from me at various times to various persons, most of whom I did not even know, such as yourself. I rejected a thousand others for no other reason than that there was no room for them. I ask, had I never lost my mind over anything else, would it not be obvious enough—more than enough—that I had lost it, from this one thing? While I reply to everyone, I initiate certain correspondences myself; and I have wasted a large part of this brief life in this business, whereas I have put off, in the meantime, so many more useful things. And now, already old, I am doing what I wish I had done when I was younger; but I decided at long last to do the opposite, and I put it in writing. For although I have no hope for a respite from the labor of study until the end, still I am putting an end to this epistolary habit, lest it always keep me from better studies, since I see that replying to all who write me is an

---

* See XVI, 2.

endless task. I desire, if there is any way, to say farewell to my follies before they say it to me; and now I am at the end; after this, even if a letter comes, even if the Roman Emperor [Charles IV] writes me—which he often has done—I would not reply otherwise than in the vernacular. But your letter, coming before the end, although close to the deadline, has deserved not only a reply, but to be stored away with the rest. The same goes for the other one, which I had long since lost, and was saved by your care rather than my negligence. It will please me and perhaps not displease you to have your name appear at least twice among the greatest names in my cupboard.

Now at last I come to your letter. You write that you were charmed to the point of heartfelt tears by certain little things I wrote, namely the book *De uita solitaria*, particularly that part where I attributed a threefold solitude to that blessed Francis whose name we both bear. I am certain it was not the power of my pen that drew you in, but your love of that name; yet I am delighted either way. For while almost all men are bad judges of their own concerns because self-love slants their judgment and they like everything that is their own, I alone of all those I know am a bad judge for the opposite reason: everything of mine displeases me because I wish it to be so good that, however it is, it does not approach what I wanted. When I learn that it has been approved by the judgment of any intelligent man, I too begin to like and approve of my own work. You will not be surprised that this can happen to me when you recall that it happened to such a man as Augustine, who would glow if his book, *On the Beautiful and the Fitting*, were approved by the Roman orator Hierius, to whom he had addressed it; but if disapproved, it would be a blow to his heart. Read the fourth book of his *Confessions*: there you will find all this not far from the end. Certainly that book of mine, about which you speak, met with such approval from that man of brilliant intellect to whom it was dedicated [Philippe de Cabassoles], that rarely have I ever seen a clearer example of that saying that lovers' judgments are blind. So much so that even after he was promoted to Cardinal of Rome, he would have it read to him at table in the presence of great men, where as a rule nothing was read except from the Holy Scriptures. If, dear friend, it is approved by you, though dedicated to another, it is no less a joy for me, or rather all the more because there is less extrinsic cause for you to approve of it or like it. Others' judgments, of course, affect the writer's mind, especially when no suspicion of either flattery or hatred is involved; and for this reason real poets, as Cicero says, have wished each of their works to be considered by the public so that, if censured, it would be corrected by many. Therefore, I add, if anything is praised by those who know, let it be held in esteem. He says that painters and sculptors used to have this done too, as is written especially about Apelles, the prince of painters.

Now about this modest book you like, you ask some things which I confess are not altogether clear; I shall still reply as I can. You say, then, that I adorned my *De uita solitaria* with many true examples and arguments; I do not know whether it is so or you just think so. Still you ask how the ascent to such a life is made easy—I am using your words—when nature or fortune is against it. What shall I say here, except that whoever does not love this life, because nature stands in the way, should start loving it and wishing for it? Next you will ask me, how can that be done? I will say briefly what I feel. There is no better way than to appraise carefully and seriously the pleasures of this life and the miseries of the opposite one—which cannot be done, I confess, except by someone who has experienced both kinds. I said some things about this there, and those who are more learned can say much more. However, if fortune interferes with good will, and this—unless I am wrong—is the other part of your doubt, again what can I say here except what is known to everyone? In any event, whatever interposes itself between the will and action, such obstacles must be removed manfully, so that, once removed, you may easily reach your goal, although I am not unaware that there is a kind of obstacle that cannot be removed in any way, such as a wife first of all, which you mention in your letter—and I have said clearly enough in that book how I feel about this, unless my memory deceives me. I could indeed say more about this, but I have nothing else to say.

Before leaving this subject, I will add one thought. Though thankful that that book of mine has reached you, I wish everything of mine had reached you along with it; for you would have a rich and unending supply of things to refute. But I am not pleased that you copied the book; to tell you why, there recently came to Venice the Grand Prior of the Camaldolensians [Giovanni degli Abbarbagliati], a man of renowned faith and joyful old age, and long since my friend through correspondence. At the home of a very close friend of mine he found that book, which happened to be the first one I had commissioned; and, as happens, all the margins were so full of additions that when the old fellow read them and saw who had been added here and there to the first draft, with friendly resentment he said, "Why did the founder of our order, Romuald, so great a lover of solitude, deserve being excluded from this book?" To this my friend said, "I know no reason, except that perhaps the writer was not acquainted with him." In no time, the prior, eager to see me, came to these mountains and asked the same question, and had the same reply from me. That was the simple truth; and after his departure, he sent me the life of Romuald with many prayers, and from it I extracted what seemed pertinent to solitude, and added one chapter to the book. I also added that most holy man to my religious calendar to venerate always and—as long as I live—to observe his feast day as one of the confessors on the nineteenth of June. Another friend of mine, prompted by this news, began complaining that I had turned my back on a certain John [St. John Gualbert], founder of the Order of Vallombrosa and my compatriot. To him also I replied that this had happened not out of negligence or disdain but ignorance of the fact; and now I am most eagerly awaiting a biography of him. If there is anything in it relating to solitude, I shall insert him too. For holiness alone will not suffice. Otherwise the thing would go on and on if I were to embrace all the saints with my pen. I remember giving that answer at times to the Preachers, who complained that Francis was in the book but not Dominic, and asserted that in this part I was on shaky ground; I said, "And so it is: this book deals with the solitary ones, and I read that Dominic was indeed a holy man, I do not read that he was a solitary." Therefore, this Romuald and perhaps that John, about whom I am still in doubt, will have to be added; and I would prefer, if it is all right, that you put off copying it; but a scholar's spirit knows no restraint. However, it is a great hunger, no doubt, that drives one to crave coarse, unseasoned food.

Next you ask me whether I hold all doctors equally in loathing and contempt. I understand: you were prompted by one word at the end of that brief letter I recently wrote to your friend and my lord, Stefano Colonna, a true nobleman, where I said, "You are joking," and that I have never believed in doctors, and never will. Yet it is a concern not unworthy of a scholar to want to know how people feel about his profession, although in the judgment of many that is of no moment, or not much. At the end of your letter you wish that I would love medicine; and it is only right, since I love you, that I should love everything of yours, unless perhaps I knew that there is something harmful in it for you. I am not your friend if I feign anything; so I truly love medicine, which as a man I have always needed, and now as an old man I need the most; but I confess to hating the lies not of doctors but of those who want falsely to be called doctors.

As you say, you have read my *Invectives*, which I poured out against that terribly talkative magpie, the Pope's doctor, who with a few vaguely understood aphorisms thought he had heaven under his feet and was contemplating nature's secrets from there. Still, it was nothing to me; I would gladly have left him to his pride and ignorance, had he not first attacked me with a bitter insult, and impertinently at that. I had written nothing to him, but had in good faith warned the Roman Pontiff, Clement VI, who was then ill, to beware of doctors, not indeed all of them but many, and to take a hint from the dying man who ordered this inscription on his tomb. "A gang of doctors killed me." I warned him to appoint not two doctors, but only one, strong not in eloquence but in knowledge and loyalty; this incidentally will suffice for your second question. But later I learned from certain doctors that this was the very advice of the doctors; whether it is so, who knows better than you? But since the Pontiff's messenger, a good fellow but uneducated, conveyed my words to him confusedly, he immediately sent him back to me, bidding that what I had sent orally I should send back more definitely in writing. I obeyed as was my duty, and wrote that letter that has been the source of all the hard feelings. Struck out of a clear sky by the taunts of an unknown man, I confess I flared up; for I was much younger then and more hot-tempered than I would be today; still, being naturally bashful and shunning quarrels, I deemed it wiser to say nothing; and indeed I would have, if one of the princes of the Church, with whom I was very friendly, had not dissuaded me from silence, saying that insolent men would attribute it not to modesty but to ignorance. He placed a pen in my hand; once I got hold of it I could not refrain from exposing that slanderer to himself. But what need is there to say more? If, as you say, you read that essay, I believe you noticed that I said nothing against medicine, but everything against false doctors, of whom he was the leader.

For who could hate medicine except a lover of illness? It is indeed venerable and lovely—not only because the Most High created it, as you write—and all the doctors are much pleased with this idea, since it applies to all the sciences and arts, of which there is none the Most High did not create. Reread the beginning of that book where that passage is [Petrarch, *Contra medicum* 1.5]; there you will find it written, "All wisdom comes from the Lord God" [Ecclesiasticus 1:1]. Proceed from this to the seventh chapter of the book; and you will find expressly that country life—that is, agriculture—was created by the Most High; and, in short, whatever would be useful to man the Most High created, and for this reason I love medicine—

because it was useful to human life, unless someone made it useless. That, therefore, is what I love, and this is what I hate: those especially who contributed to this evil; may God spare them, or rather may He not spare those whose deadly recklessness has subverted so necessary and so pure an aid to fragile nature, and transformed a mute, as Virgil calls it—that is, a real—profession into a verbal catastrophe. Then, dressed in purple and adorned with gold, they believe themselves to have gained the power of life and death over everyone. How I wish they would fool themselves at their own risk, not everyone else's, so that they might examine more deeply the causes of things and not be so hasty with deadly remedies that hide in the shadows of a foreign name and bring old-fashioned death, wrapped up in a Greek cloak, to the gullible. I admit I hate lying, in any kind of men. For it is contrary to God who is truth; but there is none I hate more, since there is no greater danger in any lie, than this one, as Pliny says. I make one exception, that which deceives in regard to religion; for just as the former is deadly to the body, this is deadly to the spirit.

Someone might say, and you do, "But do you except no one from this discrediting of doctors?" By Jove, I would like to; for I know not how it is that from no other class have I always had so many friends and I have them to this day. But not to dissemble or hide anything, until now I have sought such exceptions in vain, and have found indeed many learned and eloquent men, but no doctors. I usually seek words from orators or poets, but from doctors only health and, to put it briefly, not professors of medicine but of healing; and if I find them, I shall not only love and honor them, but nearly worship them as bestowers of a divine gift. As you yourself admit, then, I have not disparaged the princes' doctors whom you mention, nor would I ever—I am not yet so mad—provided the fame that extols them be true, and I believe it is, although testimony from within the family is not exempt from suspicion. I disparage only those who promise us health and stuff us with syllogisms.

But enough now about the doctors; when I talk about them, usually it is to themselves much more than to others, and most of the time it ends up in a joke. Among others I have one who would rise to the stars, had medicine not held him down, so lofty and so capacious is his genius [Giovanni Dondi], and such a friend to me that I could scarcely be more of a friend to myself. Three years ago when I was down with a fever, since he could not come to me for good reasons, he visited me with a letter and advised me as to what I ought to do in that condition. I, whose hot blood has abated with the years but not congealed, knew what he would write me, for I have my fill of advice from doctors. So I took up my pen before I read the letter; and after reading it I at once replied heatedly, and the altercation was long but friendly: that is, not content with the first skirmishes, we struck again with long letters in a war of words; but finally when he realized my stubbornness, he quieted down. Among other things he tried to get me to abstain from fruit that grows on trees, drinking water, and fasting, although I, who know my nature, could not live three days without drinking water. I am not so ignorant of things, unless I am mistaken, that some measly Greek or Arab, who never saw me and was buried a thousand years before I was born, knows me better than I do; in Cicero's *De officiis* there is a certain passage relating to this. He says, "Good health is maintained by knowledge of one's own body, by observing what generally hurts or helps it, by moderation in diet, and by every attention to guard the body, foregoing pleasures." Still he adds one thing that seems contrary to this when he says, "Furthermore, with the skill of those to whose knowledge this pertains" [2.24.86]. Here I wrote in the margin in my own hand (this will divert you for a moment from arguing to laughing), "And where, I ask, are they?" Perhaps there were some then, and perhaps there are today, although I myself happen not to have seen them; or, if I have, I certainly do not know them.

But to come back to that friend of mine, after our long dispute we remained I in my way of thinking and he in his. He cannot bring me to his point of view, nor can I bring him to mine. He says I would have lived longer, had I obeyed the doctors; I say I would have died sooner. For I am of a most delicate constituion that slips quickly into sicknesses and then barely comes out of it. Warned by experience, I trust in my nature more surely than in the advice of those who are called doctors. Yet I have now lived long enough already, and what little remains is uncertain. These are our daily disagreements, but his modesty yields to my persistence; and he has taken to coming here as a friend, not as a doctor, since he is unbelievably charmed by my conversations and writings of whatever sort. Still, speaking with him and with others, it so happens that I have received many words of advice from doctors, but I believe nothing; for I find nothing effective, and this was what I briefly said that caused you so much astonishment. But that is the way it is; I do not believe in words but in results which do not lie. Before a doctor crosses my threshold I know in part what advice he brings. "Eat newly hatched chicken, drink boiled water that is still warm, use that filthy remedy that doctors have learned from a shore bird," and so forth. But I have lived until this day with my one counsel from God, and shall live with it until the end; and when I have paid my debt to nature, I shall, with God's help, be safe and sound. These many things are about the profession generally; as for you, dear friend, I have nothing definite to say. I see a talented and discreet man, but I certainly do not see what kind of doctor you are; I could, if you were closer, for right now I very much need a sound doctor for my illness. But since you have taken this path, if you believe me at all, try to be not one of those who argue, but one of those who cure—if there are any.

Although we have said much, I think there is still one point in a part of your letter that I must not overlook. You wish, if you could, to share the years of your life with me so that what would be subtracted from yours would be added to mine; and you make God the witness of your secret vow. A sizable kindness indeed for a new friend, but brash confidence for one who cannot be sure of a day to want to give away years, even though it were offered by a mere boy to Nestor or to Methuselah himself, the longest-lived of men. We all die, and there is no sure measure of life or order of dying; every day young people get there ahead of the decrepit. Yet, true love compels you to say such things. So I believe it and I thank you, and from this especially I feel that I am dear to you before you know me. Therefore, may your years, dear friend, be happy and joyful; but mine, which I never wished to be very many, I begin now to wish would be few; for, to use the words of the patriarch Jacob, "Few and evil are the days of my pilgrimage" [Gen. 47:9], and when I observe the ways of our age, I hope for nothing better in the future. And, as the Satirist says, "Now every vice stands on the brink" [1.149]. Farewell.

Arquà, May 1 [1370-72].

Sen. XVI, 4.

To Philippe [de Cabassoles], Cardinal Bishop of Sabina, *on bearing the absence of friends with resignation; what is not seen with the eyes is loved nonetheless.*

I hoped for what I wished (for hope and desire generally go together): I hoped to be with you during this part of the year, both to satisfy you who often invite me, and myself who always wish to be. I had raised both your hopes and mine, but, as you see, they have failed both of us. I assure you in good faith that I have never failed you, nor am I about to now; I have tried everything in good faith, I say, but nothing has succeeded. I wanted to see whether I could go at least one mile on horseback, but I never could; and so great was my ardor that, if I could have done that, I felt confident that everything else would go well. Death has thus stripped me of my friends; what she did not do, absence fills in for her. Bear patiently, Father, to be counted among my friends; although the disparity of virtue and rank seems to disqualify you from this number, and you are for me certainly something more than a friend, yet if a friend is one who loves and is loved as long as this love is for the sake of the one loved and nothing else, you are beyond any doubt a friend; for I am no less sure of your feelings than of mine. And I know that you will not take it amiss that I be called your friend when you hear that Augustus Caesar not only allowed, but wished and urged, that Horace Flaccus, who was not only of humble origin but a freedman, be called his friend. More than that you will loftily reject the insolence of cardinals who are seized with oblivion about their mortality because of a thin crimson cloth. They are not only mortal, but in a certain way on the verge of death. Unless I do not know you after all the time you have been with me, you not only are not arrogant because of this rag, but would not be no matter what purple or crown you might have; indeed, as I know you through and through, you have become more humble and feel that all that has increased for you are the worries, and every day from your present grandeur you sigh for your ordinary life of long ago and our quiet hideaways and leisure, when we would go alone for days on end in the woods, when the servants, searching for us at lunch-time, would

---

* See VI, 5.

barely find us in the evening, forgetful of food and astonished that the day had passed so quickly.

I will not mention how great and sincere was our delight in each other's conversation, when we would speak of nothing but our salvation or literature and the memory of famous events, with all lands and all ages before our eyes at the same time, contented beyond belief with our lot and celebrating with special praises those who scorned fleeting things. Among them was Giacomo Colonna, at that time young in years, but already old in firmness of character and nearness to death; free from all ambition, he attained to the episcopate at the Pope's bidding, unaware of what was happening, not to say against his will; from there he was promoted to the patriarchate of Aquileia with the full consent and urging of the nobles and the entire population. From Rome where he was then, he wrote to his brother and to his close friends, to me among others, swearing that he had risen higher than he wanted and would not rise any further; and not much later he rose to his heavenly dignity with Christ beckoning.

That, I said, and everything of the sort, I shall leave unspoken. Answer me this, even without words. How much sweeter did the murmur of the Sorgue and the song of the birds sound then in your ears than the shouting of litigants now who make our consistories resound with hellish bellowing! Yet this is where your lot has raised you, and the foresight of that Holy Father made you known to his predecessors. They did not know you while you were so happily out of sight, but they considered the good of the Church, not yours, except that your great and pious labor, especially amidst so many impious ones, will not fail to be rewarded. Having said this first, and being in no doubt whatever about your equanimity and regard for a long friendship, however unequal, I turn to what I started to write.

May He, who brings happiness with His love, so love me that there is hardly any joy for me as great as from remembering my faithful friends, you before others; I wish I could say from conversing with you, but that is a rarer occasion. For we are so separated by too harsh a fate that you must read me more often than hear or look at me. We must make the best of our lot, and not embitter the absence with complaints nor provoke regret with impatience. It has often been said, and must be said more often, that if we were to love nothing but what we see with our eyes, no one would love God, nor his soul, nor himself except in the mirror; but I, both in my friends and in myself, love more what I do not see. And even in passing the time together, which restores me tremendously, I concentrate not so much on the faces and countenances of those present as on the inner beauty, the soul's face and features, and I know that what first in any of you strikes my eyes is not the friend but the friend's dwelling-place; for each one's spirit is himself, and not that shape that can be pointed to with a finger, as Cicero elegantly says. When Anaxarchus was in anguish, he thought about this and said to his executioner, "You are striking Anaxarchus's wrapper" [Tert., *Apol.* 50.6]; indeed he was striking the wrapper where Anaxarchus was hidden and breathing; he could not strike the philosopher out of reach in the citadel of reason and armed with patience. That thought allows me, however distant your dwelling-places, always to have you [all] present, while my spirit always is with you, and to trust that yours are with me. And not only those who are far away, but also those who are utterly gone and have now turned into a few ashes; you are here, they are alive. Thus does love ease the entire loss due to absence and death, and I see them all, whether dead or absent, and you among the first: and although I cannot come to you, I am with you, though fortune be adverse and hostile. I am not unaware too that the utmost sweetness and inestimable pleasure is in the voice itself and the gleam of the eyes, through which the friend who lives within is somehow viewed as through wide-open windows.

I perhaps seem to have used this word "pleasure" too often. However disgraced the word may be in the multitude's judgment, nevertheless, in the judgment of the more learned it can be used either way. For this we have the most eminent authorities, Cicero and Seneca, who condemn Epicurean pleasure but often attribute the very word pleasure to honorable delight, and Maro, where, embracing every kind in a general statement, he says, "Everyone is pulled by his own pleasure" [*Ecl.* 2.65]; he has a king speaking to his son as a father whose love is the greatest and purest on earth, say,

> As long as I hold you in my embrace,
> Dear boy, my last, my only pleasure. [*Aen.* 8.582–83]

But if the authority of three such witnesses does not erase the bad connotation of one word, let a fourth, too great for anyone to take exception to, come forth; not only his pleasure but even his drunkenness is sober and holy. For did not that ethereal musician, David, in singing a song of gratitude to God, after saying, "The children of men will place their hope in the shadow of your wings," immediately add, "They shall be drunk from the abundance of your house, and you will give them to drink from the flood of your pleasure" [Ps. 36:8–9]. I believe that now nothing more is required to excuse that reviled word.

You be well and rest assured that, after God and virtue, which up to now I have not so much enjoyed as yearned to enjoy, the next pleasure for me is in faithful and pure friendships.

Arquà, May 5 [1372].

Sen. XVI, 5.

To Charles IV, Roman Emperor,* concerning the falsity of the charter removing Austria from the Empire.

A lie is lame anywhere; it is easily caught, it can hardly escape the judgment of a sharp, quick mind. See how an idle, inflated document, devoid of truth, is brought forward by God knows who, doubtless no scholar or man of letters, but a tiro, a clumsy schoolteacher, prone to lying anyhow, but lacking the skill to make up a lie; if he had it, he would never have poured out such silly absurdities. Impostors of this kind like to season the false with some semblance of truth, so that what never was, because it resembles things that have been, could be believed to have been. Supposing this man believed that Roman authority and the majesty of the empire, founded and guarded by arms, laws, and virtue, could be subverted with his nonsense, which was utter madness, he at least ought to have produced artful nonsense and a prepossessing lie, which would not give itself away immediately even to bleary eyes. About that fabrication, O Caesar, I have no doubt that the whole act of that rascal was altogether manifest at once to you and to your courtiers, the wisest and most learned men, and to your chancellor among the first, who is all eyes, like a lynx. Yet because you bid me tell you what I think about this too, I obey and say what comes at the moment to my busy mind, which has been pressed and obsessed with far different cares. I consider it no slight token of your kindness that you wanted me to be in on such a great secret, and reckoned me fit to expose this fraud.

I leave out the point, however, that an equal has no power over an equal; Julius Caesar or Nero did decree not anything that you cannot by your own right decree the opposite. That threefold villain did not see this when with ridiculous cunning he invented those two authors of a most unworthy deed of independence, as though no one could rescind what the best one had done and the worst had confirmed. But I leave this part of the case to your legal advisers, or

---

* Charles of Bohemia was not officially crowned emperor until 1355, although he had been proclaimed king of the Romans in Avignon in 1346 upon his father's abdication. He was proclaimed king of Italy in Milan and emperor in Rome in 1355. Even before meeting him personally in 1354, P. had directed two appeals to him to cross into Italy. Despite its position here, this letter belongs among the thirteen addressed to the emperor in the *Familiares*.

rather to you, in whose innermost heart (as a boy I would hear this in law school) are all the laws. I come to what you are waiting for.

It says, "We, Julius Caesar, emperor, we, Caesar and worshipper of the gods, we, supreme Augustus of the imperial land," and the rest. Who anywhere is so stupid and ignorant of history as not to see already, even if blindfolded, that there are almost as many lies in this as words? For although

> all the terms we've used these many years
> To lie to our lords, that age first discovered,

as Lucan says [5.385–86], it still did not invent those words through which the lords lie to us. So, although Caesar's friends, flattering his greatness, began speaking to Caesar in the plural, which had not been done to any other before him (the custom later moved down from the emperors into the general public), still one finds that he never used to speak about himself, even with his soldiers, except in the singular. That ox did not know this; for if he had, he would have bellowed more cautiously. I own several friendly letters of Julius Caesar himself, the man in question; his many speeches in Lucan and other authors, and one in Sallust, could be said to have been dictated not by his taste but by the writers'.

He did, however, dictate the letters from which I have extracted a few passages as examples. "Caesar to Oppius and Cornelius, greetings. I am delighted, so help me Hercules, that you indicated in your letter how thoroughly you approve what was done at Corfinium. I shall gladly use your advice, and the more so because I had decided of my own accord to make sure of behaving as gently as possible" [Cic., *Att.* 9.7c]. And again: "Caesar to Oppius and Cornelius, greetings. On the ninth of March I came to Brundisium, I pitched camp by the wall. Pompey is in Brundisium; he sent Gnaeus Magnus to talk peace; I replied what I thought best; I wanted you to know this at once. When I see hope that there is some chance of a reconciliation, I shall inform you at once" [ibid., 9.13a]. Likewise, writing to Cicero, he says, "Although I judged that you fear nothing and would do nothing imprudent, nevertheless, dismayed by the rumors, I thought I should write you" [ibid., 10.8b], and so on. There exists a letter of his or a privilege, about an important matter, addressed not to individual friends but to the Sidonian nation, which runs as follows: "Gaius Julius Caesar, emperor and pontifex, and dictator for the second time, to the magistrates, the senate and people of Sidon, greetings. If you are well, fine; I too, along with my army, am well. I have addressed to you a copy of the decree of Hyrcanus, son of Alexander, the high priest and governor of the Jewish nation, so that it may be placed in your public records. I want to exhibit this, inscribed in Greek and Latin, on a bronze tablet," and immediately after, "Since I have decreed after due deliberation;" and later, "that for these reasons Hyrcanus, son of Alexander, and his sons be governors of the Jewish nation, and forever have the high priesthood of the Jewish nation according to their ancestral customs, and I decree that he himself and his sons be reckoned among those who stand by us, and among the men most friendly to us, and that he and his sons enjoy all priestly rights whatsoever," and the rest. You will find this letter, if you search, in the third book of Josephus,* a most dependable author of histories. I could press the point even more, but you see his style.

For who does not see that it is not only false but ridiculous that this Julius Caesar should call himself Augustus? I thought indeed that to all children who had so much as touched the threshold of a school, it was known that this name began with his successor. Read the history of Annaeus Florus, of Suetonius Tranquillus, of Orosius, of Eutropius, in short, any history. None was unaware of this, except this jackass now braying so rudely.

Moreover, what follows about some invented uncle or other is utterly amazing. Why should Julius Caesar's uncle thus be known only in that little document, but never read about or heard of anywhere else, especially since Caesar's own father was known to no one or to very few, which would astonish me except that I like to imagine that Caesar's glory and the splendor of his name was so great that he, just like the sun, overshone the stars around him? But I know not whence this uncle now reappears, or where he has been hiding for so many centuries, or for what crime he was deported to the ends of the earth. I am especially astonished that an unnamed witness comes to court, and that on such an important matter credibility is based upon one who lacks not only credit but even a name. More and more, the nullity of the thing is revealed, a privilege brought forward without the name of the person to whom it was allegedly granted, whereas privileges, if I recollect from my childhood, go by the letter of the law. Many things are there, then, which weaken and invalidate it; let your legal counselors see to this detail also.

---

* P. was evidently quoting from an abridged Latin version of Josephus, who had included the document in *Jewish Antiquities* 14.2 (190–94).

Unless perhaps you would call more serious the name of the "eastern area that is commonly called Austria," although austral and eastern are different things; but I would say that those names were variously given according to the location of the neighboring regions. Whether you look at the earth as a whole or the city of Rome, whence it is claimed this document emanated whereby that area was removed from the empire, the region is neither eastern nor austral, but northern.

What about the document's date, which is most obviously false? There neither a particular day is written, nor the consul's name; who except a madman would say, "Given in Rome on Friday, in the first year of our reign," and not add which day of which month? What shepherd or what plowman would write thus, let alone the great man who, besides the other works of his genius in which he was no less masterly than he was in ruling, is known to have discovered the most exact calculation of a full year?*

The words, "of our kingship," are so far from the truth that they arouse not only laughter but gall and upset the stomach. For Caesar, as you have heard, wanted to be called emperor, pontifex, and dictator—never king. We read of seven kings of Rome in the early age of the city; if any after them wanted to rule as king, they were either killed by the sword or thrown headlong from the Capitoline rock. I admit the suspicion of aspiring to be king directed against Caesar as the greatest insult by none other than his enemies. Therefore, could that man, so eager for glory and so rich in prudence, include among his titles something that brings infamy upon him? He certainly would no more call himself king or want to be so called than to be called buffoon, adulterer, pimp, or rather he would much less want to be called king; for all those are ugly and filthy, but "king" was too hateful, dangerous, and unbearable in Rome. Do you want proof of this? When the peoples of Spain offered to make Scipio Africanus king because of his greatest and most glorious achievements, out of admiration for his excellence, what then did he reply? I record the very words of Titus Livy: "He had the herald hush the crowd, and said that for him the greatest name was that of commander with which his soldiers had hailed him; the title of king, great elsewhere, was intolerable in Rome" [27.19]. Therefore, when Lucan says, "Caesar was everything" [*Phar.* 3.108], understand it to mean that upon him alone were heaped all the dignities and honors

* Namely, that the true length of a solar year is 365 1/4 days.

which were then in Rome, where without a doubt there was no king. Far be it for him to make any mention of a kingship, which he would curse and completely reject when made by his rivals. Let all this be in reply to the fable of Julius Caesar by that clumsy, silly fabricator of lies.

A good part of this applies to the hoax about Nero, which ends with the words, "given on the day of that great god Mars" [Tuesday]. O mad and shameless fellow, what if someone produced a contrary letter whose date was the day of Luna [Monday] or of Mercury [Wednesday]—which shall we call the first or which the last? Who can bear this wanton lying, or this madness? But you, O Caesar, ought to laugh and rejoice because your rebels crave more than they can handle, and want to reduce your empire and declare themselves free through a lie, but do not know how. For if that fellow knew how to lie, he would never have begun thus, "We, Nero, friend of the gods;" he would have read that Nero scoffed at all the gods. Speaking of this, Suetonius Tranquillus says in his sixth book on the Caesars, "A scoffer of all religion altogether except for the Syrian goddess, he soon came so to scoff at her that he defiled her with urine" [*Nero* 56].

These, O August Emperor, are the thoughts that occurred to me for the present without great study—quite apart from the style of both letters, which is all, from beginning to end, rough and recent. Just as it was fabricated there [in Austria], so it looks as if made there the other day by some scruffy drudge. Even if a notion of antiquity, striven for childishly, stands out in individual words, there is instead a far-fetched air of falseness, which like an unsightly erasure can almost be made out by the blind. It is all so far from what it wishes to appear—namely, from antiquity and the style of Caesar—that perhaps a credulous old woman or a hillbilly, but certainly not an intelligent man, could be deceived. But your letter which you sent me was dictated by hatred for those people, and proves to me that you are a great orator. I rejoice; it is fitting for Caesar to be as praised for his tongue and intellect as for his wars and his justice. Be well, Caesar, remember me and your empire, and live so that your people shall not want to lie to you, and your enemies fear to do so.

Milan, March 21, in haste [1361].

Sen. XVI, 6.

To Donino, grammarian of Piacenza,* that there is cause for greater hope when one's opinion of one's own knowledge is lower.

I cannot offer you a more dependable remedy than what I found effective for myself in a like illness. When I was in my early teens, there was an old countryman of mine, a man of venerable gray hair and notable gravity of manner in addition to extraordinary knowledge of literature—although he was one of that lot called the pope's scriveners—whom we recognize to be more hard-working than clever. He held that office for more than fifty years with great dedication and industry. By then, his age and integrity and above all a certain very gentle behavior and charming eloquence had gained him the utmost in good will and authority. The man's name was Giovanni, and his surname came simply from his homeland, da Firenze; this, I believe, was at the root of his love for me, for there was, to my knowledge, nothing else in me as yet for him to love. However, between good men the love of the country they share is very powerful, just as hatred of it is among evil men. Anyhow that man had become a great admirer, lover, and promoter of my limited talent. Reward him, Christ Jesus, for I owe him much; he did not live to that time of my life when I could have shown my gratitude with action. Never did he lay eyes on me without poking hot spurs into my sides and with fatherly devotion rousing my youthful spirit toward virtue, knowledge, and above all the love of God, without which he said a man can do nothing well; or rather such a man is absolutely nothing, no matter how well fortified by knowledge and power.

Well, then, one day when I was alone and deep in thought, I approached this man who was alone and intent as usual on worthy studies; that gentlest of men was thrilled to see me coming. He said, "Why do I see you more worried than usual? Am I mistaken, or has something new happened?"

I replied, "You are not mistaken, dearest Father, and nothing new has happened, but I am upset by old torments. You know the struggles and worries in my heart, you know how eagerly I have

---

* An otherwise unknown young grammarian.

always burned to raise myself above the multitude, and, to say it with Virgil and Ennius,

> I've tried the road whereby I too could rise
> Above the ground and soar, winning the praise
> Of men's mouths. [*G.* 3.8–9]

Never did I lack either the will or the dedication or the talent—so it seemed. Even if all these things failed me, was not your assurance more than enough? How often have you offered me the highest praise for outstanding talent, as many listened, so that you readily persuaded almost everyone that it was so, since they heard it from the mouth of the one who would never tell a lie? How often, taking me aside, did you warn me in a low voice to exercise such an intellect with the liberal arts and not allow such a great gift of God and nature to grow dull? Buoyed up by such a guarantor, I would struggle, and nothing seemed difficult to me any more. Still I would apply myself and spend every hour in literary studies so that not one was wasted. But dissatisfied with what I found, I would always try something new, beguiling my labor with the thought that whatever I was doing would not be in vain; I promised myself everything great and splendid. But now, although I have never interrupted my studies and believed I had reached the summit, I feel myself gradually sliding toward the bottom, and the steady flow of my talent nearly dried up. I have no idea where this unforeseen plague is from; what once seemed simple now seems insoluble; where I used to run anywhere without faltering, now I can barely walk, halting at each step and wavering over everything. Thus I have been transformed from a man of talent to a dullard, from rich to poor, from bold to fearful, from teacher to pupil; and I come to you on the verge of despair since you drove me into these straits. I own that I know nothing; and whether I abandon what I have started and grasp a new way of life, or do something else, I seek advice from no one but you."

Unable to endure any longer these and like complaints which I voiced impetuously and not without tears, he said, "Do not, son, do not, I beg you, waste in complaints the time that ought to be spent in thanksgiving; things are better than you think. You knew nothing as long as you thought you knew a great deal; but on the day you recognized your ignorance, believe me, you progressed inestimably. Now at last you begin to know something, since you believe you know nothing; the shadows that you did not see, of course, when

you felt proud of yourself, are opening up. He who climbs a mountain begins to see many things he neither saw at its foot, nor believed worthy of attention; and he who wades into the sea realizes
that the further he steps, the deeper the water, and that he needs a
boat to go further. Likewise you who at my urging—as you say and
I do not deny—have entered upon this path, go ahead with what you
have begun, with me not only urging but pushing you. God will be
with you; do not doubt it."

Hearing this as though from a heavenly oracle, I departed happier in my purpose and full of a better hope. So believe that what he
said to me was said to you, with this addition: that not to know
one's misery is ultimately the greatest of miseries, and that there are
certain illnesses the patient does not feel because he is overwhelmed
by numbness, and when he begins to wake up and to feel them,
there is hope and the beginning of recovery. Farewell.

[1373-74].

Sen. XVI, 7.

To the same person, [*] *that there are still some admirers of virtue, if any exists.*

Do not, dear friend, I beg you, do not slacken on this path you have taken, particularly on such a fine one, for the reason you allege, that virtue and the liberal arts seem to be without honor in our age. We say this age disparages anything good, I grant, and we are not lying. To be sure, a thing is disparaged when no energy is spent in acquiring it. But do you believe that virtue, in order to be honored, needs renown among men and the applause of the multitude? Believe me, if all men kept silent, if they died, if they hated it, virtue itself is its own glory. But men neither keep silent nor hate; and although no one is trying to attain it, or very few, there are still some who would admire it in others, if only there were some virtue that they could admire. Take away the miracle itself and you will take away the worshipper. Do you think that virtue was held in esteem only among our forebears? It was indeed, to the point that many would eagerly give their lives for what today hardly anyone would give a penny for. Today also the rarer it is, the more admirable and welcome it would be.

Jerome writes, as something extraordinary and eternally memorable, that he read how certain nobles from the furthest bounds of Spain and Gaul came to see Livy. Yet, was there too little reason for not only certain noblemen but the entire world to flock to see and hear him? I leave out that fount of milk that Jerome attributes to him, and that blessed fount of eloquence that Valerius attributes to his Pompey. How much, in the end, was it worth to see a man who, even if he had done nothing else in his life nor could do or say anything further, still, with his divine style and incomparable energy, (notwithstanding that Gaius Caligula thought otherwise), brought to completion in 142 volumes that immense work on the entire history of Rome from its founding. It is the next thing to a miracle; the life of one man could scarcely suffice to copy it—let alone to produce a new one like it. How much was it worth to behold the head that had dealt with so many things, and the fingers that had written of such noble things? Well, I believe, if Titus Livy himself were alive today, that not "certain ones" but very many would go to see him. Certain-

---

[*] See XVI, 6.

ly if only my health were better, as it was lately—to match my spirit—
and the roads safer, I would not be loath to seek him out not only
as far as Rome, but as far as India, starting from this city of Padua
where he came from, and where my residence has been now for
many years.

I shall reluctantly refer to another example, but I have no other
that is closer or more recent, or better known to many of my
friends, although, because of your age, it could not be known to you
unless told to you by them. Even though I may perhaps appear
boastful to those who always put the worst interpretation on everything, I still figure that just as I had a perfect right in the previous
letter to encourage you with fatherly advice in your anxiety, so do I
have it now to boast with fatherly confidence—if what has been
gotten through no merit at all of mine can be called boasting, especially since both letters involved encouraging you and propping up
your diffident spirit, for I have always cared for you like a son.
Therefore, have you not heard that I, who am nothing if compared
not, obviously, with the ancients but even with my contemporaries,
while in France and very young, was surprised to see certain nobles
and learned men coming to me from northern France as well as
from Italy? They were drawn by no other business than to see me
and speak with me. One of them, to be mentioned with respect, was
Pierre de Poitiers [Bersuire], a gentleman outstanding in religion
and letters; and, to add to my astonishment, there were some who
sent ahead magnificent gifts, as though to pave the way and open
doors through their munificence. Avignon on the Rhone, where I
then was, is in no way comparable to Rome, but the Roman Pontiff
and many emblems of the Roman state were there and are there
today, having been recently carried away in vain for a short while by
Urban V. They were what made the city famous all over the world;
still, the visitors confessed in both word and deed that they sought
nothing but me, to the point where if I happened to be away, they
would have dropped everything else and come at once to the source
of the Sorgue, where I mostly used to stay in summer. If you were
either unaware or incredulous of this, you cannot certainly have
yourself forgotten that long afterward, when I had returned to Italy,
you came to see me over not as great a stretch of road, but still
long, even though I had never seen or known you before, whence
arose this friendship; had it not lasted, or rather grown over time, I
would by no means be writing this to you intimately.

How many young men later have come to me, to this very day,
from that city most friendly to studies, Parthenope [Naples], particu-

larly those who could not see me there in the days of the greatest king [Robert], cannot be unknown to you on account of our friendship, just like the visit of the Perugian bard [Stramazzo di Perugia]. I call him that if an enormous love of letters and a truly burning spirit makes a bard—that old blind man who ran a grammar school in the town of Pontremoli. But he heard that I had gone off to Naples to the king I am speaking of, since I was puffed up with youthful pride and scorned anyone else's judgment at that time, whereas nowadays I would not turn down anyone's. Leaning on the shoulder of his only son, a lad in his teens, he too came shortly to Naples, drawn by his great longing for me. And when he announced in public the reason for his journey, the king learned of it and wanted to see him, for the appearance of the man and his fervor in the chill of old age was like a prodigy; and after staring for some time at the man's face, which was most like a bronze statue, and hearing what he was looking for, the king said, "If you wish to find the one you are looking for in Italy, hurry. Otherwise you will have to look for him in France; we have learned this from him lately as he was leaving here." The poor fellow said, "And I, unless life gives out on me, will seek him, if necessary, in India." The king, admiring and pitying him, ordered that he be given money for his journey. Retracing his steps from there with the greatest exertion, he first looked for me in Rome to no avail, and he returned to Pontremoli. There, hearing that I was still in Parma, although the winter too was now an obstacle, he crossed the snow-covered Apennines; and, sending on ahead to me some verses that were not bad, he himself was soon there.

"O what a face, how worthy of a painting!" For the one about whom the verse is written had one eye [Hannibal]; this man had none. That one was borne on the back of an elephant, this one on his own feet; that one sought Rome and the world empire that went along with it, this one sought one paltry man known to him only by reputation. And how many times do you think . . . but what am I saying? You were there in the midst of it. How many times, uplifted by the arms of his son and of another pupil he treated as a son—he used both of them for conveyance—did he kiss my head with which I had conceived those works that he said had charmed him so powerfully, how many times did he kiss this right hand with which I had written them (and how few had I written then!—although even today they are few)? I shall move on; it is a long story. He was always with me just like that for three days, and once it was known who he was and what he was doing, he filled the whole city with astonishment. I shall not omit one detail: on a certain day, out of enthusiasm, he was saying many things, among them, "Do not let me be a burden to you if I enjoy you too eagerly, since I come to see you with so much effort like a pilgrim." At that word the bystanders burst out laughing. He realized they were laughing and why; and turning to me even more excited, he added, "I want you, no one else, for my witness that, blind as I am, I see you better and more surely than any of these who have clear eyes." With these words he left them all hushed and dumbfounded.

I say no more except that the lord of that city [Francesco da Carrara], who loved me exceedingly—I doubt whether anyone on earth living in his time was more generous—was delighted by the blind man's words and the spirit, and sent him on his way with much honor and magnificent gifts. But for me all this was then more splendid to see than it is glorious now to tell. But I got into this story just to shake you out of your lethargy, if there was any, and to show you by an example known to you that there are still some who would cherish virtue, if only there were some virtue. Speak for yourself: what has stirred you to take on so much exertion at such an untoward time, if not perchance the fame of my accomplishments? If false fame was able to do so much, what would true fame not be able to do? They sought out so eagerly one whose age promised nothing praiseworthy except an inborn quality. With what energy, what fervor would they have sought out Cicero or Virgil or the one we have been talking about, Titus Livy? Therefore, study manfully and do not worry either that you will lack the talent (which hardly needs mentioning),* or that knowledge and virtue will lack honor. Farewell.

Padua, May 12 [1373].

* The precise meaning of the Latin is uncertain.

Sen. XVI, 8.

To Dom Jean [Birel], Prior of the Grand Charterhouse [at Garignano],* that he pray to God for him.

In numbness and veneration do I speak to you, O most religious gentleman, as though in you I were speaking to Christ, who undoubtedly inhabits your breast as a beatific guest, for the soul of the righteous is the seat of God. It is His gift that you shine like a new star over the world, through the thickest darkness of our age among sinful men such as the earth abounds in; you lead the life of an angel, and have an angelic reputation, and from the lofty lookout of the Charterhouse you shed light like the morning star from a mountain top in the east. But what shall I say before what occurs to me first? O wretched me, happy you! For I, to use Virgil's words, "much tossed about on land and sea" [*Aen.* 1.3], am harassed daily by the heavy storms of surging humanity; you, as Terence says, now "sail within the harbor" [*An.* 480]. I, troubled and already weary, am rambling among the thorns and byways of this life; you sit calmly on the threshold of heaven and in the vestibule of paradise. Before my eyes forever hovers the fear of death; before yours, the hope of life and the infallible pledge dwell.

What, then, shall I beg for first except what I yearn for first and need most, that you intercede for wretched me with the Lord Christ, with whom I trust you have the greatest influence? I wander now in a parched wilderness and do not find the way, hungry and thirsty, my soul failing, crying out to the Lord; if I were to be snatched from my straits and, aided by your merits, were to be led by Christ our Leader to the straight road, and, being enrolled among the citizens of heaven, were to approach the city of my abode, or if by chance I were to overcome that first temptation of ignorance, I would avoid the other three, which the text of the psalm lists in order. And, sitting in the darkness and shadow of death, tied down in beggary and fetters, humiliated in labors and weakened [Ps. 107:10, 12], again calling to the Lord, I would be led

---

* Jean Birel Limousin was prior of the famous Charterhouse north of Milan founded by Giovanni Visconti where P. spent a great deal of time during his residence in Milan. Famous for his sanctity and for the zeal with which he addressed various rulers, he was seriously considered for the papacy at the death of Clement VI.

from the darkness and shadow of death itself. And when the brazen gates have been shattered and the iron bars burst, I would be led from the path of my iniquity and from the chains of my sins. Furthermore, my soul has loathed all food; and approaching the very gates of death through spiritual privation, and again calling to the Lord, it would be rescued from perdition when He sends His word, and freed from its own straits. Finally, going down to the sea in ships and trading on the great waters, and seeing the works of the Lord and His wonders in the deep, and in turn mounting up to heaven and sinking into the abysses, and thus melting away in its plight, reeling and staggering like a drunken man, all its wisdom swallowed up and consumed, and again crying out to the Lord, who is the only true aid, first and last, in these sufferings, it would likewise be led out of its straits, and the Lord would hush the storm to a gentle breeze, and the billows of the sea would be still, and thus at last it would arrive happy and secure into the haven of its delight.

These are those four temptations which the royal prophet [David], inspired by the Holy Spirit, saw and deeply contemplated. The first, as Augustine says, is the temptation of error, the lack of truth, and the dearth of the Word; the second is that of doing good and overcoming lust; the third, contrary to the first, is that of disgust and weariness; the fourth is that of the storms and dangers in governing churches. The first three are common to everyone, but the last is peculiar to those who govern, although even the pilot is not tempted without endangering the passengers; and one who sits by the rudder of a small boat, not only faces no less hardship, but no less danger from the sea than one who steers a huge vessel. In these contrary winds and waves of temptations and storms of life, I pray you, grant me the protection of your prayers. When you approach as a holy guest the table of your Lord and mine to pray, let Him be with me in my wandering and my weariness, lest I go to ruin. May He graft upon my barren soul, to be watered and fertilized with wholesome tears, a love for Him, a contempt for the world, a hatred of pleasures, an eagerness for virtues, true piety, holy religion, unwavering faith, happy hope, burning charity, firm chastity, and worthy worship of His name. However, may He root out the works of the flesh, the whispers of demons, the consent of the unhappy soul, the remnants of bygone passions, and the terrible habit that binds me inextricably as I am being hustled to death. May He view my earthly pilgrimage with approval, and direct my wandering steps into the way of eternal salvation. May He, on the day of my departure and in that last hour of death, deign to help unworthy me, recalling not my iniquities, but graciously receiving my spirit as it departs this poor body. May He not enter into judgment with His servant, however obstinate and wretched. May He, the fount of mercy, deal with me mercifully. May He favor my cause and cover over my deformities on the very last day. Finally, may He not allow this soul, the work of His hands, to reach the haughty empire of His enemy and ours, or to be prey to foul spirits, and be a plaything for hungry dogs.

Here I have prescribed for you the form of the prayer I seek. However, I do not forbid you to vary it, for what is good for my soul I believe is better known to you than to me. These are for the most part my usual prayers every day; but I pray that with your prayers you assist mine, which are weak and afflicted by my sins. It is cruelty to deny a suppliant the help you can furnish without harming anyone and with no hardship for you. These are certainly gifts much dearer than gems and gold; I, needy and poor, await them from you, the richest and happiest in Christ.

Perhaps someone would say, "And where do you get such confidence about a man you have never seen?" This hope, I confess, does not come from my merits, but from the utterly pure love I feel for you and for your innocent flock in Jesus Christ. But if sincere love has no great merit, there is also the most devout reputation of your sanctity, which promises that you would be for me easy of access and indulgent. Nor does the fact that I have never seen you with these eyes stand in the way of that pious hope. Things that are not seen are often loved more vehemently; not without reason is it written, "Do not love things that are seen, but those that are not seen; for those that are seen are temporal, while those that are not seen are eternal." However much a sinner, I see you; and, however different from you, I see you in Him who sees both of us within, and in whom we shall see all things through His bountiful grace, and even now we see many who had passed on a thousand years before we were born. I see you in the fervor of the heart which, though cold to other things, grows warm in remembering your name. And even though I were to see you with better eyes and in a clearer light, still I wish also to gaze on you with these mortal eyes and hear you with these ears; and while I may often hear you through your exemplary deeds and from the mouths of many, like one who believes many things about you from common talk, I wish to meet and embrace you. Although I embrace you incessantly in the arms and longing of my soul, I wish with this useless and sinful hand of mine, if allowed, to touch at last that most holy right hand dedicated to God of so great a man, even though I may hold it with constant passion and squeeze it with great straining of the mind.* You are, to be sure, better known to me than you think. For you stand on high; you are observed far and wide; virtue makes you very well known to many whom you yourself do not know.

Furthermore, there is a pledge precious to me and cherished, and entrusted to your guardianship. I speak of my only brother, who is battling for Christ under you and, so to speak, under your auspices. Besides him I neither have nor hope to have any other; nothing is dearer to me of all the gifts of nature and of fortune; and I know that he is dear to you too as friend. I calmly bear his being taken away from me to become Christ's and yours; and with the hope of my brother's salvation, as I keep telling myself, I console my solitude, or rather I rejoice and boast that such a brother has been granted me. Removed from me and from the world, he was taken as a son by you and as a servant by Christ. All this then is what affords me the utmost reliance on your goodness; accordingly, how I feel toward you and toward your comrades in the holy army, Christ's servants, you will learn from the Prior of the Charterhouse of Milan, who will deliver my letter to you with his hand and my spirit with his tongue. Farewell from that very Chartherhouse of Milan, where I now dwell.

April 25 [1354-57].

---

* The meaning of the last clause is in doubt.

Sen. XVI, 9.

To the same person, * an apology for praising him while still alive.

You have given my head a good washing, as the saying goes, nor was there lacking the pungency of soap, to use Ambrose's words. I swear by Christ, who cannot be deceived, that I flattered neither you nor anyone else. And would that the swell, the heat, the disdain of my protesting spirit had not harmed me more than my fawning. Frequent are the quarrels in my works, though I would never have guessed it from the outset, such was my state of mind; frequent also my jokes, at times biting, but nowhere any flattery, for I do not include among flatteries true praises which have benefited many in the pursuit of virtue and steadfastness. It is unseemly, you say, to praise someone living—and at that, the very one you are addressing. I know that nothing that harms ought to be done. What if it does good, what if it also proves useful to the one who praises and even to the one praised? One who is blown over by a light breeze must be a lightweight; one who has his roots in solid ground, foundations set in stone, constancy of demeanor, his heart in heaven, does not fear the wind. Splendid indeed are those minds aroused by glory, as Cicero says. So it is that insults and threats drive the base to the straight path, the charming spur of glory drives generous minds; we drive the ass with sticks, the steed with clapping. A good mind is not puffed up by praises, but uplifted "and when praised, virtue grows," as Naso elegantly says [*Pont.* 4.2.35]. I speak from experience with something like this. I have of course never received praise for holiness, nor deserved it; if, however, I have had any praise for my style or talents—how much praise I do not know; I do know this: that if it is true, it cannot be much, but I feel what spurs it struck into me.

You say, "You praised me while alive, and to myself." I understand what you censure. It is written, "Do not praise a man during his lifetime." When Ambrose treats that passage, he says, "Praise after his life, exalt after its consummation;" and again, "Praise after the danger, celebrate him when he is safe." But how do I know whether I am going to outlive you? "But at least praise me to others." What if in doing this I do not leave out that either? "But by praising me you will cast me down." If I believed this, I would not

---

* See XVI, 8.

praise you. Do not feel badly if you are praised, O good and faithful servant; the praise is not yours but the Lord's. Or do you forbid me to praise Christ in what He has made? Certainly it is all right not only to be praised by another, but even to boast, but in the Lord. How often does Augustine praise Jerome? How often does Jerome praise Augustine and call him "most holy and blessed father" [*papam*]? And yet they speak not to someone else, not after death, inasmuch as they are talking to each other. But you will exclaim, "I am not Jerome;" nor am I Augustine. "I am not Augustine;" nor am I Jerome. What if you are greater to me than Augustine to Jerome or Jerome to Augustine? Do you not know that greatness and smallness are relative to one another, and small things even become great when compared to the smallest; and the great are small when compared to the greatest? Do you not know what high praises Ambrose, who forbids praising the living, lavishes on a living man while speaking to him? Read his homily on the purification of the Blessed Virgin Mary, and note how reverently he questions Augustine on the meaning of Simeon's words, what praises of his sanctity and intelligence he weaves in. You will think it is—I will not say a father speaking to a son, or a master to a pupil—a faithful general to a soldier whom he had washed with his own hands in the sacred font as he led him to the path of truth and cleansed of the ingrained dust, or rather not a scholar to a scholar, not a bishop to a bishop, not a friend to a friend, in short, not a man to a man, but a man speaking to God, and awaiting not a human utterance but a heavenly pronouncement.

At this point I could pour out philosophical or poetic examples, if I did not fear that you would very easily, as they say, with a deft flick of the shield parry them all; therefore, I turn to the examples of saints. I ask you, with what high praises and glorious words does John Chrysostom address Demetrius, and with what acclaim does he hail Isidore? Or Hilary of Arles and Prosper hail Augustine? But you will object and say that the ones they praised were at least saints. But what do you say to Paul the Apostle, the vessel of election and the teacher of the Gentiles, who sends a letter to Seneca and praises him as a man, and to Jerome who considers him among the sacred writers, when without doubt he was a pagan? Why should I not be allowed to praise not only a Christian, but a servant of Christ and an instructor of the Christian militia? Read the letters of Ambrose written to the emperors Valentinian and Theodosius; you will see his most holy severity often using the most honorific words to profane men because of some semblance of virtue.

But if perhaps you say, "Seek a saint to honor with praises, for I am a sinful man," and the rest that is often spoken by men like you, what do you say to holy Ambrose and to many others whom I consciously omit in order to be no more wordy than is necessary? Furthermore, what will you reply to those words of David, "for the saint is gone, for the truth has been shattered by the sons of men," since "there is no one who does anything good" [Ps. 12:2, 14:1]. Therefore, if I glimpse anywhere in such great darkness even a thin spark of truth, I feel I have glimpsed a new splendor of the sun, and I eagerly hasten there, praising not so much the light itself, but the Author of the light. This should be neither held against me nor, I believe, annoying to you. And indeed, if it can be proved by the testimony of many that sometimes it is all right to praise oneself without arrogance, how much more so is it to praise someone else and to be praised by someone else, and to hear someone praising you! Only let there be no fraud, insolence, rash credulity, and poisonous adulation. From these suspicions, obviously, the austerity of your life and profession should free you; and if my profession and age not free me, at least my age should, which is more removed from every youthful indiscretion. Flatteries belong to the younger years and the weaker sex; they do not befit a man's gray hair.

Since such is the case, even though a sure and infallible advisor were to whisper incessantly in your heart's ear, I shall still speak out, relying upon your patience, and say what my opinion on this is. Spit back the words of flatterers like poison besmeared with honey, and drive away the flatterer with the authority of your brow and your words so that he will not return. Accept the praises of others in this wise: if they are true, you (being aware of your human frailty and humbling yourself all the more) may glorify nothing through such praises except the one Bestower of your blessings; but if they are false, you may understand how much you lack, you will have your hands full ridding yourself of your defect and your eulogist of his lie—so try to become what he gives you credit for. Thus, you should feel the spur on both sides, toward gratitude and toward virtue, so that, either happy with the lessons learned, you thank God, or, saddened by your defect, you turn another's error to your advantage. I, being the great sinner I am, do not come to grease your head with my oil. God forbid that I should begin doing with you, dear Father, what I do not remember ever doing to anyone; but in speaking with you, let me arouse myself, if I can, and, while doing you no harm, benefit myself if perchance in praising you this cold heart of mine may burn to imitate you. For who seeks to imitate anything but what he considers worthy of unique praise? Therefore, allow yourself to be praised, that you may possibly become better and I may be eager to imitate you.

I do not deny, however, that you do very well to spurn the praises of men, especially those whom, if you wanted to repay, you could not, except with grave falsehood; and it will turn out for you what is written about Marcus Cato: the less he sought glory, the more he attained it. Yet if you give me an absolute command, I shall stop praising you, but not admiring you—although I have not praised you nor do I admire you; I praise Him in you, Him I admire and venerate who every so often takes man, in himself a wretched, tottering animal, and freely makes him praiseworthy, admirable, and venerable. But you will never succeed in stopping me from begging for the aid of your prayers. This I would not do if I thought either that my prayers were contemptible to you, or yours to Christ. For my part, I am far from Him, and, alas, for much too long a time; and I am hoarse from earthly things muffling me. You are closer to Him, your voice is louder. You will hear me, I hope; he will hear you praying for me and will heed you, I wish, above all in what I particularly ask you to seek, namely, that I be while alive what I would like to be while I am dying.

It remains for me somehow to satisfy your demands and questions. Were I to follow your example in these, I too would lose my temper, and it would not be unbecoming, would it? You bestow upon me such a blazon of talents as I neither seek nor deserve, and although you express a great deal, there is incomparably more that you leave unsaid; without saying it you proclaim it when you ask me to finish that book undertaken, you say, by Innocent III, *On the Dignity of the Human Condition*, which he promised but did not finish, and to complete another's undertaking when I have not yet been able to complete my own—as though it were easy for me to write copiously and charmingly about any matter whatsoever. Nor do you note that that man, whose virtue and intelligence raised him at an early age to the crown of the Roman pontificate, started to write on the wretchedness of the human condition and barely reached his goal, but on the opposing argument he only began to write without presenting authorities which a disappointed posterity would attack after his death. Now you tell me to fulfill his promise and to try my hand at what it is known he either did not want or was afraid to do or could not. "But who am I or what ability is in me?" as Laelius says in Cicero [*Amic.* 17]. Therefore, I am confidently undertaking what that man shrank from! Why he, even if evaluated on his own, apart from the papacy, is considered so prudent in everyone's judgment as to be numbered among the most learned; and in his pontificate was such that beyond any doubt, as I often heard it said by great cardinals of the Church, foreign in nationality and envious, who admitted—not of their free will but because the truth forced them—that after him no one dignified Peter's See to the same degree. With such a man, of such great authority and such powerful intelligence, you tell me to share this burden on unequal terms: while he was silent about the misery of the human condition, I am to deal with its opposite, and in such a way that, as no one doubts, what for him was an easy, simple subject, would for me be difficult and tricky. For human misery is vast; happiness is brief and very limited.

But since I know your mind, I think, though not your face, and I know that you have imposed this burden upon me for no other reason than some great and signal trust you have conceived about my situation and talent, suggested by that charity which makes you love me in Christ, I would obey most willingly. What better could I do than to carry out your bidding? But in my way stands a heap of responsibilities, so many that if you knew them, you would either pity me or laugh. They have been expanded not by my ambition or greed, but—I admit—by my active leisure and an insatiable thirst for literature, which, I have the feeling, will never be laid aside except with my last breath. And I am besieged on all sides by my worries; nor could you say that those words of Virgil fit anyone more, about a queen in love or a crazy, idle shepherd, "The work is stalled in the middle" [*Aen.* 4.88], and "My leafy vine is half pruned on the elm" [*Ecl.* 2.270]. Therefore, just as I would like to deny you nothing, so would I not dare make promises greater than my strength. Still, I shall try if by chance I can sneak some hours and steal them to devote to you; and I shall do so trusting not so much in my talent as in your prayers. And I shall tell you how far I have advanced, strange to say, though I have so far begun nothing: I do have a book in hand, *De remediis ad utranque fortunam*, in which, to the best of my ability, I try to soften the passions of my heart and the readers' hearts, or, if possible, to uproot them. But when the pen came to dealing with sadness and misery and I was engrossed in it, by chance it happened that the sort of sadness arising from no certain causes, which the philosophers call sickness of the spirit, I assuaged by juxtaposing its opposite—which can be done in no better way than by searching for the causes of joyfulness. That is nothing else than seeking the dignity of the human condition. On that very day your letter arrived, strongly calling for this very thing, as though you knew what I was then doing, and were adding the spur of your urging as I was running of my own will. I have therefore done so and have pressed more diligently, just as if you were constantly standing over me as I wrote, and I silently answered you, "You see, I am doing as you say." I believe this is the outline, if either the brevity of life or other obstacles forbid me to amplify and embellish it more carefully, this at least no one will take from you. But enough of this. As for your questions, in order not to bore you excessively today, I have given the answers to the one from whom you will receive this letter, surely a well-educated man who loves you deeply and me too for your sake, a man whose devotion, appearance, and conduct I like.

Fare well and happily in Christ Jesus, by whom I beseech and adjure you: whenever you are privileged to converse with Him, keep me in mind; and from your lofty stronghold of contemplation do not despise me as I call from the depths to the Lord and to you.

[1354-57].

Sen. XVII, 1.

To Giovanni Boccaccio da Certaldo.*

I had decided not to answer your letter; for although it contained practical and friendly ideas, still they were abhorrent to my way of thinking. Meanwhile, it occurred to me to write you a letter, not a short one, about something else; but, since it was crawling with erasures, I was preparing to copy it over. A certain friend took pity on me for being almost continuously sick and freed me from this task. But while he was writing I began to wonder, "What is my Giovanni going to say now? 'This fellow addresses pointless things, and does not reply to the important ones.'" Then, more on impulse than reflection, I took up once again my pen, which I had put aside; and I have written you another letter of almost the same length, in which I reply to yours. They were written almost two months ago, but no messenger was available. Now, finally, those two long ones are coming to you with this short one, and they come open so that the border guards may be spared the trouble of opening them; let whoever wishes read them provided he gives them back undamaged. They will know that we have nothing to do with wars; would that others were like us! Then the peace that is now banished would be with us. You will therefore read first the letter written in my hand, and then the one written in a strange hand; I have put them in this order. When you come to the end, you will be worn out and will say: "Is this my sick friend, that busy old man? Or someone else with the same name, a healthy young man with time to spare?" I confess I am surprised at myself and at my stubbornness. Farewell.

[June 1373].

* See I, 5.

Sen. XVII, 2.

To the same person, * that study must not be interrupted by age.*

The letter reporting your condition has reached me; and on this score it filled my heart with great, though not unusual, sadness; I have long since had my fill of these rumors. It is going badly with you, I confess, in what the multitude calls fortune's goods, but true philosophers say they deserve neither to be called nor valued as goods, although it is not denied that they are minor supports for mortal life. I am pained, and I would say I protest against Fortune if I believed she existed. Now I dare not be angry if what makes us joyful and sad does not happen at random as is commonly asserted, but by the will of a greater One who, after giving you much more than other mortals, and placing you above nearly all your contemporaries, has made you equal to many of them, and with fair perhaps, but distressing compensation makes you the Lactantius or Plautus of our time, with the utmost talent and eloquence, but with no less poverty. But if, judicious as you are, you examine this matter in depth impartially, and evaluate what has been given to you and what withheld, I think you will admit, setting everything on a scale, that on the human plane you have not been treated wretchedly, just a little too harshly.

To see this clearly, pay attention and consider, do not fool yourself: how many are there in the entire horde of men with whom you would like to exchange, I will not say your money, your health, your few acres, but everything you own put together? And, if you find very few or none at all, set your mind at rest and cheer up, thanking Him who gives abundantly to all and does not find fault. But since He would not grant you everything, He granted you the better things. For we go wrong in this, that when we see a man outstanding in virtues and culture, but lacking in other things, we marvel, we become angry and we protest. And we complain that it has happened unfairly to the one whom we consider worthy of greater things. That would be true if he had those things with which he has been adorned from himself or from someone else, not from Him who does not give everything to one, but this to you, that to another, as it is written, "distributing them to each as He wills" [1 Cor. 12:11].

---

* See I, 5.

Therefore, let it suffice to have received what is more precious, although what is cheaper has been denied to you. But to whoever glories in perishable riches, you, rich in a philosophical and poetic treasure, must say with confidence those words of Flaccus,

> You are surrounded by a thousand herds,
> Sicilian cows lowing; to you a mare,
> Fit for the chariot, neighs; you dress in wool
> Twice dipped in African
>
> Purple. To me, unerring fate has given
> A small domain and some slight inspiration
> Of Grecian music and the will to scorn
> The envious multitude. [*Carm.* 1.16.33–40]

I have often had this conversation with friends, and now I write here what I am in the habit of saying. If someone rich in virtues had perchance entered the service of a particular prince who treated him harshly and avariciously, saying, "Let your virtues suffice for you; allow me to come to the aid of the others suffering from the lack of this gift," this man would have a perfect right to reply: "If I have any virtue, I did not receive it from you. Therefore, if you wish to do me justice, you must look only at the merit in me and judge me as you find me, so that the reward may equal the virtue; nor must you give me in payment what is not yours but heaven's gift and makes me not worthy of rebuke but of good will." This cannot be said to the Lord of all, who has given us the virtues and the body and the soul itself. He indeed can justly answer anyone who seeks more, "Be quiet, be satisfied with your lot, and stop coveting everything"; and to anyone alleging his endowments, however great, He can cite those words of the Apostle, "What have you that you did not receive?" And likewise what follows, "But if you received it, why do you boast as though you had not received it" [1 Cor. 4:7]. And these so far are a few of the many examples, all so well known to you that they are hardly better known by anyone else; and from them all I reach this one conclusion: the virtuous man cannot justly complain about the lack of temporal goods.

I now come to the other part of your letter that was about me. I have often said it previously, and I hate to drive home one and the same thing so many times, but if, as your letter states, my lot were happy and rich, yours could certainly never be so meager; I wish you would impress this on your mind. Nothing is truer. Therefore,

Sea, and, what surpasses all absurdity, the Hyperboreans and the Ethiopians. Truly astonishing if a man such as you could be persuaded of this! More astonishing if you believed that I could be persuaded of it, except perhaps in the way that, in one and the same house, however tiny, all four parts of the world can be designated: South and North, East and West. I can scarcely believe I am even so fully known here at home, nor do I know whether there is anyone today on earth who entertains a narrower opinion of himself.

I wonder, dear friend, why you wish to deceive me, why you wish to make a fool of me, strictly speaking, and puff me up, unless someone else has deceived you, as I have said. It would astonish me beyond belief, since I thought there never was anyone who knew me better than you did; and still I would rather think anything than suspect something made up by one so trustworthy. But suppose I, a simple, uncultured man, were known somewhat further, or rather very far away, "even at the time of Marcus Tully when the fame of the Roman republic had not yet reached its peak," as Severinus says [*De cons.* 2.7], I must say the inadvertence of so great a writer forever astonishes me—for where Tully says this he was referring not to his own age but to that of Scipio Africanus. But be that as it may: imagine that my reputation has reached wherever you would like, just as I have seen the wisest fathers dreaming wonderful things about their sons who had no knowledge nor any prospect of knowledge. Would you believe that would put a check upon my studies? It would be a spur: the more I would see the fruit of my labors prosper, the more keenly would I apply myself; and success would render me, in my state of mind, not lazy, but restless and eager. But you, as though not content with the boundaries of the earth, say that I am even known above the ether heavens—praise fit for Aeneas and Julius. Doubtless I am known there; would that I were also loved there! Of course, I am not refusing the praise you bestow upon me for having inspired the minds of many throughout Italy— and perhaps beyond Italy—to these studies of ours, neglected for many centuries. For I am the oldest of almost all those who now pursue these studies among us. But I do not admit what you infer from this, that yielding to younger minds I should interrupt the momentum of the labors I have undertaken, and allow others to write something if they wish, lest I appear to have wanted to write everything alone.

O how greatly our opinions differ, though both our wills are the same! To you I seem to have written everything, or far more than anyone else; but to me I seem to have written nothing at all. But suppose I have written much and am writing much, how much better could I exhort the minds of those who follow me to persevere? Often examples inspire more effectively than words; certainly the aged Camillus, a most experienced general, by going off to war like a young man, inspired young men much more to virtue than if he had left them on the battlefield with orders to carry out, and retired to his bedchamber. But why do you appear worried, lest by writing on everything I would leave nothing for others to write? This is like that ridiculous fear of Alexander of Macedonia, who is said to have often dreaded that by conquering everything his father Philip would snatch from him any hope of martial glory. Crazy youth, not to know what great wars would remain for him even now, were he alive, even though the Orient had been conquered, and not to know perhaps of the generals Papirius Cursor and the Marcii. But Annaeus Seneca freed us from this fear in a certain letter to Lucilius. He says, "Much still remains to be done, and much will remain, nor will anyone born a thousand centuries from now be cut off the occasion for still adding something" [*Ep.* 64.7].

You, dear friend, with astonishing contradiction, try on the one hand to turn me away from progress on the works I had begun, by the hopelessness of finishing them, on the other by pointing to the glory I have achieved; and after saying that I have filled the world with my writings, you say, "Are you thinking, I ask, of equaling the number of volumes by Origen or Augustine?" Well, I believe that no one can equal Augustine; for who could equal him now when no one, in my judgment, was his equal in that age, so fruitful in talents? He was too great a man in every respect, too far beyond reach. As for Origen, you know I am accustomed not so much to counting as to evaluating; I would rather have written a few short irreproachable books than countless books in which there are great and intolerable errors, if his reputation is true. You tell me it is impossible to equal either of these, and I admit it, although my reason is not the same for the two of them. Against yourself, who urge me to retire my pen, as though you were thinking of something quite different, you cite some industrious old men, Socrates and Sophocles, and Cato the Censor among our people, and how many others you could have mentioned; but hardly anyone knowingly speaks against himself for long. Yet, searching on all sides for excuses for your advice and my weakness, you say that perhaps their constitution was different from mine; I would freely agree to that, although my constitution too has appeared very strong at times to those who profess knowledge of such things, but old age is stronger.

At this point you also bring up that I wasted a good part of my time in the service of princes. So that you may not err in this, here is the truth: I was with the princes in name, but in fact the princes were with me; I never attended their councils, and very seldom their banquets. I would never approve any conditions that would distract me even for a short while from my freedom and from my studies. Therefore, when everyone sought the palace, I either sought the forest or rested in my room among my books. If I were to say, "I did not lose a single day," I would be lying; I lost many days (I wish not all!) either through a kind of laziness or bodily sicknesses or mental anguish which no human skill avails to shun completely. What I lost at the princes' bidding you will now hear. For I too, like Seneca, keep account of expenses. Once I was sent to Venice to negotiate the reestablishment of peace between that city and Genoa, and I used up a whole month of the winter; later, in behalf of peace in Liguria, three summer months far away from civilization with the Roman prince [Charles IV], who was reviving, or to put it more correctly, abandoning the hopes of the—alas—collapsed empire; finally, three more winter months to congratulate King John of France, who had then been freed from an English prison. For even if on these three journeys I assiduously applied my mind to my usual concerns, still, because there was no means to write or to fix my thoughts in my memory, I call them lost days, although on my last one, while returning to Italy, I dictated an enormous letter to the elderly scholar Pierre de Poitiers [Bersuire], on the vicissitudes of fortune; it arrived too late and found him deceased. There, then, are the seven months I lost in the service of princes, an enormous loss, I do not deny, in so short a life; but would that the loss which the vanity and empty activities of my adolescence caused me were not more enormous! To this you add that perhaps our span of life is different from that of the ancients, and that it is possible that those who today are old were then called young.

What else can I say here, except what I said recently to a certain lawyer of this university, who I had learned liked to say this in the classroom in order to disparage the industry of the ancients and excuse the laziness of the moderns? Through one of his students I informed him not to say it any more, lest he himself be considered unlearned among the learned. For about two thousand years, and more, there has been no change in the length of human life. Aristotle lived sixty-three years, Cicero the same, and he would have lived longer, had it pleased the wicked, drunken Antony. And how many things he had long before discussed on the subject of his sudden and calamitous old age—he wrote a book on old age which he shared with his friend [Pomponius Atticus]! Ennius lived seventy years, as did Horatius Flaccus, and Virgil fifty-two, a short time even in our age. But Plato lived to be eighty-one; and it is said to have been considered such a phenomenon that, because he had completed the most perfect age, it was acknowledged that the Magi offered sacrifices to him as though he were more than a man, whereas today in our cities we see this kind of longevity all around; octogenarians and nonagenarians are common, and no one is astonished or offers sacrifices. If at this point you hold up to me either Varro or Cato and others who reached their hundredth year, or Gorgias of Leontini, who far surpassed them, I have some to oppose to them; but since their names are obscure, I shall mention one instead of many, Romuald of Ravenna, a very famous hermit who recently lived a hundred and twenty years, amidst the greatest labors which his love of Christ inspired in him, and many vigils and fasts—from which you are now diverting me with your advice, as best you can.

I have dwelt somewhat longer on this particular so that, except for those first fathers who are reputed to have lived at the beginning of the world, and who, as I think, had nothing to do with letters, you should neither believe nor maintain that our other ancestors lived longer than we do. They had more energy, not more life, except that life without energy is not life but a sluggish, useless lapse of time. You have prudently evaded this, with very few words, saying that if it is not a question of age, it could be of constitution and perhaps of the air or the food—finally that for these or other reasons I cannot do what they could. I fully agree and confess this to be so, but I do not equally confess what you infer from this. You gird yourself with painstaking arguments that in part, however, seem contrary to your thesis; for you say and advise that it should be enough for me—I use your very words to the letter—to have perhaps equaled Virgil in poetry and Tully in prose. Oh, if only you were led by truth to assert this, and not misled by love. You add that I have received by decree of the Senate, like our forebears, the most splendid title and rare glory of the Roman laurel, which all goes to prove that I, exalted by the success of my studies and put on the same plane as the very greatest and honored by a signal reward for my labors, should cease pestering God and men, and be satisfied with what I have achieved since my fondest prayers have been granted and nothing whatsoever has failed me. If only what love has convinced you of were either true or at any rate convincing to everyone, I would freely yield to others' testimony, and, following ordinary usage, I would believe what others say about me. But it all seems different to others, and especially to me, who think I have really not equaled anyone except the multitude; to them I would much rather be forever unknown than be like them. But that laurel crown, woven from half-fledged leaves, came to me when I was half-fledged in age and in mind. Had I been any more mature, I would not have wanted it; for just as old men love practical things, so the young love what is dazzling and do not consider the purpose. And what do you think? It brought me no knowledge or eloquence, but boundless envy, and it took away my rest—thus have I paid for my vainglory and youthful rashness. Since then nearly everyone has sharpened their tongues and pens against me, and I have always had to stand on the battleline with my banners raised, always resisting assailants now on the right, now on the left; envy turned my friends to enemies. Here I could mention many things to astonish you. In short, my laurel has afforded me this: to be known and tormented; without it I could have kept quiet and out of the public eye, which some think is the best kind of life.

The high point of your argument seems to me that I should try to live as long as I can for the joy of my friends, and—above all—to cheer your old age, because, as you say, you wish me to outlive you. Alas, our Simonides [Francesco Nelli] had also wished this; and the prayer, alas again, was fulfilled all too well since, if there were any order in human existence, he ought to have outlived me. You too, dear brother, before anyone else, wish for the same thing; and so do some of my friends make the loving prayer, but it is just the opposite of mine. I wish to die while you are alive and well, and to leave behind some in whose memory and words I may live, by whose prayers I may be helped, by whom I may be loved and missed; for besides a clear conscience I think there is no comfort more welcome than this for a dying man. But if—supposing you were perhaps to persuade me of this—you are moved by the opinion that I am truly greedy for life, you are completely mistaken. How could I wish to live long in the midst of these carryings-on, which, to my great sorrow, I have lived to see, and—not to mention the weightier things— this unsightly, obscene get-up of the shallowest men, which I often complain about only too much in writing and in speaking? But words fail me to vent the outrage and the grief I feel; though they are called Italian, and were born in Italy, they do everything to appear barbarians. And would that they were barbarians so as to free my eyes and those of true Italians from such a shameful spectacle! May God Almighty confound them, alive and dead! For them it is not enough to have lost through their laziness our ancestors' virtues and glory and all the arts of war and peace; but they also had to dishonor through their senselessness the language and dress of their homeland, so that I judge not only our fathers happy who departed from here in time, but also the blind who do not see all this.

Lastly, you ask that I pardon you for daring to advise me and to prescribe a way of life, namely, that I should abstain from mental strain, sleepless nights, and my usual labors, and nurse with luxurious ease and sleep my old age, exhausted by the years as well as by studies. Yet I do not pardon you, I thank you, being aware of your love that makes you a physician for me, which you are not for yourself. Rather I ask you to excuse me for not minding you, and thereby to be persuaded that even if I were most eager for life—which I am not—nevertheless, if I were to abide by your advice, I would perish all the sooner. Continual work and concentration are my mind's food; when I begin to rest and slow down, I shall soon stop living. I know my own strength; I am not by habit fit for other labors; to read—this is what I do—and write, which you bid me let go, is a light effort, or rather a delightful rest which makes me forget heavy labors. No knapsack is as easy to move as a pen, none more enjoyable. Other pleasures slip away, and bruise as they tickle; the pen tickles as you take it in hand, and it delights when it is put down, and benefits not only its master but many others, often even those who are far away, sometimes even those who follow after thousands of years. What I am about to say seems to me very true: of all earthly delights, just as none is more noble than letters, so none is more enduring, none sweeter, none more faithful, none that accompanies its possessor through all vicissitudes with such simple equipment and with never a bad taste. So spare me, then, dear brother, spare me; I will believe anything from you but not this. Whatever you make of me—for there is nothing that the pen of a learned and eloquent man cannot do—I must nevertheless try, if I am nothing, to be something, and if I am something, to be a little more, and if I were great, which I am not anyhow, to be greater and the greatest insofar as I can. Am I not allowed to appropriate for myself the word *greatest* of that cruel barbarian [Maximinus] who, when it was argued that he was great enough and should not work too hard, replied, "The greater I am, the harder I shall work" [*Hist. Aug.* 19.6.4–5], words worthy of not being said by a barbarian.

I have, therefore, settled this, and the next letter to you will be a sign of how far I am from counsels of idleness. For, not content with the huge projects I have begun, for which this brief life does not suffice nor would suffice, were it doubled, I daily hunt for new labors on the outside, so great is my hatred for sleep and lazy repose. But have you perhaps not heard those words of Ecclesiasticus, "When a man has done, then shall he begin: and when he leaves off, he shall be busy" [18:6]? Indeed, I seem to have begun now; whatever I may appear to you or to others, this is my view of myself. If, in the midst of all this, the end of life comes, which now certainly cannot be far off, I confess I would wish, as they say, that it find me living as though my life is done. But since, as things are, I have no hope of that, I wish that death would find me reading or writing, or, if it please Christ, praying or weeping. Farewell, remember me, and live happily, and persist manfully.

Padua, April 27 [1373], toward evening.

Sen. XVII, 3.

To the same person,* a wife's remarkable obedience and faithfulness.

I have seen the book [*Decameron*] you produced in our mother tongue long ago, I believe, as a young man; it was delivered to me— from where or how I do not know. If I were to say I have read it, I would be lying, since it is very big, having been written for the common herd and in prose, and I was too busy and time was short; and at that, as you know, I was disturbed by war breaking out on all sides. Though I am far from sympathizing with it, I still cannot avoid being disturbed by the ups and downs of the republic. Well, what of it? I leafed through it, and, like a hurried traveler who looks around from side to side without halting, I noticed somewhere that the book itself had been attacked by dogs' teeth, but admirably defended by your walking-stick and your yells. This did not suprise me. For I know the power of your talent, and I know from experience that there is a breed of men who are insolent and lazy, who rebuke in others whatever they themselves either do not want, do not know, or are unable to do; only in this are they learned and shrewd, but otherwise speechless. I did enjoy leafing through it; and if anything met my eye that was too frankly lewd, your age at the time of writing excused it—also the style, the idiom, the very levity of the subject matter and of those who seemed likely to read such things. It matters a great deal for whom you are writing, and variety in morals excuses variety in style. In the midst of much light-hearted fun, I caught several pious and serious things about which I still have no definitive judgment since nowhere did I get totally absorbed. But it happened just about as it does to runners: I looked into the beginning and the end somewhat more curiously than the rest. At the beginning you described perfectly, in my opinion, and magnificently deplored the condition of our country—I mean during that plague-ridden time, mournful and wretched, which our age witnessed worse than all before us. At the end, you placed the closing story, far different from many of the preceding ones. It has so pleased me and engrossed me that, among so many cares, it nearly made me forget myself and want to commit it to memory so that I might repeat it to myself not without pleasure whenever I wished, and to

* See I, 5.

retell it, whenever the occasion arose, to my friends, chatting, as we do. I did so a little later; and when I recognized that it was pleasing to the listeners, suddenly, in the midst of talking, I was struck by the idea that maybe such a sweet story would appeal also to those who do not know our language, since it had always pleased me after hearing it many years earlier, and I gathered it had pleased you to the point that you considered it not unworthy of your vernacular style, and of the end of your work, where the art of rhetoric tells us to put whatever is more powerful.

And so, on a certain day, when my mind was being torn as usual between various thoughts, angry at them and at myself, so to speak, I said goodbye to all of them for a time, and, seizing my pen, set out to write that very story of yours, hoping that you would surely be delighted that I would, of my own accord, be a translator of your works, something I would not readily have undertaken for anyone else. I was drawn by love for you and for the story, but not to the point of forgetting that saying of Horace in his *Art of Poetry* [133–34],

> You will not try to render word for word,
> You trusty dragoman.

I have told your story in my own words, or rather changing or adding a few words at some points in the narrative because I believed that you not only would allow it to be done, but would approve it. Although many have praised and sought the story, I decided to dedicate your work to you, not to anyone else. Whether I have deformed it or, perhaps, beautified it by changing its garment, you be the judge—for it all began there, and it goes back there; it knows the judge, the house, the way—so that you and whoever reads this may be clear on one point: that you, not I, must render an account of your works. Whoever asks me whether it is true, that is, whether I have written a history or just a tale, I shall reply with the words of Crispus, "Let the responsibility fall on the author" [*Jug.* 17], namely my Giovanni. With this preface, I now begin.

On the western side of Italy there is a very high mountain of the Apennine chain called Monviso, whose summit, piercing the clouds, rises into the pure ether, a mountain famous for its size, but even more as the source of the Po which, flowing from a tiny spring from its side, moves toward the rising sun, and soon swollen by amazing tributaries over a short downward course, becomes not only one of the greatest streams, but is called "the king of rivers" by Virgil [G. 1.482]; with its strong current, it divides Liguria, then separates Emilia, Flaminia, and Venetia, and finally empties with many huge mouths into the Adriatic Sea. That section of land, which I spoke of before, composed of both a lovely plain and interspersed hills and mountains, is equally sunny and charming throughout, and takes its name [Piedmont] from the foot of the mountain that it lies under. And it has a number of outstanding cities and towns; among them, at the foot of Monviso, the land of the Saluzzi teeming with hamlets and castles, is ruled by certain noble Marquises.

One of these, the first and greatest of them, was a certain Gualtieri to whom fell the governance of the family and of all the lands. He was in the prime of youth and beauty, and no less noble in manners than in blood; in short, a fine gentleman in all respects, except that, being content with his lot, he was most unconcerned about the future. A devotee of hunting and fowling, he become so obsessed with it that he neglected nearly everything else; and, what his people bore hardest, he shrank from the very suggestion of marriage. After they had borne this in silence for some time, they finally went to him in a body; one of them, who was more influential or persuasive and on more familiar terms with his lord, said: "Most excellent Marquis, your kindness gives us the nerve to speak with you man to man with respectful confidence any time the situation warrants. And now let my voice convey to your ears the silent wish of all, not because I have anything unique to say on this matter, but because you have proven by many tokens that you are fond of me, among others. Well then, while we like everything about you, for good cause, and always have, so that we consider ourselves happy with such a lord, there is one thing which, if you let yourself be talked into it and lend us a willing ear, will make us plainly the happiest people in the entire neighborhood: namely, that you should give serious thought to marriage, and bend your neck to that lawful yoke not just freely but with determination, and the sooner the better. For the days fly by rapidly; and, although you are in the bloom of youth, old age still pursues this bloom relentlessly, and death itself is very near at any age. No one is granted an exemption from this levy; all alike must die, and just as that is certain, so it is unsettled when it will happen. Therefore receive, we pray, the prayers of those who would never balk at any command from you. However, leave to us the job of searching for a wife; for we will find for you a woman worthy of you and born of such noble parents that one is bound to expect the best from her. Free all your people from a disturbing anxiety, we beg you, lest perchance something, humanly speaking, happen to you: you depart without a successor, and we are left behind without a God-given lord."

The pious entreaty moved the gentleman's heart, and he said, "Friends, you force me to do something that never entered my mind. I enjoyed total freedom, which is rare in marriage. However, I willingly submit to my subjects' wishes, relying on your fore-thought and loyalty. But I relieve you of the task for which you vol-unteer, to seek a wife for me, and I take it upon my own shoulders. For what does the nobility of one confer upon another? Often sons are utterly unlike their parents; whatever good there is in man is from no one else but God. Therefore, I will entrust to Him the destiny of my state and my marriage, hoping for His usual mercy. He will find for me what is expedient for my peace and well-being. And so, since it has so pleased you, I shall take a wife; I promise you this in good faith, and I shall neither disappoint your desire nor delay it. You, on the other hand, promise me one thing and keep it in mind, that whatever wife I myself shall choose, you will attend with the highest honor and veneration, nor will there be any one of you who ever challenges or complains about my choice. It was your doing that I have subjected my spirit, which you know was utterly free, to the yoke of matrimony; let the choice of the yoke itself be mine; whoever my wife will be, let her be your mistress as though she were the daughter of the Roman emperor."

They promised unanimously and joyfully that nothing would stand in the way of them eagerly undertaking to carry out most mag-nificently their lord's proclamation on a set day, whereas it seemed to them scarcely possible ever to see the longed-for wedding day. Thus the meeting came to an end, and he nevertheless assigned the responsibility for the wedding celebration to his domestics, and he proclaimed the day.

Not far from the palace there was a small hamlet inhabited by a few poor people, of whom the poorest of all was named Gian-nucolo. But since heavenly grace sometimes visits even the huts of poor people, he happened to have an only daughter, Griselda by name, outstanding enough in bodily comeliness, but so splendid in the beauty of her ways and spirit that there was nothing finer. Being reared on scanty food, always in the most terrible want, unacquaint-ed with any pleasure, she had learned to expect no luxury or ease; but in her maiden heart was hidden a brave and wise spirit. She cheered her father's dotage with inestimable love, and would pas-ture his few sheep, all the while wearying her fingers on the distaff;

and then, returning home, she would prepare vegetables and a dinner in keeping with their fortune, spread his bed on the floor, and, in short, perform in the narrow space all the chores of an obedient, dutiful daughter. Gualtieri, who often passed that way, had always cast his eyes on this maiden, not with a young man's lust, but with an old man's gravity. With his keen insight he had noticed her exceptional virtue, superior in her sex and age, and hidden from the eyes of the multitude by her humble condition, with the result that he determined at the same time to have a wife, which he had never before wanted—and to have her alone, and no one else.

The wedding day was at hand; but where the bride was to come from, no one knew; everyone was wondering. Meanwhile, he himself shopped for golden rings, crowns, and girdles; but he had expensive clothing, shoes, and everything of that sort that was needed, made to order on another girl's measurements, who was just like her in size. The awaited day came; and since no gossip about the bride was heard, everyone's astonishment had grown immensely. Meal time arrived, and the whole palace was teeming with vast preparations. Then Gualtieri, as though setting out to meet the approaching bride, stepped out of the palace escorted by a crowd of noblemen and ladies. Griselda, unaware of all that was being prepared for her, had completed her chores around the house and was carrying water from a distant spring across her father's threshold, so that, having discharged her other obligations, she might hasten with her girlfriends to see her lord's bride. Just then Gualtieri, walking deep in thought, called her by name and asked her where her father was; when she answered respectfully and humbly that he was at home, he said, "Tell him to come to me."

When the poor old man came, he took him a little aside, by the hand, and, in a low voice said, "I know, Giannucolo, that you are fond of me, and I know you are an honest man; and I believe you want whatever is my pleasure. But there is one thing I would especially like to know: whether you would have me, who am your lord, for a son-in-law by giving me your daughter to wife."

The old man, astonished by the unexpected proposal, was paralyzed, and barely gasping a few words, said at last, "There is nothing I ought to want or not want except what is pleasing to you, who are my lord."

"Then," said he, "let us go inside alone so that I can ask her about certain things in your presence."

So while the others waited in astonishment, they entered and found the girl bustling about for her father's sake and stunned by the arrival of so great a visitor. Gualtieri confronted her with these words: "It pleases both your father and me that you be my wife. I believe it would please you too. But I must ask you whether, after this is all done, which will be soon, you are ready and willing never to disagree with my will in anything, just as I agree with you in everything, and whatever I wish to do with you, you will let me with all your heart, without any gesture or word of repugnance."

To this she replied, trembling with astonishment, "I know, my lord, that I am unworthy of so great an honor. But if it is your wish and if it is my lot, I will not only never knowingly do, but not even think anything that is against your wishes; nor will you ever do anything, even if you order me to die, that I would bear grudgingly."

"That is enough," he said. So he then led her out into the open, and showed her off to the people, saying, "This is my wife, this is our lady; honor her, love her, and if you hold me dear, you are to hold her most dear."

Then, lest she bring into her new home any trace of her former condition, he ordered her to be undressed, and to be clothed from head to foot in new garments. This was carried out discreetly and speedily by the ladies in waiting, who vied in cuddling her in their bosom and on their lap. Thus this girl was dressed; her dishevelled hair was combed and braided by their hands, and she was adorned for the occasion with jewels and a crown, and, as it were, suddenly transformed so that the people could hardly recognize her. Gualtieri solemnly betrothed her with a precious ring that he had brought for this purpose, and he had her mounted on a snow-white horse and led to the palace, as the people accompanied them and rejoiced. In this fashion the marriage was celebrated and that most happy day brought to a close.

In a short while so much divine favor had shone upon the poor bride that she seemed to have been brought up and trained not in that shepherd's cottage but in the imperial court. She came to be loved and adored incredibly by all; and even those who had known her from birth could scarcely be persuaded that she had been Giannucolo's daughter, so great was the beauty of her life and her ways, the gravity and sweetness of her words with which she bound the hearts of all to her with the knot of great love. Soon her fame, with blazoning heraldry, spread her name not only within her native territory, but throughout the neighboring provinces, so that many ladies and gentlemen eagerly thronged to see her. Thus Gualtieri, graced by a humble but signal and thriving marriage, lived in utter peace at home and abroad with the utmost favor of men, and was on all sides considered a very wise man because he had with such discernment grasped the extraordinary virtue hidden under so much poverty. Nor indeed did the clever bride attend only to domestic, womanly duties, but—where the situation required—official duties as well, in her husband's absence arbitrating and settling the country's disputes and the disagreements of the nobles with such grave pronouncements, such maturity and fairness of judgment that everyone declared that the lady had been sent by heaven for the public well-being. And not much time had passed when she became pregnant and at first the people worried with anxious expectation, but then she gave birth to a very beautiful daughter. Although they would have preferred a son, yet with her fertility, which they had prayed for, she made not only her husband but the whole country happy.

Meanwhile Gualtieri, as it happens to people, after the baby had been weaned, was seized by a strange craving—how praiseworthy, let the more learned ones judge—to probe deeper into his dear wife's faithfulness, which he had already proved amply, and to keep testing it again and again. He therefore called her aside into the bedroom and spoke to her with troubled brow: "You know, O Griselda, for I do not believe that in your present fortune you have forgotten your past condition—you know, I say, how you came to this house. To me of course you are dear enough and beloved. But not so to my nobles, especially since you have borne your first child; they are utterly prejudiced against being under a mistress who is a common-er. So I, who hanker for peace with them, must obey not my own judgment but that of others about your daughter, and do what is as repugnant to me as anything could be. But I would never do it without your knowledge. I want you to adjust your thinking to mine and to apply that patience you promised from the beginning of our marriage."

Upon hearing this, unmoved in word or in countenance, she said, "You are our lord, and this little daughter and I are yours. Do as you please, therefore, with what belongs to you; for nothing can please you that would displease me; there is nothing whatever that I either hanker to have or fear to lose, except you. This I have pinned to the bottom of my heart, never to be plucked either by the lapse of time or by death; anything else can happen sooner than my mind change."

He was happy at that reply, but putting on a sad look, he left; and after a short while he sent to his wife one of his henchmen, the one he trusted the most and used to employ on weightier business, instructing him on what he wanted done. Coming to her at night the man said, "O madam, forgive me, and do not blame me for what I am forced to do. You who are so wise know what it is like to be under a master; intelligent as you are, you realize the harsh necessity to obey, even if you have never had to. I have been ordered to take this baby and to...." Here he broke off speaking, and as though expressing by silence the cruelty of his task, he said no more.

The man's reputation was suspect, his looks were suspect, the hour was suspect, and so were his words. Although she clearly understood from all this that her sweet daughter would be killed, she did not shed a tear, nor utter a sigh—a terribly hard thing even for a nurse, let alone a mother. But with unwrinkled brow she picked up the little girl, looked at her for a short while, and as she kissed her fondly, she blessed and marked her with the sign of the holy cross, and handed her over to the henchman, saying, "Go, and carry out what our lord has enjoined upon you. I beg only one thing: take care that no wild beasts or birds mangle this little body, unless, however, you have been otherwise ordered."

When he returned to his lord and told him what had been said and what had been replied, and offered him his daughter, fatherly devotion profoundly stirred his heart; yet, he did not change the original harshness of his plan. He ordered the henchman to wrap her in rags, throw her into a basket, place her on a gentle mule, and to take her to Bologna with all possible diligence to his sister, who was married to the Count of Panago, and hand her over to be reared with motherly tenderness and taught good manners, and besides hidden so carefully that no one could find out whose daughter she was. At once the henchman departed and zealously fulfilled the task assigned to him.

Meanwhile, often observing his wife's countenance and words, Gualtieri never noticed any sign of a change of heart, no less liveliness and diligence, her usual obedience, the same love, no sadness, no mention of her daughter—her name was never heard from her mother's mouth deliberately or incidentally.

Four years had gone by in this state, when there she was pregnant again and gave birth to a very handsome son, to the immense joy of the father and of all his friends. When the child, after two years, was weaned from his nurse, the father returned to his usual whim, and again spoke to his wife. He said, "Long ago you heard that my people can hardly put up with our marriage, especially since they learned of your fertility, but never more bitterly than since you gave birth to a boy. They say, and often this muttering has reached my ears: 'So when Gualtieri goes, Giannucolo's grandson will rule over us, and such a noble country will be subject to such a lord!' Many things of this tenor are tossed about daily among the people, so that I, being eager for peace and, to admit the truth, fearing for myself, am driven to dispose of this infant as I did his sister. I am forewarning you of this so that you will not be upset by a sudden unexpected grief."

To this she replied, "I have said and will repeat: I can neither want nor not want anything except what you want, and in these children is nothing of mine but the birth pangs. You are my lord and theirs, use your right over your property, and do not seek my consent. For the moment I entered your house, as I laid aside my clothes, I laid aside my wishes and feelings, and put on yours; therefore, in anything, whatever you want, I too want. Why, if I knew beforehand of your future will, whatever it might be, I would start wanting and hankering before you did. Now, I cannot anticipate what is on your mind, but gladly follow it. Imagine that I feel it is your pleasure that I die; I shall die willingly, and nothing at all, not even death, will be equal to our love."

Admiring the woman's constancy, he departed with troubled countenance, and immediately sent the same henchman once again to her who, after many excuses for obeying out of necessity and many appeals for forgiveness if he had caused or was causing her anything untoward, he demanded the child as though he were about to commit a terrible crime. With always the same bearing, whatever the condition of her mind, she took up her son, whose beauty and disposition were lovable not only to the mother but to everyone; and marking him with the sign of the cross, and blessing him as she had done with her daughter, and clinging to him with her eyes as long as she dared, she kissed him tenderly, and without revealing any sign whatever of grief, she offered him to the messenger and said, "Take him, do what you have been ordered. Now too I pray for one thing, and that is, if it can be, you protect these tender limbs of this beautiful baby from the pecking of birds and the clawing of beasts."

Returning to his lord with this charge, he drove him into more and more consternation, so that, had he not known that she loved her children very much, he could almost have suspected that this firmness in a woman proceeded from a certain savagery of heart; but, though very fond of all her people, she did not love anyone more than her husband. The henchman was ordered to Bologna, and took the boy where he had taken his sister.

These tests of conjugal affection and faithfulness could have sufficed for the most stubborn husband. But there are those who, once they begin, never stop, or rather, they press on and stick to their purpose. Thus, with his eyes fixed on his wife, he watched assiduously whether there was any change in her toward him; but he could find nothing at all, except that she daily became more faithful and obedient to him, to the point where the two of them seemed to be just one mind, and that one not shared by both, but only the husband's; for the wife had resolved never to want or not want anything for herself, as has been said.

Gradually Gualtieri's reputation had begun to grow stained because with inhuman harshness and with regret and shame for a lowly marriage, he had ordered his children killed. For the children were nowhere to be seen and no one had heard where in the world they were; wherefore that man, famous otherwise and dear to his people, had now made himself infamous and hateful to many. His fierce spirit was not bent thereby, but he went ahead in his usual sternness and that cruel lust of his for testing her. And so, after twelve years had passed following his daughter's birth, he sent messengers to Rome to bring back forged apostolic letters, with which he made known to the people that he had received permission from the Roman Pontiff, for the sake of his own peace and that of his nation, to repudiate his first marriage and take another wife. Nor was it of course difficult to persuade those ignorant mountaineers of anything whatsoever. When this news reached Griselda, saddened, I imagine, but unshaken, she stood firm, as one who had once for all decided about herself and her lot, and awaited what he, to whom she had subjected herself and her all, would decree.

He had already sent to Bologna and asked his brother-in-law to bring his children to him, while the rumor spread everywhere that that girl was being brought to him to be his wife. To carry this out faithfully, the brother-in-law took to the road on the agreed day with a brilliant escort of nobles, bringing the girl, already marriageable, of peerless beauty and richly adorned, along with her brother who was already in his seventh year.

During all this, to test his wife once again with his usual skill, and to crown her grief and shame, Gualtieri led her into the street and said in the presence of many, "I was glad enough to be married to you, looking to your character, not your background. Since I now realize that every great fortune is but a great servitude, I am not allowed to do what any peasant can. My people force me and the

Pope authorizes me to take another wife, and a wife is now on her way and will arrive shortly. Therefore, be brave, give way to another, and take back your dowry and return calmly to your former home; to man no lot is everlasting."

She replied, "My lord, I always knew that my lowliness was incompatible with your grandeur; and I never considered myself worthy of, I will not say marriage to you, but service under you. And in this house, where you made me mistress, I call God to witness I have always remained a maid at heart. Therefore, I thank God and you for this time I have been with you with great honor, far above anything I deserved. As for the rest, I am prepared to return to my father's home with a good and peaceful heart, and to spend my old age and to die where I spent my childhood, always a happy and honorable widow for having been the wife of such a man. I willingly yield to the new wife who I wish will come to you happy; and, since this is your pleasure, I depart not against my will from here where I lived most gladly. But as for telling me to take my dowry with me, I see what it amounts to, for I have not forgotten how I was once stripped of my own clothes on the threshold of my father's house, and dressed in yours I came to you; I had no other dowry whatsoever but faithfulness and nakedness; therefore, look, I take off this dress and I return the ring with which you wed me. The other rings and clothing and ornaments, with which I became the envy of all because you gave them to me, are in your bedroom. I left my father's home naked; I would return there naked, except that I consider it unbecoming that this womb, in which lay the children you begot, should appear naked to the people. Therefore, if it pleases you, and not otherwise, I pray and entreat that, in payment of the virginity I brought here and cannot take back, you let me keep one of those shifts I like to wear in your company, to cover the belly of your former wife."

Tears overflowed her husband's eyes so that he could no longer hold them back. So, turning his face, he barely uttered the trembling words, "And you may have a single shift." And so he left in tears.

Undressing herself in the front of everyone, she kept only the shift for herself, and covered by it, went forth in the presence of all, bare-headed and barefoot, and so, with many following her and weeping and blaming fortune, she, the only one with dry eyes and august in noble silence, walked back to her paternal home.

The old man had always been doubtful of his daughter's marriage, had never entertained much hope, and always thought it would happen that, once the husband had had his fill of a humble wife, he, a great man, proud in the manner of the nobles, would throw her out. So he had kept her shaggy smock, shabby with age, hidden in a corner of the house. Therefore, when he heard the hubbub not of his daughter, who came back silently, so much as of her escort, he ran to meet her at the door and covered his half-naked daughter with her old dress. She remained with her father a few days with such marvelous calm and kindness that no sign appeared of a sad spirit, and no vestige of a more prosperous situation, since indeed in the midst of riches she had always lived poor in spirit and humble.

By then the Count of Panago was approaching, and the rumor of the new marriage spread everywhere. The day when he would arrive in Saluzzo had been learned, for he had sent ahead one of his men. Therefore, the day before, Gualtieri summoned Griselda, who came most loyally, and said to her, "I wish to receive splendidly the girl who is to arrive here tomorrow for dinner, and the ladies and gentlemen who will be with her, as well as our own who will join in the banquet, so that each will be welcomed and seated according to the full honor due his rank. But I have no women in the palace fit for this job; and so, despite your poor dress, you will assume the hostess's responsibility for receiving and seating them properly, since you know my ways."

She replied, "Not only gladly, but eagerly, will I always do this and whatever I feel is your pleasure. Nor will I ever tire of this or slow down, as long as there is any breath left in me," and, as she said it, she grabbed the housemaid's broom and mop, began to sweep the house, set the tables, make the beds, and urge on the other women in the manner of a most faithful maid.

At the third hour of the next day the count arrived. Everyone vied to admire the manners and beauty of the girl and of her little brother. There were those who said that Gualtieri had made a wise and happy change, because this bride was more refined and noble and he was getting such a fine brother-in-law too. In the feverish preparations for the banquet, Griselda was everywhere on hand and attentive to everything. She was not dejected by so great a fall, nor embarrassed by her worn-out clothes; but with a serene look she met the girl at the door, bent her knee like a servant, and with lowered eyes she said reverently and humbly, "Welcome, my lady"; and afterward she received the other guests with a smile and with words of admirable sweetness. Very skillfully she so set the huge palace in order that everyone, and especially the strangers, marveled mightily at her grand manners and at the good sense beneath such dress, while she, above all, could not stop praising both the girl and the little boy, extolling in turn the girl's and the boy's refinement.

At the very time when everyone was to sit down at table, turning to her, Gualtieri said in the presence of all, in a loud voice as though joking, "What do you think, Griselda, of this bride of mine? Is she fair enough, handsome enough?" She replied, "Quite; no one fairer or handsomer can be found. Either with no one else ever, or with her, you can enjoy a peaceful, happy life; and that it may be so I wish and hope. One thing I sincerely beg of you and warn you: do not harass this one with those stings with which you harassed your other wife. For because she is younger and has been brought up more delicately, she would not have the strength, as I sense, to endure them."

As she said this, he gazed at the alacrity and weighed the constancy of the woman he had offended so often and so bitterly, feeling sorry for her undeserved lot, and no longer able to bear it, he said, "Dear Griselda, I know your faithfulness well enough, I have observed it; and I do not believe there is anyone under the heavens who has reaped such great proofs of conjugal love." As he said this, he embraced in his eager arms his dear wife, who was overcome with joyful astonishment and awakened as though from a bad dream, and said, "You alone are my wife. I have not had another, nor shall I. But the one you take for my bride is your daughter, this boy who was believed to be my brother-in-law is your son; and what you seemed to have lost one at a time, you have now recovered all together. Let those who have believed the opposite know that I am whimsical and experimental, not heartless; that I have tested my wife, not condemned her; that I have hidden my children, not killed them."

Hearing this, she nearly fainted with joy; and mad with maternal love, she rushed into her children's arms with truly joyful tears, and wearied them with her kisses and drenched them with her motherly sobbing. Quickly the ladies, surrounding her joyfully and graciously, took off her lowly clothing and put on her what she used to wear. All around resounded the happy clapping and everyone's congratulatory words; and that day was celebrated with much joy and weeping, and was more festive than the wedding day had been.

For many years thereafter, they lived in boundless peace and harmony. Gualtieri moved his poor father-in-law, whom he seemed to have neglected until then lest he should sometime interfere with the planned experiment, into his palace and held him in honor. He married off his daughter honorably and splendidly, and left his son the successor to his domain, having been happy both in his marriage and in his offspring.

I decided to retell this story in another language not so much to encourage the married women of our day to imitate this wife's patience, which to me seems hardly imitable, as to encourage the readers to imitate at least this woman's constancy, so that what she maintained toward her husband they may maintain toward our God. For although "He is no tempter of evil, and tempts no one," as the Apostle James says [1:13], still He does test and often allows us to be harassed with many heavy blows, not in order to know our spirit, which He knew before we were created, but so that our weakness may be recognized through obvious and familiar signs. I would number among the men overflowing with constancy whoever would suffer without a murmur for his God what this little peasant woman suffered for her mortal husband.

[1372-73].

Sen. XVII, 4.

To the same person,* odds and ends from the preceding letter, and on finally putting an end to this letter-writing.

My love for you has prompted me, old as I am, to write what I would scarcely have written when I was young. Whether the contents are true or fictitious I know not, since they are no longer histories but just tales; but I have done it for one reason: that they belong to you and were written by you, although, foreseeing this challenge, I prefaced that the guarantee would rest with the author, that is, with you. And I shall tell you what happened to me in connection with this story, which I would rather call a tale. A Paduan friend of ours, a man of the highest intellect and broad knowledge, read it for the first time; scarcely past the middle of the letter, he stopped, being overcome by sudden weeping; but after a while, when he took it in hand again and was about to read it through now that he had composed himself, a groan once more interrupted the reading as though it had made an appointment to come back then. So he confessed that he could not proceed, and handed it to one of his company to read, quite a learned man at that. I am uncertain how others would interpret this incident, but I interpreted it in the best light and understood the man's heart was very sensitive; for, in truth, there is no more kindly man, at least not that I know. As he was weeping and reading, those words of the Satirist came to mind [15.131–32]:

> Nature admits
> She gives the human race the softest hearts;
> She gave us tears—the best part of our feelings.

After a time, another friend of ours from Verona (just as we have other things in common, so have we friends) having heard what had happened to another while reading, wished to read the same tale. I humored our gifted friend; he read it all without stopping anywhere, nor did his brow darken or his voice break; no tears, no sobs interrupted him, and in the end he said, "I too would have wept, for the touching subject and the words fit for the subject prompted weeping, nor am I hard-hearted; but I believed, and still do, that the

---

* See I, 5.

whole thing was made up. For if it were true, what woman any-where, whether Roman or of any nation whatever will match this Griselda? Where, I ask, is such great conjugal love, equal fidelity, such signal patience and constancy?" To that I did not reply any-thing then, lest I lead the discussion from the jokes and the sweet merriment of friendly conversation to the bitterness of an argu-ment. But the answer was simple: that there are some who consider whatever is difficult for them, impossible for everyone, and they so judge everything by their own measure as to put themselves in first place; whereas there have been many, and perhaps still are, for whom things that seem impossible to the multitude are simple. For who is there, for example, who would not think the tales of Curius and Mucius and the Decii among our people are fictitious, or Codrus and the Philaeni brothers among foreigners, or, since we are speaking of women, Porcia, Hypsicratea, or Alcestis and others like them? And yet the stories are true. Well, I do not understand what one who shrugs off his own life for another could not shrug off or endure.

But I learn just now that that letter and another long one never reached you. What can I do? One must endure. One may get angry, but not take revenge. There have recently appeared throughout Cisalpine Gaul this unbearable breed of men, the border guards, or rather the bane of messengers, who open and examine letters and peruse them most fussily. Perhaps this is excused by the orders of their masters, who feel guilty of everything in a life of pride and alarm, and think that everything is being said about them and against them, and want to know everything. What is inexcusable is that if they find anything in the letter to flatter their donkey ears, some used to spend time copying it and detain the messengers, but now, with growing wantonness, to spare their fingers they order them to leave without the letter. And what is most disgusting, the ones who do this the most understand nothing and are like those who have a big gaping craw and a slow digestion, and are inviting a bad case of cramps. Nobody is more galled than I by such insolence, no one more impatient, so that often it has turned me aside from writing and often driven me to grief for what I have written, since against these literary pirates there is no opportunity for any other vengeance, with everything in turmoil and the freedom of the state in ruins. Of course, to this annoyance is added my age and weari-ness with almost everything, and I have not only had my fill of writ-ing, I am sick of it. All this together leads me to say to you, dear friend, and to all to whom I used to write—insofar as it concerns my epistolary pen—a last farewell, in order that flimsier scribblings may not to the end hinder me, as they have long done, from more worthwhile study, and that my writings not fall into the idiotic hands of these rascals, from whose mischief I shall at least be safe. If ever I need to write either to you or to others, I shall write so as to be understood but not to amuse myself.

I recall that in a certain letter of this series that I had promised from now on to be briefer in my letter writing, prompted by the lack of time, which is running out. But I did not want to keep the promise; and, as I am given to understand, it is much easier to be silent with friends than brief. So great is the zest for conversing, once we have begun, that it would be easier not to have begun than to curb the onrush of a converstion that has begun; but I did promise. Yet, is not a promise kept when one does more than was promised? When I promised, I believe I had forgotten those words of Cato in Cicero which are widely known, to the effect that old age is more loquacious by its very nature. Farewell, dear friends. Farewell, dear letters.

Amidst the Euganean Hills, June 8, 1373.

Sen. XVIII, 1.

To posterity, an account of his background, conduct, and the development of his character and studies.

Francis Petrarch to posterity, greetings. Perhaps you will have heard something about me, although this too is doubtful, whether a petty, obscure name would reach far into either space or time. And perhaps you will wish to know what sort of man I was, or what were the results of my labors, especially of those whose fame has reached you or whose bare titles you have heard. On the first point men's opinions will vary. For almost everyone speaks as his pleasure, not the truth, impels, and there are no standards for either praise or blame. But I was one of your troop, a poor mortal man, neither of too great nor of base origin, but of an ancient family, as Augustus Caesar says of himself; by nature, anyhow, I was of neither foul nor shameless temperament, had the habits caught from others not harmed it. Adolescence misled me, youth swept me away, but old age set me right, and taught me by experience that truth I had read long before: that adolescence and pleasure are vain; or rather, it was the Creator of all ages and times who set me right. He sometimes allows wretched mortals, puffed up with nothing, to go astray so that, being aware of their sins, however late, they may know themselves. In my youth my body was not very strong, but quite supple. I do not boast of being especially handsome, but enough to be pleasing in my greener years—with a clear complexion, between light and dark, lively eyes, and for a long time very keen vision, which unexpectedly abandoned me after the sixtieth year, so that, to my disgust I had to resort to glasses. Old age invaded my body, which had been very healthy in every age, and surrounded it with the usual array of ills.

I was born in exile in Arezzo in the year 1304 of this last age, which began with Christ, at dawn on a Monday, July [20], of honorable parents, Florentine in origin, of modest fortune, and, to tell the truth, verging on poverty, but driven from their homeland. I am a confirmed despiser of riches, not because I would not wish for them, but because I hated toil and worry, the inseparable companions of wealth—not that access to a fancy dinner requires such worry! I have led a happier life with plain living and ordinary fare than all the followers of Apicius, with their elaborate feasts. What are called banquets, since they are revels, injurious to decency and good manners I have always disliked. I considered it irksome and useless to invite others for that purpose, and no less so to be invited by others. But dining with friends is so delightful that I have thought nothing more welcome than their unexpected arrival, nor have I ever willingly taken a meal without a companion. Nothing has displeased me more than pomp, not only because it is evil and contrary to humility, but because it is troublesome and distracting. I struggled in my adolescence with the most intense but constant and honorable love, and would have struggled even longer, had not a premature but expedient death extinguished the flame that was already cooling. I wish, of course, I could say I was utterly free of lust, but, if I did, I would be lying. This I shall say with confidence, that, though carried away by the fervor of that age and of my temperament, I have always cursed such vileness in my heart. But as soon as I was approaching my fortieth year, while I still had plenty of ardor and strength, I so completely threw off not only that obscene act, but the very recollection of it, that it seemed I had never looked at a woman. I count this among my greatest blessings, thanks be to God who freed me, while still sound and vigorous, from so vile and hateful a slavery.

But I turn to other matters. I have perceived pride in others, not in myself; and unimportant though I have been, in my own judgment I have always been even less important. My anger has very often hurt me, but never others. I have been a most eager and faithful devotee of honorable friendships. Fearlessly, because I know I speak the truth, I boast of being hot-tempered, but very forgetful of wrongs and ever mindful of kindnesses. I was fortunate to the point of envy in my associations with princes and kings, and in my friendships with nobles. But this is the penalty for growing old: to weep ever so often over the deaths of your dear ones. The greatest rulers of this age have loved and courted me; but I know not why—let them explain it. And I stayed with some of them in a way that they were, so to speak, my guests, so that I derived many advantages and no annoyances from their eminence. I fled, however, from many of those whom I loved a great deal; such love for freedom was implanted in me that I studiously avoided anyone whose very name seemed incompatible with it.

I had a well-balanced rather than a keen intellect, fit for all kinds of good and wholesome study, but especially inclined to moral philosophy and poetry. Yet in the course of time I abandoned the latter, when I found delight in sacred letters, in which I felt the hidden sweetness I once despised; for I limit poetry to embellishment only. I have dwelt single-mindedly on learning about antiquity, among other things because this age has always displeased me, so that, unless love for my dear ones pulled me the other way, I always wished to have been born in any other age whatever, and to forget this one, seeming always to graft myself in my mind onto other ages. I have therefore been charmed by the historians, though I was no less offended by their disagreements; and, when in doubt, I followed the version toward which either the verisimilitude of the content or the authority of the writers pulled me. My style, as some have said, was clear and powerful, but it seemed to me weak and obscure. In ordinary conversation with friends or relatives I have no concern for eloquence, and I marvel that Augustus Caesar did take such pains. But when the subject itself or the place or the listener seemed to demand otherwise, I have exerted myself a little, how successfully I do not know; let them judge in whose presence I spoke. As long as I lived well, I would care little how I had spoken; to seek fame merely from verbal elegance is but empty glory.

Either luck or my will has up to now divided my time in this fashion. The first year of my life I spent partially in Arezzo, where nature had brought me to light; the six following years in my father's country home in Incisa, fourteen miles above Florence, after my mother had been recalled from exile; my eighth year in Pisa, the ninth and thereafter in Transalpine Gaul, on the left bank of the Rhone in the city called Avignon, where the Roman Pontiff holds, and has long held, the Church of Christ in shameful exile, although a few years ago Urban V seemed to have led her back to her own See. But it came to nothing, as is obvious; and what I bear all the harder, it was even while he was alive, as if he repented of his good work. Had he lived a little longer, he would doubtless have learned how I felt about his retreat. My pen was already in hand, but that unhappy man abruptly deserted that glorious undertaking along with his life. How happily he could have died before the altar of Peter and in his own home! For had his successors remained in their See, he would have been the author of that fine achievement; or had they left, his virtue would have been all the nobler, the more obvious their fault. But this complaint is too long and not to the point.

There, then, on the bank of that very windy river, I spent my boyhood under my parents, and then my whole adolescence under my follies, but not without long absences. During this time I spent four whole years in the small city of Carpentras, a little to the east of Avignon; and in these two cities I learned as much of grammar, logic, and rhetoric as my age could, or rather, as is usually learned in school; and you, dear reader, know how little that is. Then I set out for Montpellier for the study of law, staying another four years there; then to Bologna where I spent three years and heard lectures on the whole body of civil law, and would have been a young man with a great future, as many thought, had I concentrated on the project. But I abandoned that subject altogether as soon as my parents abandoned me [because of their death]. Not that I did not like the dignity of the law, which is doubtless great and replete with Roman antiquity which delights me, but that practicing it is perverted by men's wickedness. It therefore irked me to master something I did not want to use dishonestly, and could scarcely use honestly; and had I wanted to, my good intentions would have been ascribed to inexperience.

So at the age of twenty-two I returned home. I call home that place of exile, Avignon, where I had been since my later childhood, for habit is like second nature. I already had begun to be known there, and my friendship sought by great men. Just why, I confess I do not now know, and marvel at it, though I did not marvel then, being of an age when I thought myself most worthy of every honor. I was sought primarily by the distinguished and generous Colonna family, which then frequented the Roman Curia, or rather, gave it luster. They summoned me and held me in great esteem which, however it may be now, I certainly did not deserve then; and that illustrious and incomparable man, Giacomo Colonna, then Bishop of Lombez, whose peer I know not whether I have ever seen or shall see, who took me to Gascony, where I spent a nearly heavenly summer in the foothills of the Pyrenees; my master and his retinue were so charming that I always sigh as I remember that time. Returning from there, for many years I was under his brother, Giovanni Cardinal Colonna, not as under a master but under a father, or rather, not even that, but with a most loving brother or with myself in my own home.

At that time a youthful craving drove me to travel through France and Germany; and although I invented other reasons to have my elders approve my journey, the real reason was my ardor and curiosity to see many things. On that journey I saw Paris for the first time and was delighted to inquire what was true and what was mythical in the stories told about that city. On my return, I went to Rome, which I had ardently longed to see since childhood. There I so waited upon Stefano Colonna, the noble head of the family, a man equal to any of the ancients, and I was so well received that you would say there was no distinction between me and any of his sons. The love and affection of that excellent man for me always remained constant until the last day of his life; and even now it lives in me, and will never end, unless I come to an end first.

When I again returned from there, since I cannot bear the nausea and hate for all cities implanted in my heart by nature, and above all for that most disgusting city [Avignon], I sought some refuge as though it were a haven; and I discovered a tiny valley, secluded and delightful, called Vaucluse, about fifteen miles from Avignon, where the king of all springs, the Sorgue, rises. Taken by the charm of the place, I moved my books and myself there. It will be a long story if I go on to describe what I did there over many, many years. To be brief, almost all of the works I have let fall from my pen were either completed or begun or conceived there. They have been so many that even at this age they vex and weary me. For my mind, like my body, has been capable of versatility rather than strength. Therefore, many things that were easy for me to plan I have laid aside because of the difficulty of realizing them. The very looks of the place prompted me to undertake a silvan work, the *Bucolicum carmen*, and the *De uita solitaria* in two books, dedicated to Philippe [de Cabassoles], always a great man, but then the modest Bishop of Cavaillon, now the great Cardinal Bishop of Sabina, who is the only survivor of all my old friends, and has cherished me and still does, not as a bishop, as Ambrose cherished Augustine, but as a brother. As I wandered in those mountains on a certain Good Friday, the idea gripped me to write something poetic in heroic verse about Scipio Africanus the Elder, whose name had been wonderfully dear to me since my earliest childhood. But having taken this on with great enthusiasm, I soon dropped it because I was distracted by various tasks; I entitled it *Africa* from its subject, a work which, through some kind of luck, either its own or mine, was loved by many before they ever saw it.

While staying in that spot, there came to me on the same day, strange to say, a letter from the Senate of the city of Rome and from the Chancellor of the University of Paris, vying to invite me, one to Rome and one to Paris, to receive the laurel crown of poetry. In my youthful elation, I judged myself worthy of whatever such great men did; and, while giving weight not to my merit but to others' testimony, nevertheless for a short while I hesitated over which of the two to heed. By letter I sought the advice of Giovanni Colonna, the cardinal mentioned above. For he was so near that, even though I wrote him late in the day, I received his reply the next day before the third hour [midmorning]. Following his advice, I decided that the authority of the city of Rome must have prefer-

ence above all others; my two-part letter to him about my accept-
ance of his advice still exists. Therefore I set off; and although, in
the manner of youth, I was a most indulgent judge of everything of
mine, I still blushed to follow my judgment concerning myself, or of
those by whom I was invited: they would doubtless not have done it
unless they had judged me worthy of the honor offered. So I decided first to head for Naples, and came to that eminent king and philosopher, Robert, as famous for his culture as for his rule, and the
only king of our age who was at once the friend of knowledge and
of virtue, so that he might declare what he thought of me. I still
marvel, and you, reader, I believe, will marvel if you know how I was
received and welcomed by him. Having heard the reason for my
coming, he was wonderfully exhilarated, thinking of my youthful
confidence, and perhaps thinking that the honor I sought would
redound to his glory, since of all mortals I had chosen him alone as
a fit judge. Why say more? After talking over ever so many things,
and after being shown my *Africa*, which delighted him so much that
he asked me to dedicate it to him as a great favor—which I could not
deny him, and certainly did not wish to—he assigned to me a certain
day for the primary purpose of my visit, and kept me from noon
until evening. Since the subjects grew and the time seemed short, he
did the same on the next two days. Having thus tested my ignorance
for three days, on the third he judged me worthy of the laurel. He
offered it to me in Naples, and with much entreaty urged me to
agree. My love for Rome overcame the august insistence of so great
a king. And so, seeing that I was inflexible in my purpose, he gave
me letters and envoys for the Roman Senate, whereby he expressed
with great favor his judgment of me. The royal judgment was then
in agreement with that of many, and especially my own. Today I do
not approve either of his judgment or of mine or of everyone's who
felt the same. Love and partiality for my age prevailed in him over
devotion to truth.

Nevertheless, I came [to Rome], and, however unworthy, relying
upon so high a judgment and trusting it, to the utmost joy of the
Romans who could be present for the solemnity, I was given the
poetic laurel while still an ignorant student. About all this I have
also written letters in verse and prose. This crown earned me nothing in the way of knowledge, but very much in the way of envy. But
this too is a longer story than is warranted here. So, after leaving
Rome, I came to Parma and spent some little time with the lords of
Correggio, who were most kind and generous to me, but could not
agree among themselves; they then ruled that city with a govern-

ment such as that state had never had in man's memory, and I surmise will not have in this age. Mindful of the honor that I had accepted, and worried lest it seem to have been conferred on an unworthy person, one day when I happened to be climbing a mountain across the river Enza in the territory of Reggio, I came to a forest called Selvapiana. Suddenly struck by the beauty of the place, I turned my pen to the interrupted *Africa*; and reawakening the enthusiasm which seemed to have died down, I wrote a little that day. Then, day after day I wrote something, until, returning to Parma, and finding a quiet, secluded house, which I later purchased and is still mine, I brought that work to completion with such ardor, in a relatively short time, that I myself am now amazed. From there I returned to the source of the Sorgue and to my transalpine solitude, after I had just finished my thirty-fourth year and had stayed at Parma and Verona a long time; and everywhere, thank God, I was held dear much more than I deserved.

Later on, the blazon of fame won me the good will of a fine man; I do not know whether among the lords of his time there has been anyone like him, or rather I know there has been none—I mean Giacomo da Carrara the Younger, through whose messengers and letters I was wearied with such earnest entreaties beyond the Alps when I was there, and wherever I was throughout Italy for many years. I was so urged into friendship with him that, though I hoped for nothing from the well-to-do, I decided at last to go to him and see what this insistence on the part of a great man, unknown to me, meant. Thus, I came, though late, to Padua, where I was received by that man of illustrious memory, not just kindly, but as the blessed souls are greeted in heaven, with such joy and such inestimable love and fondness, that, since I cannot hope to equal it with words, it is better to cover it with silence. Among many things, knowing that I had led a clerical life since childhood, he made me a canon of Padua in order to bind me more tightly not only to himself but to his city. In short, had his life been longer, it would have been the end of all my wandering and journeys. But alas, among mortals nothing is enduring; and if anything sweet appears, it soon ends in bitterness. In not quite two years, God, who had sent him to me, to his fatherland, and to the world, took him away; neither I nor his fatherland nor the world—I am not blinded by love—was worthy of him. And although he was succeeded by his son, a most prudent and eminent man who, following in his father's footsteps, always loved and honored me, still, after the loss of the one with whom I had been better matched, especially in age, I again returned to

France, incapable of staying still, and not so much with a yearning to see again what I had seen a thousand times, as with an effort to cope with stiffness—as sick people do—by a shift of position.*

[1370-74].

---

* The unfinished draft breaks off at this point.

INDEX

Note: If the title of a work is translated in the text, it will appear in translation in the index. Otherwise, all titles of classical works are given in the abbreviated form specified by the *Oxford Classical Dictionary.*

Abdera, 484
Abraham, 38, 246
Abruzzi, 90
Absalom, 390, 448
Acciaiuoli, Niccolò 3, 93
Achaia, 255
Achates, 142, 143
Achilles, 17, 122, 300, 376, 450, 451, 577
Adige (river), 290
Adrastus, 212, 220
Adriatic (sea), 10, 71, 138, 190, 430, 599, 657
Aegean (sea), 190, 254, 256
Aeneas, xv, 122, 142, 143, 146, 147, 150, 300, 381, 648
Aeneid, see Virgil
Aeolia, 156, 300
Aeolian Isles, 375
Aeolus, 140, 141, 190, 255, 375
Aesculapius, 23, 174, 214, 439, 440, 456, 458
Aesop, 600
Afranius, Lucius, 62
Africa, 50, 105, 251, 252
Africa, see Petrarch
Agamemnon, 450

Agave, 157
Aghinolfi, Donato, 504
Aghinolfi, Giovanni (d'Arezzo), 483
Agnes, St., 219, 261
Agrippa, Marcus, 537, 566
Agrippina, 565
Ajax, 122, 450
Albano, 12, 243
Albanzani, Antonio, 179, 392, 409, 489
Albanzani, Donato (Apenninigena), 90, 92, 108, 156, 158, 177, 180, 182, 186, 189, 292, 377, 386, 392, 398, 487, 489, 583, 584
Albanzani, Solone, 179, 378
Albinus (Alcuin), 172
Albinus, Clodius, 48
Alcestis, 670
Alcibiades, 49
Alcides, *see* Hercules
Alcinous, 213
Alcuin, *see* Albinus (Alcuin)
Alexander, King of Epirus, 122
Alexander, King of Macedonia, 17, 69, 70, 122, 123, 125, 128, 252, 258, 297, 341, 356, 433, 448, 451, 512, 565, 577, 649

Alexander, *see* Severus Alexander
Alexandria, xv, 112, 113, 302, 481
Alps, 10, 41, 97, 119, 152, 240, 242, 250, 251, 319, 328, 373, 441, 503, 678
Alps, Noric, 10
Ambrose, St., 18, 21, 46, 55, 67, 85, 164, 194, 210, 233, 235, 288, 292, 319, 417, 505, 515, 531, 575, 637–39, 647, 676; *De excessu* 2.32–34, 18; 2.40, 21; *De obitu Val.* 10, 647; *On the Passing of the Emperor Theodosius*, 531
Ambrose, St. (church of), 67
Ameil, Pierre d', 225
Amnon, 390, 448
Amphiaraus, 565
Anarcharsis, 512
Anaxagoras, 24, 46, 417, 484
Anaxarchus, 619
"Androclas," 267
Anna, 144
Annaeus, *see* Seneca, Lucius Annaeus
Annibaldeschi, Paolo, 382, 388, 392
Antenor, 150
Anthony (of Padua), St., 533
Anthropophagi, 562
Antigonus, King, 384
Antilochus, 382
Antioch, 481
Antiochus, 218
Antipodes, 433
Antisthenes, 296
Antoninus Pius (Titus Aurelius F. B. Antoninus), 252, 538
Antoninus, Diadumenus, 48
Antoni[n]us, *see* Aurelius Antoninus, Marcus
Antony (Marcus Antonius), 448, 449, 650
Antony (the Abbot), St., 294, 444, 646
Apelles, 29, 611
Apennines, 10, 41, 72, 97, 187, 319, 441, 656

Apicius, 316, 672
Apollo, 23, 39, 88, 167, 211, 458
Aponus, 91
Apostle, *see* Paul, St.
Apostles, 254, 304, 307, 308, 322, 336
Apostolic See, *see* Peter, See of
Appius Caecus, *see* Claudius Caecus, Appius
Apuleius Madaurensis, 563; *Asclepius* 41.33, 563
Aquileia, 91, 441, 618
Aquilo, 255
Aquitaine, 367
Arab, 615
Arabia, 62, 169, 337
Arabs, 456, 471–73
Archemorus, 292
Archimedes, 24, 33
Archytas of Tarentum, 151, 474
Arelatensis, *see* Provence
Aretino, Federigo, 139, 297
Arezzo, 268, 360, 369, 483, 484, 486, 672, 674
Arezzo, Giovanni d', *see* Fei, Giovanni, and Aghinolfi, Giovanni
Arganthonius, King, 384
Arians, 417
Aries, 299
Aristarchus, 43
Aristides, 205
Aristotle, 42, 55, 66, 67, 122, 146, 164, 172, 206, 216, 323, 325, 394, 451, 466, 468, 472, 484, 490, 565, 593, 651; *Economics*, 325, 541; – 1.6.1345a13–17, 325; *Ethics*, 241, 468; – 1.1.1095a.1–2, 241; *On Good Fortune*, 285; *Rhetoric*, 206; *Secrets*, 207
Armenia, 62, 112, 371
Arno, 363
Arpinum, 484
Arquà, 478, 485, 491, 498, 505, 517, 518, 552, 557, 581, 587, 607, 616, 620
Artaxerxes, King, 215

Heb. 9:27, 551
James 1:13, 668; — 4:4, 356
1 John 2:15-16, 356; — 4:19, 355
Apocalypse, 219
Birel, Jean, 633, 637
Bitias, 148, 212
Black Sea (Euxine Sea), 61, 119, 290, 346
Blaesilla, 423
Boccaccio, Giovanni (Giovanni da Certaldo), 21, 22, 14, 15, 37, 75, 92, 98, 100, 107, 152, 157, 167, 177, 189, 191, 263, 302, 391–93, 443, 444, 582, 643, 644, 655, 656, 669; *Decameron*, 655
Boethius, Anicius Manlius Severinus, 153, 264, 417, 472, 588; *De cons.* 1.1, 264; — 1.4, 553; — 2.7, 648
"Bolanus," 193
Bologna, 84, 230, 268, 287, 319, 362, 363, 366, 484, 601, 662, 664, 675
Bologna, University of, 230
Bolsena, Lake, 240
Boniface VIII, 243, 247, 248
Bordelais, 303
Borgo San Sepolcro, Dionigi di, 581
Borysthenes (river), 562
Bosphorus, 61, 190, 256
Brabant, 367
Brahmins, 446
Britain, 17, 136, 241, 566, 603
Broaspini, Squaro dei (Gasparo di Verona), 519, 520, 591
Brossano, Francesca (P.'s daughter), 378
Brossano, Francesco (P.'s grandson), 379
Brossano, Francesco (P.'s son-in-law), 188, 378
Brundisium, 622
Bruni, Francesco, 27, 54, 58, 193, 328, 397, 400, 404, 410, 506, 509, 590

Brutus, Marcus Junius, 67, 124, 320, 525; *On Virtue*, 67
Burgundy, 251, 309
Byzantium, 100, 176, 186, 190, 257, 291

Cabassoles, Philippe de, 154, 197, 199, 225, 227, 228, 257, 331, 339, 357, 365, 402, 403, 425, 492, 502, 506, 517, 560, 592, 596, 609, 610, 617, 676
Cadiz, 61
Caecilius, 117, 127, 129, 130, 223, 274, 451
Caesar, Gaius Julius, xv, 55, 118, 119, 121–25, 127, 130, 259, 261, 282, 314, 351, 416, 420, 433, 448, 451, 469, 522, 523, 526, 527, 535, 536, 547, 550, 551, 564, 565, 621–25, 648; *BCiv.* 3.91.3, 523
Calabria, 186, 389, 412
Calabrians, 412
Calanus, 17
Caligula (Gaius Julius Caesar Germanicus), 80, 527, 529, 545, 629
Calpurnius Bestia, Lucius, 223
Camaldolensians, 74, 611
Camilla, 211, 384
Camillus, Marcus Furius, 123, 127, 320, 649
Campania, 45
Cannae, 122
Capaneus, 190
Capella, Felix, 588
Capitoline, 37, 131, 260, 300, 301, 536, 624
Capitolinus, Julius, 566; *M. Aur.* 18.4, 566
Capra, Enrico, 492
Capri, 368
Capua, 319, 441
Capuans, 569
Caracciolo, Berardo, 201; *Dictamina*, 201
Carbo, Gnaeus Papirius, 228

Cicero, xiv, xvi, 17, 19, 40, 43, 45–
47, 54, 55, 58, 67–69, 85, 88,
107, 117, 118, 121, 123–26, 130,
135, 151, 161, 164, 172, 185,
194, 201, 204–6, 208, 216, 222,
237, 264, 265, 271, 274–76, 278,
283, 284, 285, 293, 315, 326,
334, 351, 361, 377, 379, 381,
385, 392, 394, 406, 417, 423,
429, 432, 438, 440, 443, 445,
451, 454–56, 458, 463, 465, 466,
472, 477, 484, 496, 507, 521,
522, 525–527, 529, 536, 544,
545, 548, 549, 556, 566, 576,
578, 586, 589, 593, 599–607,
609, 610, 615, 619, 622, 632,
637, 640, 648, 651, 671; *Academics*, 604; *Ad Brut.* 1.4a, 525; *Amic.*
9.31, 545; – 14, 477; – 17, 640;
– 28, 429; – 59, 477; *Att.* 9.7c,
622; – 9.13a, 622; – 10.8b, 622;
Diu. 1.30.63, 45; *Fin.* 5, 21, 58,
647; *Hortensius*, 293; *In Praise of
Philosophy*, 604; *Leg. Man.*, 10,
118; – 11–14, 126; *Nat. D.*,
1.160, 507; *Off.*, xvi, 43, 54, 208,
222, 285, 432, 522, 526, 527,
536, 549, 615; – 1.22.74, 549; –
1.25, 54; – 1.28.97, 43; –
1.29.101, 536; – 1.68, 208; –
1.123, 432; – 2.6.19, 285; –
2.7.23, 526, 527; – 2.7.24, 526; –
2.24.86, 615; *On Consolation*, 19,
604; *On Glory*, 605; *On the Laws*,
548, 549, 605; – 3.14.31, 549;
On the Orator, 68, 605; – 2.24,
68; *Phil.*, 380, 522, 526, 529,
550; – 1.4.33, 526; – 2.4.112,
529; – 9.5.10, 549; – 9.14–15,
380; *Rep.*, 19, 69, 276, 525, 529,
604; – 6.1.13, 525; – 6.15, 276;
– 6.16, 529; – 6.25, 69; *Rhetoric*,
601; *Sen.*, 5, 463, 465, 578; – 17,
264; – 19, 602; – 20, 228; – 66,
206; – 83, 271; *Tusc.*, 18, 19,
272, 381, 440, 443, 551, 552,

577; – 1.15.34, 577; – 1.31, 440;
– 1.38, 381; – 1.48, 18, 551, 552;
– 1.48.115, 551, 552; – 5.35.100,
443; – 5.62, 272
Cicero, Quintus Tullius, 522
Cincinnatus, Quintius, 124
Circe, 145, 156, 212, 214, 414
Cisalpine Gaul, xv, 1, 41, 153, 368,
670
Cistercians, 350
Claudian (Claudius Claudianus),
255; *De IV Cons. Hon.* 299–300,
549; *Panegyricus de tertio consulatu
Honorii Augusti* 93–98, 255
Claudius (Tiberius Claudius Nero
Germanicus), 253, 542, 555, 565
Claudius Caecus, Appius, 24, 166,
445
Clazomenae, 484
Cleanthes, 24, 46, 451
Clement V, 360
Clement VI, 13, 38, 103, 241, 368,
463, 613
Clement VII, 228
Clonus, 212
Codrus, 123, 670
Colchians, 210
Colchis, 61, 470
Colonna (family), 601, 675
Colonna, Agapito the Elder, 556
Colonna, Agapito the Younger, 338
Colonna, Giacomo, 7, 366, 601,
602, 618, 675
Colonna, Giovanni, 241, 571, 596,
602, 605, 675, 676
Colonna, Stefano, 338, 341, 368,
388, 401, 402, 467, 556, 557,
602, 612, 675
Colonna, Stefano the Younger,
338, 556, 557
Comic [Poet], *see* Terence
Commodus, Lucius Aelius Aure-
lius, 546, 566
Constantine, 55
Constantinople, 101, 255, 346, 411
Constantius, Flavius Valerius, 538

Drusus, Nero Claudius, 577
Durance (river), 256

Earth, Mother, 446
Easter, 591
Eden, Garden of, 244
Edward III, King, 367
Egypt, 62, 302, 304, 371, 447
Egyptians, 267
Elagabalus (see Heliogabalus)
Elea, 484
Emilia, 103, 250, 657
Empedocles, 184
Empire, 39, 232, 235, 313, 349, 484
England (see Britain)
Ennius, Quintus, 186, 455, 526, 627, 651
Enza (river), 678
Epaminondas, 120, 122, 532
Ephebus, 149
Epicurus, 46, 541, 561; *Frag.* 466–67, 561
Epiphany, 494
Epirus, 122, 255
Epistolae sine nomine, see Petrarch
Erebus, 102
Erichthonius, 532
Eriphyle, 223
Este, Niccolò d', 435, 476
Este, Ugo d', 420, 435, 476
Ethiopia, 337
Ethiopians, 251, 385, 648
Etna, 41, 184, 441
Etruria, 373, 484
Euboea, 255
Euganean Hills, 415, 424, 451, 493, 496, 497, 516, 534, 586, 599, 671
Euripides, 190, 527, 552; *Cresphontes*, 552
Europe, 369
Eurydice, 322, 565
Eurytus, 212
Eusebius, 253; *On Chronology*, 253
Eutropius, 538, 623; − 11.2, 538
Euxine Sea, *see* Black Sea (Euxine Sea)

Fabius Maximus, Quintus, 50, 121, 124, 346, 451
Fabius Sabinus, 550
Fabricius Luscinus, Gaius, xv, 40, 114, 123, 205
Falerno, 368
Familiares, see Petrarch
Fates, 145, 214, 286, 288
Faustinus, St., 319
Fei, Giovanni (d'Arezzo), 483, 486
Felix, 542
Ferrara, 135, 136, 369, 435, 476
Festus, Porcius, 165
Fiano, Francesco da, 491
Firmicus Maternus, Julius, 33, 85, 266, 267; *Astrology*, 266, 267
Flaccus, *see* Horace
Flaminia, 250, 657
Flanders, 367
Florence, 3, 78, 80, 89, 370, 484, 511, 674
Florentines, 520
Florus, Lucius Annaeus, 623
Fortune, 1, 6, 59, 75, 76, 195, 228, 284–86, 288, 297, 298, 300, 383, 478, 570, 641, 644
Fracassetti, Giuseppe, xiv
France, 311, 338, 362, 494, 581, 630, 631, 675, 679 (*see also* Gaul)
Francesco da Siena, 608, 609
Francis, St., 55, 184, 282, 417, 610, 612
Frederick II, 39
Frignano, Tommaso da, 416, 419

Galba, Servius Sulpicius, 530, 541
Galen, 175, 456
Galilee, 261
Ganges, 62
Garda, Lake, 242
Garignano, 633
Gascony, 367, 602, 675
Gasparo di Verona, *see* Broaspini, Squaro dei (Gasparo di Verona)
Gaul, xv, 1, 17, 41, 66, 68, 97, 104, 153, 173, 175, 241, 244, 311,

26.47.4, 536; — 27.15.1-2, 543

Padova, Giovanni da, *see* Dondi, Giovanni (da Padova)
Padua, 9–11, 36, 71, 73, 74, 91, 95, 104, 128, 172, 179, 185, 195, 293, 344, 369, 376, 391, 393, 396–99, 402, 404, 407, 419, 420, 423, 424, 426, 432, 435, 437, 482, 486, 488, 493–95, 497, 501, 519–21, 534, 559, 589, 591, 608, 630, 632, 654, 678
Palladius, Rutilius Taurus Aemilianus, 67, 445
Pallas, 38, 142, 147, 150, 542
Panago, 662, 666
Papacy, 313
Papinian, Aemilius, 550
Papirius Cursor, Lucius, 121, 124, 649
Papirius, Fabianus, 161
Paraclete, *see* Holy Spirit (Paraclete)
Paris, 150, 157, 367, 469, 675, 676
Paris, University of, 676
Parma, 187, 369, 464, 472, 631, 677, 678
Parma, Giovanni da, 464, 472
Parnassus, 160
Parrhasius, 29
Parthenope, *see* Naples
Parthia, 222
Parthians, 127, 433
Patras, 133
Paul, St., 20, 25, 104, 107, 116, 144, 145, 164, 165, 184, 206, 221, 222, 236, 238, 254, 261, 264, 282, 309, 315, 324, 336, 348, 354–56, 396, 401, 417, 425, 443, 448, 449, 504, 526, 550, 638, 645, 646
Paul, St. (basilica), 236
Paul, St. (hermit), 294, 444
Paulinus, Bishop of Nola, 461
Paullus Macedonicus, Lucius Aemilius, 122, 276, 389
Paullus, Julius, 550
Paullus, Lucius Aemilius, 122, 427
Pavia (Ticinum), 82, 151–53, 156, 175, 176, 179, 188, 210, 226, 269, 280, 288, 289, 291, 303, 330, 369, 380, 397, 409, 435, 442, 504, 557
Peligni, 90
Peloro, 441
Penna, Luca da, 599
Penthesilea, 76, 211
Pergamum, 169, 561
Persia, 62
Persians, 68, 277, 434, 445, 448, 546
Persius, 214, 215, 575; *Sat., Prol.* 10, 575; *Sat.* 2.58, 214; – 2.59–60, 214; – 2.69, 215
Pertinax, 541
Perugia, 369, 631
Peter, King of Cyprus, 302, 481
Peter, See of, 103, 211, 244, 248, 253, 307, 315, 325, 335, 342, 502, 513
Peter, St., 100, 117, 210, 236, 254, 258, 261, 309, 313, 315, 320, 336, 354, 396, 401, 446, 510, 514, 557, 641, 674
Peter, St. (basilica of), 236
Peter, St. (church in Pavia), 210
Petrarca, Gherardo, 357, 571
Petrarca, Giovanni (P.'s son), 4, 8
Petrarch, xiii, xiv, xv, xvi, 672; *Africa*, 38, 215, 676–78; *Bucolicum carmen*, 52, 676; *De remediis utriusque fortune*, 285, 300, 641; *De uita solitaria*, 67, 155, 179, 197, 225, 357, 403, 503, 517, 596, 610, 611, 676; *Epistolae sine nomine*, 19; *Familiares*, xiii, xiv, xvi, 1, 19, 21; V, 19, 444; – X, 3, 357; – XI, 7, 373; – XIV, 5, 360; *Invective contra medicum*, 444; – 1.5, 613; *Invective*, 588, 612; *Librorum Francisci Petrarce annotatio impressorum*, xiv; *Posteritati*, 20, 21; *Seniles*, xiii, xiv, 19, 20, 22; – VIII, 1, 443; – VIII, 8, 443; – XIII, 13, 20; – XVI, 3, 20, 23; *Variae* 15, 20
Petremoli, 631